SO-AZC-552

LUTHERANS AGAINST HITLER

LUTHERANS AGAINST HITLER

THE UNTOLD STORY

Lowell C. Green

CONCORDIA PUBLISHING HOUSE · SAINT LOUIS

ACADEMIC PRESS

For my beloved wife, Vilma, and our dear children, Daniel Green,
Katharine Olah, Sonja Link, and Barbara Savereide

 Published 2007 by Concordia Publishing House
3558 S. Jefferson Ave., St. Louis, MO 63118-3968
1-800-325-3040 • www.cph.org

Copyright © 2007 Lowell C. Green

All rights reserved. No part of this manuscript may be reproduced, stored in a retrieval system, or transmitted, in any form or by any means, electronic, mechanical, photocopying, recording, or otherwise, without the prior written permission of Concordia Publishing House.

Unless otherwise noted, translations from the original languages (including Bible passages and quotations from the Lutheran Confessions) have been supplied by the author.

The author's translation of the Bethel Confession (chapter 7) is based on the document as it is found in *Berlin, 1932–1933*, vol. 12 of *Dietrich Bonhoeffer Werke*, edited by Carsten Nicolaisen and Ernst-Albert Scharffenorth (Güterslow: Chr. Kaiser, 1997). Translated into English with the permission of Augsburg Fortress.

Quotations marked KJV or noted as "Authorized Version" are from the King James or Authorized Version of the Bible.

Library of Congress Cataloging-in-Publication Data

Green, Lowell C., 1925–
  Lutherans against Hitler : the untold story / Lowell C. Green.
    p. cm.
  Includes bibliographical references (p.   ) and indexes.
  ISBN-13: 978-0-7586-0877-2
  ISBN-10: 0-7586-0877-2
  1. Lutheran Church—Germany—History—20th century. 2. Friedrich-Alexander-Universität Erlangen-Nürnberg. Theologische Fakultät. 3. Hitler, Adolf, 1889–1945. 4. Church and state—Germany—History—1933–1945. 5. Christianity and politics—Lutheran Church—History—20th century. 6. Christianity and politics—Germany. 7. World War, 1939–1945—Religious aspects—Lutheran Church. 8. Germany—Church history—1933–1945. I. Title.
  BX8020.G74 2007
  284.1'43'09043—dc22

2006034613

1 2 3 4 5 6 7 8 9 10   16 15 14 13 12 11 10 09 08 07

CONTENTS

List of Maps and Illustrations

Foreword

Even before the Third Reich came to its smoldering end, an extensive discussion had developed about how such an evil regime could ever have come to power and how it could have repeatedly used that power, without any real challenge, to commit its horrifying crimes. This discussion has lasted to the present day, and no consensus has been met. One reason for the length of this debate is that while the issues seem to be easily simplified, in actuality they are quite complex. Hence, the simple explanations have been regularly refuted by available evidence. But another reason is that some components are still, after all these years, misunderstood.

An instructive example of this refutation of simple explanations has to do with the lack of any coherent and unified anti-Nazi effort by Germany's religious leaders. The facts are not in dispute. Leaders of all the Christian churches in Germany have acknowledged and repented their failures. What makes the issue perplexing is that there never should have been such failures, for Adolf Hitler's basic beliefs and actions were as anti-Christian as it is possible to be. He promoted hatred, lies, theft, murder—even idolatry. The Christian clergy, in all variations, had preached against every one of these sins, yet very few Christian clergymen were willing to declare publicly that Hitler and his movement represented a frontal assault upon the Ten Commandments and the teachings of Jesus. So we face a conundrum. It is logical to suppose that adherents of the Christian faith ought to have united instantly around its basic precepts and denounced Hitler. But they did not. Why not?

Helping us to analyze this mystery is the great contribution of Lowell C. Green's book. By examining one religious denomination, the Confessional Lutheran Church, and by explaining its behavior not on the basis of our assumptions but on its terms and by drawing on extensive inside knowledge, Professor Green shows us what is distorted in the analysis I have just summarized above.

9

Despite their common adhesion to several fundamental principles, the Christians of Germany cannot be put together as a bloc. Even setting aside the deep divisions between Catholics and Protestants, one cannot accurately categorize even all Protestants as forming a coherent entity. Instead, one must comprehend what divided the various Protestant churches and understand how those divisions were based upon deep theological commitments plus intense and never-forgotten historical experiences. As one reads through Lowell C. Green's book, one increasingly grasps this central fact: The inherited divisions formed the prime impediment to collective action.

Upon reflection, this should not surprise us. Adolf Hitler came to power by exploiting the divisions of Germans—political, social, and economic. He kept his hold over Germans because they continued to be divided. One of his central propaganda themes—and a classic "big lie"—was that he had unified the country: *ein Volk, ein Reich, ein Führer*. In reality, his great weapon was the classic formula for power: divide and rule.

What Lowell C. Green has done is illustrate how these divisions affected even Germans who were fundamentally anti-Nazi: the Lutheran leaders. These leaders included men who were Professor Green's teachers while he studied theology at the University of Erlangen after World War II, so his insights are based upon a close acquaintance with the key actors. Further, as an ordained Lutheran minister and a specialist on the history of the Reformation, Green has a deep understanding of the theological positions that were at the core of the behavior of the Lutheran leaders. This helps make the book uniquely useful.

But this book will also cause considerable controversy, though it should elevate the level of current debates. The author's interpretations are presented with great vigor, and I certainly do not agree with everything he has written. For example, I think Professor Green is wrong to blame the theories of Charles Darwin for contributing to Nazi ideology. I would certainly agree that the "social Darwinists" should be blamed, though what they primarily did was to provide a new vocabulary and some pseudoscientific justifications for preexistent racist ideas. They did that by seriously distorting Darwin's theories.

But this and most of my other quibbles are minor in comparison to the major contributions Lowell C. Green has made. This is an important book that will significantly strengthen our understanding of Nazi Germany. It will not end the long-standing and ongoing discussion about how the Third Reich could have happened. No single book will ever do that. But it does point us firmly in the right direction for comprehending the apparently puzzling behavior of Christians in Germany under the Hitler dictatorship.

William Sheridan Allen
State University of New York at Buffalo

Preface

How did a scholar who specializes in Renaissance humanism and the theology of the Lutheran Reformation come to write a book about Germany during Hitler's Third Reich? As William Sheridan Allen has indicated in the foreword, it was my privilege to study at the University of Erlangen during one of the greatest periods in its illustrious history. Among my teachers were renowned scholars such as Werner Elert, Paul Althaus, Walther von Loewenich, Walter Künneth, Friedrich Baumgärtel, and Wilhelm Maurer. As the book unfolds, the reader will discover these names falling into place. But why should I have even thought of undertaking the arduous task of writing such a book? This pursuit was goaded by the words and actions of postwar historians who wrote essays that were derogatory to those professors to whom I owed so much and were historically inaccurate of the church of my fathers, back to the days of Martin Luther.

Previous histories about the terrible days of the Third Reich had imbibed the propagandistic practices of the Fascists, Soviet Communists, and National Socialists, in which denunciation played a prominent role. For me, as a citizen of the United States, it was intolerable to hear the denunciations by those living in an easy post-Hitler era who were scolding those who had done their best in dark and cloudy times—especially when these detractors suppressed historical documents and facts that gave an entirely different picture. And when one of the later historians at the University of Erlangen led student radicals in a demonstration against the former home of Werner Elert, which had subsequently become a student hospice, and demanded that the "evil" name of Elert be taken down—an act that the Frankfurt newspaper called "dirtying one's own nest"—his credibility as an impartial historian was completely destroyed. I felt that the distortions that appeared in this man's essays needed to be counteracted with the facts as I knew them.

William Sheridan Allen mentions my personal acquaintance with many of the chief actors in the story. Besides those named above, I have spent time with people such as Bishop Hans Meiser, Theodore and Eva Baudler, Alfred Drung, Eduard Putz, Hilmar Ratz, Ernst Kinder, Jan and Charlotte Bender, Carl Stange, Martin and Eva Schmidt, Karlmann Beyschlag, Wilhelm and Hanna Elert Gerhoh, Rudolf Hermann, Hans Volz, Emanuel Hirsch, Theodor Strohm, Heinrich Grüber, Julius Bodensieck, and, last but not least, Paul Leo, his wife, Eva (née Dittrich), and his daughter, Anne Leo Ellis. More brief encounters were with Friedrich Gogarten, Friedrich Hauck, Heinrich Bornkamm, Hanns Rückert, Friedrich Wilhelm Hopf, Julius Schieder, Martin Niemöller, Hans Asmussen, Karl Barth, Paul Tillich, Heinrich Vogel, and Bruno Doehring. In some cases it was merely a glimpse, in others there was a conversation, and in still others there were many and prolonged discussions. All these connections have given me insights into the task at hand. Thus when Carl Stange related to me how Karl Barth had offended his colleagues at Göttingen by his imperious ways, this seemed to confirm my own appraisal of the Swiss theologian.

Spending several years as a graduate student in Germany, living in the Martin Luther Heim among other theological students (all of whom had vivid memories of the Third Reich and World War II), visiting places that were involved in the story, seeing the war's destruction evidenced in the bombed buildings, talking with people who had come through the war, traveling to Berlin and Hamburg and Bremen and Basel and many other places, and hearing hundreds of anecdotes that people were still relating all gave me a rich store of memories from which to draw. Only the reader will be able to decide whether these experiences enhance the book or detract from its worth.

In the pages that follow, most of the translations from German texts are my own. Where there are exceptions, I have tried to give due credit to the translator. In rendering German lines, I have generally tried to give equivalent meanings in idiomatic English rather than supplying literal translations, but where I have thought it crucial, I have given literal renditions.

Acknowledgments are owed to many people. Karlmann Beyschlag, Wilhelm and Hanna Elert Gerhoh, Gerhard Althaus, and Niels-Peter Moritzen (director of the Theological Archives at Erlangen) provided documents and valuable comments. Ronald Feuerhahn of Concordia Seminary, St. Louis, Missouri, expressed support for this project from the start and repeatedly encouraged me as new problems arose. Charles Ford of St. Louis University provided important insights into the position of Dietrich Bonhoeffer.[1] William Sheridan Allen of the State

---

1 Charles E. Ford wrote the important article, "Dietrich Bonhoeffer, the Resistance, and the Two Kingdoms," *Lutheran Forum* 27, no. 3 (August 1993): 28–34. This issue of

University of New York at Buffalo encouraged my publishing efforts. Karlmann Beyschlag assisted with gathering the photographs, and Karl E. Schmidt, also of Buffalo, New York, assisted in drawing the maps. Lois Elert Veseley, an American member of the Elert family, provided me with rich genealogical information about the family's origins in Pomerania.

Grateful recognition is owed the many librarians who went far beyond the normal demands of duty and without whose help this book could not have been written. Special mention must be made of David O. Berger of Concordia Seminary, St. Louis, Missouri, and Robert V. Roethemeyer of Concordia Theological Seminary, Fort Wayne, Indiana, and the library staff at the State University of New York at Buffalo, who were always helpful and who solved many problems expeditiously. Special thanks are owed Nancy Haberly and Jacques Berlin, leaders in the Computer Society of Western New York, who gave me indispensable help with computer problems.

Finally, I owe a debt of gratitude to my dear wife, Vilma, whose warm, loving care was a constant inspiration. She patiently put up with many lonely evenings while I was at the computer desk and encouraged me in many different ways. To all these and to many others who helped, my heartfelt thanks.

Lowell C. Green
State University of New York at Buffalo

Lutheran Forum also included significant essays on Bonhoeffer by other writers. Ford also brought to my attention the paper by Uriel Tal, "On Modern Lutheranism and the Jews," which had appeared in *Luther, Lutheranism and the Jews: A Record of the Second Consultation between Representatives of The International Jewish Committee for Interreligious Consultations and The Lutheran World Federation* held in Stockholm, Sweden, 11–13 July 1983, edited by Jean Halpérin and Arne Sovik (Geneva: Department of Studies, The Lutheran World Federation, 1984). We shall take up Tal's study in greater detail in chapter 5.

Abbreviations of Literature

In citing works in the footnotes, short titles or abbreviations have been used as listed below.

AELKZ	*Allgemeine evangelisch-lutherische Kirchenzeitung*
AGK	Arbeiten zur Geschichte des Kirchenkampfes. More than 55 vols. Göttingen: Vandenhoeck & Ruprecht, 1958ff.
Althaus, *Stunde*	Paul Althaus. *Die deutsche Stunde der Kirche*. Göttingen: Vandenhoeck & Ruprecht, 1933.
Althaus, *Th. Ord.*	Paul Althaus. *Theologie der Ordnungen*. 2d ed. Gütersloh: Evangelischer Verlag "Der Rufer," 1935.
Althaus, "Volkstum"	Paul Althaus. "Kirche und Volkstum." Pages 113–43 in *Evangelium und Leben: Gesammelte Vorträge*. Gütersloh: Carl Bertelsmann, 1927.
ATF	Archives of the Theological Faculty of the University of Erlangen.
Beyschlag	Karlmann Beyschlag. *Die Erlanger Theologie*. Einzelarbeiten aus der Kirchengeschichte Bayerns 67. Erlangen: Martin Luther Verlag, 1993.
Bonhoeffer	Dietrich Bonhoeffer. *Dietrich Bonhoeffer Werke*. Vol. 12: *Berlin, 1932–1933*. Edited by Carsten Nicolaisen and Ernst-Albert Scharffenorth. Gütersloh: Chr. Kaiser, 1997.
BSKO	*Bekenntnisschriften und Kirchenordnungen der nach Gottes Wort Reformierten Kirche*. Edited by Wilhelm Niesel. 3d ed. Zürich: Evangelischer Verlag, 1938.
BSLK	*Die Bekenntnisschriften der evangelisch-lutherischen Kirche*. Göttingen: Vandenhoeck & Ruprecht, 1930.

Carter	Guy Christopher Carter. "Confession at Bethel, August 1933—Enduring Witness: The Formation, Revision and Significance of the First Full Theological Confession of the Evangelical Church Struggle in Nazi Germany." Ph.D. diss., Marquette University, 1987. (Printed by Ann Arbor: Dissertations Information Service, 1988.)
Dietzfelbinger	Hermann Dietzfelbinger. *Veränderung und Beständigkeit: Erinnerungen.* Munich: Claudius, 1984.
EKL	Heinz Brunotte and Otto Weber, ed. *Evangelisches Kirchenlexikon.* 4 vols. Göttingen: Vandenhoeck & Ruprecht, 1956–1961.
ELC	Julius Bodensieck, ed. *The Encyclopedia of the Lutheran Church.* 3 vols. Minneapolis: Augsburg, 1965.
Elert, *Ausgang*	Werner Elert. *Der Ausgang der altkirchlichen Christologie: Eine Untersuchung über Theodor von Pharan und seine Zeit als Einführung in die alte Dogmengeschichte.* Posthumously edited by Wilhelm Maurer and Elisabeth Bergsträßer. Berlin: Lutherisches Verlagshaus, 1957.
Elert, *BBB*	Werner Elert. *Bekenntnis, Blut und Boden: Drei theologische Vorträge.* Leipzig: Dörffling & Franke, 1934.
Elert, *Christian Ethos*	Werner Elert. *Christian Ethos.* Translated by Carl J. Schindler. Philadelphia: Muhlenberg, 1957.
Elert, *Ethos*	Werner Elert. *Das christliche Ethos: Grundlinien der lutherischen Ethik.* Tübingen: Furche-Verlag, 1949.
Elert, *Ein Lehrer*	Werner Elert. *Ein Lehrer der Kirche: Kirchlich-theologische Aufsätze und Vorträge.* Edited by Max Keller-Hüschemenger. Berlin: Lutherisches Verlagshaus, 1967.
Elert, *Zwischen Gnade*	Werner Elert. *Zwischen Gnade und Ungnade: Abwandlungen des Themas Gesetz und Evangelium.* Munich: Evangelischer Presseverband für Bayern, 1948.
ELKZ	*Evangelische Lutherische Kirchen-Zeitung.* Successor to *AELKZ.*
Eyjólfsson	Sigurjón Arni Eyjólfsson. *Rechtfertigung und Schöpfung in der Theologie Werner Elerts.* Arbeiten zur Geschichte und Theologie des Luthertums, new ser., 10. Hanover: Lutherisches Verlagshaus, 1994.
Hamm	Berndt Hamm. "Schuld und Verstrickung der Kirche: Vorüberlegungen zu einer Darstellung der Erlanger Theologie in der Zeit des Nationalsozialismus." In *Kirche und Nationalsozialismus*, edited by Wolfgang Stegemann. Stuttgart: Kohlhammer, 1990.

Helmreich	Ernst Christian Helmreich. *The German Churches under Hitler: Background, Struggle, and Epilogue.* Detroit: Wayne State University Press, 1979.
Hermelink	Heinrich Hermelink. *Kirche im Kampf: Dokumente des Widerstands und des Aufbaus in der evangelischen Kirche Deutschlands von 1933 bis 1945.* Tübingen: R. Wunderlich, 1950.
JMLB	*Lutherische Kirche in der Welt. Jahrbuch des Martin-Luther-Bundes.* Berlin: Martin Luther-Verlag, 1969–.
Kater	Horst Kater. *Die Deutsche Evangelische Kirche in den Jahren 1933 und 1934: Eine rechts- und verfassungsgeschichtliche Untersuchung zu Gründung und Zerfall einer Kirche in nationalsozialistischen Staat.* Arbeiten zur Geschichte des Kirchenkampfes 24. Göttingen: Vandenhoeck & Ruprecht, 1970.
KJahr 1932	*Kirchliches Jahrbuch für die evangelischen Landeskirchen Deutschlands 1932.* Ein Hilfsbuch zur Kirchenkunde der Gegenwart 59, edited by Hermann Sasse. Gütersloh: Carl Bertelsmann, 1932.
KJahr 1933–1944	*Kirchliches Jahrbuch für die Evangelische Kirche in Deutschland 1933–1944.* Single volume edited by Joachim Beckmann. Gütersloh: Carl Bertelsmann, 1948.
Klügel, *Dokumente*	Eberhard Klügel. *Die lutherische Landeskirche Hannovers und ihr Bischof, 1933–1945: Dokumente.* Berlin: Lutherisches Verlagshaus, 1965.
Klügel, *Landeskirche*	Eberhard Klügel. *Die lutherische Landeskirche Hannovers und ihr Bischof, 1933–1945.* Berlin: Lutherisches Verlagshaus, 1964.
Korblatt	*Korrespondenzblatt für die evangelisch-lutherischen Geistlichen in Bayern.*
Künneth, *Abfall*	Walter Künneth. *Der große Abfall: Eine geschichtstheologische Untersuchung der Begegnung zwischen Nationalsozialismus und Christentum.* Hamburg: Friedrich Wittig, 1947.
Künneth, *Lebensführungen*	Walter Künneth. *Lebensführungen: Der Wahrheit verpflichtet.* Wuppertal: R. Brockhaus, 1979.
Künneth, *Politik*	Walter Künneth. *Politik zwischen Dämon und Gott: Eine christliche Ethik des Politischen.* Berlin: Lutherisches Verlagshaus, 1954.
Künneth and Schreiner, *Die Nation*	Walter Künneth and Helmuth Schreiner, ed. *Die Nation vor Gott: Zur Botschaft der Kirche im dritten Reich.* Berlin: Wichern, 1933.

KZ	*Kirchliche Zeitschrift.* Published since 1876. Pertinent volumes edited by Johann Michael Reu. Columbus: Lutheran Book Concern, 1930–1943.
Lau, *"Äußerliche Ordnung"*	Franz Lau. *"Äußerliche Ordnung" und "weltlich Ding" in Luthers Theologie.* Studien zur systematischen Theologie 12. Göttingen: Vandenhoeck & Ruprecht, 1933.
Lau, "Two Kingdoms"	Franz Lau. "The Lutheran Doctrine of the Two Kingdoms." *Lutheran World* 12 (1965): 355–72.
Loewenich, *Erlebte Theologie*	Walther von Loewenich. *Erlebte Theologie: Begegnungen, Erfahrungen, Erwägungen.* Munich: Claudius, 1979.
Meier, *Deutschen Christen*	Kurt Meier. *Die Deutschen Christen: Das Bild einer Bewegung im Kirchenkampf des Dritten Reiches.* Göttingen: Vandenhoeck & Ruprecht, 1964.
Meier, *EKK*	Kurt Meier. *Der evangelische Kirchenkampf.* 3 vols. Göttingen: Vandehoeck & Ruprecht, 1976–1984.
Meier, *Kirche und Judentum*	Kurt Meier. *Kirche und Judentum: Die Haltung der evangelischen Kirche zur Judenpolitik des Dritten Reiches.* Göttingen: Vandenhoeck & Ruprecht, 1968.
Meiser, *Verantwortung*	Hans Meiser. *Verantwortung für die Kirche: Stenographische Aufzeichnungen und Mitschriften von Landesbischof Hans Meiser 1933–1955.* Edited by Hannelore Braun and Carsten Nicolaisen. Vol. 1: *Sommer 1933 bis Sommer 1935.* Vol. 2: *Herbst 1935 bis Frühjahr 1937.* Göttingen: Vandenhoeck & Ruprecht, 1985–1993.
Niemöller, *Evangelische Kirche*	Wilhelm Niemöller. *Die evangelische Kirche im Dritten Reich: Handbuch des Kirchenkampfes.* Bielefeld: Ludwig Bechauf, 1956.
Reese	Hans-Jörg Reese. *Bekenntnis und Bekennen: Vom 19. Jahrhundert zum Kirchenkampf der nationalsozialistischen Zeit.* Arbeiten zur Geschichte des Kirchenkampfes 28. Göttingen: Vandenhoeck & Ruprecht, 1974.
Sasse, *In Statu Confessionis*	Hermann Sasse. *In Statu Confessionis.* Edited by Friedrich Wilhelm Hopf. Vol. 1: *Gesammelte Aufsätze.* Vol. 2: *Gesammelte Aufsätze und Kleine Schriften.* Berlin: Verlag die Spur, 1975–1976.

Schäfer, *Wurm*	Gerhard Schäfer, comp. *Landesbischof D. Wurm und der nationalsozialistische Staat 1940–1945: Eine Dokumentation.* Stuttgart: Calwer, 1968.
Schäfer, *Württemberg*	Gerhard Schäfer, comp. *Die Evangelische Landeskirche in Württemberg und der Nationalsozialismus: Eine Dokumentation zum Kirchenkampf.* 6 vols. Stuttgart: Calwer, 1971–1986.
Schmidt, *Bekenntnisse*	Kurt Dietrich Schmidt. *Die Bekenntnisse und grundsätzlichen Äußerungen zur Kirchenfrage.* Vol. 1: *Des Jahres 1933.* Vol. 2: *Das Jahr 1934.* Vol. 3: *Das Jahr 1935.* Göttingen: Vandenhoeck & Ruprecht, 1934–1936.
Schmidt, *Dokumente*	Kurt Dietrich Schmidt, ed. *Dokumente des Kirchenkampfes II: Die Zeit des Reichskirchenausschußes 1935–1937.* 2 parts. Arbeiten zur Geschichte des Kirchenkampfes 13–14. Göttingen: Vandenhoeck & Ruprecht, 1964–1965.
Scholder, *Kirchen*	Klaus Scholder. *Die Kirchen und das Dritte Reich.* Vol. 1: *Vorgeschichte und Zeit der Illusionen, 1918–1934.* Frankfurt am Main: Ullstein, 1977. Vol. 2: *Das Jahr der Ernüchterung 1934, Barmen und Rom.* Berlin: Siedler, 1985.
Simon	Bettina Simon. *Ausgegrenzt, entrechtet, verraten: Paul Leo—Biographische Spurensuche im Kontext des Verhaltens der ev.-luth. Landeskirche Hannovers (1933ff.) gegenüber ihren Pastoren jüdischer Herkunft* (*Ostracized, Delegalized, Betrayed: Paul Leo—Biographical Traces in the Context of the Procedure of the Evangelical Lutheran Land Church of Hanover (1933ff.) regarding Its Pastors of Jewish Descent*). Hausarbeit im Rahmen der Ersten Staatsprüfung für das Lehramt an Gymnasien. Universität Göttingen. Göttingen, unpublished thesis, June 12, 1996.
Tutzing	Paul Rieger and Johannes Strauß, ed. *Tutzinger Texte.* Edited for the Evangelische Akademie Tutzing. Vol. 1: *Kirche und Nationalsozialismus zur Geschichte des Kirchenkampfes.* Munich: Claudius, 1969.
WA	Martin Luther. *D. Martin Luthers Werke. Kritische Gesamtausgabe.* 65 vols. Weimar: Hermann Böhlaus, 1883–1993.
ZwKK	Helmut Winter, ed. *Zwischen Kanzel und Kerker: Augenzeugen berichten vom Kirchenkampf im Dritten Reich.* Munich: Claudius, 1982.

Abbreviations of Organizations

AELK	*Allgemeine evangelisch-lutherische Konferenz*	General Evangelical Lutheran Conference
AVSPW	*Arbeitsgemeinschaft Völkisch-Soziale Pfarrer Württembergs*	Study Association of *Völkisch-* Social Pastors in Württemberg
BDL	*Bund deutscher Lutheraner*	Federation of German Lutherans
CDB	*Christliche-Deutsche Bewegung*	Christian-German Movement
CVDP	*Christlicher Volksdienst Partei*	Christian *Volk*-Service Party
DEK	*Deutsche evangelische Kirche*	German Evangelical Church; Reich Church
DEKB	*Deutscher evangelische Kirchen Bund*	German Evangelical Church Federation *or* Federation of German Evangelical Churches
DGB	*Deutsche Glaubens-Bewegung*	German-Faith Movement; the German-Faithful
DNVP	*Deutschnationalen Volkspartei*	German National *Volk* Party
DVP	*Deutsche Volkspartei*	German *Volk* Party
EKD	Evangelische Kirche in Deutschland	Evangelical Church in Germany (after WWII)
EKU	*Evangelische Kirche der Union*	Evangelical Church of the Union
GDC	*Glaubensbewegung Deutscher Christen*	German-Christian (Faith) Movement
HJ	*Hitler-Jugend*	Hitler Youth
JB	*Jungreformatorische Bewegung*	Young Reformation Movement

KDC	*Kirchenbewegung Deutsche-Christen*	Church Movement of German-Christians (Thuringia)
LWF		Lutheran World Federation
NSDAP	*Nationalsozialistische Deutsche Arbeitpartei*	National Socialist German Workers Party; National Socialists; Nazi Party
PNB	*Pfarrernotbund*	Pastors Emergency League
RKA	*Reichskirchenausschuß*	Reich Church Commission
SS	*Schutzstaffel*	Nazi elite guard
VELKD	*Vereinigte evangelische-lutherische Kirche in Deutschland*	United Evangelical Lutheran Church in Germany
VKL	*Vorläufige Kirchenleitung*	Provisional Church Leadership

INDEX TO GERMANY IN 1935

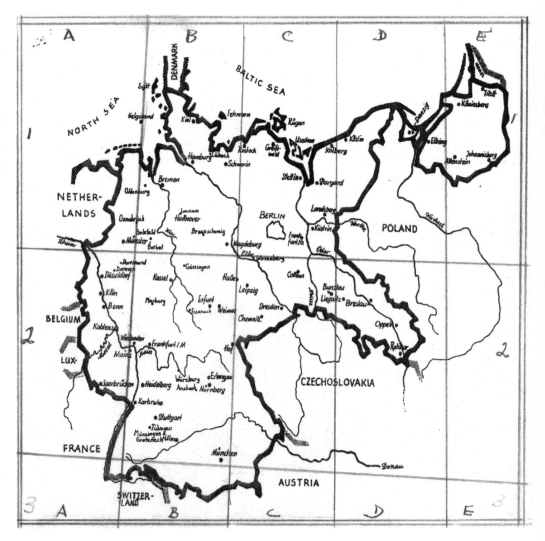

Fig. 1: Germany in 1935

INTRODUCTION

Much has been written about the Christian churches in Germany during the Hitler years. A bibliography published in 1958 on the history of the church struggle from 1933 to 1945 listed 5,566 titles already available at that time, and hundreds, if not thousands, of books and articles have appeared subsequently. So why has the present volume been written at all? Briefly, there are three reasons behind this book. First, though Lutherans comprise the majority of the German population, the history of the Confessional Lutheran churches during the Third Reich has never been written. Second, the fragmentary discussions of Lutherans in some of the more general histories of this period have been unsatisfactory and call for a correction. Third, important new historical sources that have recently become available shed a different light upon the teachings and actions of Lutherans under Adolf Hitler.

In the pages that follow, the viewpoint of the Confessional Lutheran churches and their leaders and theologians will be presented. Occasionally, this will lead to pointing out where Lutheran teachings and practices differed from Calvinism, Barthianism, and the Prussian Union. Because previous histories generally presented Reformed Protestant thinking, the present book offers a new perspective. This history could not have been written without noting these distinctions because the behavior of the Confessional Lutherans would be inexplicable in isolation from their ideology. Some stricter Lutherans, for example, feared that participation in the attempted German Evangelical Church advocated by Hitler would drag them into a new Union church. Their resistance was not necessarily the result of personal virtue; the restraints came from their understanding of what comprised the church. That the author sees himself as a Confessional Lutheran will doubtless be discernible, but the intention of this book is to explain why German Lutherans were cautious of attempts at unification and how this led them to act as they did.

Church Rivalries in Germany

Since the Protestant Reformation of the sixteenth century, there has been unfriendly rivalry between Lutheran and Reformed or Calvinist church bodies. It has been difficult for German Lutherans to forget the aggressive, deep inroads made by Calvinism into Lutheran church bodies throughout the preceding centuries. Almost every Protestant territory that later became a Reformed or Union land church[1] (*Landeskirche*) had once been Lutheran and had been "converted" by a Calvinist or Reformed ruler or by a Crypto-Calvinist theologian. The list of those Lutheran territories is long and includes, among others, the Palatinate, Anhalt, Bremen, East Friesland, and Galicia. On the other hand, there was scarcely a case in which Lutherans subverted Calvinist territories. Moreover, the Electorate of Saxony twice fell to a takeover by deceptive Crypto-Calvinist theologians, takeovers that were later reversed. Lutherans often wondered why the Reformed were constantly seeking church fellowship despite their almost contemptuous attitude toward the "Catholic" character of Lutheran doctrine and liturgy.

A Great Misfortune: The Prussian Union

Then came the greatest aggression of all: the Prussian Union, engineered by Frederick William III, a Hohenzollern king of the Reformed faith.[2] Frederick had married a Lutheran woman, with whom he could not receive Communion in the Lutheran Church. He was determined to overcome the long-held rule that Lutheran altars are only for Lutheran communicants. Beginning in 1817, the king carried out his unification program, which included his *Union Agenda* (a book that was supposed to provide uniform services in Lutheran and Reformed churches) and the implementation of his political structure that forcibly united

---

1 The use of the term "land church" or "territorial church" denotes a church of a particular territory or region of the German federal union.

2 Occasionally in the literature, the royal Prussian Church formed by Frederick William III is designated as the "Old Prussian Union" to differentiate it from later territorial and political manifestations, including the church body formed by the German Empire and the socialist interim government from November 1918 to August 1919. The Union church that survived into the Weimar Republic (1919–1933) remained historically based on the earlier Church of the Prussian Union. Therefore this book simplifies the discussion by using the "Prussian Union" to describe the consistent theological and cultural motifs of unionism throughout various political epochs.

the members of 7,000 Lutheran congregations with fewer than 130 Reformed congregations. This structure was called the Prussian Union.

Although approximately 98 percent of the Prussian Union consisted of Lutheran congregations, the Prussian crown introduced measures that strongly discriminated against Lutherans. In fact, it became illegal to recognize a Lutheran church within the Prussian Union. During a period of stern persecution, a group that called itself the "Old Lutherans" withdrew from the state church and established its own denomination, the Free Lutheran Church. At first the members of the Free Lutheran Church were bitterly persecuted by the state church, but later the Old Lutherans won toleration.[3] Seeking to avoid the persecution befalling Lutherans who adhered to the Confessions, other Old Lutherans, looking for religious liberty, immigrated to the United States or to Australia. It is estimated that about 8,000 people came from Prussia to the United States during this period of persecution.[4] Most of these immigrants joined one of two conservative bodies: either The Lutheran Church—Missouri Synod or the Buffalo Synod, which today is part of the Evangelical Lutheran Church in America.

The forced merger (*Gleichschaltung*) in Germany of Lutherans and Calvinists into one state church established the pattern for Adolf Hitler's endeavor a century later to herd all German Protestants into one Reich Church that would be submissive to him. As a mixture of conflicting confessions, the Prussian Union lacked unity in doctrine and practice. It was actually a bureaucratic system of church administration more than it was a real church. As a huge ecclesiastical umbrella, the Prussian Union destroyed the former paternalistic system in which the members of a small German territorial church, governed by a Lutheran prince, felt

---

3 The classic example of persecution of Lutherans under the Prussian Union took place in the church at Hönigern, Silesia. After four months of resistance by the people, during which time their dauntless pastor was imprisoned, the lay leaders still refused to accept a Union pastor or to turn over the keys of the church. On December 22, 1834, the Prussian Union authorities returned with 400 infantry soldiers, 50 cuirassiers, and 50 hussars. When the leaders of the congregation continued to refuse to turn over the keys, the military smashed open the church doors with battering rams and seized possession of the building. On Christmas Day 1834, the new pastor, fortified by the presence of several officials of the Prussian Union, conducted the service according to the *Union Agenda*. After this violent introduction of the Prussian Union, the church life of the congregation at Hönigern declined rapidly (related in Sasse, *In Statu Confessionis*, 2:184–93). The Prussian Union and events at Hönigern are also described in Hans Preuß, *Von den Katakomben bis zu den Zeichen der Zeit* (Erlangen: Martin Luther-Verlag, 1936).

4 See Jobst Schöne, "Georg Philip Eduard Huschke (1801–1886): Ein Rückblick," *Lutherische Beiträge* 6, no. 3 (2001): 205–13; for numbers of immigrants to the United States, see Schöne, "Huschke," 207.

themselves united with their ruler in one faith. The people lost their sense of ownership as their historic church was replaced and their Lutheran faith was suppressed in the interest of "unity." Thus church life declined alarmingly in the Prussian Union. Moreover, the Prussian state, with its militarist and expansionist policies, spread its tentacles over neighboring German territories, such as Saxony, Schleswig-Holstein, Rhineland, Westphalia, Hanover, and Hesse.

Even as the political leaders fought the Prussian advance, unwilling churchmen in these neighboring territories struggled against a takeover by the Prussian Union Church. These church leaders justifiably feared a loss of confessional integrity and a repetition of the Lutheran persecutions that had occurred in Prussia. This led to the formation of federations between members of the Confessional Lutheran land churches and Lutherans within the "destroyed" churches that already had been absorbed into the Prussian Union. Out of this situation, a rivalry developed between the leaders of the Lutheran land churches and those of the Union land churches who owed their power to the Prussian state.

The Confessional Lutherans, mindful of the past aggressive behavior of the Prussian Union, found themselves faced with a threefold threat to their independence during the Third Reich: the German Evangelical Church or Reich Church, the Confessing Church, and the Barmen Declaration. The Confessional Lutherans also were surrounded by the so-called German-Christians, whom they came increasingly to recognize as henchmen of the Nazi Party.[5] What stance should Confessional Lutherans take toward the formation of the German Evangelical Church or DEK (*Deutsche evangelische Kirche*)? Some of the professors at the University of Erlangen regarded the DEK as a harmless reorganization of the old Federation of German Evangelical Churches. These professors, including Werner Elert and Paul Althaus, thought that within this new organization the Lutheran Church could retain its identity and even assume its rightful place as the dominant Protestant denomination in Germany. Other professors at the University of Erlangen, including Hermann Sasse and Friedrich Ulmer, took a more negative

---

5 *Christliche-Deutsche Bewegung* (CDB), the original title for the Christian-Germans, is a hyphenated title in which *Christliche* and *Deutsche* are adjectival and therefore bound together with the hyphen. They are translated accordingly into English. Most Christian-Germans espoused traditional Christianity and refrained from political activism. The *Glaubensbewegung Deutscher Christen* (GDC), which is not adjectival in the German, translates into English as the "German-Christian Faith Movement" or, more succinctly, "German-Christian Movement" (because *German* and *Christian* are adjectival in the English translation, the hyphen is added). Because many German-Christians sympathized with the Nazis and infiltrated the churches to hamper legitimate work, the retention of the hyphen should help to remind the reader that these Germans opposed traditional Christianity.

attitude, regarding the DEK as a Trojan horse that would later bring the Lutheran land churches into an enlarged Union church.

Although the Confessional Lutheran land churches of Bavaria, Hanover, and Württemberg avoided a takeover by the National Socialists, the Prussian Union, with its unwieldy size and its ambiguity in faith and practice, fell with little resistance into the hands of the German-Christians in 1934. Henceforth, its huge bureaucracy was controlled by the Nazis. Church leaders who refused to recognize the Nazi leadership in the Prussian Union formed the Confessing Church, which was also a unionistic church. Out of its circles, and strongly influenced by the theological system of Karl Barth, came the leading ideas of the Barmen Declaration, which placed the Lutheran and Reformed creeds on the same level, calling them both "Reformational confessions." This declaration was stoutly rejected by most Confessional Lutherans.

STRUGGLES WITHIN THE UNION CHURCHES

One can feel the shame and pain of those Lutheran members of the Prussian Union as their denomination, its backbone removed and robbed of its theological integrity by King Frederick William III, skidded into Hitler's Reich Church and became a puppet sect. With their denomination in the ruthless hands of German-Christians, those who cared about truth and integrity built and participated in, at great personal peril, an underground church, the Confessing Church (*Bekennende Kirche*). Courageous members of the "destroyed" Prussian Union churches rejected the new official Nazi church bureaucracies that were dominated by the German-Christians. Instead, they set up governing systems that they called "Brethren Councils" (*Brüder-Räte*). Confessing Church members lived under the constant threat of the fury of Hitler's puppet churchmen. Many church leaders landed in concentration camps or found a martyr's death, desolate and removed from family and friends.

Members of the Confessing Church often resented the fact that the intact churches did not develop underground systems to work closely with the Brethren Councils of the destroyed churches. However, many leaders in the destroyed Lutheran land churches were wary of involvement in the Brethren Councils, which they regarded as a form of the Prussian Union operating within the Confessing Church. Therefore the leaders in the destroyed Lutheran churches turned to their colleagues in the intact Lutheran land churches for support. To avoid becoming part of the Union churches, they set up "Luther Councils" (*Luther-Räte*) after the pattern of the Brethren Councils. This development was deeply resented by some leaders of the Confessing Church, particularly by those involved in its more radical wing, the Dahlem Front, which was led by Martin Niemöller.

Instead of being jealous of and angry with the Confessional Lutheran churches, some of the leaders of the Confessing Church, such as Wilhelm Zoellner, recognized the need to correct the weaknesses in doctrine and practice of the Union churches. After the fall of Nazism in 1945, some members of the Dahlem Front, still resenting Confessional Lutheran solidarity, resumed the church struggle (*Kirchenkampf*), this time against the Lutheran land churches. Local Brethren Councils became a lobbying force by which zealots of the Confessing Church countermanded conservative Lutherans and their duly constituted church governments.

GUARDING AGAINST WRITING HISTORY OUT OF CONTEXT

After World War II the rivalry between the Union churches and the Confessional Lutheran churches was reflected in the early histories of the church struggle. Church historians with Union church leanings chronicled the events under the Third Reich in a manner that discredited the Confessional Lutherans. Nowhere is this more apparent than in the discussions concerning the Lutheran opposition to the Barmen Declaration. Perhaps it was not always the deliberate intention of historians to present the Lutheran churches and their people in an unfavorable light. A history of Confessional Lutherans during the Third Reich was lacking and much important information was unavailable. Especially in the first two decades following World War II, historians lacked access to source materials. But this has changed. For example, Bishop August Marahrens and the Church of Hanover had been presented as shameless collaborators with the Nazis, but studies by Eberhard Klügel and his publication of important documents relating to Marahrens and the Hanoverian church did much to exonerate the bishop and to provide a more balanced picture.[6] Another important event was the publication of the journals of Bishop Hans Meiser and the papers of Bishop Theophil Wurm; both projects have provided a different picture of Confessional Lutherans during the Third Reich.[7] Because the thrust of Prussian anger has been directed against the three intact Lutheran land churches of Bavaria, Württemberg, and Hanover,

---

6 See p. 17 for bibliographic information on Klügel's work. Klügel's positive assessment of Marahrens was challenged by Gerhard Besier, *"Selbstreinigung" unter britischer Besatzungsherrschaft: Die Evangelisch-lutherische Landeskirche Hannovers und ihr Landesbischof Marahrens 1945–1947* (Göttingen: Vandenhoeck & Ruprecht, 1986). Of course, the years covered by Besier do not fall within the scope of the present study, which ends with the fall of Nazism in 1945.

7 For the papers of Bishop Hans Meiser, see Meiser, *Verantwortung*. For the papers of Bishop Theophil Wurm, see Schäfer, *Wurm*; see also Schäfer, *Württemberg*.

the discovery and availability of these primary sources makes a fresh study mandatory.

Moreover, some previous writers, besides holding an undue bias in favor of the Prussian Union, lacked a sense of the historical context or what is called in the science of historiography a "historical frame of reference." Some writers were too quick to judge people from the past without proper attention to circumstances during the Third Reich. These writers harshly condemned their subjects on the basis of the far better conditions prevailing in the 1960s or 1970s. The time has come for a historical treatment in which the writer avoids judging the motives of Christians who struggled during the Third Reich and a treatment in which a broader understanding is given to the difficulties of those who suffered in the Nazi police state.

It is difficult for us to place ourselves in the historic circumstances of those who lived in Hitler's totalitarian state. The Germans who by 1938 or 1940 were strongly against Hitler could not see the danger in 1933.[8] For example, Friedrich Baumgärtel, a professor at the University of Erlangen who had been an officer in the German army during World War II and who was noted for his steadfast opposition to National Socialism, once told me that a U.S. journalist had asked him, "How could you have been an army officer at Hamburg and have done nothing to stop the goings-on in the concentration camp there?" Baumgärtel responded, "Sir, as one coming from a free society, you have no concept of what it was like to live in a totalitarian state, where all information was controlled by an evil government and where everyone was moved by fear." He then told the young reporter, "I did not know that there was a prison camp near Hamburg, but if I had found out about it, I can assure you that I wouldn't have told a single soul." It is almost impossible for us to imagine the anxiety and fear imposed by a terrorist police state. The scholarly historian must, of course, chronicle the vices as well as the virtues that are a part of the story. The historian must control the temptation to judge those who lived in a fascist state so there can be an understanding of what really happened.

Paul Althaus, in his classroom lecture on Christian ethics, commented in 1953 about the problems that earnest Christians faced during the Third Reich. He

---

8 Even Karl Barth, who severely castigated the Confessional Lutherans after 1945 for not recognizing Hitler's agenda earlier, admitted an inability in 1938 to see the true dangers of Nazism, describing "how the two great opponents in this struggled . . . confronted each other, how in this meeting at first neither side understood the other, and how then both the church as well as the state revealed themselves in their true nature, how they got into conflict and what, at the end, on the part of both sides, became the final result of the controversy" (*Not und Verheißung im Deutscher Kirchenkampf* [Bern: Buchhandlung der Evangelischen Gesellschaft, 1938], 3).

pointed out that many government officials found themselves in positions in which the Nazi government demanded actions the officials felt to be wicked. Such calls to action demanded officials make a decision between right and wrong, obedience or disobedience, and conscience and the ruling party. These officials also had to take into consideration the personal consequences of the decision, as well as the consequences that might be applied to their families or others. If an official resigned, what kind of person would the replacement be? Thousands who defied orders wound up in concentration camps and their positions were given to corrupt Nazis who followed diabolical orders without question and who chose to inflict additional suffering on the people with whom they dealt. Therefore many earnest Christians tried to pursue a moderate course, avoiding trouble by pretending to support the Nazi cause but attempting to mitigate evil measures whenever possible.

SEVERAL PREVIOUS STUDIES

At this point, let us look briefly at the works of several previous writers. One of the most widely known books on the churches during the Third Reich is the two-volume *Die Kirchen und das Dritte Reich* by Klaus Scholder.[9] Scholder must be commended for his painstaking and detailed research. Unfortunately, he is strongly biased against the Confessional Lutherans and favors those who support the Union church and the Barmen Declaration. Thus Scholder's stance leads him at times to a misleading presentation of the facts. For example, he often lumps Paul Althaus with Wilhelm Stapel, Emanuel Hirsch, and Friedrich Gogarten as members of a group of "political theologians." This "guilt by association" grouping is misleading, not only because Stapel was not a theologian but also because Althaus rejected the extreme positions of these three writers. Actually, Karl Barth, whom Scholder places in a favorable light, was the political theologian *par excellence*. Unfortunately, Scholder's work was never completed; it stopped in the year 1934 because of Scholder's untimely death.

A similar prejudice is visible in Arthur C. Cochrane, an American pupil of Karl Barth. Cochrane authored *The Church's Confession under Hitler*.[10] Cochrane regards the Barmen Declaration as the only "confession under Hitler," quite oblivious to its contradictions of Lutheran theology. Although he acknowledges that Hermann Sasse was the first to write against Nazi ideology (in 1932), Cochrane

---

9 See p. 19 for bibliographic details. The English translation is *The Churches and the Third Reich,* trans. John Bowden, 2 vols. (Philadelphia: Fortress, 1987–1988).

10 Arthur C. Cochrane, *The Church's Confession under Hitler* (Philadelphia: Westminster, 1962).

blames even Sasse for rejecting the Barmen Declaration in favor of Lutheran Confessional theology, as if one does not have the right to speak out as a Lutheran.

The German Churches under Hitler, the impartial and fair monograph by another American, Ernst Christian Helmreich, is perhaps the most useful book on the subject in English. More evenhanded than Scholder is the massive three-volume work completed by Kurt Meier, *Der evangelische Kirchenkampf.* Moreover, whereas the early death of Scholder prevented his work from going beyond the year 1934, Meier's massive work covers the entire period in great detail. Meier presented much material found nowhere else, and his large work is a valuable mine of historical information, to which the present writer gladly confesses his indebtedness, as is shown by the large number of acknowledgments to Meier in the notes of this work. Also helpful are Meier's earlier monographs on the Jewish people and on the German-Christians; much of the material in these smaller books was incorporated into his later three-volume history.[11]

The publications of Wilhelm Niemöller and Berndt Hamm are highly partisan and one-sided. Niemöller published one of the earliest accounts of the church struggle in his monograph *Die evangelische Kirche im Dritten Reich.*[12] Hamm, Werner Elert's successor in the chair of church history at the University of Erlangen, writes extremely disparaging accounts of Elert and Althaus. Hamm's essays are marked by three fatal weaknesses: (1) In criticizing his subjects, he fails to consider the historical context of the difficult times under Hitler and condemns people from a postwar vantage point. (2) He seems to manipulate historical facts to achieve his purpose, leaving out details prejudicial to his own interests. (3) He exhibits an accusatory style that some people in the Confessing Church learned from their Nazi opponents.

Friedrich Baumgärtel of Erlangen sounded a warning against manipulating the facts of history. Initially, he wrote only a book review of Niemöller's monograph, pointing out some serious discrepancies in Niemöller's work. After Niemöller angrily responded to the book review, Baumgärtel expanded his study into a small book published in 1959 as *Wider die Kirchenkampf-Legenden.*[13] Baumgärtel criticized Niemöller, noting that he had selected material that made the Confessional Lutherans look bad and had suppressed evidence that was unfavorable to the Prussian Union, of which Niemöller was a member. Although Baumgärtel's slim volume provoked much anger from the Dahlem Front, sober historians have lauded its accuracy. Karlmann Beyschlag, a professor at the Uni-

---

11 See p. 17 for bibliographic details on the work by Helmreich and p. 18 for details on the work by Meier.

12 See p. 18 for bibliographic details.

13 Neuendettelsau: Freimund, 1959; repr., 1976.

versity of Erlangen, published a valuable history entitled *Die Erlanger Theologie*.[14] In an appendix, he provides important documents regarding Althaus and Elert during the *Kirchenkampf*.

---

14 See p. 15 for bibliographic details.

CHAPTER ONE

THE BACKGROUND OF THE CHURCH STRUGGLE (*KIRCHENKAMPF*)

This opening chapter introduces the players in the drama of the *Kirchenkampf*: the different churches, the various organizations linking church leaders with the social and political currents, and the National Socialist Party (Nazi Party). This chapter defines the tenets of the Confessional Lutheran churches, the Prussian Union and other Union churches, the Confessing Church and its councils, as well as the other Protestant churches that were present when Adolf Hitler seized political power in Germany in 1933. After a brief review of the political and religious currents of the time, especially the role of the National Socialist Party and the Christian-German and German-Christian Movements, the focus turns to the various ways church leaders tried to respond to the challenge of the Nazi Party. Finally, the chapter closes with a look at the theological faculty at the University of Erlangen, which was the most prominent voice of Lutheran theology during the Third Reich.

THE PROTESTANT CHURCHES OF GERMANY IN 1933–1934

In Germany all the state churches were abolished as such in 1918 and replaced by twenty-seven autonomous land churches, besides the provincial churches of the Prussian Union.[1] Together, Protestants made up about 60 percent of the total German population in 1933. Lutherans, both in confessional churches and in Union churches, made up almost all of this number.

---

1 A list of the Free Lutheran churches is given in Hermelink, 29–30.

The following list identifies the Confessional Lutheran land churches and their membership by state.

State	Membership	Percentage of Total Population
Bavaria	1,598,442	21 percent
Württemberg	1,722,295	67 percent
Hanover	2,414,232	92 percent
Schleswig-Holstein	1,420,777	94 percent
Free State of Saxony	4,465,880	89 percent
Mecklenburg (two land churches combined in 1934)	731,081	94 percent
Thuringia (numerous smaller territorial churches combined in 1920)	1,412,013	92 percent
Braunschweig	464,175	94 percent
Oldenburg	101,513	95 percent
Schaumburg-Lippe	45,001	98 percent

The old Hanseatic cities reported as follows:

City	Membership	Percentage of Total Population
Hamburg	1,006,206	85 percent
Lübeck	121,093	95 percent

Besides this, the ecclesiastical territories formerly belonging to the bishop of Lübeck, centering in the cities of Eutin and Oldenburg, had 45,895 Lutherans representing 97 percent of the population. Aside from a heavy plurality of Lutherans in the Union churches, the Confessional Lutheran churches in Germany totaled about 14,200,000 members in 1933.

There were relatively few purely Reformed land churches in Germany. Nineteenth-century Prussia had had only about 130 Calvinist congregations, and when they were forcibly united with 7,000 Lutheran congregations by Frederick William III into the Evangelical Church of the Prussian Union, their identity was seriously impaired. As more Union churches were formed, Reformed congregations disappeared. In 1933–1934 a Reformed church remained in the state of Hanover with 228,775 members, which comprised 7 percent of the population. Birkenfeld, a former territory about 40 miles north of Saarbrücken, also had a Reformed church that had 43,721 members, which represented 79 percent of the population. The

Reformed church in the state of Lippe had 154,050 members or 94 percent of the population; however, a separate "Lutheran Class" included eleven staunchly Confessional Lutheran congregations. The largest Reformed city was Bremen, though the Reformed members were contained within a Union church. Additionally, though many of the churches were Reformed, the cathedral and several parishes in Bremen had remained Lutheran after the forceful introduction of Calvinism. In Bavaria there also were several Reformed congregations, including the Huguenot church in Erlangen and St. Martha in Nuremberg.

There were various separate Union churches. The Prussian Union, which numbered about 20,000,000 members, was divided among the following provincial churches:

State	Percentage of Total Population
East Prussia	82 percent
Brandenburg	91 percent
Pomerania	94 percent
Posen	62 percent
Silesia	50 percent
Saxony Province	89 percent
Westphalia	46 percent
Rhineland	29 percent
Memel	92 percent
Danzig	56 percent
Poland	12 to 13 percent
Upper Silesia	19 congregations[2]

In several cases, the merger of Lutherans and Calvinists took place during a Prussian military occupation and was subsequently never rescinded. In 1933, there were four Union churches in Hesse with membership totaling about 2,541,000 members. In Baden there was a Union church of 895,469 members that represented 66 percent of the population. The Union Church of Anhalt, with a strong Reformed presence, had 319,129 members, embracing 91 percent of the population. The church with the longest name was the United Protestant Evangelical Christian Church of the Palatinate, which had 544,991 members or 53 percent of the population. The Palatinate was strongly Calvinist.[3]

---

2 The exact percentile, a tiny fraction of the total population, was not supplied.

3 All the preceding statistics are from *KJahr 1932*, 561–69. For the sake of completeness, the list of Prussian Union churches includes Upper Silesia; however, Upper Silesia

Eight Free Lutheran churches were listed in the 1932 *Kirchliches Jahrbuch*.[4] The incomplete figures listed 4,900 members besides those of the Evangelical Lutheran Church in Prussia (Old Lutheran), which had 57,000 members and 153 churches.

Other denominations in Germany in 1933 included the Moravians with 9,640 members; the Mennonites with 21,390 members; the Baptists with 68,000 adult members; the Methodists with 51,396 members; the Salvation Army, which listed 189,440 employees and adherents; and several smaller evangelical groups that totaled fewer than 50,000 members.[5]

In 1866 the rule of Prussia had spread, and as it expanded, so did the tentacles of the Evangelical Church of the Prussian Union. It moved into previously Lutheran territories and took over or absorbed churches in Schleswig-Holstein, Hanover, and Hesse. Because the minister for culture and education (*Kultusminister*) exerted a strong influence over higher education, the universities of Kiel, Göttingen, and Marburg became staffed with professors who were friendly to the Prussian Union and critical of Confessional Lutheranism. These universities never regained their status as strong centers of Lutheranism. Three universities remained the bulwark of Lutheran theology: Erlangen, Leipzig, and Rostock. At times, Greifswald and Dorpat (Tartu, in Estonia) were also centers of Confessional Lutheranism.[6]

Hermann Sasse, who had grown up in the Prussian Union and served in it before moving to the University of Erlangen in 1933, wrote in 1945 that the Prussian Union had for a long time been a political instrument of the state, that its theologians had been the spokesmen of an ideology of ecclesial subservience to the civil order, and that these theologians had thereby distorted the teaching of Luther.[7] Sasse pointed out that not only had Luther called civil rulers "heroes and miracle men" but also that he had sometimes named them "God's jailors and hangmen" and that on occasion he pilloried them as "usually the greatest fools or the most evil rascals on earth." Sasse charged that in the 1930s not only Prussian Union theologians but also Confessional Lutherans were prone to quote Luther's complimentary descriptions of political leaders and keep his biting criticisms of rulers well hidden in a drawer.[8]

---

had only a small number of churches and the percentage of the population is not provided.

4 *KJahr 1932*, 588.

5 *KJahr 1932*, 590–94.

6 Sasse, *In Statu Confessionis*, 1:293.

7 Sasse, *In Statu Confessionis*, 1:298.

8 Sasse, *In Statu Confessionis*, 1:297.

Wilhelm Zoellner, a prominent Lutheran churchman who was part of a Prussian Union church, made the following indictment of the Union church system:

> There are really three confessions in the Church of the Old Prussian Union: the Lutheran, the Reformed, and the United. Hitherto the Union in Prussia has not brought it together to create a true confession for itself. But if for the renewal of the church we are to go back to the Confessions of four hundred years ago, we can do this only if these Confessions become a living presence for today. Gogarten was right when he said: "Confession always includes the testimony of the Gospel against something within." We have different intellectual streams today than those at the time of the Reformation, and therefore the confession of the Gospel over against them will often be not a mere repetition of the old Reformational Confessions, but from the answer of the church from that time, it must come to the answer of the church of today . . . . The Union constitution that we have today in Prussia could only arise out of indifference regarding the confession, and therefore the confession, as a living soul, has been switched off.[9]

Zoellner thought the Lutherans and the Reformed could make a real contribution to the projected German Evangelical Church, but his own group, the Union Church, would have little to give: "A Reich Church upon the basis of the Confessions would yield a church with a Lutheran type and with a Reformed type, extending into its top leadership, but it is not appropriate for the supporters and friends of the Union to perpetuate their type within this church."[10]

When we speak of Confessional Lutherans, we must not forget that the vast majority of the members of the Evangelical Church of the Prussian Union were Lutheran and that many of them were strong Confessional Lutherans, including Zoellner and Hermann Sasse. Lutherans in the Union churches organized themselves regionally into Lutheran Associations or Lutheran Conferences (*lutherische Vereinen* or *lutherische Konferenzen*). These groups held regular meetings and tried to keep the Lutheran consciousness alive in the Prussian Union.[11] If all the Lutherans in Germany were added together, their number would have comprised about 60 percent of the German population in 1933.

Some Union churches were only administrative unions in which congregations continued to exist separately as either Lutheran or Reformed (e.g., in Westphalia, Brandenburg, or Pomerania). In other cases, a consensus union occurred in which the Lutheran, Reformed, and Union confessions were upheld on a basis

---

9 *KZ* 57 (1933): 375.

10 *KZ* 57 (1933): 376. See also the negative judgment of the Union churches by Max Glage, pastor of the independent St. Anschar Lutheran Church of Hamburg, in the January 21, 1934, *Anscharboten*, reprinted in *KZ* 58 (1934): 246–49.

11 Meiser, *Verantwortung*, 1:1–2; reference to Reese, 77f., 84f.

of parity (e.g., Baden, Rhineland, Palatinate). In the Synod of Halle in 1937 (see below), steps were taken toward converting the Prussian Union into a consensus union. As we have seen, more German Lutherans in 1933 were under the jurisdiction of Union churches than were in Confessional Lutheran churches.

AN EARLY PROTESTANT POLITICAL MOVEMENT

One of the earliest groups that investigated the political scene from a Christian perspective was the Study Association of *Völkisch*-Social Pastors in Württemberg (*Arbeitsgemeinschaft Völkisch-Soziale Pfarrer Württembergs* [AVSPW]).[12] As the name indicates, this was an association for study purposes, not a political action group, as the German-Christians would be. The declaration of the AVSPW began with this quotation from Luther: "I was born for my Germans, and I want to serve them." The opening was followed by the assertion: "The Germanism [*Deutschtum*] to which we confess ourselves is that which was born out of the Reformation. We see the fundamental presupposition for every recovery of our *Volk* as lying in a recovery of Luther's spirit within our *Volk*: piety, trust in God, the courage to fight."[13] Next followed a rather theocratic statement: "Our primary goal is therefore this: That Jesus Christ again become the ruling power in public life according to the understanding of the Gospel as it was returned to light through the Reformation."[14] The document continued with a repudiation of all forces that destroyed "this religious-moral good," listing the following foes: (1) "the growing Jewish influence upon German intellectual life," with its anti-Christian attitude that "works against the purity and honor of the German soul"; (2) the "counter-Reformational" Roman Catholic Church, with its power plays that, "under the cloak of religion," were trying to destroy the "freedom of faith, conscience, and thought" of the Germans; (3) the religious sectarians who were corrupting "the German life of faith" with the stamp of "superficial Anglo-American piety"; (4) the covetousness that "rules the whole political life and economy," dividing the people and causing class struggle; (5) the "dreadful lack of character" of concepts of international brotherhood that were preached under the flag of a humane liberalism but which in fact ended in the politics of a lack of national worth.[15] This declaration presented attitudes that would later lead to trouble.

---

12 Schäfer, *Württemberg*, 1:71.

13 Schäfer, *Württemberg*, 1:71. For an understanding of the use of *Volk* and its derivatives in this book, see pp. 109–11.

14 Schäfer, *Württemberg*, 1:71.

15 Schäfer, *Württemberg*, 1:71–72.

THE CHRISTIAN-GERMAN MOVEMENT

The *Christliche-Deutsche Bewegung* (CDB), or the Christian-German Movement,[16] should not be confused with the German-Christian Movement, which will be treated later.[17] The CDB was organized as a group in which Christians might study and discuss political issues; however, the group refused to endorse any single political party. It disbanded after the antics of the 1933 election.

There were two branches of the CDB: the South German branch, which was a rather popular movement and included people from various walks of life,[18] and the North German branch, which was more elitist and counted many prominent leaders. The North German branch was founded in 1930 by Pastor Walter Wilm, landowner Ewald von Kleist-Schmenzin, Court Preacher Bruno Doehring of Berlin, and several individuals from the circles of the *Stahlhelm* (the militaristic Steel Helmets). Its numbers included members of the German National *Volk* Party (*Deutschnationalen Volkspartei* [DNVP]). There were a number of university professors in the CDB, including Paul Althaus, Emanuel Hirsch, Heinrich Bornkamm, and Heinrich Rendtorff. Rendtorff, who had become land bishop of Mecklenburg-Schwerin in 1930, was a principle leader of the CDB. In 1930 the only member of the Nazi Party in the CDB was Friedrich Wieneke. Althaus's connection with the CDB ended when the movement collapsed in the summer of 1933.

After the CDB disbanded, Wieneke joined the German-Christian Movement. Because the CDB avoided taking political sides, it is curious that though Otto Lohss, leader of the South German branch, denounced the Center Party, Althaus, a member of the North German branch, supported Heinrich Brüning and the Center Party. Althaus once told Helmut Thielicke that he, a Lutheran, had voted for the Roman Catholic party because he thought that members of the Center Party were the only ones who could hold together the splintered fragments of the Weimar Republic.[19] Thus James A. Zabel is correct when he writes: "The CDB did

---

16 The following works provide valuable information on the Christian-Germans. Hermann Sasse, "Die Kirche und die politischen Mächte der Zeit," in *KJahr 1932*, 74–76; James A. Zabel, *Nazism and the Pastors: A Study of the Ideas of Three Deutsche Christen Groups*, Dissertation Series of the American Academy of Religion 14 (Missoula, MT: Scholars Press, 1976), 21–24; Meier, *Deutschen Christen*, 10–12; Meier, *EKK*, 1:65–70; and Schäfer, *Württemberg*, 1:71–102. Unlike Meier and Zabel, Schäfer discusses related groups going back to the mid-1920s.

17 The false claim that Paul Althaus was a German-Christian was partly caused by the inaccurate association of the Christian-German Movement, of which he was a member, with the German-Christian Movement.

18 A document from 1931 is perhaps the earliest position statement of the South German branch of the CDB.

19 Helmut Thielicke, "Äusserung über Herrn Professor D. Paul Althaus, Erlangen," March

not actively support the Nazis before 1933," in which year, of course, the CDB dissolved its organization.[20]

In 1931 Hanns Rückert, a member of the CDB, moved from Leipzig to Tübingen, where he became a member of the German-Christian Movement (GDC). Althaus refrained completely from joining the German-Christians after the CDB disbanded in September 1933. Emanuel Hirsch belonged to the GDC for a few weeks and was briefly a member of the Thuringian *Kirchenbewegung Deutsche-Christen* (KDC) in 1934. But he soon left both groups because he felt they restricted his independence.

Although the CDB denied that it favored any political party, its two leaders came out in favor of National Socialism. Otto Lohss, who led the South German branch, endorsed National Socialism in 1931, and Heinrich Rendtorff, bishop of Mecklenburg-Schwerin, the leader of the North German branch after 1932, later issued a similar statement. Both men hoped that National Socialism would bring solutions to Germany's serious problems. The following statement likely came from Lohss: "We see in the German Freedom Movement [of Adolf Hitler] an instrument in the hand of God."[21] Rendtorff wrote in the *Mecklenburgische Zeitung*: "The Evangelical Church knows herself to be obliged to place the fundamental powers of the National-Social movement under the Word of God."[22]

One thing that greatly troubled the Germans in 1933 was the ruthless advance of world Communism. Germany stood geographically much closer than the United States to the savage measures of Soviet collectivization and its horrible atrocities. Germans had personal contact with Soviet people who were being terrorized by Bolshevik brutality. Beginning in 1928, Joseph Stalin had begun to push through his program of abolishing private property and collectivizing agriculture and industry under the Soviet state, and he arrested and deported to Siberia those who disagreed with his policy. The Soviet government confiscated the food raised by the peasants; as a result, millions starved to death. The famine became acute among the Volga Germans by 1933. *Brüder in Not* (*Brethren in Need*), a Berlin publication, reported that in 1933 the evangelical churches in Germany had received about 100,000 letters from German-Russians describing the famine and appealing for help.[23] Therefore when the National Socialists pre-

---

28, 1947, page 4, from Althaus Papers, file "Entlaßung 1947," in possession of Gerhard Althaus.

20 Zabel, *Nazism and the Pastors*, 23.

21 Dated April 26, 1932, quoted in Schäfer, *Württemberg*, 1:86.

22 Dated April 23, 1931, quoted in Schäfer, *Württemberg*, 1:91.

23 Robert Conquest, *The Harvest of Sorrow: Soviet Collectivization and the Terror-Famine* (New York: Oxford University Press, 1986), 281, 386 n. 47.

sented themselves as the only viable alternative to Bolshevism and excoriated the Center Party of Heinrich Brüning as being soft on Communism, they won many votes from people who were not otherwise in favor of Nazism.

The fear of Bolshevism colored a report issued by the CDB at Stuttgart on September 29, 1931, which included the following statements based on reports of Soviet terrorism: "We see how the Bolshevist 'Godless Movement' shamelessly and impudently blasphemes all that is high and holy and drags it into the dust. We hear how Bolshevism announces with brutal openness a battle of annihilation against the Christian Church and all Christian culture." The report referred to a declaration Stalin made in 1930 regarding collectivization, which proclaimed that within five years "no private property, no marriage, no family, no church and no other faith would be found in Russia other than faith in communism." Stalin added that anything preventing the achievement of this goal must be annihilated. The CDB report asserted that, under the principles of international Communism, what the Bolshevists wanted for Russia, they also wanted for Germany. This led to the inference that in the coming German elections the voters would have to decide between atheistic communism on the left or "a renewal of *Volk* and state upon a national and Christian basis" under Nazism on the right.[24]

Lohss sent a list of the CDB's goals—signed by Rendtorff, Wilm, Rittmeister H. von Viereck-Dreveskirchen, and Heinz Pflugk—to Land Church President Theophil Wurm on December 10, 1931. The list included:

> The Christian-German Movement is a free gathering of men and women who are bound together by the same faith. . . . We affirm the Evangelical faith. . . . We learned in a hard school that neither faith in the state nor in the economy, neither faith in parties nor in movements, neither faith in our race nor in the good intentions of German people, can suffice to deliver the German *Volk*. . . . We affirm the German freedom movement under the cross. On the basis of faith we can recognize only one Lord, the living God. All humanity is right only when it serves Him. Also the German *Volk* and Reich do not have their own purpose or final worth, but they call to service for God, for obedience under the will of God. If the German *Volk* denies this obedience, it stands under the judgment of God and will be repudiated. If the German *Volk* confesses itself to this obedience, then it may view its life and history as an order of God the Creator, as an entrusted talent, as a task appointed to it by God, as a place of his forgiveness, as the field of the hope of faith. . . . We want to gather and educate the Christian people of Germany to such an attitude of faith. Our combat circles [laypeople] and our study fellowships [pastors] are to do their helpful service in all German lands.[25]

---

24 Quotations in Schäfer, *Württemberg*, 1:75.

25 Quoted in Schäfer, *Württemberg*, 1:81–83.

Hermann Sasse reprinted the above objectives of the CDB in the 1932 *Kirchliches Jahrbuch* and concluded with the following characterization of the CDB:

> This movement is greeted with much joy in wide circles of the church. Its starting point, the presupposition of the church and churchly confessions, is undoubtedly right. One can only wish that it will fulfill its mission in an ongoing deepening of its program . . . . In National Socialist circles, there is lively opposition against the program [of the CDB].[26]

THE GERMAN-CHRISTIAN MOVEMENT

There was a noteworthy verbal distinction between the titles of the CDB and the GDC. Whereas the CDB placed the word *Christian* first in its title (*Christian-*German Movement), the GDC placed *German* at the start (*German-*Christian Movement). The confession of the GDC was faithful to the principles of National Socialism. The Nazis had promised tolerance in the 1924 party platform. The following words of section 24 were regarded by many as supportive of the churches:

> We demand freedom for all religious confessions in the state, so far as they do not endanger its existence or conflict against the ethical and moral feelings of the Germanic race. The party as such presents the standpoint of a positive Christianity, without binding itself confessionally upon any particular confession. It fights against the Jewish-materialistic spirit in and outside us and is convinced that a permanent revitalization of our *Volk* can only follow from within upon the basis of public benefit or of self-interest.[27]

Except for a few people—including Otto Dibelius, Dietrich Bonhoeffer, Hermann Sasse, and Richard Karwehl—almost no one saw the danger in a Nazi Party with such a program. Sasse perceptively wrote as early as 1932 that on the basis of section 24 a conflict was inevitable between Christianity and Nazism because the doctrine of original sin and unworthiness of the sinner would offend the "ethical and moral feelings" of the Germanic race.[28]

Sasse's words predicted the rousing refutation of the doctrine of original sin that occurred at the Conference on the Heathen-Religious Wrestling of Our Time in Berlin at the end of January 1934.[29] This conference was led by radical representatives of the German-Christian and German-Faith (*Deutsche Glaubens-Bewegung*) Movements.[30] A protest was given in words that seem borrowed from Sasse's

---

26 *KJahr 1932*, 76.

27 Hans Liermann, *Kirchen und Staat* (Munich: Isar, 1954), 15.

28 See *KJahr 1932*, 65–66; Sasse, *In Statu Confessionis*, 1:262.

29 *KZ* 58 (May 1934): 309–11.

30 On the *Deutsche Glaubens-Bewegung*, see pp. 46–49 and *EKL*, 3:1683–85.

prophecy: "The [Christian] doctrine of [original] sin and the guilt of mankind is an insult to the Germanic person." Ernst Bergmann stated: "We do not believe that we were conceived and born in sin. We do not believe that God became man in Jesus." Instead of speaking of "fallen mankind," one should speak of "ascending mankind." To the future belongs the elevation to a "higher, nobler, superman type. We must ourselves become Christ."[31]

The mainstream of German-Christians consisted of two major groups. The first was the Thuringian group or the Church Movement of German-Christians (*Kirchenbewegung Deutsche-Christen* [KDC]). This movement began in 1927 under the leadership of two Lutheran pastors with Pietistic or even neo-Pentecostal leanings: Julius Leutheuser and Siegfried Leffler. In later years, the KDC became increasingly radical and aligned with Nazi ideology. The group that was most directly connected with the Nazi annexation of churches was the German-Christian (Faith) Movement (*Glaubensbewegung Deutscher Christen* [GDC]), which was originally led by the Berlin pastor Joachim Hossenfelder.

Generally speaking, the German-Christians had these goals: to adapt Christian teachings to the Nazi program, to sway the churches into accepting National Socialism, and to seize control of the land churches and bring them into the German Evangelical Church (DEK) or Reich Church (the program of annexation was called *Gleichschaltung*).

Leutheuser and Leffler, the founders of the German-Christian Movement in Thuringia, came out of the Lutheran Land Church of Bavaria and had studied theology at Erlangen at the feet of Werner Elert and Paul Althaus.[32] At Erlangen, they faced a Confessional Lutheran theology that insisted that God gave a complete divine revelation of the Gospel in the Bible and that in respect to the doctrine of salvation there could be no further revelation. However, the Erlangen theologians also taught that God makes himself known to man through human reason, history, nature, and the orders of creation, the knowledge that belonged to the Law, not to the Gospel.

Leutheuser and Leffler had strong leanings toward neo-Pentecostalism and the belief in ongoing direct revelation or prophecy from God. Both men left more conservative Bavaria to work in the Lutheran Land Church of Thuringia, a new and unstable amalgamation of eight small land churches, in which their enthusiastic leanings would be less restricted. Leutheuser and Leffler developed an ideology based upon the belief that concepts such as *Volk*, race, blood, and soil were divinely inspired. More prominent writers such as Wilhelm Stapel, Emanuel

---

31 *KZ* 58 (1934): 310.

32 Elert reports that Leffler and Leutheuser had been in his seminar at Erlangen. See Elert's November 17, 1937, report to Rector Fritz Specht in ATF, file "Elert" by date.

Hirsch, and Friedrich Gogarten expounded similar views. Later we shall see how Elert and Althaus found it necessary to differentiate their position from the two extremes of German-Christian ideology and Barthian theology. Althaus marked this task in *Theologie der Ordnungen* (*Theology of the Orders*) and Elert did this in his *Bekenntnis, Blut und Boden* (*Confession, Blood, and Soil*). In chapter 9 we shall return to a more complete examination of these two books.

THE GERMAN-FAITH MOVEMENT

More radical than the German-Christian Movement was the German-Faith Movement (*Deutsche Glaubens-Bewegung* [DGB]). Members of this group were called the *Deutschgläubige*, or "German-Faithful," in analogy to the Roman Catholic concept of the "faithful" as those who accept, believe, and follow the teachings of the papal church. Formally organized in 1933, the DGB came out of a number of earlier groups. The German-Faithful openly opposed both Jewish and Christian doctrines and produced ideologies based upon elements from the old Germanic religions, the Nordic gods and goddesses, pantheism, and mysticism. The DGB talked often about a Nordic or Aryan religion and turned traditional Christian festivals into commemorations of heathen festivals.[33] For example, the DGB inaugurated a Nordic cult at the tomb of Henry the Lion in the venerable cathedral of Braunschweig. Something similar was done in the tenth-century abbey church at Quedlinburg. Although the DGB regarded Alfred Rosenberg as one of its own, the movement failed to achieve recognition from the Nazi Party.[34] Hitler really was not interested in religion; rather, he sought control of the churches because they were powerful institutions. The Berlin Sport Palace rally on November 13, 1933, in which the DGB was involved, quickly offended the churches. Thus the DGB lost most of its adherents and became of little further interest to Hitler.

A short German Apostles' Creed by Ernst Bergmann, a DGB leader, stated: "I believe in the God of German-Religion, who works in nature, in the lofty human spirit, and in the strength of his *Volk*. And in the helper, Krist [*sic*], who fights for the nobility of the human soul. And in Germany, the pedagogical land of a new humanity."[35] Another example of the DGB position is found in Hermann Mandel's 1934 Theses for a German Reformation. Mandel rejected traditional Chris-

---

33 Helmreich, 80. For a more detailed exposition see Meier, *EKK*, 2:12–35.

34 Alfred Müller, "Völkisch-religiöse Richtungen," *EKL*, 3:1,683–84.

35 "Ich glaube an den Gott der Deutschreligion, der in der Natur, im hohen Menschengeist und in der Kraft seines Volkes wirkt. Und an den Nothelfer Krist, der um die Edelkeit der Menschenseele kämpft. Und an Deutschland, das Bildungsland der neuen Menschheit" (Schmidt, *Bekenntnisse*, 1:131). Note how the Greek spelling *Christ*

tianity and in its place advocated a return to Germanic heathen practices. He promoted an organic worldview, which is a symptom of romanticism: "We confess . . . an organic worldview, in which God is the living unitary basis of the world [and] the world is an organism permeated by God as its leading unity and entirety."[36] Mandel added: "Faith, in the conditionality of the life of the soul and the spirit through race and estate, does not denote for us 'blood superstition' and materialism, but the natural consequence of an organic worldview."[37] Mandel rejected the biblical doctrine of creation and replaced it with evolution: "We do not believe that man was created directly by God, but that he came into being with all creatures by a mediation out of the God-foundation [*Gottesgrunde*]."[38]

Mandel explicitly rejected orthodox trinitarian theology and Lutheran Christology as expressed in Articles I and III of the Augsburg Confession (1530). He repudiated "all pessimism regarding sin in Paul and in Lutheran theology" and insisted that "Jesus gives a positive call to the human will for a change of heart, and he believes in the possibility of our so doing."[39] Taking up the statement of section 24 in the 1920 Nazi Party platform, Mandel advocated a "positive Christianity" that would be "far from the world-denying, will-disabling Christianity of dogmatic orthodoxy" and would be "a life-affirming Christianity in deed, which, in the imitation of Jesus, would be ready to give one's self as an offering and dedication of self."[40]

Mandel spoke approvingly of the policies of the Prussian Union and its apotheosis into the Reich Church: "We believe in one German *Volk* Church for our future, in which we all can and must live together as brethren, and, since we are called into one fellowship of life, we can and must be bound together in one religious understanding of life, in spite of the various beliefs and worship practices."[41] One marvels to see how Mandel, having easily disposed of traditional doctrinal differences, spoke in grandiloquent and empty phrases on the value of a Prussian Union Church in which Christian beliefs have been retained on a level of parity, though reduced to the least common denominator in practice.

---

becomes the more Germanic form *Krist*. Nazis often replaced the letter *C* with the more Teutonic letter *K*.

36 Hermann Mandel, "Thesen deutscher Reformation," § 15, quoted in Schmidt, *Bekenntnisse*, 2:181.

37 Mandel, "Thesen," § 21, in Schmidt, *Bekenntnisse*, 2:182.

38 Mandel, "Thesen," § 22, in Schmidt, *Bekenntnisse*, 2:182.

39 Mandel, "Thesen," § 43, in Schmidt, *Bekenntnisse*, 2:183.

40 Mandel, "Thesen," § 44, in Schmidt, *Bekenntnisse*, 2:184.

41 Mandel, "Thesen," § 49, in Schmidt, *Bekenntnisse*, 2:184.

At this point, it is important to discuss the November 13, 1933, event at the Berlin Sport Palace. In this rally, the German-Faith Movement (DGB) destroyed the power of the more moderate German-Christian Movement (GDC), which was headed by Joachim Hossenfelder. To the disgust of the DGB, Hossenfelder had made himself bishop of Brandenburg a few weeks earlier. The DGB saw his actions as a return to the state church of earlier years. Instead of the territorial or land church system, the DGB wanted a Reich Church run by the laity and featuring the most radical elements of Nazism. Dr. Reinhold Krause, the Nazi district leader *(Gauleiter)* of Berlin, turned against Hossenfelder in a newspaper article that appeared several days before the meeting in the Berlin Sport Palace. In the article, Krause lamented that the laypeople had not been included in the reorganization of the churches and criticized the use of the "Führer principle" as the reactionary principle of previous times. Krause added these words, ominous for Hossenfelder and the more conservative German-Christians: "If those who have been called are not willing to lead, then a few nontheologians will have to take over the leadership. Our Lord and Savior chose fishermen after the theologians refused to follow him."[42]

Krause delivered a sensational address at the November 13, 1933, Berlin Sport Palace rally before 20,000 spectators. He called for the abolition of all "un-German" elements in doctrine and liturgy, including the abolition of the Old Testament because of its stories of pimps and cattle dealers and reward-based "Jewish morality." Krause also demanded a cleansing of the New Testament from all "obviously distorted and superstitious reports" and for the rejection of the "scapegoat and inferiority-complex theology of Paul the Rabbi." Krause warned against an "exaggerated presentation of the Crucified One," for one did not need humble servants but proud men for the Third Reich. When properly presented, Krause thought one could see the close connection between the Nordic spirit and the heroic Jesus-spirit. It should become clear that the Reformation of Martin Luther would experience its final fulfillment in the victory of the Nordic spirit over the Oriental materialism of orthodox Christianity.[43]

The rabid speech of Krause awakened sober churchmen to the dangers of the GDC. Although Krause spoke for a radical minority, his actions discredited the less-radical parts of the GDC. Whereas the German-Christians had been regarded by Bishop Hans Meiser[44] as rather benign members in the Land Church of Bavaria, Krause's speech became a wake-up call to all involved. Hundreds of German-Christians in the land churches of Bavaria and Württemberg forsook the

---

42 Scholder, *Kirchen*, 1:702.

43 Scholder, *Kirchen*, 1:702–5.

44 Künneth, *Lebensführungen*, 114–15.

movement, and church leaders such as Meiser and Theophil Wurm became suddenly aware of the threat posed by the GDC. The Sport Palace Debacle, as it came to be known, also dealt irreparable damage to the image of Reich Bishop Ludwig Müller, whose usefulness to Hitler was greatly diminished and who henceforth slipped into obscurity. Nevertheless, we shall see that even after 1934 Müller remained able to inflict great damage upon the German Protestant churches.

A SURVEY OF VARIOUS GROUPS OF LUTHERAN THEOLOGIANS BETWEEN THE TWO WORLD WARS

In the period after World War I, there were at least three underlying currents in Protestant theology: (1) old liberalism, which was represented by Adolf von Harnack, Hans Lietzmann, and Emanuel Hirsch; (2) dialectical theology, which was led by Karl Barth, Emil Brunner, Friedrich Gogarten, Rudolf Bultmann, and Georg Merz; and (3) Confessional Lutheran theology, which, besides the Erlangen group, included scholars such as Ernst Sommerlath, Martin Doerne, Adolf Köberle, Karl Heim, and Carl Stange. The most prominent Confessional Lutheran group was at the University of Erlangen, where the scene was dominated in 1933 by Elert, Althaus, and Otto Procksch, as well as Sasse, Friedrich Ulmer, and Hans Preuß. Hermann Strathmann, the well-known biblical scholar and politician at Erlangen, did not champion the Confessional Lutheran position. We shall discuss the faculty of the University of Erlangen at greater length in chapter 15.

Karl Holl led the Luther Renaissance—a group that included Emanuel Hirsch, Heinrich Bornkamm, Hanns Rückert, Hans Volz, Robert Stupperich, and Erich Vogelsang. Holl expressly rejected the doctrine of forensic justification as taught by Philip Melanchthon and the Formula of Concord. Instead, Holl taught that justification was based upon an "analytical judgment," that is, the ethical qualities of the believer himself or herself. To support his teachings, Holl turned to the pre-1518 writings of the young Luther. Moreover, some of Holl's pupils became prominent supporters of Hitler and the GDC, notably Hirsch and Vogelsang. Neither Althaus nor Elert accepted Holl's position on justification.

Protestant theology had been both invigorated and lamed by the liberalism that had been dominant in Germany for fifty years. Brilliant liberals included Hermann Gunkel, Harnack, Hirsch, Lietzmann, and Bultmann. The greatest blow to liberalism was the emergence of dialectical theology under the leadership of Karl Barth. Barth advocated a radical return to biblical theology. He also insisted that religious truth is dialectical in nature, that is, truth lies between two extremes. Lutheranism emphasized a theology of creation and the immanence of God, but Barth adhered to the Reformed maxim that the infinite is not compatible with the finite (*finitum non capax infiniti*) and insisted on the remoteness of God from the things of this world. Some of Barth's early followers included Gogarten, Merz, Brunner, and Bultmann.

Barth was extremely influential. Politically a Socialist (he joined the Social Democratic Party in 1932), Barth was sympathetic with the goals of Lenin and the Soviet Union. He was marked ideologically by theocratic ideas of the involvement of the church in society. All this led Barth to urge the German churches to become involved in political and social activism.[45] Whereas most theologians and church leaders during 1933–1934 did not recognize the threat in Hitler and instead directed their opposition against the German-Christian Movement, Barth, like Sasse and Dietrich Bonhoeffer, saw that the underlying enemy was Hitler and that the dictator stood behind the GDC. Thus Barth became the primary leader at the historic meeting in Barmen in May 1934 and the principal architect of the Barmen Declaration.

The Barmen Declaration was unacceptable to Confessional Lutherans because of the Lutheran distinction between Law and Gospel, their understanding of the two governances (inaptly called the "two kingdoms"), and their concept of God's active involvement in his creation. Consequently, the declaration was rejected by Althaus, Elert, Sasse, Wilhelm Maurer, Friedrich Baumgärtel, Carl Stange, Christian Stoll, Martin Doerne, Heinz Brunotte, and countless other Lutheran thinkers. Nevertheless, the Barmen Declaration became the rallying call of many people in the Confessing Church in their opposition to Hitler. The Barmen Declaration will be analyzed in chapter 8, but in leaving it at this point, it can safely be said that Barmen was the watershed between the Confessional Church and the Confessing Church. Meanwhile, Barth became entangled in conflict with National Socialism, was obliged to leave Germany, and followed a call to Basel in Switzerland. While there, he wrote polemics against the Confessional Lutherans and carried on his own program. Barth even criticized the Confessing Church for what he regarded as the cowardice of its pastors, though he praised the positions of certain Communists.

---

45 Barth was more radical politically than many people have realized; see George Hunsinger, ed. and trans., *Karl Barth and Radical Politics* (Philadelphia: Westminster, 1976). The centerpiece of Hunsinger's book is an essay by Friedrich-Wilhelm Marquardt, "Socialism in the Theology of Karl Barth," 47ff. Barth's 1911 treatise "Jesus Christ and the Movement for Social Justice" is included (p. 19ff.). Barth contended that socialism is God's program, and he propounded the theocratic thesis that it is the duty of the state to foster socialism so the kingdom of God will come. Marquardt writes that as a young pastor Barth practiced a radical socialism. His later theology was developed as an ideological basis for his praxis. Helmut Gollwitzer, Marquardt's mentor, presents an essay in which he essentially agrees with the findings of his pupil. Gollwitzer himself was a pupil of Karl Barth and a supporter of the Barmen Declaration.

It should be stated that none of the full professors[46] in the inner ring of the theological faculty of the University of Erlangen belonged to either the Nazi Party or the GDC. Two men who were loosely connected with the theological faculty were Nazis: Wilhelm Vollrath—an instructor for practical theology, to whom Hans-Albrecht Molitoris, the Nazi-appointed "Leader of Council of University Instructors," gave the title "Representative of the Council"—and Paul Sprenger, the professor for Reformed theology. Because Sprenger was not a Lutheran, he did not belong to the inner faculty. Elert, theological dean during this period, regarded Vollrath as a spy and managed to exclude him from most faculty meetings.

---

46 Also known as an "ordinary professor," that is, one whose position was "according to the order" or academic plan. Thus an "extraordinary professor" was one who was outside the order and did not possess full benefits.

CHAPTER TWO

THE RISE OF ADOLF HITLER

Many Germans supported Adolf Hitler because they had a deep fear of the Communists, fears that were nourished by reports of terrorism in the Soviet Union. For example, Joseph Stalin had deliberately imposed famine and starvation in the Ukraine and elsewhere. Many of the Ukrainian peasants affected had close cultural and ethnic ties to Germany. Conservative estimates say that 14,500,000 peasants died from the famine.[1] Germans who were aware of the situation cherished the hope that Hitler would provide a good government that would check the spread of Soviet communism.

HITLER'S GRADUAL ASSUMPTION OF POWER

In 1920 Adolf Hitler was sent by German army intelligence to investigate a socialist political party in Munich. Impressed by the group, Hitler joined and quickly became one of its leaders. The group blossomed into the National Socialist German Workers Party (*Nationalsozialistische Deutsche Arbeiterpartei* [NSDAP]) or

---

1 On German colonies in Russia, see Karl Cramer, "Die deutschen Kolonisten an der Wolga," *Lutherische Kirche in Bewegung: Festschrift für Friedrich Ulmer zum 60. Geburtstag*, ed. Gottfried Werner (Erlangen: Martin Luther-Verlag, 1937), 168–83. The terrible Soviet atrocities of that time are detailed in Robert Conquest, *The Harvest of Sorrow: Soviet Collectivization and the Terror-Famine* (New York: Oxford University Press, 1986), where death roll statistics are given on pp. 300–301. Western government leaders preferred to ignore the flow of information that continued to spread despite Soviet attempts to suppress it. As a schoolboy in the late 1930s, I found access to books published in the United States that described the terrible events, but U.S. leaders, including Franklin Roosevelt, seemed unaware or unwilling to know or admit the truth about Stalin.

the Nazi Party. Hitler and the NSDAP attracted an increasing number of followers. The party fomented resentment against the Treaty of Versailles, spoke of the unemployment and hunger prevalent in Germany, pilloried the failures of the Weimar Republic, blamed Jewish people for Germany's woes, fanned the fires of nationalism, and aroused pride in the Germanic race as a Nordic *Volk*. After many reverses, the NSDAP had its first real victory in the election of September 14, 1930, when it captured 107 seats in the German parliament (*Reichstag*). On January 30, 1933, Field Marshal Paul von Hindenburg, who had served as president of the Weimar Republic since 1925, swore Hitler into the position of German chancellor.

Nazi supporters were jubilant at Hitler's appointment to the chancellorship. Few of those who were later to oppose Hitler were alarmed. Karl Barth wrote his mother on February 1, 1933:

> I do not believe that this will mean the beginning of big changes in any direction. Germany is both inwardly and outwardly a body that is much too slow for such variations in its facade really to change anything. Furthermore, the persons concerned have too little for which they are outstanding. There is too little courage among the German people that would be necessary in leading to a revolution as was the case with the rule of Mussolini.[2]

But Barth, and many others, had grossly underestimated the new chancellor. With singleness of purpose, Hitler sought to consolidate his gains. Because he lacked a majority in key government positions, Hitler had Hindenburg dissolve the *Reichstag*, calling for new elections on March 5, 1933. Meanwhile, parliament was undermined when its building in Berlin, the *Reichstagsgebäude*, was burned down by an unidentified arsonist on February 27. It was widely thought that the Nazis had ordered the fire to block parliamentary government, but the Nazis called the fire an attack on the government. They used the occasion to justify the suspension of civil liberties and to create the foundation for the ensuing dictatorship.

From its origins, the NSDAP had been rather hostile to religion and the church. However, the party adopted new tactics in its endeavor to win the 1933 parliamentary elections. On the one hand, the NSDAP supported the organization of the German-Christian Movement as the religious arm of the Nazi Party. On the other hand, the NSDAP made positive overtures to the Protestant churches and other Christian denominations as Hitler made himself out to be an advocate of religion. On March 4, 1933, the day before the national election that put the NSDAP into full power, Hitler gave a speech in Königsberg, East Prussia, in which he quoted the Bible and referred to God repeatedly. Holding up a political tract,

---

2 Barth, cited in Scholder, *Kirchen*, 1:280.

Hitler said: "I read here on this sheet of paper, sent out by the Center [Roman Catholic] Party, these words: 'We know that except the Lord build the house, they labor in vain that build it. Everything depends upon God's blessing.' "[3] Then Hitler proceeded to say that God's blessing had been withheld from the Weimar Republic (which had been established in 1918) because it had been built upon lies, perjury, and treason. He urged the people to vote the next day for the NSDAP. He concluded: "Then there will again be a German *Volk* of whom it can be said: People, lift your heads high and proud again; thou art no longer enslaved and without freedom, but thou art free again and can say with justice: 'We are all proud that, by God's gracious help, we have become true Germans again.' "[4] Immediately thereafter, the assembly sang the theocratic lines of the Netherlands folk song "We Gather Together to Ask the Lord's Blessing," a hymn used repeatedly by Hitler.

This program was broadcast on national radio, and, as one reporter stated, "Millions of Christians in Germany heard it and sang along, and as the great bells of the Königsberg cathedral rumbled forth, prayers everywhere soared heavenward as never before in the history of Germany."[5] However, witness Wilhelm Griessbach relates that the common people of Königsberg laughed because they knew that the church had refused to ring the bells for the Nazi Party rally and that the peal heard on the radio had been taken from a recording.[6] Agnes von Zahn-Harnack wrote a statement warning against Hitler's exploitation of religion, which was read on March 1, 1933, in the presence of the committee of the *Deutsche evangelische Kirche* (DEK) presided over by Bishop Theophil Wurm.[7] But few minds were as alert as that of Miss Harnack. Most people went along with the frenzy of the hour.

The election of 1933 was not an overwhelming victory for the NSDAP. Despite all its efforts to manipulate public opinion, the Nazi Party won only 44 percent of the votes on March 5. However, Hitler was able to increase his support to a 52 percent majority in the *Reichstag* by means of an alliance with the German National *Volk* Party (*Deutschnationalen Volkspartei* [DNVP]) and the German *Volk* Party (*Deutsche Volkspartei* [DVP]), which was called the "Battle Front Black-White-Red."[8]

---

3 Hitler's speech quoted in *KZ* 57 (1933): 303–6.

4 Hitler's speech quoted in *KZ* 57 (1933): 303–6.

5 Quoted in *ZwKK*, 109–10; see p. 19 for bibliographic details.

6 See *ZwKK*, 109–10.

7 Schäfer, *Württemberg*, 1:250; see also Scholder, *Kirchen*, 1:290. Hermann Sasse identifies Agnes von Harnack as the daughter of Adolf von Harnack; see *In Statu Confessionis*, 2:195.

8 Scholder, *Kirchen*, 1:284.

HITLER CONSOLIDATES HIS POWER
DURING A TIME OF APPEASEMENT

Hitler was given an unprecedented amount of power during his early months in office. The virtual authority of a dictator was placed in his hands by events such as the burning of the *Reichstag* building; the state of emergency declared on February 27, 1933, which suspended the freedoms required in the German Constitution; and the Enabling Act of March 23, which gave Hitler the power to enact legislation by decree. On April 7, a law was passed that created the office of Reich governor (*Reichstatthalter*), by which power was seized from the various German states and centralized within one office (*Gleichschaltung*). This posed a threat to the independence of the corresponding land churches within those states and led Lutherans to fear the designs of the Prussian Union for a corresponding ecclesiastical consolidation.[9]

However, despite his amalgamation of governmental and institutional power, Hitler still depended upon the favor of the German people and world opinion. During his first year, he proceeded slowly as he tightened his grip on political power. As historians have described it, Hitler initiated a "time of appeasement" of leaders at home and abroad.

Walter Künneth, an eyewitness, describes how the Western powers tried to appease Hitler by taking part in the triumphal procession that he staged at the 1936 Olympic Games in Berlin:

> At the head of the representatives of various countries came Hitler, standing in his automobile, greeting the people like a victor, immediately followed by the Americans in gray cylinder hats, and the other nations. All of these took part and made their contribution to the glorification of the "Führer." How could the great mass of the common folk see through this grandiose illusion and regard Hitler as a "criminal" while the representatives of the Western powers so very apparently stood at his side?[10]

The general effect of Hitler's promises during his first year was to build trust in the minds of church leaders. When some outrageous step was taken by the new government, there was a tendency to place the blame for these radical acts upon the GDC or the Nazi Party, to accept Hitler's reassurances, and to sigh, "If only the Führer knew what these extremists are doing, he would be shocked and would put a stop to it." By the time church leaders became aware that Hitler was in full accord with the drastic changes and attacks upon ecclesiastical independence, it was too late to resist. The dictator had become so firmly entrenched that they were

---

9 Meiser, *Verantwortung*, 1:3–4 and n. 15.

10 Künneth, *Lebensführungen*, 95–96.

powerless to head him off. It became increasingly clear that dissidents could expect to end up in a concentration camp. Some pastors who nevertheless openly opposed the wrongs of the Nazi Party were seized by the Gestapo and were never heard from again.[11] Before long, Germany would be in the grips of a police state that exerted a reign of terror.

EARLY CAUTIOUS OPTIMISM AT HITLER'S PROMISES

The August 11, 1919, Constitution of the German Empire that established the Weimar Republic disestablished the state churches by announcing that "[a] state church does not exist" (section 137).[12] The former state churches were henceforth called "land" churches. The Evangelical Church of the (Old) Prussian Union also became a "land" church; thus its constituent church bodies became known as "provincial" churches. During the fifteen years of the Weimar Republic, the new land and provincial churches underwent many difficult experiences. But they also learned to cherish their independence from the state, a factor important to their survival during the church struggle under Hitler.

The churches considered the Weimar Republic to be hostile toward religion. One source of dissatisfaction had been the apparent opposition of some government officials toward the teaching of religion in the schools. The German public schools had traditionally provided teachers who taught religion to children on the basis of their Christian affiliation, whether Roman Catholic or Lutheran. The Weimar government had organized some "secular schools" (*Weltanschauungsschulen*), which had abolished the teaching of religion. In the Free State of Saxony many people keenly resented the presence of these secular schools.

In late February 1933, just before the crucial March elections, Hitler's government ordered religious instruction to be restored in all schools as of April 1, and it took steps to abolish 295 secular schools in Prussia in which no religious instruction was given.[13] Especially in Saxony, where enmity against religious instruction was strong, all secular schools were closed. The Reich administrator issued the following order for Saxony: "I make it the official duty of every teacher and educator in the Land of Saxony to be aware at every moment that he is responsible for the

---

11 This was the case with the father of my friend Professor Theodor Strohm of Heidelberg. Strohm's father, a Lutheran pastor at Lindau in southern Bavaria, was known to be critical of the Nazi regime. Late one night, the Gestapo knocked on the door of the parsonage and seized Pastor Strohm from the arms of his family. There was no due process of law and he was never heard from again.

12 Hans Liermann, *Kirchen und Staat* (Munich: Isar, 1954), 12.

13 Helmreich, 129.

education of German youth in regard to concepts of the nation and the people, in regard to Christianity, and regarding genuine fellowship among the people."[14]

Ludwig Ihmels, the aged Lutheran land bishop (*Landesbischof*) of Saxony, prepared a statement to be read from all the pulpits of Saxony on March 26. In part, his response was as follows:

> The church can only admonish: be joyful, move bravely forward, that the old Gospel become a new power in the life of the people. In fact, this is an hour of paramount decision[15] which we are experiencing. Coming generations will want to hear how we have used this hour. We read of wasted hours of world history, of wasted hours also in the history of the church. This hour dare not have come in vain. For this, we are responsible.[16]

Nearly all those who later opposed Hitler were his supporters in 1933: the Niemöller brothers (Martin and Wilhelm), many theological professors at the University of Erlangen and elsewhere, and a number of church leaders, including Ihmels, Heinrich Rendtorff, and Theophil Wurm. They all wanted to believe Hitler, and they hoped for the best.[17] Rendtorff, land bishop of Mecklenburg-Schwerin, wrote:

> Many members of the Evangelical Church today live with all their thought and feelings in the National Socialist Movement. The Evangelical Church through its calling to seek out and to serve individuals is therefore obligated to seek them out in the circle in which they live, and that means also in the National Socialist Movement.[18]

Because so many were oblivious to the dangers Hitler posed to church and society, we should not be surprised that the writings of many theologians during Hitler's first year expressed an optimism that, at last, Germany was arising from its post-Versailles slump. With the best of intentions as Christian citizens, these church leaders sought to legitimize the new government and encourage Germans

---

14 Quoted in *KZ* 57 (1933): 316.

15 The notion of an important "hour of decision," or decisionism, which was heard frequently at this time, will be discussed in the presentation on political romanticism in chapter 5. Decisionism was a form of political romanticism and of the dialectical theology of Barth, Gogarten, and others of that group, among whom the oft-recurring word was *Entscheidung*, that is, "decision." Political romanticism and decisionism is also discussed in Kater, 22–26.

16 Quoted in *KZ* 57 (1933): 316.

17 How church leaders in 1933–1934 were misled by Hitler's deceptiveness—"the wish became the father of the thought"—is described in Erich Beyreuther, ed., *Die Geschichte des Kirchenkampfes in Dokumenten 1933/45* (Wuppertal: R. Brockhaus, 1966), 23–25.

18 *Evangelische Wahrheit* (1931–1932), 205, quoted in Klügel, *Landeskirche*, 7.

to support it. To be sure, the Nazis had issued dubious statements and committed questionable acts since the 1920s, but at this point, there was a willingness to overlook these "mistakes" and to place one's trust for the future in the new government.

EARLY NAZI SEIZURE OF LAND CHURCHES

German Lutheran leaders tended to be distrustful of democratic polity. They looked back with dismay at the political foundering of democracy in the Weimar Republic and agreed that the new German church could best be governed by a strongly centralized church polity led by bishops. The Lutheran leadership did not think that the new Reich bishop and other church leaders should be chosen by the general population in a public election; rather, they wanted the new occupants of church offices to be chosen by the called leaders of the respective land churches. Reformed groups, on the other hand, had a long history of self-government. Thus they were strongly opposed to leadership by bishops and insisted on popular elections.[19] Hitler heard their voice, and though he was opposed to democratic processes, he correctly saw that he would be able to manipulate a general election. Therefore Hitler supported the Reformed demand for the election of all German church officials by popular vote. The result was disastrous.

The Reformed insistence upon democratic practices prevailed in the Prussian Union and helped to bring about the fall of all the Union churches into Nazi hands. Johannes Pfeiffer writes that "the arrangement whereby elections to church assemblies were conducted like political conventions (according to party 'tickets') proved to be fatal for the church in 1933."[20] The Nazi propensity for seizing control of land churches was foreshadowed as early as 1933 when the land churches of Prussia, Mecklenburg, and Saxony were temporarily seized.

The Prussian Union was the first to fall to Hitler and his cohorts. Unfortunately, Hermann Kapler, president of the Prussian Union's High Consistory (*Oberconstorialrat*) and also chair of the commission to form the new German Evangelical Church, had chosen to retire on June 30, 1933. The leaders of the Prussian Union appointed as temporary president Ernst Stoltenhoff, a Rhenish churchman. Because the constitution of the Prussian Union required that the civil government be consulted before appointing a president, the church leaders had violated their own constitution in the appointment of Stoltenhoff.[21] This

---

19 See the discussion of the Führer principle in chapter 4. Karl Barth was especially vocal in this matter. On democratism and antihierarchicalism in the Reformed churches and their role in the formation of the DEK, see Kater, 69–71.

20 Johannes Pfeiffer, "Berlin-Brandenburg," in *ELC*, 1:213.

21 See *KZ* 57 (August 1933): 508–9. Why did the Prussian Union railroad Stoltenhoff into

gave the Nazis an excuse for intervention, thus avoiding an election to seize control of the High Consistory. On June 24, 1933, the Nazi Party replaced the Upper Church Councilmen (*Oberkirchenräte*) with its own man, August Jäger, as land bishop of the Prussian Union and Reich *kommissar*. Jäger at once dismissed Otto Dibelius as general superintendent. Friedrich von Bodelschwingh, feeling pressure from Hitler, resigned as Reich bishop on the same day. Ludwig Müller was waiting on the sidelines and soon seized the position of Reich bishop for himself.[22]

Two other land churches were also taken over by the Nazis in 1933, but under different circumstances. In Saxony, a leadership vacuum arose during the infirmity and death of Bishop Ludwig Ihmels. Friedrich Coch, a sinister leader, helped arrange the "incorporation" of the Land Church of Saxony on May 7, 1933, and after Ihmels died on June 7, he attempted to seize control. On June 30, Karl Fritsch, the minister for internal affairs in Saxony, issued an order by which Friedrich Coch was made *kommissar* bishop of Saxony.[23]

The situation in Mecklenburg was different.[24] Prior to the appointment of August Jäger as Reich *kommissar* in Prussia, Walter Bohm, a Nazi, had been appointed state *kommissar* over the Land Church of Mecklenburg-Schwerin on April 22, 1933. However, on April 27, Bohm's appointment was withdrawn.[25] Bishop Heinrich Rendtorff had led protests that had reached the ears of German President Paul von Hindenburg, who forwarded the complaints to Hitler. As a result, the Reich administrator was withdrawn and promises were made to Rendtorff that won his approval. Subsequently, Rendtorff publicly applied for admission to the Nazi Party. However, because of a series of intervening events, his membership was never finalized.[26]

After the seizures of the land churches in Prussia and Saxony, Friedrich von Bodelschwingh conferred with Hindenburg about the critical situation in Prussia. On June 30, Hindenburg corresponded with Hitler, demanding that the seizures be reversed. On July 14, Hitler complied and restored rightful church govern-

---

the position in violation of its own constitution? Perhaps this was an example of the unhappy rivalry between Confessional Lutheran and pro-Union factions. Stoltenhoff was a militantly pro-Union man who insisted that the projected DEK must include full communion among Lutheran, Reformed, and Union churches, a position that was unacceptable to Confessional Lutherans.

22 Chronicle and documents in *KZ* 57 (1933): 508–9, 561–72. See also Hermelink, 41–45. Hermelink includes Hindenburg's June 30, 1933, protest to Hitler (p. 44).

23 Joachim Fischer, *Die sächsische Landeskirche im Kirchenkampf 1933–1937,* AGK 8 (Göttingen: Vandenhoeck & Ruprecht, 1972), 16–17.

24 See Meier, *EKK,* 1:91, 550 n. 347.

25 Meiser, *Verantwortung,* 1:512.

26 Helmreich, 134.

ment to the land churches by removing the state *kommissars* and their dictatorial powers. This action restored church government in Prussia and Saxony according to their old constitutions.[27] However, Friedrich Coch remained in Saxony and succeeded in having himself elected land bishop. In 1934, Coch finally presided over the incorporation of the Land Church of Saxony into the DEK.

---

27 Künneth, *Lebensführungen*, 110; Carter, 291.

CHAPTER THREE

LUTHERANS ADDRESS THE CHALLENGE FROM THE GERMAN-CHRISTIANS—1933

Only gradually did people in the church became aware of the dangers of the Nazi Party and its religious branch, the German-Christian Movement. However, as early as 1932, voices were speaking out against the racism and the violence that accompanied Hitler's operations. This chapter presents some of these earliest challenges, beginning with the Altona Confession of the Lutheran churches in Holstein. Next we will survey several groups in the Land Church of Hanover: the Osnabrück Circle; the Churchly Gathering (*Kirchliche Sammlung*); and a group that developed out of the Churchly Gathering, the Confessional Fellowship (*Bekenntnisgemeinschaft*). Then the focus turns to the Young Reformation Movement, followed by a look at the Kapler Commission, which met at Loccum to prepare the groundwork for the constitution of the German Evangelical Church (DEK). A later chapter is devoted to the Bethel Confession, the first great manifesto in the struggle of the Lutherans against the German-Christians. Although Karl Barth and his followers shunted aside the Bethel Confession in favor of their own Barmen Declaration, the Lutheran statement at Bethel remains the best reply written against Nazi ideology.

THE ALTONA CONFESSION

On "Bloody Sunday," July 17, 1932, a conflict between Social Democrats, Communist members of the Nazi Party, and the Socialist Party took place in Altona, a suburb of Hamburg populated by industrial laborers and a center of Social Democrats and Communists. The battle was deliberately fomented by Nazi storm troopers (*Sturmabteilung*), who staged a propaganda march of 10,000 men that became violent. As the procession neared Altona, the Communists met the marchers with gunfire. A street battle commenced in front of the principal Lutheran church, where an afternoon service was being conducted by Hans Asmussen. His text was the Fifth Commandment: "Thou shalt not kill."[1] Outside the church, the police could not restore order until evening. Seventeen people were killed and more than one hundred were injured, some of them seriously.[2]

Four days later, on July 21, the members of the neighboring Lutheran churches gathered for an emergency Divine Service to reflect upon the bloody tragedy that had occurred in their midst. Immediately following the service, members of the church in Altona asked for a statement that expressed the church's position in this political situation. The pastors were also of the opinion that a statement was needed. As a result, five pastors, led by the 34-year-old Asmussen, were commissioned to prepare a declaration regarding the recent events. It was intended that this formal statement would suggest an official Lutheran position on the class conflicts that had bedeviled Germany under the Weimar Republic. The statement would also address the Nazi exploitation of class antagonism to obtain voter support. The commission began its work in late July and produced a document named "Word and Confession," which was handed to Adolf Mordhorst, bishop of the Lutheran Land Church of Holstein.[3] On January 11, 1933, Georg Sieveking, church provost of Altona, read the Altona Confession before a capacity crowd where twenty-one Lutheran pastors signed the declaration.

In the days that followed, the major German newspapers discussed this event. The Nazi Party and Communist newspapers denounced the confession, but elsewhere it found strong approval. On January 28, the church leadership and 213 pastors of the Lutheran Church in Mecklenburg presented the confession to their congregations. On February 14, the Lutheran Church of Lübeck followed suit. In March, the Young Evangelical Conference of the Lutheran Land Church of Hanover declared themselves "in solidarity with the word of Altona."[4]

The Altona Confession, or "Word and Confession of the Altona Pastors in the Trouble and Confusion of Public Life,"[5] opens by pointing to a recent assault on public life, a reference to the riot on Bloody Sunday. It adds that the church can-

---

1 See Scholder, *Kirchen*, 1:784 n. 42.

2 *KZ* 57 (March 1933): 189–92; see also Scholder, *Kirchen*, 1:226.

3 Scholder, *Kirchen*, 1:23–34.

4 Quoted in Scholder, *Kirchen*, 1:237.

5 The German title was "Wort und Bekenntnis Altonaer Pastoren in der Not und Verwirrung des öffentlichen Lebens." The full document is given in Schmidt, *Bekenntnisse*, 1:19–25. An abbreviated form is included in *KZ* 57 (1933): 189–92.

not speak out simply to legitimize partisan political views because ". . . the church has the task of sharpening consciences and proclaiming the Gospel."[6] The church must overcome its previous hesitancy to speak out on contemporary issues, "for the recovery to health of our people and its eternal salvation depends upon people, who are now living, of having God's Word spoken by the church regarding their needs, and that this be heard and believed by them." The writers then assert that this arrangement (*Ordnung*) is willed by God and therefore given in the Holy Scriptures.[7] After the opening prologue, the Altona Confession goes more thoroughly into five articles.

Article 1 presents the Lutheran doctrine that preaching is the oral Word of God and asserts that "this eternal Word of God takes place from the Holy Scriptures in this way, that it is proclaimed by a human being." The authors of the confession assert that Christians hear this preaching, confess their unrighteousness, and trust the promise that God for the sake of Christ is mighty in the forgiveness of their unrighteousness. In this faith they are justified. Jesus Christ himself is present in this Christian church and is its might: "Therefore the church cannot be shaped or borne in its essence by the state, by some party, or from scholarship, or from some sort of worldview [*Weltanschauung*]. Thereby, nothing dare be surrendered from its proclamation." A clear word is spoken against the desire of some that the church put its stamp of approval upon Nazi ceremonies. Article 1 asserts that the church must not be used to achieve political purposes: "Whoever places the proclamation of the church under the influence of political power thereby makes the political power into a religion that is hostile to Christianity."[8]

Article 2, entitled "On the Limits of Man," proclaims that in creation God made man the lord of the earth and that man must carry out his lordship to the extent that he is able. However, because of sin, God has placed limitations upon humanity. The writers attack the dream of "a classless society without hunger, weariness, or suffering," that is, Communism. The confession's authors state that we must not rise up against the limitations God has set for us because of sin; instead, we must expect trouble in this present life. A world of righteousness without war will not come on earth: "All these things God has reserved for the new world which he will give through Jesus Christ our Lord."[9]

Article 3 deals with the state and maintains that, regardless of the form of government, the duty of the people is to be obedient citizens. Because the writers assert that "God is the Creator of the state. . . . Not the state as a concept, but the

---

6 Schmidt, *Bekenntnisse*, 1:19.

7 Schmidt, *Bekenntnisse*, 1:19–20.

8 Schmidt, *Bekenntnisse*, 1:20–21.

9 Schmidt, *Bekenntnisse*, 1:22.

existent state, is there by God's power as Creator," it could be understood that God created the forthcoming Nazi state. However, as if in response to the possibility of a tyrannical state, Article 3 proceeds: "We are called to be obedient toward the superior power [*Obrigkeit*]. But if the case should come in which the superior power itself should act contrary to 'what is best for the state,' then each one must decide whether the moment has come at which one should obey God more than men."[10] This statement seems to suggest that the individual has the authority to decide what is against the state's own best interest and to disobey the state.[11]

Article 4 discusses the tasks of the state. The Altona Confession acknowledges that one's present life is a gift from the Creator and states that God has given to the state the task of ordering the way in which citizens live together. "But our life and the condition of our state is threatened by the problem of unemployment and the destruction of the economy. The government is commanded by God to do all that it can to give help. It is dealing with human life, which God has given." According to Article 4, political parties "stand under the command of God to maintain our political system, not to destroy it. They will have to answer to God for their opposition." Instead of inciting the people to make unrealistic demands of what the government should do for them, political parties should inculcate the values of thriftiness, cleanliness, order, and faithfulness.[12]

Article 5 brings the Altona Confession to an end with a discussion of God's commands: "We believe, teach, and confess that it has pleased God to reveal in his commandments what he requires of us and what life asks of us. Even if it is impossible to keep the commandments, still everyone shall exert every effort to do that which the commandments require." A few lines later, Article 5 presents a Lutheran theology of the order of creation. The traditional order of creation—civil authority, parents and the family, labor and industry, and ecclesial authority—are presented in the following: "We believe that it corresponds to the Creation when a German regime rules in Germany . . . . We confess that marriage is a divine order . . . . We believe that labor is a divine order."[13]

The Altona Confession makes firm statements about respect for life and about concern for the poor working class: "Since we believe that God is the Creator of life, we must repudiate all contempt for life as sin . . . . We make this judgment on the basis of our faith, and not on the basis of the value that an individual life and the nation present, but in view of the Creator who has created it." The confession

---

10 Schmidt, *Bekenntnisse*, 1:22.

11 Asmussen has in mind Acts 5:29, the so-called *clausula Petri*: "We ought to obey God rather than man." For a different position on Acts 5:29, see Elert, *BBB*, 34–35.

12 Schmidt, *Bekenntnisse*, 1:23–24.

13 Schmidt, *Bekenntnisse*, 1:24–25.

also speaks in support of laborers: "We repudiate it as sin when employers and employees, the state and its officials are seen as objects for exploitation. We also regard it as sin when someone can be satisfied in the face of dominant unemployment." The confession then gives a noble view of the dignity of humankind:

> We believe that honor is an indication that man was created in the image of God. We repudiate it as sin when robbing a person of his honor becomes a means of political propaganda, when the employer is dishonorable to the worker or the worker is dishonorable to his employer, or when the rich man is dishonorable to the poor man or the poor man to the rich man.[14]

Despite some weaknesses, the Altona Confession can be held in high regard for its strengths. Commonly acknowledged to have been one of its authors, Hans Asmussen played a significant role in the German Lutheran church for the next twenty years. However, Asmussen was hardly a representative Lutheran. He expressed his own theological ambivalence in a letter to Werner Elert on February 23, 1928: "It is indeed peculiar that Lutheranism has so little agreement within its own ranks that some people feel more at home with me among the Calvinists around Barth than in Lutheran circles which bear that name."[15]

THE OSNABRÜCK CONFESSION

The North German city of Osnabrück has enjoyed a strong church life, nurtured by the healthy rivalry between Roman Catholics and Lutherans—with each denomination comprising about half of the population. The Catholics occupy two old Romanesque churches: the cathedral and St. John's. The Lutherans inhabit two Gothic edifices—St. Mary's and St. Katharine's—as well as several more recent edifices. At the center of Osnabrück is the venerable city hall where one of the treaties of the Peace of Westphalia was signed (1648), ending the terrible Thirty Years' War. During the Third Reich, the Osnabrück Circle included about thirty Lutheran pastors. Hans Bodensieck, one of the group's leaders, was head pastor of St. Mary's.[16] the Osnabrück Circle also included Paul Leo,[17] Julius Ruprecht von Loewenfeld, Wilhelm Thimme, and Richard Karwehl.

---

14 Schmidt, *Bekenntnisse*, 1:25.

15 From a letter to Werner Elert, in ATF, file "Werner Elert Papers."

16 On Hans Bodensieck, see Klügel, *Landeskirche*, 50–52, 491ff., 511. Hans was a half-brother of the U.S. theologian Julius Bodensieck, who was president at Wartburg Seminary, Dubuque, Iowa, during much of this period. After Hans's mother died, his father married Minna Niemack, a woman of Jewish descent, who was Julius's mother. Both brothers were friends of Paul Leo.

17 Eventually Leo would teach at Wartburg Seminary, Dubuque, Iowa.

Karwehl was a brilliant theologian, strongly influenced by Karl Barth, and one of the first to perceive the evils of Nazism. Thus Karwehl criticized the Nazi Party and National Socialism as early as 1931:

> Always the point of departure is the autonomous person. . . . This is not changed by the fact that the idea is crowned with God, who created the miracle of the "Aryan man." . . .

> But a god whose factual significance consisted therein could not be God but is rather an idol. In any case, this god has nothing to do with the real God of biblical revelation.

Karwehl added: "The National Socialist concept of the state, as we saw, was purely invented by man, and here once again as in the picture of the Beast out of the abyss"—a derogatory association of Nazism with the apocalyptic incarnation of evil in Revelation 13.[18]

Karwehl was the principal author of the Osnabrück Confession, which offered convincing declarations about the autonomy of the church and its central message of sin and redemption, stating: "The only authority in the preaching of the church is the crucified and risen Lord. He is believed and testified to be alive and ever present in preaching and the sacraments."[19] This confession also includes a clearer distinction of the two governances than the earlier Altona Confession: "The kingdom of God and an earthly kingdom are two different things. Therefore we reject every confusion of the two, and every mingling of the kingdom of God with any earthly kingdom whatsoever."[20]

ZOELLNER'S SUMMONS TO LUTHERANS AND THEIR RESPONSE TO THE GERMAN-CHRISTIAN CHALLENGE

The influential Lutheran Christian Heinrich Wilhelm Zoellner (1860–1937) was superintendent of the Evangelical Church of Westphalia from 1905 until his retirement in 1930. Although the Lutheran church in Westphalia was imbedded within a Union church, Zoellner inexorably criticized the existence of the Prussian Union and was regarded as one of the most eloquent and outspoken Confessional Lutherans in all of Germany. But Zoellner wanted to work toward a church that simultaneously united German Protestants and maintained confessional integrity for Lutherans. In contrast, Hermann Sasse supported the concept of a Confessional Lutheran church in Germany that would be international and

---

18 Richard Karwehl, "Politisches Messiastum: Zur Auseindandersetzung von Kirche und Nationalsozialismus," *Zwischen den Zeiten* 9 (1931): 527, 537; quoted in Simon, 50–51.

19 Schmidt, *Bekenntnisse*, 26.

20 Schmidt, *Bekenntnisse*, 27.

ecumenical in character and would avoid the snares of nationalism. Had Sasse's recommendations been followed instead of Zoellner's, the formation of the nationalistic DEK, Hitler's Reich Church, might have been prevented, thus avoiding the struggles of the *Kirchenkampf.*

Nevertheless, Zoellner had good intentions when, on April 13, 1933, he issued an appeal for Lutherans to work together for German church unity in the emerging church crisis. Zoellner insisted:

> The confessional basis of the various Evangelical churches is inviolable. But [confessions] have not only their significance as boundaries marking the differences, but also as the basis for fellowship. Also in leadership and teaching, in proclamation and instruction, the form of church life must take place on the basis of the church's confession. What unites us is that we bow under the Word of God in the testimony of the Holy Scriptures. Therefore, we long for the formation of an Evangelical church of the German nation upon a clear confessional basis.[21]

Referring to Hitler's promise that the church would have complete freedom to carry out its work without interference from the state, Zoellner defined that work as follows:

> It has to do again today with the old task, which must be dealt with in every time, of testifying to the message from the cross and Christ and the certainty of the resurrection from the dead in this world of sin and death. Thus, the church stands with its commission in the midst of the nations as the front line of God against death. This is the church's service to creation.[22]

In his conclusion, Zoellner announced that he was bringing his appeal to the entire Christian public and that he would soon put together a group of church leaders to launch this task.[23] It appears that Zoellner himself, for all his eloquence, did not actually bring about a Lutheran gathering to discuss his proposal.

Heinrich Weinel, who was a professor at the University of Jena and who held Union church propensities, responded with an energetic protest against Zoellner's statement. Weinel wrote: "This plan is a dreadful distortion of the concept of the Reich Church; it is demonic, for it tears open again the old wounds of the confessional divisions in Germany and adds, to the split of our German Christianity into land churches, the much more dreadful splitting into Confessional churches."[24] Weinel was espousing the case of a nationalistic German church versus a Lutheran

---

21 Quoted in Schmidt, *Bekenntnisse,* 140.

22 Quoted in Schmidt, *Bekenntnisse,* 140–41.

23 See Schmidt, *Bekenntnisse,* 141.

24 Kater, 68. As early as 1915, Weinel had proposed founding a unionistic German Reich Church, a proposal that brought Weinel into conflict with Hermann Bezzel, presi-

church that understood itself as an international movement with ties to the ecumenical movement and especially to world Lutheranism. The argument that Germans who sought ties with Confessional Lutherans in other countries were unpatriotic was raised repeatedly by fervent supporters of the DEK and its postwar reincarnation, the Evangelical Church in Germany (*Evangelische Kirche in Deutschland* [EKD]). It is not surprising that Emanuel Hirsch argued against German Lutheran participation in the ecumenical movement because it was dominated by Anglican and Reformed elements that had little understanding of the Lutheran distinction between Law and Gospel.[25]

Confessional Lutherans, on the other hand, responded positively to Zoellner's summons in one of two ways. Men such as Althaus and Elert, like Zoellner, favored a Reich Church that would include Lutheran, Reformed, and Union churches and all their "Reformational confessions" but that would be a Confessional Lutheran church at the national level. There would be special provisions to protect the interests of the Reformed and the consensus Union churches within such an organization. The Kapler Commission, which will be discussed later in this chapter, laid the groundwork for such a constitution. Others—including Sasse, Friedrich Ulmer, and Fritz Kollatz—rejected Zoellner's proposal as having a political rather than a theological agenda; they saw it as a politicization of the church. The theses of Kollatz provided a critical reply to Zoellner. In opposition to Zoellner's call to found a Reich Church, Kollatz insisted that doctrine was not negotiable for Lutherans.[26]

Nevertheless, the General Evangelical Lutheran Conference (*Allgemeine envagelisch-lutherische Konferenz* [AELK]) issued the following statement:

> In view of the total rebuilding of the German Reich, the AELK with its bishops, professors, and related churchly organizations calls for a new beginning in the church as an Evangelical Church of the German Nation. This Church of the German Nation can only be a Lutheran Church . . . . We therefore expect the following of the men who are now working in a responsible place for building a German Evangelical Reich Church: (1) that they take a stand for the

---

dent (later, land bishop) of the Church of Bavaria and a supporter of the Lutheran Confessions. See Lowell C. Green, trans., "The Confessions and the Unity of the Church," by Hermann Sasse, in *The Lonely Way: Selected Essays and Letters (1927–1939)* (St. Louis: Concordia, 2001), 351–67. Emil Lind, a spokesman in Thuringia for the German-Christians (*Nationalkirchlichen Bewegung DC*), said in April 1937: "Our theology is grounded upon [Friedrich] Schleiermacher, [Adolf von] Harnack, [Ernst] Troeltsch, and [Heinrich] Weinel" (Meier, *EKK*, 2:449 n. 860).

25 On Hirsch, see A. James Reimer, *Emanuel Hirsch und Paul Tillich: Theologie und Politik in einer Zeit der Krise* (Berlin: de Gruyter, 1995), 83.

26 Schmidt, *Bekenntnisse*, 141–42; Carter, 36–37.

Lutheran Confessions, (2) that they build the German Reich Church as a Lutheran Church with Lutheran leadership, without damaging the rights of the other confessions.[27]

Hans Meiser, who had become land bishop of Bavaria on May 4, 1933, saw a real danger in the following official announcement, which appeared in the press in early May 1933: "The Reformational Confessions . . . call us today to make an act of confession [*einem Akt des Bekennens*] in the language of our time [*in der Sprache unserer Zeit*], as it is needed in the questions confronting us today."[28] What was so troublesome about this and other statements was the apparent intention to bypass the historic Lutheran Confessions and to speak, instead, in one's own words as an act of "confessing." Meiser feared that doctrinal differences among the historical confessions might be watered down and that the forthcoming DEK would actually become another Union church. Meiser also was alarmed at the efforts of specific German-Christians to achieve a supreme head (*Summepiskopat*) of the evangelical churches, so he summoned all Confessional Lutherans in Germany to attend an emergency meeting held on short notice at Würzburg on May 14. One purpose of the meeting was to strengthen the hand of the "Commission of Three Men," or Kapler Commission, and to let Bishop August Marahrens know they stood behind him. At the meeting in Würzburg, Meiser presented his agenda in these words:

Our task presents itself to me as follows:

(1) The joining together of the Lutheran churches must become still stronger.

(2) In order to strengthen Marahrens, the following must be said in some manner: (a) that the newly forming church must, according to our will and according to our demand, have a Lutheran stamp, without repressing any other confession (the wretchedness of not having any confession must not be built into the new structure . . .); (b) the personal head of the church must be a Lutheran clergyman, who must not be chosen by a popular election; (c) the church cannot simply retreat to the confession of the fathers but must also be expressed in a doctrinal form that moves Christendom at this time; but that is a task which cannot be completed in eight days.[29]

At this meeting in Würzburg, the groundwork was laid for the future United Evangelical Lutheran Church in Germany, an organization that would be firmly

---

27 Meiser, *Verantwortung*, 1:xxvi.

28 Meiser, *Verantwortung*, 1:xxvi–xxvii. From the very beginning, the advocates of a "Confessing Church" rather than a "Confessional Church" were presenting their case against the Lutheran Confessions.

29 Meiser, *Verantwortung*, 1:xxvii.

grounded in Confessional Lutheran principles. The following statement was released:

> We wrestle and pray that the new beginning of the nation will mean also a new breakthrough to God. Therefore, we see ourselves obligated to speak to our people the message of the Lutheran Reformation: It is God who has ordered our nation [*Volkstum*] and the civil authorities. It is God who in his judgment and in his grace leads to forgiveness of sins, and only by this, to true freedom. It is God who brings to realization true fellowship and discipline in his church.[30]

Although the conference at Würzburg marked an important beginning, by September 1933 it had become clear that the formation of a Lutheran Bishops Conference was a dream that could not be fulfilled as long as the bishops were of two different persuasions. Some of the bishops were committed to the GDC whereas others were opposed to it; it was impossible for such disparate groups to work closely together. Little could come from these efforts until after the fall of the Third Reich in 1945.[31]

THE YOUNG REFORMATION MOVEMENT

After the return of the World War I veterans, a spate of federated youth movements reappeared in Germany. Young men unable to identify completely with the existing church bureaucracies sought new allegiances in theology and Christian action. Among these was the Hanoverian Conference of Younger Theologians, later called the Young Evangelical Conference (*Jung-evangelische Konferenz*). Members of this group grounded themselves in the Lutheran Reformation but also listened to contemporary theologians such as Karl Barth, though they did not completely follow the Swiss theologian. Out of this movement came the Sydowa Brotherhood (*Sydower Bruderschaft*), which called for a renewal of the church through careful study of the writings of Martin Luther, and the St. Michael Brotherhood, which fostered liturgical renewal.[32] Hanns Lilje, general secretary of the Christian Student Movement (*Deutsche Christliche Studenten-Vereinigung*), and Walter Künneth, leader of the Seminar for Apologetics in Berlin, belonged to this younger generation. They became organizers of the Young Reformation Movement (*Jungreformatorische Bewegung* [JB]) in Berlin, which brought the youth movement under new leadership and played an important role in resistance to Hitler.

---

30 Klügel, *Landeskirche*, 43.

31 Meiser, *Verantwortung*, 1:xxxii; Klügel, *Landeskirche*, 43–44.

32 Klügel, *Landeskirche*, 12–14.

Two days before Hans Meiser's Lutheran conference at Würzburg, a youthful group gathered to organize the JB. Twenty-eight men and women signed the JB summons of May 9. Some of the more prominent names included Martin Doerne, Eduard Ellwein, Theodor Ellwein, Friedrich Gogarten, Theodor Heckel, Künneth, Lilje, Wilhelm Lütgert, Karl Bernhard Ritter, Wilhelm Stählin, and Heinz-Dietrich Wendland.[33] This group aimed to strengthen the German church by renewing the principles of the Lutheran Reformation.[34]

In his doctoral dissertation, Peter Neumann claims the "high church" Berneuchen Circle, led by Stählin and Ritter, and the Sydowa Brotherhood, led by Georg Schultz, played a significant role in founding and leading the JB.[35] However, the presence of neither organization is visible in the records. In fact, prominent leaders of the JB such as Künneth, Martin Niemöller, and Lilje had little interest in the high liturgical views of the Berneuchen Circle.[36] Additionally, Schultz's views did not receive the attention they might have deserved. Ultimately, Neumann's claim that the Berneuchen and Sydowa groups were dominant in the formation of the JB lacks foundation.

At first, the JB was headed by a triumvirate of Künneth, Lilje, and Gerhard Jacobi, who was pastor of Kaiser Wilhelm Memorial Church in Berlin. However, when Jacobi transferred to another location, he was replaced by Martin Niemöller. Künneth served as administrator for the JB because, as the leader of the Apologetics Center in Berlin, he had an office staff.

The JB seemed to appeal to individuals who were concerned about how the churches could remain independent from the strong political pressures originat-

---

33 For the complete list, see Peter Neumann, *Die Jungreformatorische Bewegung*, AGK 25 (1971), 23. This book was the reworking of a doctoral dissertation submitted in 1968 to the Kirchliche Hochschule in Berlin.

34 Künneth, *Lebensführungen*, 109.

35 The Sydowa Brotherhood encouraged pastors to study Luther's writings. Neumann discusses the involvement of the Berneuchen Circle and the Sydowa Brotherhood in the JB and the program of Georg Schultz in *Die Jungreformatorische Bewegung*, 29–33.

36 Few traces of the Sydowa Brotherhood are to be found in the writings of the JB. Künneth also disavows the position of the Berneuchen Circle in *Lebensführungen*, 72–73. Others who knew Lilje well have denied that he had anything to do with the ultra-liturgical goals of the Berneuchen Circle. Thus Wilhelm Gerhold, who worked under Lilje after the war as an upper church councillor (*Oberkirchenrat*) of the Land Church of Hanover, said that his bishop had absolutely no connections with the Berneuchen Circle and its high-church practices. Instead, Lilje's position in 1933 was characterized by his work in the student movement and by Pietistic tendencies. After he became land bishop in Hanover, Lilje took a more strongly Lutheran position. Wilhelm Gerhold, telephone conversation, December 15, 1998.

ing in the GDC. From its beginning on May 9, 1933, the JB grew within a week to three thousand people.[37]

Peter Neumann writes that in April and early May 1933 the JB and the German-Christians were differentiated only by the fact that the JB adhered to the doctrine of two governances instead of the theocratic or single-governance doctrine of the GDC. According to the GDC position, the church would be essentially absorbed into the state.[38] However, the JB increasingly differentiated itself from the GDC as the German-Christians took a radical course in late May 1933. Additionally, after the controversy over who should become Reich bishop and Hitler's interference with the church elections in July, the JB found itself clearly at odds with the GDC.[39]

The JB established a journal, *Junge Kirche*, issued a statement supporting Friedrich von Bodelschwingh for Reich bishop; and entered actively into the preparations for the church election of July 23, 1933. In a July 12 letter to German President Hindenburg, Hitler had promised free elections for the leadership of the emerging DEK. On July 14, the JB sent a mailing to the congregations under the heading "Gospel and Church" ("*Evangelium und Kirche*"). The pamphlet included guidelines from the JB for the new church and a list of candidates recommended by the JB for the new positions in the DEK. Barth, who vehemently opposed the JB, weakened the effort by producing his own rival list of candidates. The GDC also went on the offensive. In a confidential letter to all local leaders of the German-Christians, Joachim Hossenfelder wrote:

> It is important to prove that the German evangelical folk want a new church which understands itself called to dedicate itself to the folk . . . . The men of yesterday coming out of the dusty corners of the old church want to hinder the emergence of the German *Volk* to the last depths of faith . . . . It is necessary everywhere to work in closest touch with representatives of the Party.[40]

Finally, though Hitler had promised not to interfere in the election, on the night before the vote, he gave a radio address in which he denounced Künneth's group by name and called on the German people to vote only for German-Christian

---

37 Scholder, *Kirchen*, 1:409; Künneth, *Lebensführungen*, 109.

38 Neumann, *Die Jungreformatorische Bewegung*, 109.

39 Neumann gives a detailed presentation of the growing JB mistrust of the GDC; see *Die Jungreformatorische Bewegung*, 108–12. In 1933 people viewed the JB and the GDC as being on opposite courses; see the report in *Bonhoeffer*, 12:81–88, from the instructive conference *Kirche im Kampf* in Berlin, dated "after June 26, 1933." In this report, Studentenpfarrer Ernst Bronisch-Holtze speaks for the JB and contrasts its aims with those of the GDC. The opposing GDC position, expressed in that report by Erich Vogelsang, is also of interest.

40 Künneth, *Lebensführungen*, 111.

Fig. 2: Wilhelm Zoellner
(photo courtesy of Karlmann Beyschlag)

Fig. 3: Walter Künneth
(photo courtesy of Karlmann Beyschlag)

Fig. 4: Martin Niemöller
(photo courtesy of Karlmann Beyschlag)

Fig. 5: Loccum Abbey
(photo by permission of Landeskirchliches Archiv of Hanover)

candidates. This implied that anyone voting for the candidates proposed by the JB would be guilty of political resistance against the will of the Führer.[41]

With the pressure brought to bear by Hitler and with their opponents divided, it was not surprising that the German-Christians won a two-thirds majority in the July election. Künneth related years later in his memoirs that the JB was undercut by the German-Christians and hindered "in every imaginable way." All the Nazi Party organizations supported the German-Christians "with every possible chicanery."[42] Some writers have claimed that opposing the GDC was not necessarily the same as opposing Hitler. No doubt some who opposed the GDC had supported the Führer for a time. But in 1933, Hitler worked hand-in-hand with the GDC. He had handpicked Ludwig Müller to be Reich bishop and August Jäger to be legal administrator of the DEK, and until these leaders crashed their own program in October 1934, Hitler and the Nazi Party provided full backing to the GDC. Thus Hitler made it clear that the members of the JB were his political foes.

Hitler's negative comments and the results of the July 23 election uncovered the weaknesses of the JB. It was not a political crusade; it had no strategies for carrying out its program in the face of political opposition. Lilje recalls: "The *Jung-reformatorische Bewegung* . . . was changed into the 'Pastors Emergency League' (*Pfarrernotbund* or PNB) under the leadership of Martin Niemöller."[43]

TWO LUTHERAN MOVEMENTS IN HANOVER

Although the Osnabrück Circle issued a reply to the German-Christian threat on April 27, 1933, it does not appear to have exerted a widespread influence. But two other groups did become influential: the Land Church Gathering (*Landeskirchliche Sammlung*) and the Confessional Fellowship (*Bekenntnisgemeinschaft*).

The first meeting of the Land Church Gathering was held on June 26, 1933. It issued a set of guidelines, among which was the statement that the group endorsed the nomination of Friedrich von Bodelschwingh as Reich bishop.[44] The chairman of the gathering was Pastor Hans (Johannes) Bosse and the business manager was Friedrich Denting, who was also the leader of the Confessional Fellowship. At the time of its organization, the Land Church Gathering included about 300 of the 1,050 pastors of the Land Church of Hanover. By October the number had increased to 450. By contrast, the GDC had 265 members among the pastors. The Confessional Fellowship was more conservative than the Pastors

---

41 Künneth, *Lebensführungen*, 113.

42 Künneth, *Lebensführungen*, 111.

43 Künneth, *Lebensführungen*, 118–19; Lilje in *ELC*, 1:526.

44 Klügel, *Landeskirche*, 49–50.

Emergency League headed by Niemöller; therefore there were often disagreements between the two groups, though the Fellowship supported the Confessing Church movement.[45]

THE PASTORS EMERGENCY LEAGUE

Many supporters of the JB entered the Pastors Emergency League (*Pfarrernotbund* [PNB]), which was organized under the leadership of Martin Niemöller on September 21, 1933. Whereas the JB had been a group of both laypeople and pastors, the PNB was a clerical organization. It was to become associated with the Dahlem Front of the Confessing Church Movement, which became increasingly liberal and increasingly committed to the theology of Barth and the Barmen Declaration. Opposition by Barth and the Barmen Declaration to the doctrine of two governances separated the PNB from other Lutherans and kept Künneth and others from full participation in the PNB and the Dahlem Front.

One of Niemöller's first actions as leader of the 2,000 members of the PNB, people "who were not part of the German-Christian Movement," was to issue a telegram of congratulations to Hitler for leaving the League of Nations. From this point forward, the PNB had its ups and downs. By January 1934, it had reached an enrollment of 7,036 members. However, when the Lutheran bishops and other church leaders met with Hitler on January 30, 1934, the bishops unexpectedly made concessions to Hitler and agreed to allow Ludwig Müller to remain in office as Reich bishop.[46] Afterward Niemöller denounced the bishops so strongly that 1,200 Bavarian, 250 Württembergian, and 350 Hanoverian pastors withdrew from the PNB. Moreover, the Württemberg branch of the league soon dissolved itself. This left the PNB with 5,256 members, a number that remained rather constant. After this January meeting, the Lutheran bishops were cautious about working with Niemöller, who often chided the bishops of the three intact churches for being more concerned with strengthening their own churches than in following him. Ernst Helmreich, a historian from the United States, comments: "Their policies often weakened the opposition [of Niemöller] to official Berlin policy, but on the other hand, had the bulwark which their churches constituted fallen to

---

45 Klügel, *Landeskirche*, 79–81.

46 Niemöller's actions in the meeting were the result of a telephone conversation he had participated in earlier that day with Künneth. In the conversation, Niemöller had made derogatory remarks against Hitler that were intercepted by the Gestapo. These comments were reported to Hitler at the meeting in front of the bishops. Niemöller's indiscretion scuttled the bishops' plan to call for the dismissal of Müller as Reich bishop. Afterward, Niemöller blamed the bishops for yielding to Hitler.

Berlin [Nazi] domination, the government authorities could have worked their will with greater dispatch and ruthlessness throughout the nation."[47]

The policy of Marahrens, Wurm, and Meiser was to give first consideration to serving their own churches and then to give a hand to Niemöller's movement. In the long run, by meeting their own needs, the intact churches proved better able to combat National Socialism than if they had neglected their work to help Niemöller's projects. In later years, the PNB devoted most of its energy to helping individual pastors under attack in the "destroyed" churches.

THE KAPLER COMMISSION

In the middle of May 1933, the Kapler Commission convened in Hanover to begin formulating the new Reich Church. Before adjourning to the quiet locale of the nearby Loccum Abbey, Chaplain Ludwig Müller of Königsberg became the commission's uninvited guest. Because he represented the Nazi state and because he had ambitions to become Reich bishop of the new church body, Müller's presence proved a hindrance and an embarrassment to the appointed participants.

During the proceedings, the role of the confessionally ambivalent Union churches in the new organization was a major problem. For August Marahrens, it was important that the Lutheran Confessions possess not merely a nominal but an actual authority in the organization. Therefore he believed the name of the new entity should be the Federated German Evangelical Church (*Bündische Deutsche evangelische Kirche*) and that the several churches should be included as a Lutheran branch, a Reformed branch, and a Union branch (three-pillars theory). Wilhelm Zoellner, a staunchly Lutheran churchman from the Union Church in Westphalia, insisted that there should be only two confessions, the Lutheran and the Reformed, and that the Union churches should not be recognized as a confession because they had nothing to contribute to the confessional makeup of the new church. Zoellner did not want the way opened for a "consensus union" in which there would be a Union church confession beside those of the Lutherans and the Reformed. Matters were not so simple, however. In fact, consensus unions already existed.[48] Ultimately, the manifesto took no position concerning the confessional basis of the new church body.

The Loccum Manifesto, which was published by the Kapler Commission on May 26, 1933, established the basic guidelines for the constitution of the forthcoming DEK.[49] The brief statement opens with effusive comments that were

---

47 Helmreich, 156.

48 On the problematic three-pillars theory, see material in Klügel, *Landeskirche*, 31–33, with footnotes.

49 For the text of the Loccum Manifesto, see Schmidt, *Bekenntnisse*, 153–54.

common during the first six months of Hitler's rule: "Our hotly beloved German fatherland has experienced a powerful raising up by the providence of God." Next, the manifesto discusses matters of polity of the new church. The DEK was to do away with the splintering that had marked German Protestantism in the past. The new entity would be only a federation, however, because the various territorial churches would retain their independence within their confessional positions—the several "Reformational confessions" would hold an inviolable position in the DEK. The Loccum Manifesto stipulated that there should be a Reich bishop of the Lutheran confession. He was to work with a "spiritual ministerium" (*Geistliches Ministerium*), which would include members of all confessions. Thus there would be an authority ready to serve as representative for the Reich bishop when non-Lutheran entities required attention. There was also to be a representative body, the German National Synod, which would have responsibility in legislative matters. It also would make appointments in the church government. Additionally, there would be advisory boards to enlist the creative work of the "German evangelical *Volkstum*." The Loccum Manifesto ended with a fine statement on the Trinity; unfortunately, this part was omitted when the final constitution for the DEK was drafted.

CHAPTER FOUR

The Founding
of the German Evangelical Church
(*Deutsche evangelische Kirche*)

Germany entered the twentieth century with dozens of Protestant territorial churches, which were disestablished in 1918. However, for many church leaders, the burning question remained: How could they further church unity and bring about a consolidation of these numerous church bodies? Some members of the Union church thought all Protestants—whether Lutheran, Reformed, or Union—should simply be "united" by decree, as in the 1817 Evangelical Church of the (Old) Prussian Union. The Confessional Lutherans, however, insisted that doctrinal agreement must precede church fellowship.[1] An important step toward outward unification had been taken in the founding of the German Evangelical Church Federation (*Deutscher evangelische Kirchen Bund* [DEKB]) in 1923, but when Adolf Hitler came to power in 1933, he wanted more than a fed-

---

1 Scholder faults "the great distrust of Lutherans regarding all unionism, their traditional friendliness to the state, the openness to 'political theology from the right,' the provincial self-interest of the land churches, and the anti-Prussian prejudices" (*Kirchen*, 1:417–18). By regarding the stronger convictions of the Confessional Lutheran churches as a weakness and the doctrinal indecision of the Union churches as superior tolerance, Scholder unconsciously endorses the principle of *Gleichschaltung* and blames the Confessional Lutherans for that which enabled them to remain intact. If Bishops Hans Meiser, Theophil Wurm, and August Marahrens had adopted Scholder's advice and imitated the Union churches, they would have advanced Adolf Hitler's totalitarian goal.

eration. Hitler called for all Protestants to combine into one German Evangelical Church (*Deutsche evangelische Kirche*)—the DEK or Reich Church.

The Prussian Union held decisive power in the administration of the DEKB. When the DEK was founded in 1933, the Prussian presence was again predominant.[2] It was unfortunate that an inordinate amount of power was exercised in the Prussian Union by Wilhelm Kube, an influential church member, a member of the Nazi Party, and a leader among the German-Christians. In 1932, Kube had called for the German-Christians to register voters among the inactive members of the Land Church of Prussia to ensure a victory for National Socialism.[3] Kube and his cohorts were successful in their endeavor to turn out the people for the election, an effort that provided the victory that he sought. The German-Christians won approximately 60 percent of the positions in Brandenburg in the 1932 church elections. The time would soon be ripe to seize the whole Prussian Union and to "incorporate" the other land churches of Germany into the new DEK.

EVENTS PRECEDING AND ACCOMPANYING THE FOUNDING OF THE DEK IN 1933

The formation of the DEK in general has been presented with great detail elsewhere.[4] In the limited space allotted to this matter, this section is confined to several specific developments that relate to the purpose of the present study.

On April 25, Hermann Kapler, president of the Supreme Council of the Prus-sian Union and chairman of the DEKB, called a meeting of the administrative committee of the DEKB. This committee approved Kapler's proposal for turning the DEKB into the German Evangelical Church (DEK) and for appointing a committee to draw up a new constitution. Kapler appointed himself to the committee (representing the Prussian Union), Bishop August Marahrens (a Lutheran from Hanover), and Dr. Hermann Hesse, a Reformed church leader from Elberfeld.[5]

On the same day, Hitler named Ludwig Müller to be his Plenipotentiary for the Concerns of the Evangelical Churches. Müller had given Hitler a "memoran-

---

2 Scholder writes: "The decisions of German Protestantism, as also the decisions of the *Reich*, were made in Prussia" (*Kirchen*, 1:249). Hermann Sasse declares that the leading force in 1933 for establishing the DEK came from the Prussian Union.

3 Scholder, *Kirchen*, 1:256.

4 The genesis of the DEK constitution is traced and documents marking the various stages of the development of the DEK are presented in detail in Kater. Also important are Meiser's notes in *Verantwortung*, 1:1ff.

5 See pp. 70–72, 79–80, for more information on the Kapler Commission.

dum" discussing occasions in church history when the state had intervened in churchly matters. Written by Erich Vogelsang, a brilliant pupil of Karl Holl who was now an instructor at the University of Königsberg, the paper was read by Hitler "with great eagerness."[6] Hitler placed Müller over the German-Christians on May 16 to temper the extremism of Joachim Hossenfelder's leadership. Also on May 16, the AELK called for the establishment of a Lutheran Reich Church under Lutheran governance, "without prejudice to the rights of evangelical people of other confessions."[7]

A week later, the Loccum Manifesto was published. At that time, the council of the DEKB met to discuss the constitution for the DEK. The council's members gave their approval to "the steps undertaken by those who had been so authorized" (namely, the Kapler Commission); approved the Loccum Manifesto; declared "themselves in agreement that the work which had been begun should be continued"; and urged the completion of the new constitution for the DEK under the participation of the designated Reich bishop, Friedrich von Bodelschwingh, and Hitler's representative, Müller.[8] Then the council of the DEKB repeated its endorsement of Bodelschwingh as Reich bishop.[9]

Eight meetings were held between June 1 and June 17, 1933, under the leadership of Reich bishop-designate Bodelschwingh to complete the DEK constitution.[10] The June 24 seizure of the Prussian Union by the German-Christians and the resulting uncertainty interrupted the work, but German President Paul von Hindenburg intervened, the seizure was reversed, and the planning of the constitution resumed with meetings on July 4, 8, and 10. On July 10, President Hindenburg urged the conclusion of the discussions. The group needed to address who would authorize the new constitution. On July 11, the decision was made that the authorization should come from all the land churches and that the authority previously vested in the DEKB would now flow into the DEK. The bishops or chief leaders of the respective land churches signed the new constitution,[11] and on July 14 a Reich decree confirmed the constitution and set July 23 as the date for new elections.[12]

---

6 Kater, 77.

7 Kater, 67.

8 Kater, 80.

9 Kater, 80.

10 Kater, 82.

11 The text of the DEK constitution is supplied by Hans Liermann, *Kirchen und Staat* (Munich: Isar, 1954), 17–20, and in *KZ* 57 (1933): 572–76. The DEK constitution in its final form and in four preliminary versions is given in an appendix in Kater, 195–213.

12 Kater, 80.

CONTROVERSY OVER THE ELECTION OF THE REICH BISHOP

Hitler wanted Ludwig Müller chosen as Reich bishop of the new DEK.[13] Despite this fact, the Kapler Commission nominated Friedrich von Bodelschwingh for the position. On May 19, Walter Künneth, on behalf of the JB, nominated Bodelschwingh as Reich bishop before a press conference in Berlin.[14] On May 26 the council of the DEKB repeated the nomination of Bodelschwingh and supported him rather than Müller by a vote of 91 to 8. With the exception of Württemberg, Mecklenburg-Schwerin, and Hamburg, all the land churches voted for Bodelschwingh. Strangely, Bodelschwingh was opposed by Bishops Theophil Wurm, Heinrich Rendtorff, and Simon Schöffel.[15]

The Reich bishop-designate came from a remarkable family. The first Friedrich von Bodelschwingh (1831–1910) was the founder of Bethel, a complex of institutions of mercy near the Westphalian city of Bielefeld. He had been a leader in inner missions and an advocate of social justice who spoke out on behalf of the laboring classes. His son, a man with the same name, was a gifted organizer and a man of action who became the director of Bethel after his father's death in 1910. The second Bodelschwingh was one of the most highly regarded church leaders in Germany. It was not at all surprising that when the bishops and other representatives of the land churches met on May 27, they elected this distinguished Lutheran as Reich bishop. Bodelschwingh accepted the position.

Hitler was not pleased with this selection. The National Socialists and the GDC began a campaign against Bodelschwingh. As a result, some church leaders withdrew their support, and on June 24 Bodelschwingh felt compelled to resign as Reich bishop. Had he been able to remain as head of the DEK, some of the later turmoil would likely have been avoided. Nevertheless, Müller was elected Reich bishop in September 1933.

Who was Ludwig Müller? Born in Gütersloh on June 23, 1863, he was reared a Lutheran in the Union church in Westphalia. He spent most of his career as a military chaplain, and from 1926 until 1933 he was head of military chaplains in East Prussia. On April 25, 1933, Hitler made Müller his plenipotentiary over the German evangelical churches. In October 1934, following the unsuccessful attempt to overthrow Bishops Hans Meiser and Theophil Wurm, Hitler quietly shunted Müller

---

13 The GDC nominated Müller for the position of Reich bishop on May 23, 1933. Müller's critics considered this a conflict of interest because he was already Hitler's plenipotentiary, head of the GDC, and now aspired to be Reich bishop. Those concerned for the independence of the churches opposed Müller's nomination.

14 Meier, *EKK*, 1:95.

15 Scholder, *Kirchen*, 1:419–20. Considerable data on Bodelschwingh and Müller and the choice of the DEKB are given in Meiser, *Verantwortung*, 1:15 n. 36.

aside. Although he was now deprived of recognition (other than that from some within the GDC), Müller still considered himself the Reich bishop. During the closing days of World War II, Müller committed suicide in Berlin on July 31, 1945.

THE "FÜHRER CONCEPT" AND ITS ASSOCIATED PROBLEMS

In its initial form in the Loccum Manifesto and through all its stages, the DEK constitution disregarded a Reformed concept of democratic leadership and instead preferred leadership by a Reich bishop of the Lutheran confession. This preference for a single strong leader was called the "Führer concept." Lutheran churches in Scandinavian countries had long been led by bishops, and such a structure had slowly been implemented in the German Lutheran churches after the 1918 collapse of the territorial churches. Thus when Friedrich Veit, the last "president" of the Lutheran Land Church of Bavaria, retired in May 1933, he was replaced by Hans Meiser, who was the church's first land bishop (*Landesbischof*). Similarly, Theophil Wurm, who became president of the Lutheran Land Church of Württemberg in 1929, was made its land bishop in 1933. August Marahrens had held the title of land bishop in Hanover since 1925.

A land bishop often had a much larger territory than a Roman Catholic diocesan bishop. The power and prestige conveyed by the title "land bishop" were important factors in the ability of Meiser, Wurm, and Marahrens to keep their land churches intact and to thwart the covetous impulses of the Nazis. Land churches without strong, centralized heads became the victims of incorporation into the Nazi state (*Gleichschaltung*). Nevertheless, the word *Führer* was problematic in ecclesial usage because it was seriously tainted by Hitler's activities. We shall return to the Führer concept in chapter 12.

The administrators and theologians in the Reformed churches rejected the concept of a strong leader. But their insistence upon filling church offices by means of democratic elections backfired when the Nazis rigged the elections in Prussia and the vacant positions were filled by German-Christians. This led to the Prussian Union becoming a "destroyed" church through its 1934 incorporation into Hitler's Reich Church.

According to the DEK constitution, the Reich bishop was to have had a Spiritual Ministerium (*Geistliches Ministerium*). This administrative core would be balanced by a representative gathering, the National Synod. When in recess, the Synodical Board would speak for the synod's interests. Unfortunately, this system of checks and balances was never effectively enacted. Instead, it was counteracted by the Nazi Party and the GDC, which exploited the Lutheran preference for strong leadership. Last-minute efforts were made by Meiser, Hans Meinzolt, Reformed church leaders, and even Karl Fezer, a prominent German-Christian, to restore the checks and balances, but interference from the state foiled these attempts. In the constitution's July 10, 1933, form, the powers of the Spiritual Ministerium for amending the constitution had been restricted and the power to call the National Synod was left to the will of the Reich bishop. An attempt by Meiser to establish a Council of Bishops to participate in the formation of legislation was also defeated. The Nazi state was determined to hold control over the DEK.[16]

THE DEK CONSTITUTION AND ITS CRITICS

The DEK constitution was signed by church leaders and was published on July 11, 1933. On July 14, the civil government approved the constitution and called for church elections on July 23.[17] Much of the constitution was dead upon arrival, however.

Werner Elert delivered a public lecture at the University of Erlangen on July 21, 1933, on "The Constitution of the German Evangelical Church."[18] In his introduction, Elert declared that he and the Erlangen faculty had had no part in drawing up the DEK constitution that had been published on July 11. He thought the Erlangen theological faculty should speak out because Berlin, "once proclaimed the guardian of Luther's theology, can now be compared only to the famous 'Robber Synod of Ephesus' (*Latrocinium Ephesinum*)." This bold denunciation on Elert's part alluded to the seizure of the Prussian Union by Nazi and GDC intrigue a month earlier.[19]

In his lecture Elert made an ironic statement of approval of the GDC. It is one of the few positive statements about this movement that can be found in any of his writings: "It was a deed of first rank in the history of the church that the 'German-Christians' in their first proclamation on May 5 of this year formulated this demand for the first time: 'The Reich Bishop, corresponding to the vast majority of church people, shall be Lutheran' § 7." Citing the German-Christians, whom he disliked, was an obvious gambit for Elert. He pointed out that the statement made by members of the GDC that acknowledded the rights of the Lutheran majority had not been allowed in the repressive Prussian Union. Elert's reasoning was as follows: If even the German-Christians acknowledge Lutheran rights in Prussia, then the government of the Prussian land church ought to follow suit.[20] Elert

---

16 Kater, 93.

17 Helmreich, 140.

18 Elert, "Die Verfassung der Deutscher evangelischen Kirche," in *Ecclesia militans: Drei Kapitel von der Kirche und ihrer Verfassung* (Leipzig: Dörffling & Franke, 1933), 40–53.

19 Elert, "Die Verfassung der Deutscher evangelischen Kirche," 40.

20 Elert, "Die Verfassung der Deutscher evangelischen Kirche," 47–48.

also stated the wish that the oppressive Prussian Union would finally recognize this principle and grant its Lutherans toleration in doctrine and liturgical practice. Elert added: "And we assure our fellow Lutherans in the Old Prussian Union that, in the battle over the real authority of the Lutheran Confessions, which is guaranteed to them in the constitution of the German Evangelical Church, we will support them to the fullest."[21]

When Elert reached Article 6, paragraph 3, on the powers of the Reich bishop, he uttered some grave warnings. According to the DEK constitution: "The Reich Bishop has the right to consummate every pastoral act." In his lecture Elert added: "One asks, deeply shocked: Where? According to the wording one might be reminded of the most fatal consequences of the 'power of jurisdiction in the universal church' accorded the pope, a direct jurisdiction which was to be followed without exception by 'all churches, pastors, and the faithful.'" Elert commented: "This means that the pope may undertake official acts over the head of the bishops in all the dioceses of his church. Were the fathers of our new constitution clear that they opened the door to the Vaticanization of the German Evangelical Church with this provision? We want to hope not. But clarity must be created over this matter so that this right of the Reich Bishop applies only to his own diocese, which was provided for in this constitution."[22]

Two of Elert's Erlangen colleagues, Hermann Sasse and Friedrich Ulmer, were even more critical of the constitution. They objected to the ambiguous language whereby, already in the prologue, the DEK was called at one place a "church" and in another place a "federation of churches" that were autonomous in doctrine and liturgy. In an essay that appeared in *Theologische Blätter* in September 1933, Sasse voiced determined opposition to the DEK constitution, showing how it violated the principle of Article VII of the Augsburg Confession, which called for agreement on Word and Sacrament before union. Sasse pronounced the constitution to be the extension of the Prussian Union over the Lutheran land churches. He wrote:

> It belongs to the attributes of every Union church that its confession [doctrine] is of less importance than its constitution [polity], which is the only real bond of unity. This applies also to the new church. The church's unity depends upon its constitution, not upon unity of teaching; for the equality of the differing confessions is emphasized repeatedly, which established the differences in the doctrines of the churches.[23]

---

21 Elert, "Die Verfassung der Deutscher evangelischen Kirche," 48.

22 Elert, "Die Verfassung der Deutscher evangelischen Kirche," 49–50.

23 Sasse, *In Statu Confessionis*, 1:268–69.

Ulmer wrote: "That the new church shall be a 'Union and Unity church,' and therefore unambiguously a Union Church, no words or assurances can help remove, because of and in spite of the citation of Eph. 4:5–6."[24]

The criticisms by Sasse and Ulmer were echoed by Johann Michael Reu, editor of *Kirchliche Zeitschrift* and a German-American observer in Dubuque, Iowa. In his regular column of news and comments on the church situation in Germany, Reu cited Hans Lauerer, rector of the deaconess house in Neuendettelsau, who spoke at Stuttgart before the Evangelical Lutheran Conference of Wurttemberg on November 29, 1933: "Above all else, it is necessary that we recognize the seriousness of the situation in which Lutheranism finds itself. It is undoubtedly once more a time in which all storms are blowing over our Lutheran Church." Lauerer noted that Müller, supposedly a Lutheran and head of the DEK, was simultaneously land bishop of the non-Lutheran Evangelical Church of the (Old) Prussian Union. Lauerer recalled with thanks that a number of Lutheran bishops had protested the situation, but he expressed concern that a number of new German-Christian pastors had received placement during the past year, a movement that damaged the unity of the Lutheran Church. According to Lauerer, this also harmed relations with Lutheran churches in other countries: "Lutherans beyond German borders do not conceal the concern with which they observe the development of church conditions in Germany, and they hold the impression that the Union movement is spreading throughout Germany."[25] Lauerer acknowledged that Lutheran consciousness had been weak of late, and he advocated that Lutherans speak out more. He also advocated that the AELK should be employed to bring together the scattered Lutheran churches of Germany and help them speak and work together.[26]

After presenting Lauerer's address, Reu gave his own viewpoint as an observer from the United States. In calling the Prussian Union responsible for much of the current trouble in Germany, Reu cited a church leader from Neuendettelsau: "Mission-Director Dr. [Friedrich] Eppelein explained with refreshing clarity that the Union is the enemy, which, in the interest of the German state as well as the German church, must be aimed at and fought against; yes, even the constitution of the new church brings conditions that are intolerable for Lutherans."[27] Reu continued with a quotation from Eppelein, protesting that all Protestant pastors are expected to vow allegiance to the new constitution of the DEK:

---

24 Friedrich Ulmer, "Was wird aus unserer Kirche? Zur neuen Kirchenverfassung," quoted in Sasse, *In Statu Confessionis*, 1:266 n. 4.

25 *KZ* 58 (1934): 117–18.

26 *KZ* 58 (1934): 120.

27 *KZ* 58 (1934): 121–22.

Now one should make clear the following situation for all pastors of a Lutheran Church within the German Evangelical Church: On the one side they are obligated, by their ordination, to the Lutheran Confessions, which reject all false doctrine, including that of the Reformed; on the other side, they are obligated to the constitution of the great German Evangelical Church, in which the Lutheran and Reformed confessions are regarded as of equal validity. We cannot imagine how a conscientious, careful theologian could readily accept such an untruth. What evangelical Christian of strong character who loves the truth can endure it that the worm of falsehood and of theological superficiality, of confessional vagueness, gnaws at the root of the German Evangelical Church and also at the root of German Lutheranism?[28]

Reu cited the noted New Testament scholar Paul Feine of Halle, who wrote: "One should now completely abandon the Union. It is not a good structure. The Lutherans have suffered much damage from it up until the present day."[29] Then Reu turned to a statement by Christian Keyßer of Neuendettelsau: "Experience has shown us that a church which deviates in some chief doctrine from the hard-fought confession of our fathers stands in danger more easily to surrender other truths. The newest occurrences in the German Reich Church are proof that, in the Old Prussian Union, intolerable conditions prevail. . . . Away with the Union!"[30]

Günther Koch, a young Dortmund clergyman, called for the dissolution of the Union church and the founding of a Lutheran Reich Church.[31] Wilhelm Zoellner also called for the dissolution of the Union church:

The Union presents itself as the most disruptive and difficult thing which hinders the establishment of a Lutheran Church. I stand in the old line that we can never come to a real Lutheran Church if we do not succeed in dividing the Union back again into its parts and rebuilding it again upon this basis. We did not receive our commission from a church that is really a church.[32]

It is said that even Otto Dibelius, the postwar land bishop of the Union church in Berlin and Brandenburg, was averse to the Prussian Union and that he had seriously considered dismantling it and establishing separate Lutheran and Reformed church bodies. He was dissuaded from this action by the plight in which the Reformed minority would find itself, should they through this action be left alone in a hostile communist state. Ironically, the hostility of the Soviet regime toward

---

28 *KZ* 58 (1934): 122.

29 *KZ* 58 (1934): 123.

30 *KZ* 58 (1934): 124.

31 Scholder, *Kirchen*, 1:373.

32 Meiser, *Verantwortung*, 2:138–39.

the name "Prussian" forced church leaders to rename themselves the "Evangelical Church of the Union" (EKU) after World War II.[33]

LAUNCHING THE DEK

On July 23, 1933, elections were held to fill positions in the new German Evangelical Church. On July 22, Hitler, despite his pledge not to interfere in church affairs, delivered a radio speech in which he urged that only German-Christians should be elected. Two-thirds of those who were elected did in fact belong to the GDC. Members of the GDC also were successful in electing Ludwig Müller as Reich bishop in place of Friedrich von Bodelschwingh. Müller was installed as Reich bishop at the National Synod in Wittenberg on September 27, 1933. Although his election was declared unanimous, at least one man, Bishop August Marahrens, voted against Müller. Regardless, the high plurality shows that the church leaders had not yet lost their confidence in Müller.[34]

The seizure of the Prussian Union and the Land Church of Saxony in 1933 had been reversed by the intervention of German President Paul von Hindenburg, but an official program of incorporation of territorial churches into the Reich Church (*Gleichschaltung*) was reintroduced on March 2, 1934, when the Reich bishop issued a decree that merged the Prussian Union with the DEK. This action provoked a protest from Bishop Theophil Wurm,[35] which led Wurm and Hans Meiser to hold a second meeting with Hitler on March 13. Nevertheless, Reich Bishop Müller proceeded with his attempt to merge all the German Protestant churches.[36] Eventually the Prussian Union and the DEK became so thoroughly integrated structurally as the Reich Church that members of the Union churches made up the majority of the resultant underground movement known as the Confessing Church.

---

33 Julius Bodensieck, interview by author, in Berlin-Dahlem, December 26, 1952, referring to an earlier conversation of Bodensieck with Dibelius. The 1953 reorganization of the Prussian Union and its renaming as the EKU is discussed by Helmreich, 415–16. A young Confessional Lutheran pastor in the Union church of Westphalia, whose name must remain anonymous, related to me that many people in the EKU today see it as a useless, harmful, and expensive bureaucratic fossil that they intend to abolish (from an interview with the author, August 28, 1997).

34 Kater, 134.

35 This action was protested by the Evangelical Church High Council (*Evangelischer Oberkirchenrat*) in a letter written by Wurm (in Schäfer, *Württemberg*, 3:85–86).

36 The only German land churches that presented successful resistance to the Nazi takeover were the three Confessional Lutheran land churches of Bavaria, Württemberg, and Hanover.

It is significant that when the DEK was officially launched in the National Synod at Wittenberg on September 27, 1933, the Lutheran bishops Meiser, Wurm, Marahrens, and Simon Schöffel; the Reformed president Otto Koopmann from Aurich; and other leaders and bishops pointed out that the Prussian Union had taken over almost all the offices in the new Reich Church.[37] The repressive methods of the Prussian Union, as carried out by the DEK, were soon to lead to disaster and to the debacle known as the Reich Church.

THE GROWING CONFLICT BETWEEN REICH BISHOP MÜLLER AND THE PROTESTANT CHURCHES

Since 1933 there had been growing conflict between Müller and the Protestant churches. This was caused by several circumstances, including Müller's clandestine efforts to prevent the election of Bodelschwingh as Reich bishop, the 1933 attempt to seize the Land Church of Saxony and the Prussian Union, the controversy surrounding Müller's installation as Reich bishop, and the GDC debacle at the Berlin Sport Palace on November 14, 1933, which was followed by massive withdrawals from the movement. Müller recovered from some of his losses and tried to restore his power in December 1933. In the process, however, his dictatorial behavior provoked fierce opposition from duly constituted church leaders. Two notorious actions as 1933 drew to a close and 1934 began brought forth vehement opposition: the merger (*Gleichschaltung*) of the church's youth movement with the Hitler Youth and the "muzzling decree."

On December 19, 1933, Müller entered a unilateral agreement with Baldur von Schirach, leader of the Hitler Youth (*Hitler-Jugend*), which transferred the Evangelical Youth Organization from the church to the Hitler Youth. During succeeding weeks, the pan-Lutheran journal *Allgemeine evangelisch-lutherische Kirchenzeitung* (*AELKZ*) was filled with attacks upon Müller's action. Bishop Meiser of Bavaria, in a statement dated December 31, 1933, denounced Müller's action as counter to church law and therefore invalid. Meiser mentioned that on December 19 Müller had given his word that he would consult with church leaders if he envisioned any changes concerning youth work; thus Müller's actions completely contradicted his words.[38] Despite these cogent arguments, the seizure of the Evangelical Youth Organization was not rescinded.

By early 1934, Müller was experiencing much opposition, so on January 4, 1934, he tried to silence his critics by enacting the notorious "muzzling decree" (*Maulkorberlaß*). Entitled "Ordinance for the Restoration of Orderly Conditions

---

37 *KZ* 57 (1933): 700.

38 *AELKZ* 66 (1934): 61–62.

in the German Evangelical Church," the decree forbade pastors from discussing current controversies during church services, specifying that church services were to be used only for preaching the Gospel, not for discussing church-political matters.

On January 3, 1934, one day before the issuance of the muzzling decree, the much-discussed Steinacher Conference of Bavarian Lutheran pastors met with 300 pastors in attendance. The principal speakers were Bishop Meiser and Hans Lauerer, rector of the deaconess institution at Neuendettelsau. At this meeting, Meiser pointed out that there had been serious controversy since the July 23, 1933, DEK elections, obviously blaming Müller for the trouble. Meiser also excoriated the incorporation of the church's youth work into the Hitler Youth, which had been done deceitfully and against the wishes of church leaders. Meiser insisted that the two organizations could exist side by side but must not be merged into one entity. Then Lauerer explained how his December 2, 1933, nomination to become a member of the Spiritual Ministerium (*Geistliches Ministerium*) of the Reich Church had been blocked. At the end of the meeting, Friedrich Klingler, a pastor from Nuremberg and a leader in the group, proposed a resolution thanking Bishop Meiser for his leadership and expressing continued confidence in him; after the motion had carried unanimously, Meiser thanked the pastors for their support.[39] It was occurrences such as these that made Müller shake in his boots and caused him to threaten all who might oppose him.

In the following letter to Wilhelm Frick, Hitler's minister of the interior, Bishop Theophil Wurm of Württemberg expressed his continuing trust in Hitler but insisted that Müller must be removed from office:

> I had thought that the church, which had received such strong assurances from the state regarding its right to exist, was obligated to prefer the confidant of the *Führer* over other candidates. But now it is becoming increasingly clear that the Evangelical Church has gotten an incapable and unworthy leader in this man. This could be foreseen neither by the state nor by the church . . . . In broad National-Socialist circles the blame is leveled against those who oppose Müller that they are not ready to give to the state what belongs to the state and that when they oppose the *Reich* Bishop, they also oppose the *Reich* Chancellor. Cannot this ugly insinuation be put to an end from a high place? . . . What wish could fulfill us more than this, that the state of Adolf Hitler should strengthen its position as the state of righteousness, of honor, and of peace?[40]

After the events of late December 1933 and early January 1934, church leaders requested and secured a meeting with Hitler on January 25, 1934. Present at the

---

39 *AELKZ* 67 (1934): 68.

40 Schäfer, *Württemberg*, 2:1,045–46.

meeting were the Reich bishop; the land bishops of Saxony, Hanover, Württemberg, Bavaria, Thuringia, and Hamburg; the church leader of Mecklenburg (later identified as Bishop Schultz); the president of the Reformed Church of Hanover; the president of the Provincial Synod of Westphalia; Martin Niemöller; Otto Weber; Hermann Wolfgang Beyer; Friedrich Werner; Karl Fezer; and, besides Hitler, several of his cohorts, including Rudolf Bultmann, Wilhelm Frick, and Hans Heinrich Lammers. Of those in attendance, Weber, Beyer, and Fezer had all left the GDC following the Sport Palace scandal.[41] At this new meeting, the church leaders had intended to tell Hitler that they could no longer tolerate Müller as Reich bishop and to ask that he be replaced.

Events transpired far differently than the church leaders anticipated because of an indiscretion by Niemöller. The meeting became nasty when Hermann Göring interrupted the proceedings to play a tape of an intercepted telephone conversation that had occurred earlier that morning between Niemöller and Walter Künneth.[42] In this conversation Niemöller had criticized Hitler and the government. At his wife's prompting, Niemöller had suggested to Künneth that President Hindenburg was about to give the "last rites" to Hitler. Niemöller was present as Göring spoke, and he acknowledged making the indiscreet remarks, which led to a tense confrontation between Hitler and Niemöller, as well as with the other church leaders. Niemöller's blunder effectively forestalled the first attempt by the bishops to get rid of Müller, and it provided a boon for Hitler. Having gained the tactical advantage in the meeting, Hitler now urgently asked the church leaders to accept Reich Bishop Müller and to work with him.[43] Wurm, Meiser, and the other church leaders agreed to give Müller another chance and promised him their following and cooperation. Later, their word of acquiescence was called the "Capitulation Statement" (*Unterwerfungserklärung*).[44] Immediately after this "capitulation," both Meiser and Wurm were overcome by shame and regret. Nevertheless, Niemöller disclaimed responsibility for the debacle at the meeting and denounced the Lutheran bishops for yielding to Hitler. As a result, as was seen in chapter 3, nearly 2,000 pastors withdrew from the PNB in protest over Niemöller's actions.

---

41 Wurm's eyewitness account of the meeting is given in Schäfer, *Württemberg*, 2:1,053–56.

42 Künneth relates this conversation and its unexpected results in his autobiography, *Lebensführungen*, 133. Künneth also discusses his discomfort with Niemöller's machinations with church politics and his eventual break with Niemöller. This discomfort reflected the ongoing problem of a single-governance view, or theocracy (Niemöller), versus the two-governances teaching (Künneth).

43 Wurm's account of this stormy audience with Hitler is given in Schäfer, *Württemberg*, 3:100–101.

44 *ZwKK*, 83; see p. 19 for bibliographic details.

A week later, on February 1, 1934, at a pastoral conference in Nuremberg, the chairman attempted to pass a resolution that would put the stamp of approval on Meiser's Capitulation Statement. Karl Steinbauer, a young vicar, objected, saying, "In the church we live by the forgiveness of sins." He added that the bishop had sinned and must do penance. The young man brashly demanded that the bishop return to Berlin and renegotiate with Hitler and Müller. Afterward, in a letter to the land church council (*Landeskirchenrat*) dated February 4, Steinbauer wrote: "The Christian, and with him the church as an entirety, lives from the Third Article, from faith and the forgiveness of sins, but not from a dishonest, unbelieving job of painting and pasting over sin with a resolution of approval."[45] Steinbauer also carried out energetic attacks on other prominent people, such as his former teacher Werner Elert.[46]

Steinbauer's public attack on Meiser and his letter to the land church council had strong repercussions. Eduard Putz, an eyewitness, describes how, at the following meeting, Meiser expressed his feelings of shame and regret before the plenary meeting of the land church council:

> Meiser burst into tears and said that after such a fall he could no longer be a bishop and he therewith offered to resign. He confessed his guilt. But all of us, young and old alike, were of the opinion that it would be a successful blow of the devil if Wurm and Meiser should resign. We declared as with one voice that, just as with Peter's denial, so in the present case the Savior's power would supply forgiveness. We suggested that the promise to *Reich* Bishop Müller should be kept for the time being, but that the *Reich* bishop would soon break his word and again come out with false doctrine and breach of the law. Then both Meiser and Wurm would have freedom of action again.[47]

---

45 *ZwKK*, 83.

46 After the war, Steinbauer is said to have blamed Elert for not preventing his deportation to a concentration camp. But it appears that Elert, who steadfastly refused to join the Nazi Party, had no influence in such matters. In a review of Elert's public lecture "Paulus und Nero," Steinbauer attacked Elert for his doctrine of the two governances and his insistence that secular government was ordained by God; see Steinbauer, "Paulus und Nero: Bedenken zu dem dritten in *Zwischen Gnade und Ungnade* erschienenen Vortrag von Werner Elert," *Korblatt* 65, no. 3 (February 15, 1950): 9–11, and *Korblatt* 65, no. 4 (February 28, 1950): 13–16. For Elert's reply to Steinbauer, see "Unter Anklage," *Korblatt* 65, no. 14 (July 31, 1950): 55–56, and *Korblatt* 65, no. 15 (August 15, 1950): 59–60. There was also a short postscript, "Zur Auseinandersetzung Prof. Elert—Pfr. Steinbauer," by Karl-Heinz Becker (*Korblatt* 65, no. 15 [August 15, 1950]: 82). Along with Steinbauer, Becker had signed a declaration (*Erklärung*) prepared by some Bavarian pastors and directed against Elert. Thus Becker's postscript expresses his dissatisfaction with Elert's response.

47 Putz, "Der Weg zum Barmer Bekenntnis," in *ZwKK*, 25–26.

Meanwhile, Wurm also had to give an accounting to his pastors in Württemberg. He told the pastors that he had gone to Berlin prepared to make concessions to the GDC, and he went to Hitler hoping to win his support for those concessions. Wurm described the intercepted telephone conversation between Niemöller and Künneth as "irresponsible gossip about the reception of the *Reich* chancellor [Hitler] by the *Reich* president [Hindenburg], which made a just presentation of our complaints almost impossible."[48] Wurm continued:

> These were the hardest days of my life. I rejoiced that I was allowed to look the *Führer* in the eyes. And now this meeting became an hour of greatest painfulness .... He is a responsible man, and we were caught up in the passion with which he speaks of Germany .... Despite the situation, we freely expressed our complaints. I in particular pointed out that the speeches of the *Reich* bishop have made a very poor impression.[49]

Then Wurm proceeded to outline his new position: that German-Christians should be recognized, peace must prevail, and "I dare say that also the political leaders, at least in Württemberg, are imbued on both sides with the will for righteousness and are intent upon removing reasons for conflict."[50]

Wurm's new approach was hailed by supporters of the GDC[51] but was greeted with dismay by opponents of the GDC. Thus Pastor Ernst Lachenmann of Stuttgart criticized Wurm's actions in an open letter.[52] Lachenmann's misgivings were speedily justified. Two months later, the German-Christians brought forth a major conspiracy against Wurm. He was arrested on the first of two occasions, was "deposed" by Müller's henchmen, and was replaced as bishop by a German-Christian. However, Wurm prevailed over the attacks in April 1934. In September and October 1934, he again proved himself a formidable opponent of the German-Christians and, though not always fully aware of the true foe, of Hitler and National Socialism. Following these two standoffs, Wurm remained in office and led his church through 1945 and into the postwar years.

Among Lutheran leaders there was a growing awareness during the course of 1934 of the dangers that were at hand. It became increasingly apparent that Reich Bishop Müller intended to combine all churches—Lutheran, Reformed, and Union—into one overarching Reich Church, regardless of confessional differences, and bring all church matters under his control. The Erlangen theological faculty expressed itself in the following opinion of May 18, 1934: "A dissolution of

---

48 Schäfer, *Württemberg*, 3:21–22.

49 Schäfer, *Württemberg*, 3:22–23.

50 Schäfer, *Württemberg*, 3:23.

51 See Schilling's letter quoted in Schäfer, *Württemberg*, 3:24–26.

52 Lachenmann's letter is quoted in Schäfer, *Württemberg*, 3:27–29.

Lutheran churches in the German Evangelical Church contradicts the doctrine of the church in the Lutheran Confession so long as the Lutheran character of the German Evangelical Church is not secured. According to this confession, there is no church unity without union of churchly teaching."[53] The votum was signed by Paul Althaus, Elert, Hans Preuß, Otto Procksch, Sasse, and Ulmer. A pointed statement against the ambitions of Müller was sounded in this May 19 statement from the Lutheran theological faculty at Leipzig: "In this last hour we implore the government of the German Church and particularly of the Reich Church, if the German *Volk* are to be served, that they abstain from the dictatorial use of the *Führer* principle in church matters and that they return to the clear legal basis of the German Church constitution of July 14, 1933."[54] This statement was signed by twelve men, including Albrecht Alt, Otto Clemen, Gerhard von Rad, Ernst Sommerlath, and Horst Stephan.

---

53 Hermelink, 102–3.
54 Hermelink, 103.

CHAPTER FIVE

Romanticism in Politics, Religion, and the Ideology of *Volk* and Race

Nineteenth-century romanticism and its child, nationalism, were the soil in which International Socialism (Communism) and National Socialism (Nazism) were spawned. Existentialism and social Darwinism, both by-products of romanticism, were ingredients of Nazi ideology.[1] In fact, in 1931 Hermann Strathmann of the University of Erlangen labeled National Socialism a "vulgar" form of "biological materialism."[2] The French occupation of German soil after

---

1 In his foreword, my colleague William Sheridan Allen has taken issue with the fact that I name Darwinism as an ingredient of National Socialism. Allen is correct in his opposition, strictly speaking. It was the distortion of Darwin's thought by his disciples, the social Darwinists, that brought about such havoc and fomented imperialism, racism, and opposition to social reform. This reveals a distinction between Darwin and the later developers of Darwinism. Still, the application, however faulty, of Darwin's biological concepts to the social and political scene helped prepare the way for National Socialism.

2 In 1931 Strathmann contended: "In Nazi literature, Christianity is openly rejected. Instead of love, hate is preached. The Old Testament and Paul must be abolished. Jesus is an Aryan; not a sufferer but a fighter . . . . The fanatical anti-Semitism cannot be harmonized with Christianity. The National Socialist ideology is a vulgar biological materialism which deifies its own people and its power" (cited in Loewenich, *Erlebte Theologie*, 160–61). That Strathmann was vilified after the war and deposed as a Nazi sympathizer shows the weakness of perception in the denazification procedure. The students at Erlangen used to say that Strathmann had been discharged by the Americans because he was a member of the Nazi Party (*Parteigenosse*). However, Strathmann did not belong to the Nazi Party but to the *Christlicher Volksdienst*

1800, followed by the successful overthrow of Napoleon, brought not only liberty but also a new infusion of nationalism and the call for German unification. The idealization of German character and the development of *volkisch* ideology followed. Under National Socialism, all these qualities were magnified and distorted into a bigoted racism, which was a prominent feature of Nazi writers who spoke of a "Jewish race" and "German race." However, as Marion Berghahn has cogently observed, these are not separate races at all; the entity of *Homo sapiens* constitutes one race. Therefore it is incorrect to speak of the Jewish people as a separate "race." Instead, Jewish people should be considered an ethnic group within the totality of mankind.[3]

It is now time to turn to the influence of romanticism and existentialism upon the ideologies both of dialectical theology and of the political and religious teachings of National Socialism. In the following, Darwinism as a form of romanticism, as well as the racism and *volkisch* ideology that it fomented, will be considered.

POLITICAL ROMANTICISM AND DECISIONISM

Decisionism was a symptom of political romanticism among theologians of this era as well as civil leaders. When reading the essays and speeches of Germans from the 1920s and 1930s, one is struck by frequent references to the gravity of "the present hour" or "the German hour" (*die deutsche Stunde*) and the drastic importance of "making the right decision" (*die rechte Entscheidung*). "The hour of decision" also was mentioned repeatedly. One finds such references among politicians and philosophers, both friends and enemies of National Socialism, and among theologians representing all sides of the debate. It was said that Germany was at a crossroad, that Germans had experienced bad times in the past but now held in their hands the choice for a better future. Therefore it was crucial that the individual, or the whole German *Volk*, make the right decision in the "present hour."

In the mouth of Adolf Hitler, this call to make a choice meant an uncompromising decision for National Socialism and the new totalitarian government. In the mouth of an evangelist, this call to make a choice might mean a decision for Jesus Christ. In the mouth of Karl Barth, this call to make a choice meant following his lead in dialectical thinking or "crisis theology." In the mouth of Friedrich Gogarten, an erstwhile confederate of Barth, who, like Barth, championed a politi-

---

Partei (Christian *Volk*-Service Party [CVDP]), a group that opposed National Socialism.

3 Marion Berghahn, *Continental Britons: German-Jewish Refugees from Nazi Germany* (Oxford: Berg, 1988), 9–10.

cized theology, this call to make a choice meant using dialectical thinking to support Hitler's program. Gogarten belonged to the proponents of political romanticism, an ideology that made much of decisionism. Decisionism grew out of romanticism; therefore a look at nineteenth-century thinkers provides some historical background.

Where did political romanticism originate? The Enlightenment and rationalism of the eighteenth century destroyed people's certainty regarding abiding truths; then romanticism replaced truth with love as the ideal to be sought and the motivation behind actions. The great Russian romantic Fyodor Dostoevsky wrote masterful novels in which an underlying motive was the need to decide between truth and love. Some thinkers have described Hitler's position as the rejection of God and his Law (truth), which was replaced by a fanatical egotism and ambition for the German race (love). When Hitler saw in 1945 that Germany was losing the war, his love turned to hatred for the Germans.

Political romanticism was marked by a strong element of irrationality and antinomianism, both of which were prominent marks of Hitler's thinking. These ideological features led Hitler to pursue a course that defied conventional wisdom (reason) and Judeo-Christian morality (law). For Hitler, genocide, eugenics, abortion, and euthanasia, as programs to advance the German race, were more important than biblical prohibitions against racial persecution and disregard for human life (antinomianism). Although common sense (reason) suggested that Hitler could not conquer the entire world, his zeal for Germany and his unbounded egotism led him into ruinous actions (irrationalism). Irrationalism and antinomianism are are also found in the theology of decisionism, a spinoff of political romanticism. Søren Kierkegaard, the nineteenth-century existentialist philosopher, understood life as a continuous moment of decision and characterized Christian faith as a consequent "leap into the dark." This path led to the theology of Barth and the Barmen Declaration. There was much of the romantic philosophy of Kierkegaard in the thinking of Martin Heidegger, Barth, Gogarten, and Rudolf Bultmann.

Theodor Strohm, a professor at Heidelberg, wrote a brilliant study of romanticism in politics and theology.[4] His work shows how Protestantism converged with conservatism in nineteenth-century Germany under men such as Friedrich Julius Stahl and Otto von Bismarck. Stahl interpreted Lutheran political ethics in terms of the "feudal-royalist order" of the Prussian state, and Bismarck carried out that program. Strohm points out that "Stahl gave the Conservative Party, as the collective basin of churchly and royalist groups, the justification for their deter-

---

4 Strohm, *Theologie im Schatten politischer Romantik: Eine wissenschafts-soziologische Anfrage an die Theologie Friedrich Gogartens* (Munich: Kaiser-Grünewald, 1970).

mination to resist democracy on the basis of constitutionalism, and thereby with their own weapons."[5] Strohm adds: "Bismarck succeeded in making conservativism the predominant political style in Germany and even in those places where this contradicted the prevailing trends."[6]

In his book, Strohm notes the description of political romanticism by Carl Schmitt. Schmitt found a bond between political romanticism and conservative Lutheranism: "From the structure of romanticism, the concept of 'decision' results: the total incompatibility of the romantic with any moral, legal, or political norm." Therefore, Strohm notes, Schmitt concludes that "in romanticism, every feeling of boundaries of reality for the state as well as for the individual is lacking."[7]

Strohm writes that during the time of particularism, when Germany was divided into hundreds of small territories or city-states, the Lutheran Church in its many local congregations had held much attraction for the German people. The tiny political units of the patriarchal states, which controlled the localized territorial churches, were reflected in the intimacy of the familiar parishes. But as smaller territorites fused together—particularly in the rise of Prussia—the familiarity of the small patriarchal territory was lost in the newly enlarged governmental jurisdictions. In the church, the personal qualities of previous generations were replaced by a state-church bureaucracy that alienated individuals and led to religious indifference.[8]

The most noteworthy bureaucratic force that offended many church members was, of course, the Prussian Union—the unwilling amalgamation of Lutherans and Calvinists into one unionistic church. The "union of throne and altar" under an elector-king of the Reformed faith had taken the predominantly Lutheran population captive, had suppressed the Lutheran Confessions and liturgy, and had superimposed confessional pluralism and a Reformed liturgy upon the Lutheran majority. This measure caused much cynicism among pastors and church members. Because the sprawling Prussian Union encompassed a large plurality of German Lutherans, it placed the Protestant churches at a significant disadvantage when the storms of National Socialism blew over the horizon. The Prussian Union, with its confessional ambivalence, was unable to resist Hitler; therefore it became his ecclesiastical tool. After all, any bureaucracy will be loyal to its benefactor.

---

5 Strohm, *Theologie im Schatten politischer Romantik*, 29.

6 Strohm, *Theologie im Schatten politischer Romantik*, 31.

7 Strohm, *Theologie im Schatten politischer Romantik*, 42.

8 Strohm, *Theologie im Schatten politischer Romantik*, 36.

DECISIONISM IN THEOLOGY

Decisionism, existentialism, dialectical theology, and crisis theology are all words or phrases that characterize the theology of Karl Barth, the Barmen Declaration, and the Dahlem Front of the Confessing Church. These thinkers turned their backs on tradition and considered the church and its confession as a present "event" (*Ereignis*). This kind of thinking pervaded both the DEK and its postwar continuation: the Evangelical Church in Germany (EKD). All these movements were more or less marked by irrationalism and its concomitant, antinomianism, which also are characteristics of political romanticism. And these movements saw history as a series of disjointed events, which sacrificed the view of history as a continuum that had marked the church since its beginning, replacing it with a punctiliar view of history.

For Barth, historic creeds or confessional statements were relative. He saw confession as a present act (*Ereignis*) that didn't have any direct connection with the Reformational confessions. This position was embraced by many in the Confessing Church, in which the traditional creeds and confessions were rarely used or followed but were replaced with the concept of confessing as an act, regardless of the content of such "confessing."

Decisionism was also prominent in National Socialism—with its emphasis upon Hitler as the great leader—because it indicated that there was a necessary moment for the decisive action of the citizens in favor of the Führer's cause. The concept of *kairos* as decisive time, or the hour of decision, became popular among thinkers as disparate as Paul Tillich, Emanuel Hirsch, and several New Testament scholars.[9] Another mark of decisionism was the understanding of the church as *aktuell* (consisting in an action), or the event-nature of the church (*Ereignis-Charakter der Kirche*), which is the opposite of its permanent or continuous character. Such a concept of the church contradicts its ecumenical and international character and reduces it to a local and temporary phenomenon. There was much "contemporary" talk of the church as "a now event."

The concept of the church as a present event supported the nationalist position of Hirsch, who resisted ties with churches in other lands. Hirsch foiled the attempts of Hermann Sasse to avoid the nationalization of the German Lutheran churches and instead to become involved in the Lutheran World Convention

---

9 On the concept of time as κάιρος, see the following: Oscar Cullmann, *Christ and Time: The Primitive Christian Conception of Time and History* (Philadelphia: Westminster Press, 1950), 39–44 and throughout. See also the magisterial article by Gerhard Delling on κάιρος in *Theologisches Wörterbuch zum Neuen Testament*, ed. Gerhard Kittel (Stuttgart: W. Kohlhammer, 1938), 3:456–65. Ethelbert Stauffer, *Die Theologie des Neuen Testaments* (Gütersloh: Bertelsmann, 1948), 59–62.

(since 1945 the Lutheran World Federation) and the Faith and Order Movement of the World Council of Churches. Elert stoutly opposed the reduction of the church to an event or series of actions and of downsizing its message to what is modern or contemporary (*zeitgemäß*): "The character of the church as event permits absolutely no permanence."[10] Interestingly, the view of history as a continuum has returned in the newer eschatological thinking of theologians such as Walter Künneth and Oscar Cullmann.

The Barthian group sometimes also spoke of their thought as crisis theology. They thought of individuals as standing at the crossroad where a proper decision must be made between at least two choices. This crossroad stood within the framework of a nonlinear view of time, punctuated by a series of unconnected and impending events (*Ereignis-Charakter*) before which the church or the individual believer must choose the proper alternative (decisionism). This aspect of crisis theology was partly the legacy of Kierkegaard (faith as a leap into the dark) and existentialist philosophy, which emphasized the singular importance of the present moment.

Ideological decisionism, irrationality, rejection of the Law-Gospel dialectic in favor of the Law as part of the Gospel, the relativization of the Law with resultant antinomianism, and the furtherance of one-kingdom political thought (theocracy) all diminished the differences between Barth and National Socialism. Hitler, too, spoke of the great hour, warned against overlooking its import, and admonished the people to make a sweeping decision for his program. Hitler also indulged in irrationalism and antinomianism. The Ten Commandments meant little to the Führer. Hitler's call was heard not only by Barth—who rejected National Socialism—but also by a number of men who had learned a theology of decision from Barth and who urged Christians to embrace the doctrines and practices of National Socialism.

DIALECTICAL THINKING IN OTHER THEOLOGIANS

Although Barth, together with Eduard Thurneysen, Emil Brunner, Georg Merz, and Gogarten, is often regarded as the founder of dialectical theology, there has been much generic dialectical thought in the contemporary theology of various thinkers who were opposed to Barth and who were not members of the inner circle of crisis theologians. This generic dialectical theology was also wary of propositional statements, believing instead that because theology deals with spiritual matters, which are beyond the powers of reason, sacred truth is best described "dialectically," that is, in terms of its opposites. This trend had been foreshadowed in Luther's separation of the theology of glory and the theology of the cross, his

---

10 "Die Kirche und ihre Dogmengeschichte," in Elert, *Ausgang*, 321.

distinction of Law and Gospel, his dialectic between the hidden and revealed God, his insight that the believer is simultaneously saint and sinner, his two-governance thinking, and so forth. Accordingly, Luther scholar Paul Althaus sometimes called himself a dialectical theologian, though he steadfastly opposed the Barthian school. There also was a strong dialectical quality in the theology of Elert, who upheld a rigorous distinction between Law and Gospel. However, in the present context, "dialectical theology" is restricted to the group around Barth.

THE DIALECTICAL THEOLOGY
OF GOGARTEN IN RELATION TO NATIONAL SOCIALISM

Although he was a Lutheran, Friedrich Gogarten was a member of the original group of dialectical theologians surrounding Barth. However, Gogarten eventually differed greatly from Barth in his position toward National Socialism. Like Barth, however, Gogarten may be called a political theologian. Unlike Althaus or Elert, Gogarten belonged to the GDC for a short period (spring 1933 to fall 1933).[11] He simultaneously belonged to the Young Reformation Movement (JB), which tried to counteract the extremism of the GDC and which supported the nomination of Friedrich von Bodelschwingh for Reich bishop rather than Ludwig Müller, the German-Christian candidate.[12] Gogarten had a strong philosophical bent, which sometimes led him away from a strictly theological position; however, as a Lutheran, he made much of the distinction of Law and Gospel.

Fortunately, Gogarten did not accept all the positions of National Socialism. A former pupil, Theodor Strohm, describes his reservations about Nazism as follows: "He decisively opposed all attempts toward a nationalistic foundation of the state, and simultaneously condemned the racist ideology as a cruel perversion."[13] Gogarten opposed notions of a nationalistic foundation of the state because the root of the state should be sought instead in the theology of creation. Not only did

---

11 Strohm, *Theologie im Schatten politischer Romantik*, 158. Gogarten's temporary membership in the GDC, which he terminated after the Berlin Sport Palace debacle, is mentioned in Meier, *EKK*, 1:298.

12 Barth personally disliked the JB and claimed that the organization was just another form of the GDC; see Barth's assessment in *Theologische Existenz heute!* (Munich: Christian Kaiser, 1933), 30–34. He deprecated Künneth for attempting a truce with the German-Christians at a time when no one knew where these matters were heading (*Theologische Existenz heute!* 30). But Barth influenced younger scholars, including Rolf Neumann and Guy Christopher Carter, to carry on his negative view of the JB and of Künneth, its leader. Künneth's movement was largely absorbed into Niemöller's Pastors Emergency League (PNB). The Dahlem Front, a subset of the PNB, followed a rigidly Barthian line.

13 Strohm, *Theologie im Schatten politischer Romantik*, 151.

he insist upon a divine rather than a human origin of the state, but Gogarten also argued that the state must subject itself to moral discipline. Strohm adds: "As a theologian, he totally rejected every form of racial ideology and racial anti-Semitism."[14] Therefore one must use discretion in calling Gogarten a Nazi theologian.

Gottfried Voigt presents a penetrating evaluation of Gogarten's thought in which he describes Gogarten's view of history as follows: "The concept of 'history' means 'the living-together of people, in which they are bound-to-one-another and committed-to-one-another, and without this, there is no human life and no such thing as history.' "[15] Voigt continues:

This being bound-to-one-another and this being committed-to-one-another dictates the Law to us in every moment. There is no such thing as a general, timeless demand nor any ethics that could be enclosed within a textbook. "God is our eternal Lord, but it has pleased him to be present in time and in history . . . he puts his claim upon us within the mask of earthly rule and earthly claims." Thus, all earthly authority becomes for me a law. I have always to place myself at its demand. I do not have any law that is universal and could always be applied at every time and every place. "Thus, God's Law meets us under the mask of that which is demanded of us, in command and in obedience, to that which is demanded of us in the estates: in the orders of the state and marriage and the family."[16]

Gogarten asserted "the truth of myself as law." He thought of one's obligation to God and one's fellow man as being *hörig*, that is, in bondage both to God and one's neighbor. He believed that the ethical occurs in concrete relations between people, that is, in the responsibility that one takes toward the neighbor. According to Gogarten, the Law is a matter of the indicative, not the imperative: "This becomes most clear in that I am not only, in truth, my very own self when I am obedient in trust, loyalty, and love with my neighbor, but also in cases where I am disobedient, disloyal, or hateful to him."[17] Gogarten doubted that one could speak of a "material ethics" in the traditional sense because that would obscure "the commandment of the hour" in which the Christian had to respond to ever-new situations: "God's creative work and God's Law takes place through people, through being one-another-obedient. If I forsake this bondage—Thou shalt love thy neighbor as thyself—then I therewith forsake

---

14 Strohm, *Theologie im Schatten politischer Romantik*, 155.

15 Voigt, "Gottesgesetz und Volksgesetz: Ein Vergleich zwischen Gogarten und Luther," *Luthertum* 50 (1939): 114ff. (quote, 117).

16 Voigt, "Gottesgesetz und Volksgesetz," 117–18.

17 Voigt, "Gottesgesetz und Volksgesetz," 119.

God, whom I am to believe and trust with all my heart." He adds: "This recognition does not bring to light a special 'law of God' over against the 'law of men.' The Law of God, rather, is enclosed within the law of men as its last sense, recognizable only to faith."[18]

Gogarten takes the final and fatal step: "The law 'is given in our *Volkstum*.' We therefore have the task 'to work on the perception and justification of the law which the present generation meets concretely again in the National Socialist movement in the state and in its people.' "[19] How could Gogarten reach such a point? For him, the Law of God and the law of the *Volk* are the same materially, but they differ functionally.[20] One can and must fulfill the civil law, but the very same law, as God's Law, cannot be fulfilled. Behind every command of "Thou shalt" stands the devouring holiness of the Lawgiver. Voigt adds the following comment from Gogarten: "The First Commandment casts its light upon the law of my *Volk* and supplies it with its divine qualification. It is the least common denominator against which every other commandment is placed, and it gives worth and importance to all folk laws [*Volksnomoi*]. . . . The law of our *Volk* is thereby a schoolmaster to bring us to Christ."[21]

One might well stand aghast at how far Gogarten drifted from biblical teachings toward Nazi ideology. His form of antinomianism, with a fideistic trust that the law of the *Volk* is the Law of God, had tragically misled him. The law of the *Volk* (National Socialists) actually militated against the Law of God and against common human decency.

---

18 Voigt, "Gottesgesetz und Volksgesetz," 121.

19 Voigt, "Gottesgesetz und Volksgesetz," 123.

20 Regarding the difference between the material and the functional aspects of the Law, see Voigt, "Gottesgesetz und Volksgesetz," 114, 124.

21 Voigt, "Gottesgesetz und Volksgesetz," 125. Here Gogarten is skating on thin ice. The American reader will be reminded at this point of Joseph Fletcher, whose "situation ethics" was marked by relativity, and the American Pragmatism of William James, John Dewey, and Shailer Mathews. Dewey and Mathews rejected any *a priori* basis for morality and taught that one derived laws of conduct from personal experience. American Pragmatism was related to the ethical relativism of another purveyor of Darwinism—Herbert Spencer (1820–1903). On Spencer's philosophy and ethics, see B. A. G. Fuller and Sterling M. McMurrin, *A History of Philosophy* (New York: Holt, Rinehart & Winston, 1966), 2:406–11. Although one must differentiate Gogarten's teaching from American Pragmatism and Darwinism, it seems that he, too, made the demands of the Law relative and claimed that the law of the people is the Law of God. This autonomous ethics was dangerous in the hands of National Socialism.

OTHER FORMS OF ROMANTICISM IN NAZI IDEOLOGY
AS DESCRIBED BY KÜNNETH

Walter Künneth was the leader of the Seminar for Apologetics in Berlin and a major analyst of modern thought during the 1930s. He devoted much attention to National Socialism and claimed that little was new. Instead, Nazism had borrowed its leading thoughts from ideologues of the previous century. Künneth named several important men who had made a significant impact on Nazi ideology, including Charles Darwin, Friedrich Nietzsche, and Houston Stewart Chamberlain.

Künneth frequently referred to Oswald Spengler's two-volume philosophy of history *Der Untergang des Abendlandes* (*Decline of the West*), which was widely read in Germany and the United States and which furthered feelings of pessimism and hopelessness. Since the fall of the Hohenstaufen emperors, and for 700 years afterward, the Germans—the most populous people in Western Europe—had been divided into hundreds of petty national states (particularism). Therefore Germany had been subject to aggression from more unified nations, such as France. Since the time of Johann Gottlieb Fichte (1762–1814), who had tried to awaken a slumbering German nationalism, a number of powerful writers had attempted to call attention to the lack of national coherency or a sense of unified purpose. Prior to 1871 and in the absence of a national state, these writers could only inculcate pride in their own "race," their biological and social entity—the German *Volk*. The suppression of political unity and power that had been imposed upon Germany by outside entities (the thirteenth-century papacy, competing national states such as France) led many writers to focus upon ethnicity and to compensate with the concept of *Volk*, which would have disastrous consequences.

Künneth perceived in Spengler a "biologism," or biologization, that is, a tendency to see human society in biological terms with physical, rather than spiritual, values. Spengler thought of man as an animal—a being who must fight. But Spengler was only part of a larger movement that thought of man in biological terms. Künneth regarded Social Darwinism as an important part of National Socialism. He charged that popular Darwinism, "a mixture of mythology and science," had been applied to the concept of society and had yielded the notion that man was only an animal, that men should fight like the beasts, and that society would be improved by the elimination of the weak through the domination of the strongest elements of the human race.[22] Compared to the biblical teaching that

---

22 Künneth, *Abfall*, 34–36. In a similar tone, Ernst Wolf, criticizing the dehumanization of German society, wrote: "The race theory of previous years, truly the 'theory' of a politicized Darwinism as an illusionary view, may suffice as example for the practical consequences of dehumanization" ("Menschwerdung des Menschen? Zum Thema

"all men have been one in Adam" (see Genesis 1–2; Romans 5:12ff.), some racial evolutionists have argued that those of African descent developed separately from other lower species.

In *Evangelist of Race: The Germanic Vision of Houston Stewart Chamberlain,* Geoffrey G. Field points out that Karl Vogt, one of Chamberlain's teachers at the University of Geneva,

> insisted that the different races were descended from different anthropoid ancestors, as did Paul Topinard . . . thus the white European could at least be affiliated with a smarter ape than the rest. The external forces which nourished polygenist thinking—the gulf between the "civilized" white and the "savage" black, and the need to justify white imperialism—were strengthened after 1860, while specific racial problems such as miscegenation or the infertility of mulattoes still produced strong backing for essentially polygenist viewpoints in scientific circles.[23]

Künneth believed that National Socialism also took over certain concepts from Nietzsche, whose *Übermensch,* or superman, had been patterned after Jakob Burckhardt's portrayal of the Italian tyrant (Machiavelli), as well as Arthur Schopenhauer's hero worship.[24] Furthermore, Nietzsche's rejection of Christianity and its ethical teachings, which he thought inculcated servile weakness among believers, laid the groundwork for the rejection of Christian faith and morality by Hitler's ideologue, Alfred Rosenberg.[25] Thus as the theologian Wilhelm Lütgert observed, "Nietzsche's philosophy became a criticism of all morality . . . . Immorality became his principle."[26] Nietzsche regarded "Christian love" as a weakness based upon false ideas of mercy and goodness. In place of traditional

---

Humanismus und Christentum," 1946 lecture at the University of Hamburg, reprinted in *Peregrinatio* [Munich: Christian Kaiser, 1954], 2:136). Also Hans Ehrenberg, a Christian pastor of Jewish descent, criticized Darwinism as a root of anti-Semitism; see Schmidt, *Bekenntnisse,* 1:67–69.

23 Geoffrey G. Field, *Evangelist of Race: The Germanic Vision of Houston Stewart Chamberlain* (New York: Columbia University Press, 1981), 205. Cf. Marion Berghahn, *Continental Britons: German-Jewish Refugees from Nazi Germany* (Oxford: Berg, 1988), 9–10.

24 Künneth, *Abfall,* 45.

25 Künneth, *Abfall,* 48. Against those who have denied that Rosenberg had any real standing in National Socialism, see Heinz Brunotte, "Kirchenkampf als 'Widerstand,' " in *Reformatio und Confessio: Festschrift für D. Wilhelm Maurer zum 65. Geburtstag am 7. Mai 1965,* ed. Friedrich Wilhelm Kantzenbach and Gerhard Müller (Berlin: Lutherisches Verlagshaus, 1965), 317. Brunotte asserts that Rosenberg was officially commissioned on January 24, 1934, to the task of confronting Christian leaders with an ersatz religion.

26 Künneth, *Abfall,* 49.

morality, Nietzsche advocated a utilitarian ethics with the sole concern of accomplishing a desired result, such as political aggrandizement.[27] This was expressed also in Nietzsche's philosophy of death, specifically that each person should decide when he wanted to die. Nietzsche wrote: "The sick person is a parasite on society. In a certain condition it is indecent to live any longer. The continual vegetation in an everlasting dependence upon physicians and medical practices, after the meaning of life, the right to life, has been lost, should be regarded by society with deep contempt. . . . It is the most worthy thing that there is when one kills himself."[28]

These teachings of Nietzsche regarding the importance of the strong and mighty and the uselessness of the weak and the sick pointed the way for Nazi policies of euthanasia and the destruction of the weak to reserve food for the strong. Although there were many important points at which Nietzsche's thought was incompatible with National Socialism, his radical teachings decisively shaped the course of the Nazi Party.[29]

Künneth also discussed the unfortunate influence of the English expatriate Houston Stewart Chamberlain. Künneth warned the reader against an overly hasty judgment of Chamberlain, pointing out that Chamberlain had cautioned against exaggerating the racial issue and that he did not share the negative views of Christianity held by Rosenberg and other Nazi ideologists.[30] Nevertheless, Künneth highlights five points at which Chamberlain affected the thinking of National Socialism for the worse.

- *The concept of race.* Using the suggestions of Darwin and Nietzsche as a point of departure, Chamberlain, in view of what he called Nordic superiority (which made the Germans the greatest of all people), advocated racial breeding for the improvement of Germans according to the principles employed in the breeding of plants and animals.

- *Low esteem for Jewish people.* Chamberlain recognized differences among Jewish people, but he asserted that most did not come from the fine Hebrew lineage that had experienced the time of the Maccabees in Jerusalem. He thought that most Jewish people were descended from the inferior sort who had come from the diaspora of other countries. Chamberlain claimed that Jewish people tended to take control of a country and were unwilling to give up their "peculiar" customs; therefore they threatened to replace "true German ways." Nevertheless, Chamberlain stated that one must not abuse

27 Künneth, *Abfall*, 49.

28 Nietzsche, quoted in Künneth, *Abfall*, 50.

29 Künneth, *Abfall*, 50–51.

30 Künneth, *Abfall*, 52–53.

Jewish people but must uphold true responsibility by not allowing these "strange people" to corrupt true German ways.[31]

- *The new portrayal of Jesus.* Chamberlain claimed that Jesus was of Aryan descent, not Jewish, and proclaimed him a part of Nordic culture. He portrayed Jesus as an unusually gifted man with an unheard-of mightiness and elevation of conviction—therefore Jesus stood at the highest point of the pyramid of humanity. This concept of Jesus was taken over with a few changes in Rosenberg's portrayal of Jesus as the great Nordic hero.[32]

- *A tendency to oppose dogma and the church.* As a youth, Chamberlain had attended services of the French Calvinists at Versailles. After he settled in Germany, he was indifferent to German Lutheranism. Chamberlain simply rejected the apostle Paul and his teachings because Paul, the mightiest builder of the Christian church, had replaced the simple religion of Jesus with an involved system of dogma that, in Chamberlain's view, prepared in the Christian church "a place of refuge for all the superstitions of antiquity and of Judaism." Chamberlain advised his readers: "Let us therefore close our ears against the chaos of the credal confessions."[33] With this thinking, Chamberlain had unconsciously provided the basis on which the Nazis would carry out their storm against the church.

- *The concept of the religious soul.* Chamberlain based his argument upon Luke 17:20–21: "The kingdom of God comes not with outward observation . . . the kingdom of God is within you." From this Chamberlain concluded that true Christianity is free of externals, such as the church and its dogma, and is instead the religious inwardness that a person finds in himself. This concept was developed by Rosenberg into the notion that the soul is like unto God and that religious truth lies within the individual.[34]

The Concept of *Volk* as Seen in *Völkisch* Ideology

During the nineteenth century, a new concept of *Volk* had arisen in Germany, nurtured by three factors: (1) the Napoleonic wars, which had awakened a deep dissatisfaction with Germany's political fragmentation and its vulnerability to exploitation by foreign militarists and had increased the yearning for a unified

---

31 Künneth, *Abfall*, 53–54.

32 Künneth, *Abfall*, 54–55.

33 Künneth, *Abfall*, 55.

34 Künneth, *Abfall*, 56–57.

national state; (2) the acquaintance with Jewish separatistic practices, which had suggested racist concepts to German ideologues; and (3) the *Völkisch* ideologies that had strongly racial overtones and were fostered by a number of extreme nationalists. These factors converged to produce the fanatical concept of *Volk* that was embraced by Hitler.

PHILOLOGY OF *VOLK*

Anglophones must come to grips with the exact meaning of the German word *Volk*, for which there is no exact English equivalent. If it cannot be defined, at least it must be explained. An obvious English translation of *Volk* would be its cognate, "folk." In the absence of an exact English equivalent, the German word will primarily be retained. Considering the varying contexts—such as nationality, people, nation, or race—can help to clarify this term. More difficult are the derivatives of *Volk*, such as *Volkstum* (literally, "folkdom") and *völkisch* (literally, "folkish" or "pertaining to the *Volk*"). The German-Swiss theologian Emil Brunner gives the following explanation of *Volk*:

> The word *Volk* has undergone a big change in meaning in the last hundred years. Luther used the term mainly in the sense of a multitude, "many people" [*Volk* as related to *vulgus*]. Between him and us lies the period of romanticism and modern ethnology. Romanticism brought the historical individuality of the *Volk* according to its intellectual and spiritual side into consideration, whereas ethnology brought the biological term of race into importance.

Brunner continues:

> The foundation of being a *Volk* is, first, the spatial nearness . . . and, second, the blood relatedness. A *Volk* cannot exist without an inner kernel of blood-related families and tribes . . . . The seed germ of the *Volk* is the family. . . . *Volk* exists, third, only as a fellowship of those who have been brought together by destiny [*als Schicksalsgemeinschaft*]. A common destiny exists as the common denominator for people only through the state. Only the *Volk* that has been brought together in a state can experience history as its common destiny.[35]

Here it can be seen how the word has changed and how it has come to differ from the English cognate, *folk*. In the United States, we can speak of country folk or city *Volk*, regardless of race—whether African American or East Indian, Italian or Swedish. Indeed, there is no "American folk" in the racial sense noted by Brunner, for the colonists and immigrants that settled this land came from many nations and races. Consequently, there is no "spatial nearness" and no "blood-relatedness" in people who now claim the United States as their country of origin.

---

35 Brunner, *Das Gebot und die Ordnungen: Entwurf einer protestantisch-theologischen Ethik* (Tübingen: J. C. B. Mohr, 1932), 440–41.

From this circumstance arose the once popular concept of the "American melting pot." Thus the English word *folk* does not hold any real racial significance. Therefore because a true English equivalent is lacking, the German word *Volk* and its derivatives (*Volkstum, völkisch*) will be retained in this book as loan words to show that they are being used in the context of the Third Reich. Thus *Volk* means variously the folk, the expanded family, the tribe, the people, or the nation.

THE NATIONAL SOCIALIST *VÖLKISCH* IDEOLOGY AND RACISM

The Nazi concept of *Volk* excluded non-Aryans—specifically Jewish people—and it included the concepts of race and nationality. Racism developed out of theories of the German *Volk*, against which other "races" compared unfavorably. Chamberlain borrowed concepts from Social Darwinism and other sources to mold an extreme anti-Jewish racism. Social Darwinism, beginning in England, built upon Darwin's evolutionary hypotheses for biology. Adapted to sociology and developed upon German soil, these principles led to sociobiological views of *Volk*, *Führer*, and *Blut und Boden* ("folk," "the strong leader," "blood relationships and German soil") that were to prove fateful under National Socialism. Darwinism taught the survival of the fittest. In Nazi ideology, this became the survival of the strongest, the concept of the superman, the Führer principle, the master race, the value of force and violence, and the need to suppress "inferior" races. Chamberlain's thought was eagerly applauded by men such as Hitler and his ideologist, Rosenberg.

It was an embarrassment to racists that the founder of Christianity, Jesus Christ, was Jewish and that Christians held Judaism in high esteem. Some racists went to great lengths to counteract this, claiming that Jesus was not Jewish. These writers included Fichte, Richard Wagner, and Chamberlain—even Adolf von Harnack played with the idea that Jesus was an Aryan. Fichte, the romantic philosopher, was among the first to claim that Jesus was not Jewish and to propound the idea of an Aryan Christianity. He claimed that the apostle Paul had corrupted the pure religion of Jesus and had personally created Christianity. Fichte called the Gospel according to John, in contrast to the writings of Paul, the authentic, non-Jewish Gospel in which Jesus was "correctly" presented. In fact, John was said to have denied that Judaism was ever the true religion.[36]

The noted Jewish scholar Paul Lawrence Rose recounts how in 1878 Wagner, the famous composer, after reading Arthur Schopenhauer, embraced the notion that Christianity was an Aryan religion that had been taken over by Jewish people. Wagner wrote: "That the God of our Savior should have been identified with the

---

36 See the discussion in Paul Lawrence Rose, *Wagner: Race and Revolution* (New Haven: Yale University Press, 1992), 143.

tribal God of Israel is one of the most terrible confusions of world history . . . . If Jesus is proclaimed Jehovah's son, then every Jewish rabbi can triumphantly confute all Christian theology."[37] In the 1870s, Paul Anton de Lagarde had claimed that Jesus was not Jewish but the son of a Roman soldier. Hitler echoed this when he commented in the 1940s: "Galilee was a colony where the Romans had probably installed Gallic legionaries and it's certain that Jesus was not a Jewish person. The Jews, by the way, regarded him as the son of a whore—of a whore and a Roman soldier . . . . He set himself against Jewish capitalism. That's why the Jews liquidated him."[38]

Wilhelm Marr (1819–1904), an atheist and anarchist, was ambivalent in his attitude toward Jewish people. At times he presented himself as a philo-Semite and at other times he seemed to be anti-Jewish. Marr regarded it as a grave misfortune that Jewish people had entered modern history as a self-segregated race within a nationality. The only solution that he could come up with was intermarriage between Jews and Germans until Jewish people had been fully integrated into German society.[39] Marr presented this as a means for the racial "ennoblement" of the Jewish people, but integration was not an acceptable program from the standpoint of Judaism. Rose criticizes Marr as follows: "What Marr required in return was the suicide of Jewry, both as a religion and as a people. To join the Germans, the Jews must first abjure themselves. This was the price of redemption."[40] Apparently, desegregation was a higher price than Jewish people were willing to pay. Marr wrote: "No reproach against Jewry, I repeat. It lies in the race, in the blood, as it has since remote antiquity. The Jew cannot honestly sacrifice himself to us."[41] At any rate, the difference between Marr and Rose suggests to the reader that there really was a "Jewish problem" or "Jewish question" in Germany that required some kind of attention. It would appear that to acknowledge the existence of such a dilemma should not be called "racism." If Jewish people were unwilling to be absorbed into the German *Volk*, they could hardly complain of having been left behind. Just how the "Jewish problem" should be resolved remained an unanswered question.

According to Rose, the term "anti-Semitism" was coined in 1860 by a Jewish person, M. Steinschneider, though it was first introduced into the discussions by Marr. By 1877 the 60-year-old Marr had been married to three Jewish women in

---

37 Rose, *Wagner*, 142.

38 Rose, *Wagner*, 143.

39 Paul Lawrence Rose, *Revolutionary Antisemitism in Germany from Kant to Wagner* (Princeton: Princeton University Press, 1990), 284.

40 Rose, *Revolutionary Antisemitism*, 285.

41 Quoted in Rose, *Revolutionary Antisemitism*, 291.

succession, though by that time he was married to a non-Jewish woman. From this point onward, he repudiated the idea of assimilation and became determinedly anti-Jewish. In 1879 Marr founded the League of Anti-Semites. But Marr attacked Christianity as well as Judaism. He claimed that Judaism, like its offspring Christianity, was zealous in persecuting one's fellow man. Marr called both religions a "disease of human consciousness."[42]

National Socialism borrowed messianist aspirations from Judaism and designated the German *Volk* as the chosen people. In its deification of the *Volk*, Nazism showed itself to be a theocratic religion, and in its postulation of the thousand-year reign, it embraced a secularization of Jewish and Christian eschatologies. Theocratic tendencies were also found in the theology of Barth and his followers who, when they attacked Luther's doctrine of the two governances, were unconsciously weakening the case against the German-Christians. A theocracy confounds the Lutheran understanding of the two governances. The single-kingdom and theocratic arguments that were leveled against Lutheran leaders weakened the case against the theocratic enthusiasm of Hitler. What was needed instead was an ideology that advocated the separation of government and religion, of state and church, which was the virtue of the correct understanding of the Lutheran doctrine of the two governances.

To be effective, the doctrine of the two governances had to be kept free from corruption by those who exempted the state from divine authority. Luther had spoken of a God-ruled, or theonomous, secular governance. The German-Christians corrupted this by advancing the concept of an autonomous state that did not need to follow the Law of God. As will be seen in a discussion of the order of creation, a sound theological approach rules out the autonomy or exemption of any state from divine governance and Law.[43] However, Barth was extremely influential when he rejected every concept of the order of creation, whether theonomous or autonomous. For him, there was little room for a theology of the First Article (theology of creation).

NATIONAL SOCIALISM'S ACCELERATION OF THE OPPRESSION OF JEWISH PEOPLE

During the first third of the twentieth century, there was a rising tide of discrimination against Jewish people in Germany, the United States, and elsewhere. As a

---

42 Quoted in Rose, *Revolutionary Antisemitism*, 288.

43 The error of Gogarten was that he envisioned an autonomous state as an order of creation. Althaus properly insisted that the state, as an order of creation, must remain obedient to the Law of God. The latter position was also taught by Künneth, Sasse, Elert, and many other Lutherans.

child growing up in the U.S. heartland, I heard complaints that Jewish people were supposedly working against the Christian observance of Sunday and wanted to make Sunday a shopping day, that Jewish businessmen engaged in ruthless practices in commerce and in the stock market, and that Jewish industrialists had brought on World War I to profit from the manufacture of weapons. In the great universities of the United States, quotas were established to restrict the matriculation and graduation of Jewish students. Journals carried articles detailing how Jewish people were thought to be stifling competition and favoring others of Jewish heritage in world financial affairs.[44]

The Nazi Party was anti-Jewish from the start, and it grew increasingly rabid in its attacks. There were at least five periods or successive steps in Nazi actions against Jewish people:

1. Between 1918 and 1933 the National Socialists fulminated continuously against Jewish people. In their 1920 Party Program, Point 4 stated: "A citizen of the state can only be one who is a member of the nation [*Volksgenosse*]. A member of the nation can only be one who is of German blood, without regard to religious confession. No Jew therefore can be a member of the nation." Point 5 added: "Whoever is not a citizen of the state can only live in Germany as a guest and must stand under the laws for aliens."[45] In *Mein Kampf,* Hitler expressed sentiments such as the following: "When we let all the causes of the German collapse pass before our eyes, the last and most decisive one remains the nonrecognition of the race problem and especially of the Jewish threat." Compare that with this inflammatory statement: "Whoever wants the German *Volk* of today to be freed from the originally alien expressions and faults must first of all redeem it from the foreign provokers of these expressions and faults. The restoration of the German nation will not take place again without a clear knowledge of the race problem and with it of the Jewish Question."[46]

2. After Hitler came to power, one of his first actions against the Jewish people came on April 1, 1933, when he proclaimed a boycott against Jewish businesses, physicians, and lawyers.[47] April 7, 1933, brought the "Decree

---

44 For a statement critical of Jews by an American writer, see Friedrich Braun, "Der jüdische Einfluss in Deutschland," *KZ* 45 (1921): 724–26.

45 Points 4 and 5 of the 1920 Party Program and a number of anti-Semitic statements in Hitler's *Mein Kampf* are collected in Meier, *Kirche und Judentum,* 64.

46 Quotations in Meier, *Kirche und Judentum,* 64.

47 See Meier, *Kirche und Judentum,* 11.

for the Restoration of the Professional Civil Service," the so-called Aryan Paragraph. The first clause stated: "Officials who are not of Aryan descent must be discharged . . ." The second clause provided exceptions for "those who were already in office on August 1, 1914, or who served in the World War on the front lines for the German Reich or its allies, or whose fathers or sons fell in the World War." The third clause offered a racial definition: "By non-Aryan is meant whoever is descended from non-Aryan, especially Jewish, parents or grandparents. It is enough if only one parent or grandparent is not Aryan. This is especially to be assumed when one parent or one grandparent belonged to the Jewish religion."[48] An additional attack against Jewish people came several weeks later. The "Decree against the Crowding of German Schools and Institutions of Higher Learning" was announced by the Nazis on April 25, 1933. This decree stipulated that enrollment must be monitored so the number of pupils or students of Aryan blood was not surpassed by those of non-Aryan descent. This restriction upon pupils and students did not apply to any who were half Jewish or less.[49]

3. Restrictions against Jewish people were greatly increased in the so-called Nuremberg Racial Decree of September 15, 1935, so named because Hitler promulgated them at a Nazi rally held in that city. These decrees applied the restrictions of the "Decree for the Restoration of the Professional Civil Service" to other occupations, making it increasingly difficult for Jewish people to find suitable employment. The Nuremberg Racial Decree also severely limited social interaction between Jews and Aryans. Subsequently, further restrictions were added: Jewish people were deprived of the normal privileges of German citizenship; they could not marry Germans; non-Jewish women under the age of 45 could no longer work in Jewish households or businesses; and Jews could not display German flags. As Nazi rule continued, new measures were added to the Nuremberg Racial Decree, and it was enforced with increasing severity. By 1943 Jewish people were deprived of virtually all human rights. The beautiful city of Nuremberg, where church resistance to National Socialism and popular support for Bishop Hans Meiser were especially strong, was unfortunately beloved by Hitler. Thus its fair name became besmirched by the Nazi government's terrible actions.

---

48 The text of the "Decree for the Restoration of the Professional Civil Service" is reprinted in Künneth and Schreiner, *Die Nation*, 92.

49 This decree is reprinted in Künneth and Schreiner, *Die Nation*, 92.

4. *Kristallnacht* ("Night of Broken Glass"), November 9, 1938, was a major attack on Jewish people. It was so named because of the shattering of the windows of Jewish homes and businesses. In one night 7,500 Jewish businesses were destroyed in Germany. During the persecution that followed, 300,000 Jewish people emigrated. By the time World War II broke out in 1939, only 215,000 Jewish people were left in Germany.[50]

5. The "final solution" in Nazi policy was the liquidation of all Jewish people. As early as January 30, 1939, Hitler had given a speech that addressed the need to destroy all the Jewish people in Europe.[51] After 1940 this program was carried out ruthlessly in Germany and in other countries under the countrol of the Nazis. Jewish people were gathered from Nazi-occupied countries, including Poland, and sent to extermination camps. The loss of such great numbers of gifted and talented people was a catastrophic setback, not only for the German nation but also for the rest of Europe and all humanity.

Lutheran Writers Voice Early Warnings about the Coming Racism

Long before the Nazi takeover of Germany, thoughtful writers had tried to warn Jewish and non-Jewish people alike of the coming danger in Germany. Uriel Tal[52] tells how, in the late 1920s and early 1930s, some German Lutheran theologians tried to counteract the threat of racism and anti-Semitism. These writers identified two roots of racism: first, the teachings of Jewish people who considered themselves the chosen people (*auserwähltes Volk*) and who kept themselves separate from other Germans (the Gentiles or *goyim*) and, second, the development of *völkisch* ideologies by extreme German nationalists during and after the nineteenth century. German nationalism had coalesced in the nineteenth century in the wake of the wars of deliverance from the French armies of Napoleon. These

---

50 Meier, *Kirche und Judentum*, 12–14.

51 Meier, *Kirche und Judentum*, 14.

52 The discussion that follows is adapted from, and the quotations in the subsequent paragraphs are taken from, a published address by Tal in *Luther, Lutheranism, and the Jews: A Record of the Second Consultation between Representatives of The International Jewish Committee for Interreligious Consultations and The Lutheran World Federation*, ed. Jean Halpérin and Arne Sovik (Geneva: Department of Studies, The Lutheran World Federation, 1984). Tal defined his subject as follows: "[It] is about the Lutherans who opposed racial antisemitism, yet drew a common denominator between the Jew and the racist, that I would like to address [in] this meeting today" (p. 49).

theologians, as presented by Tal, clearly foresaw the coming of an ideology of race and *Volkstum* as it was emerging in the teachings of the National Socialists. It originated in the separatist concepts held by Jewish people, and it linked with an equally exclusionist doctrine of the Aryan race to produce the deadly theory and practice that brought on the persecution of Jewish people.

Tal describes some of the writers who warned about the dangers of the racist practices of the National Socialists: "Karl Auer of Berlin, while discussing the significance of his anthology, *From Herder's Message for Our Times*, stated that both the Jews and the growing *völkisch* movement should heed Herder's warnings against all forms of 'pride and prejudice' so symptomatic of ethnic and national groups." Tal also mentions Hans Hofer, an "ardent opponent of the *völkisch* movement," who warned that it turns "the nation and nationality . . . into a religious value." Hofer charged that "there are Germans who simply deify [*vergöttern*] our peoplehood [*Volkstum*] . . . peoplehood should not be exalted as if it were divine." Hofer pointed out that the worship of one's nation is a "degradation" and a "falling down to the low levels of Judaism." Hofer opined that the Old Testament people fell away when they idolized their own nationalism. Tal writes: "The irony, Hofer concluded, is that that very Judaism to which the *völkisch* have sunk is the main target against which they themselves and the Nazis struggle."

Tal mentions "another anti-*völkisch* Lutheran" by the name of Ernst Moehring, a friend and defender of German Jews, an "outspoken opponent of racist antisemitism and of Nazism . . . [who] compared and equated Jewish nationalism with Nazism on the grounds that both movements were 'a regress from universal humanness.'" Another supporter of the Jewish defense association was Heinrich Frick, a professor of theology at Giessen, who "warned German Jewry against both the *völkisch* [elements], including the Nazi movement, and the Zionists . . . Frick defined Jewish nationalism and Nazism as two movements which turned earthliness, this-worldliness and materialism into metaphysical entities, i.e., into religion." Frick noted that "Zionism and Nazism shared the conviction that Germany could not tolerate Jews in its midst, whereas for Christians, as well as for humanists, the very integration of Jews into German society, culture and national state would bear witness to the integrity of Germany." Tal also mentions Willy Stärk, a professor at Jena. Stärk opposed racism and warned against the Zionist movement. He found that both Jewish racism and Nazi racism consisted in "a physical crudeness, as Flesh and Blood and Soil." Eduard Lamparter, a Stuttgart pastor, according to Tal a "devoted, consistent and able defender of Judaism against prejudice, discrimination and antisemitism," wrote in 1928:

> The Nazi slogan of a Third Reich, consecrated and to last a thousand years—
> that is to say, a state of grace chosen to fulfill an eschatological political mission—and Jewish nationalists' yearnings for a messianic kingdom to be

restored in an earthly, this-worldly Zion—both constituted an abuse of the millennial metaphor of Revelation 20:1–3 on the origins of the thousand-year symbol.

Tal also notes that Richard Karwehl, in an address given on June 10, 1931, called both Jewish and Nazi dreams of a thousand-year reign a "secular eschatology" and a "political messianism."

At a time when it was fashionable to deliver accolades on the superior Nordic *Volk*, what led these Lutheran writers, who had positive views of the Old Testament, to warn their Jewish friends against the dangers of racism in their own thinking? The Old Testament had taught the uniqueness of the Hebrew people as the chosen people of God and had urged them not to mingle with others. Some Jews interpreted this concept of the chosen people as meaning they were chosen to affirm God, if necessary at the cost of their own lives.

Althaus presented a short discussion on "the Jewish question" in *Leitsätze zur Ethik* (*Principles of Ethics*).[53] He expressed moderate alarm at the incursion of atheistic Judaism into German society in his address at Königsberg on June 17, 1927, and exhorted that the church "must have an eye and a word for the Jewish threat to our *Volkstum*. The wild anti-Semitism that has blindly overtaken many in our *Volk* today will not be overpowered if one is unwilling to see the actual problem of our *Volk* or if one tries to cover it up."[54] Althaus stated expressly that he opposed the hatred of Jewish people and that he only opposed "the threat given by a corrupt and corrupting urban intelligentsia whose people are chiefly of the Jewish *Volk*."[55] Althaus's concern here was not with Jewish people of the synagogue who faithfully practiced their religion but with hardened capitalists, whether Jewish or Gentile, who he believed had abandoned the moral teachings of their religion, possessed remarkable talents in the world of business, and had become unscrupulous and ruthless in taking over world business and industry.

A remarkable statement comes from Paul Leo (1893–1958), a noted scholar and direct descendant of the famous Jewish philosopher Moses Mendelssohn through his granddaughter Fanny Hensel, who was the sister of composer Felix Mendelssohn.[56] As a man of candor and humility and a Lutheran pastor in the

---

53 Althaus, *Leitsätze zur Ethik,* 2d ed. (Erlangen: R. Merkel, 1928), 54–55.

54 Althaus, "Volkstum," 130–31.

55 Althaus, "Volkstum," 131.

56 Leo was the son of a professor of classical scholarship at Göttingen and a nephew of the noted Privy Counselor (*Geheimrat*) Paul Hensel, who was professor of philosophy at the University of Erlangen. At first Leo served as an institutional chaplain in Osnabrück, but after his work was made untenable by Nazi interference, he was given a post as assistant pastor at historic St. Mary Lutheran Church, whose head pastor,

Land Church of Hanover, Leo published a memorandum in May 1933 in which he stated that some of his fellow Jews had been harmful to Germany. After noting that serious charges had been brought against Jews, Leo wrote:

> We will best prepare ourselves for a fair assessment of this anti-Jewish attitude if we first of all frankly admit that sincerely thinking Judaism cannot avoid a confession of guilt in regard to the German people [*Volkstum*]. Certainly, in the past and present, there have been numerous Jews who have stood in the front ranks as moral personalities and intellectual powers, and besides them there have been a large number of unpretentious and obscure people of Jewish origin who were only a benefit for the German *Volk*. On the other hand, one must also say that the emancipation of Jews brought not only a blessing, but also, in some respects, caused damage and became a curse to [German] culture. That there has been also an evil Jewish influence in the history of German intellectual life and business affairs can simply not be denied.[57]

Leo's statement on Jewish shortcomings can be compared with the following statement published in 1932 by Paul Fiebig of Leipzig: "The bearers of Jewish religion and ethics until the present, the individual representatives of the Jewish *Volk* know exactly where the failures of their people and their history lie, but do not also the Aryans, the Nordics, the Germans, the pastors, and the church members also know their own shortcomings?"[58]

After pointing to the faults of some Jews, Leo suggested in a statement that must have offended some of his readers that Jewish people should convert to Christianity. After stating that a true solution could only come when the Jews listened to the Bible, Leo added:

> By this it is also said that there is only one legitimate way by which the Jew can break through his destiny [*Schicksal*], a way that can be done under the Jewish Law: not through assimilation and the dissolution of his faith, but through conversion, which is the entry into Israel according to the spirit. Thereby, one remains a Jew according to the flesh, likely a Jew with a fundamental German education—one must not forget this, our citizenship, let alone deny it—but one thereby belongs as such to the church of Jesus Christ, in which there is neither Jew nor Greek, and already in this present earthly condition [*Ver-*

Hans Bodensieck, strongly supported Leo. Leo was placed in charge of two rural congregations that were served by the pastors of St. Mary's. On the life of Leo, see the sketch in Simon, esp. 61–67, 80–81, 87–105, *passim.*

57 Meier, *Kirche und Judentum,* 83–84. Hans Ehrenberg of Bochum, another pastor of Jewish descent, also criticized the policy of emancipation as misguided philo-Semitism, which he rejected along with anti-Semitism (Schmidt, *Bekenntnisse,* 1:68).

58 Meier, *Kirche und Judentum,* 77.

faßtheit]. However, Jewish people will remain a problem for themselves and, in spite of their lofty worth, a problem for the other peoples [*Völker*].[59]

Leo wrote pointedly that despite the fact that the National Socialists had made vicious attacks upon Jews for many years, the Evangelical Church had still taken no decisive stand in support of his beleaguered people. It was unthinkable for the church to remain silent. Leo challenged his church to provide its answer to the hateful attacks on Jews by the Nazis:

> It is to be lamented that the Evangelical Church up to this time has not deter-mined, and perhaps is unable to determine, a public position regarding the treatment of Jews by today's government. Many Jews of Evangelical faith, as well as the unbaptized, have waited with pain, and feel themselves forsaken and betrayed by the absence of such a message from the church. There is all the more reason to demand that there be a new confessional statement that pro-nounces a clear word over these matters . . . . Finally, the church must ever keep in mind how severely Judaism has suffered psychologically and economically under those measures, which perhaps seem viable from the standpoint of polit-ical considerations. As defender of this severely suffering part of the people [*Volksteil*], and particularly of the baptized who belong to a congregation, the church must contact the state, simply out of the principles of Christian love.[60]

Leo's analysis invites both admiration and skepticism. Here is a man who tried to be both honest and critical of his own beloved Jewish people. Such a statement would be politically impossible today, even by one living in a land of free speech. When Leo suggested that the church might be unable to determine a proper posi-tion toward the Jews, he was being eminently realistic. The hands of church leaders were tied, as we shall see again and again.[61] In Leo's own Land Church of Hanover, Bishop August Marahrens tried to be fair in his dealings with people of Jewish background, both lay and clergy.[62] He prevented the incorporation of the discrim-inatory Aryan Paragraph into the DEK constitution. If the paragraph had been included, it would have prevented pastors of Jewish descent from serving in the church. Leo thanked Marahrens personally for this effort.[63]

---

59 Meier, *Kirche und Judentum*, 84.

60 Meier, *Kirche und Judentum*, 84–85.

61 Leo is cited in Meier, *Kirche und Judentum*, 83–85. See also Klügel, *Dokumente*, 94, 133–34, and especially Leo's longer article, "Kirche und Judentum," in Klügel, *Doku-mente*, 189–96.

62 Klügel, *Landeskirche*, 491–99; see especially Marahrens's statement in Klügel, *Landes-kirche*, 499; Klügel, *Dokumente,* 202–3.

63 Klügel, *Landeskirche*, 492.

Leo served as teacher in an underground seminary that operated under the auspices of the Confessing Church. Bettina Simon, who remarks that she has little information about this institution, affirms that there were ten students.[64] Leo related that the institution had no permanent location but moved from place to place to evade the Gestapo. Thus one week Leo and his students might meet in a barn, the following week in a tavern, and the third week someplace in the woods. Leo's arrest in his home on *Kristallnacht* and his transportation to the concentration camp at Buchenwald cut short his participation in the underground seminary. At the time of his arrest, Leo managed to keep a personal Bible, and he led Bible studies for the prisoners at the concentration camp. Soon the guards began to sit in on his lectures. Perhaps to get rid of this "dangerous fellow," Leo was freed in January 1939.[65]

How did Marahrens deal with Christians of Jewish background in general? Although Nazi regulations since the Nuremberg Racial Decree had forbidden the association of Aryans with non-Aryans, Marahrens refused to adhere to this rule and required his pastors to accept non-Aryan people as members in their congregations.[66] Marahrens wrote an impassioned plea to the Reich minister of the interior to end the discrimination against mixed couples of Jewish and non-Jewish blood and against their children.[67]

Marahrens took a cautious position concerning the placement of non-Aryan men as pastors in German congregations.[68] Rejecting the Aryan Paragraph, he said that each case must be decided on its own merits; some congregations were happy to have a non-Aryan pastor, but a man of Jewish descent should not be forced on an unwilling congregation.[69] Marahrens had five pastors of Jewish descent in his

---

64 Simon, 91.

65 During Leo's incarceration, his daughter, Anna, was cared for by a friend, who sent her to a children's home in Holland. After being freed, Leo left Germany for Holland on February 9, 1939. In Holland, Leo met his fiancée, Eva Dittrich. Leo emigrated to the United States, where he taught in a Pittsburgh seminary. Eva could not obtain a visa to the United States, so she traveled with relatives to Venezuela, where Leo traveled in the summer of 1940 to marry Eva. The couple returned to Pittsburgh before Leo took a pastorate at Fredericksburg, Texas, in 1943. In 1949 Leo took a call as professor of New Testament theology at Wartburg Theological Seminary in Dubuque, Iowa, where he spent the rest of his life.

66 Klügel, *Landeskirche*, 497.

67 Klügel, *Dokumente*, 202–3; see also Klügel, *Landeskirche*, 496f. Strangely, Marahrens differentiated between mixed couples who had children of mixed blood and those with no children at all, asking that at least in the latter case the couples be allowed to continue to live together.

68 Klügel, *Landeskirche*, 491–96.

69 Klügel, *Landeskirche*, 493. This was similar to the position expressed by Bultmann, who

land church. In addition to Leo, who served at Osnabrück, Bruno Benfey served at Göttingen and Rudolf Gurland served in Meine (later at Hermannsburg). In 1937, when Rinteln was annexed by the Land Church of Hanover, Gustav Oehlert was added to the list of rostered pastors of Jewish descent.[70] Marahrens intended to allow these pastors to continue in their positions as long as possible, hoping that no disturbance might arise, but his hands were tied. Additionally, Marahrens also tried to abet the ordination of another Lutheran of Jewish descent, Otto Schwannecke, a theological student from Gifhorn. Marahrens's efforts, however, were hindered by Nazi opposition. He later attempted to get Schwannecke a call in the United States, but these negotiations were prevented by the outbreak of World War II. Schwannecke was drafted into the army and fell in battle at Düsseldorf on March 3, 1945.[71]

Georg Cölle, a member of the Nazi Party, had taken control of the financial offices of the Land Church of Hanover. Time and again, Marahrens was involved in unpleasant struggles with Cölle. For example, until Marahrens was blocked by the *Schwarze Korps*, the official SS newspaper, he ensured that Leo received his salary, even after Leo was forced to resign at Osnabrück.[72]

One of the first Germans to confront Nazi ideas of racism and its oppression of Jewish people was Heinz Kloppenburg, a young Lutheran pastor in Oldenburg.[73] While serving as a pastor in Rüstringen, Kloppenburg circulated the following theses, entitled "Christian Faith and Race Research," in the *Oldenburgisches Kirchenblatt*. He showed a remarkable freedom from the racism and *völkisch* ideology of the day, as demonstrated by the following excerpts:

Section 3: The Christian believes and confesses that through the atoning sacrifice of Jesus Christ, all people of all races are, in the same way, participants by faith in the love of God. Although he knows the irremovable differences of the races, the Christian rejects every haughty looking down upon others by his own race as irreconcilable with his faith.

Section 4: The Christian believes and confesses that all racial differences of people belong to the "appearance of this world," which will be abolished at the end of days. Therefore, the weakness of his own race is no ground for despair,

---

rejected the Aryan Paragraph out of hand but who also said that the deciding question must be whether placing a Jewish pastor in a parish might make the churchly task unfulfillable. See chapter 6 for a more complete discussion of Bultmann's position.

70 Klügel, *Landeskirche*, 504. See also Simon, 107.

71 On the tragic case of Schwannecke, see Klügel, *Landeskirche*, 495.

72 Klügel, *Landeskirche*, 494.

73 Interestingly, for a short time Kloppenburg was a member of the GDC. In June 1933 he threatened to leave the movement when it opposed Friedrich von Bodelschwingh as Reich bishop (Meier, *EKK*, 1:100, 555).

nor is the strength of his race any ground to feel himself to have been especially chosen by God . . . .

Section 5: In response to the Creator, the Christian must maintain and strengthen the good genetic strains of his own *Volk*. Therefore, the church must always pay attention to the results of scientific race research. However, the Christian remains on his guard lest the science of race research be robbed of its strictly scientific character and be changed into a worldview [*Weltanschauung*]. Race research belongs to natural science and it corresponds to the fact that as such it knows its own boundaries.

Section 6: . . . Every attempt to construct a "religion out of blood" the Christian rejects as idolatry and a figment of the imagination.

Section 8: The Christian knows that religion as a spiritual good is not limited to a single race, a single classification. Race research confirms that there is such a thing as an "adoption," i.e., an appropriation and assimilation of spiritual possessions from one race to another.

Section 9: In conclusion, the Christian knows that the ineradicable racial makeup of his *Volk* is formed and stamped by the rule of the living God in history.[74]

Kloppenburg's theses had been published on December 7, 1932, and the entire essay from which they had been extracted appeared in May 1933.[75]

The voice against racial discrimination in the church was taken up in the "Summons for the Young Reformation Movement" of May 1933: "We confess faith in the Holy Spirit and we therefore fundamentally reject the exclusion of 'non-Aryans' from the church, for such exclusion rests upon the confusion of state and church. The state judges; the church rescues."[76] Here a distinction was made between what the state could do and what the church could do. The state could make its own rules and could decide not to hire non-Aryans; the church had no authority to decide whom the state should or should not hire. However, when it came to the areas in which the church had jurisdiction, that is, in its own staffing, no hiring policy could be allowed that discriminated against people of Jewish descent. This attitude underlies the statements of Künneth, Dietrich Bonhoeffer, Martin Niemöller, Hans Freiherr von Soden, and the Erlangen Opinion on the Aryan Paragraph. In each of these statements, it was asserted that the church should not interfere with the hiring policies of the state but that such discrimination could not be tolerated within the church itself. It was only later, when the demonism of Nazi racism had begun the relentless persecution of Jewish

---

74 Schmidt, *Bekenntnisse*, 1:18–19.

75 Schmidt, *Bekenntnisse*, 1:18.

76 Schmidt, *Bekenntnisse*, 1:146.

people, that theologians became more clear and wanted to oppose racial discrimination as a whole—but by that time it was too late to accomplish much.

After the conflicts had begun between the National Socialists and the German churches, Kloppenburg took a prominent position in the church struggle. He was leader of the Confessing Church in Oldenburg from 1934 to 1945. In 1937 he was deposed from his pastoral position by the Nazi authorities, though he continued to lead in his church.

BIBLICAL CONCEPTS CONCERNING THE JEWS AS A SEPARATED PEOPLE

The concept of *Volk* had appeared in the Old Testament, where it was suggested that the people of Israel were the chosen people of God and that they were to avoid mixing with other ethnic groups. In their understanding of themselves as a unique *Volk*, the Israelites spurned the Philistines and Canaanites, and the Jews in the New Testament despised the Samaritans, the Romans, and other Gentiles. The early Christians were persecuted by the Jews, and when they got the upper hand, some Christians persecuted Jews. The history of the European Middle Ages includes disgraceful stories of prejudice, harassment, oppression, and persecution of Jews by Christians. During this historical period, Christians justified their activities by claiming that Jews were responsible for the death of Jesus.[77]

From among the many Bible passages that speak of the Jews as God's chosen people, the pivotal words of Deuteronomy 7:6 stand out: "For thou art an holy people unto the Lord thy God," which is rendered "Denn du bist ein heilig Volk Gott, deinem Herrn" in Luther's German Bible. Passages such as this show the roots of a *völkisch* ideology in the Hebrew Bible. One might find parallels in the New Testament, particularly in Acts 5–8, which describes how Jewish priests led the persecution of the earliest Christians. For nearly two thousand years, even after the destruction of Jerusalem and the loss of Palestine, Jewish people had retained their identity as a separate people, prohibiting marriage with non-Jews and refusing to be assimilated into the nations into which they had been dispersed. The Jewish people kept religious rites such as circumcision and Passover, observed dietary restrictions and maintained separate kosher foods, preserved

---

77 Confessional Lutheran theology protests against blaming the Jews for the death of Jesus. Ecclesiastical detractors of the Jews who issue such blame have corrupted the New Testament teaching that Jesus' death was brought on by the sins of the whole world and that Christ's sacrificial death brought forgiveness and reconciliation for all people and all races, including Jews and Gentiles. However, true toleration includes both the right of Christians to teach that Christ is the only way to heaven, also for Jews, and the right of Jews to reject that message and to follow a different teaching.

the Hebrew language, worshiped on the seventh day, resisted marriage with non-Jews, and attempted to advance causes for people of Jewish descent. This made the Jewish people a distinct ethnic group and led to widespread discussions of "the Jewish problem." The Lutheran authors who were cited by Tal[78] sounded the warning that Germany must not fall prey to *völkisch* ideologies and racism, whether the roots were in Judaism or in German nationalism and regardless of their likes or dislikes for Jewish people or Nazis.

Propaganda based on the superiority of the German people, rabid racism, and the persecution of Jewish people and other minorities marked the Nazi rule of Germany. Most citizens seemed undisturbed by Nazi claims about the superiority of the Aryan race or by the denigration of other peoples, particularly the Jewish people. Many Germans in 1933 seemed unaware of these aspects of National Socialism, and because the new government received free rein, it gradually increased in power and evil.

EVANGELICAL CHURCHES AND THEOLOGIANS ADDRESS THE CONCEPT OF *VOLK* AND RACE

During the 1920s, prominent scholars such as Emanuel Hirsch, Friedrich Gogarten, and Wilhelm Stapel wrote of the uniqueness of the German *Volk*. But Paul Althaus advised great caution in using this terminology. Althaus delivered a widely discussed lecture at Königsberg in 1927 in which he expounded upon *Kirche und Volkstum* ("the church and the *Volk* movement").[79] This address is crucial for this investigation because it shows Althaus's thoughts on *Volk* in relation to the church a few years before Hitler came to power and at a time when the National Socialists were trying to influence German thinking. Althaus avoided the entrapment of racism when he discussed *Volk* in relation to the church. In his views, though the church is not *of* this world, it is *in* the world. In serving its people, the church works within the context of nation and *Volk*. The church must proclaim the Gospel to the people wherever they are as persons, members of families, and members of the entire nation or *Volk*. To be sure, the church must acknowledge the actuality of the "Jewish threat," but this dare never lead to anti-Semitism.[80] Althaus insisted that the church cannot follow the earthly political notions of racial discrimination, particularly in relation to Jewish people.[81]

---

78 See the discussion on pp. 116–18.

79 Althaus, "Volkstum," 113–43.

80 Althaus, "Volkstum," 130. Here Althaus is perhaps thinking in terms of the revolutionary anti-Semitism introduced by the socialist Wilhelm Marr. Paul Lawrence Rose dis-

Staunch Confessional Lutheran Hermann Sasse, who edited the prestigious and widely distributed *Kirchliches Jahrbuch für die evangelischen Landeskirchen Deutschlands* (*Church Yearbook for the Evangelical Land Churches in Germany*), provided a clearheaded disavowal of *völkisch* enthusiasm as early as 1932. Historians have often praised Sasse for his trenchant disclosure that true Christianity, with its doctrine of original sin, was an unavoidable insult against the Nazi idolization of the Teutonic race. However, in the same essay they have often overlooked Sasse's wry observation that the Nazis were using the *Volk* as a commodity. Sasse actually ridiculed the whole concept of *Volk* when he wrote:

> The modern [concept of] leadership [*Führerschaft*] is nothing but the reverse side of the decay of real authority. This is in part the actual decay and in part the lack of understanding with which the men of today, including the theologians, stand in relation to this basic fact of human life. The other aspect is connected in this way: the masses belong to leadership [*Führerschaft*] just as the *Volk* belong to the authority of the true powers that be: magistracy. Herein lies one of the fundamental questions of National Socialism: Can the masses again be melted down into a genuine *Volk* with an organic membership, or can they only be "organized"? It [National Socialism] has been unable to supply an answer to this question, but has continuously vacillated between an almost religious veneration of the *Volk* and a contempt for the "masses," which are both composed of the same people.[82]

When he wrote these words, Sasse was a pastor at historic St. Mary Lutheran Church in Berlin. Remarks such as these led the Nazis to suspend publication of *Kirchliches Jahrbuch*. Curiously, Sasse's attacks on National Socialism were overlooked by the Nazi government when it approved him in 1933 for the call to the theological faculty at the University of Erlangen.

Sasse also co-authored the August 1933 Bethel Confession. Article IV:2 in that document deals with the orders of creation, under which it includes *Volk*.[83] When Article VI:4 discusses *Volk*, it follows the generic rather than nationalistic use of the term:

---

tinguished between International Socialism (Communism) and National Socialism (Fascism) and showed ways in which they were related, including their aversion to Jews.

81 Heinz-Dietrich Wendland, a Union church theologian and instructor at Heidelberg, presented various points related to *Volk* and *Volkstum* in a significant article that appeared in Künneth and Schreiner, *Die Nation*, 106–37.

82 Sasse, "Die Kirche und die politischen Mächte der Zeit," in *KJahr 1932*, 31–32 n. 1; repr. in Sasse, *In Statu Confessionis*, 1:252–53 n. 1. Concerning the juxtaposition of the *Volk* and the masses, Sasse cites a February 3, 1932, speech by Hitler at the University of Halle (*KJahr 1932*, 100–101).

83 See the Bethel Confession in *Bonhoeffer*, 12:375.

The message of the Gospel is equally accessible or equally inaccessible to all peoples [*Völkern*]. For only God the Holy Spirit can work faith in men and awaken the consensus of a right confession. The fellowship of the confessing church transcends the boundaries of nations [*die Volksgrenzen*]. The church lives in every *Volk* to which the message of the church has come. The *Volk* is not the church; but the people who belong to both are bound to both in an indestructible solidarity.[84]

---

84 Quoted in *Bonhoeffer*, 12:399.

CHAPTER SIX

OPPOSITION TO THE ARYAN PARAGRAPH
AND OPPRESSION OF JEWISH PEOPLE

THE ARYAN PARAGRAPH PREPARED AND ADOPTED
BY THE CHURCH OF THE PRUSSIAN UNION

The statements on racism by Heinz Kloppenburg, Walter Künneth and other people of the Young Reformation Movement, and Paul Leo were disregarded by leaders of the Prussian Union, which, during the summer of 1933, came under the control of the German-Christians. Instead, during a September 5–6, 1933, meeting, the Prussian Union adopted a copycat Aryan Paragraph based upon the state's "Decree for the Restoration of the Professional Civil Service." This was the official beginning of racial discrimination against pastors of Jewish descent or pastors married to Jewish wives. The application of the Aryan Paragraph also led to discrimination against lay church members of Jewish background. The decree began with this preamble: "The General Synod of the Evangelical Church of the Old Prussian Union has passed the following church law." The following are excerpts from the Aryan Paragraph of the Prussian Union:

Section 1, 1: Only he may receive a call as clergyman or as an official of the general church government who possesses the preparatory training required for his career and who commits himself unreservedly to the national government and the German Evangelical Church.

Section 1, 2: He who is not of Aryan descent or who is married to a person of non-Aryan descent cannot be called as a clergyman or as an official of the general church government. Clergy and officials of Aryan descent who become married to a person of non-Aryan descent are to be discharged. How it is determined that a person is of non-Aryan descent is determined according to the rules of the statute of the Reich [i.e., the "Decree for the Restoration of the Professional Civil Service"].

Section 3, 1: Clergymen and officials who cannot provide the guarantee from their previous activity that they have unreservedly committed themselves to the national government and the German Evangelical Church can be forced to resign.

Section 3, 2: Clergymen or officials who are of non-Aryan descent or who are married to a person of non-Aryan descent are to be forced to resign.

Section 3, 3: The application of ¶ 2 can be overlooked if there are special merits regarding the edification of the church in the German spirit.

Section 3, 4: The rules of ¶ 2 do not apply to clergymen and officials who already on August 1, 1914, were clergymen or officials of the church, of the Reich, of a province, or of another body of public law, or who served the German Reich or its allies on the battlefront in the World War, or whose fathers or sons fell in the World War.

Section 8, 1: In cases where someone is forced to resign or is discharged . . . the final decision is made by the government of the Land Church without due process of law.

Section 11: The rules of §§ 1 and 3 apply essentially to the members of the church bodies as well as to those who bear honorary offices in the church.[1]

Because Union churches governed more than half of German Protestantism, this development had far-reaching consequences. It was expected that the Aryan Paragraph would be adopted by the DEK at its constituting convention on September 27, 1933, an expectation that was thwarted. Although only twenty-nine pastors of Jewish descent served in the Protestant churches of Germany in 1933,[2] the Aryan Paragraph inflicted serious damage upon the standing of lay church members of Jewish descent, as well as on pastors who were part Jewish or whose wives were Jewish or partly Jewish. The devastating effect is evidenced in the final years of the famous writer Jochen Klepper, who along with his wife and daughter committed suicide in 1942.[3]

The Aryan Paragraph of the Prussian Union provoked strong criticism from non-Union churches, as well as from several provincial churches. Strong disap-

---

1 Text in *KJahr 1933–1944*, 24–25; also in Meier, *Kirche und Judentum*, 86, and somewhat abbreviated in Schmidt, *Bekenntnisse*, 1:178–79, 183. An abbreviated English text is found in Helmreich, 144.

2 This number given by Meier, *Kirche und Judentum*, 26.

3 Klepper will be discussed on pp. 152–54.

provals were registered by Künneth, Martin Niemöller, Rudolf Bultmann, and Dietrich Bonhoeffer, not to mention the opinions (*Gutachten*) of the theological faculties at Marburg and Erlangen. These writers generally regarded the civil "Decree for the Restoration of the Professional Civil Service" as a matter that belonged to the civil government, and they largely restricted their opposition to the Aryan Paragraph of the Prussian Union.[4] Thus Bonhoeffer held that the state and the church each had to work out the racial problem in its own way and that the church was not in the position to praise or blame the state. Bonhoeffer wrote in the spring of 1933:

> [The church] knows of the basic necessity for the use of force in this world and of the necessarily "moral" unrighteousness of certain concrete acts of the state. The church, primarily, cannot directly engage in political actions, for the church claims no knowledge of the necessary historical precedence thereto. [The church] also cannot speak a direct word to the state regarding the Jewish Question of today and demand from it a certain different kind of action. But that does not mean that the church passively lets all political action go on without its participation; precisely because the church does not moralize in an individual case, it can and must ask the state ever and again whether it can justify its actions as a *legitimate civil* action, that is, as action in which law and order, not lawlessness and disorder, are created. . . . [The church] must raise this question in full clarity today in regard to the Jewish Question. . . . So long as the state acts according to law and order—be it also new law and new

---

4 In their responses, both Künneth and Bonhoeffer started from the premise that the "Jewish problem" had two differing aspects: a political and a religious consideration. On April 11, 1933, Künneth presented a paper, "Die Kirche und die Judenfrage in Deutschland," before a conference of all the superintendents and presidents of the Prussian Union. Künneth stated: "The position of the church on the Jewish problem is not regulated by a political point of view but rather by the concerns of the Christian congregation. . . . From this comes the obligation of the church to serve all members of the congregation in the same manner. . . . A deviation means the surrender of the Gospel" (quoted in Scholder, *Kirchen*, 1:348–49). Noting that these distinctions still partly hold in the post-World War II era, Scholder describes Bonhoeffer's position on the distinctive powers as follows: "The actions of the state remain free from the interference of the church. There is no room here for a pedantic or an aggrieved objection by the church. History is not made by the church but rather by the state" (Scholder, *Kirchen*, 1:350). See also Künneth's May 9, 1933, statement reflecting Bonhoeffer's position, in "Die 16 Thesen der Jungreformatorischen Bewegung," section 7: "We confess our faith in the Holy Spirit and therefore we reject fundamentally the exclusion of non-Aryans out of the church, for it rests upon the confusion of state and church. The state has the work of judging but the church has to rescue" (Schmidt, *Bekenntnisse*, 1:146). Künneth further discusses this in his memoirs, *Lebensführungen*, 106–9. Künneth regards this action, in which he was joined by Niemöller and Hanns Lilje, as the real beginning of the Confessing Church.

order—the Church of the Creator, Reconciler, and Redeemer cannot act in a directly political way against it. [The church] of course may not hinder the Christians who find themselves summoned against such action to accuse the state of being "unhuman" [*sic*] but, as church, it will only ask whether the state had followed order and law or not.[5]

THE REQUEST OF THE UNION CHURCH IN HESSE FOR THEOLOGICAL OPINIONS ON THE ARYAN PARAGRAPH

The Aryan Paragraph of the Prussian Union presented a serious problem that had to be addressed. Many members in the Union Church in Kur-Hesse (Electoral Hesse), which had come under the heel of Prussian domination in the early nineteenth century, were uncomfortable with the Aryan Paragraph. Thus at their conference (*Landtag*) in Marburg on September 11, 1933, they passed a resolution that requested opinions from two theological faculties—Marburg and Erlangen—on whether the Aryan Paragraph was in accord with the teachings of the Bible and the confessions of the church. The following are the responses that they received.

THE MARBURG RESPONSE

The opinion of the theological faculty at the University of Marburg was the most direct and incisive. It stated:

All of church history, as well as the laws of the state and the laws of the church among all nations, has known the term of Jew until now not in the sense of a race but exclusively in the sense of a religious confession, that of the Jew who has not acknowledged the Christ of God. The Jew who has recognized the prophecy of Christ in the Law and Prophets of his people, who has converted and been baptized, is no longer a Jew for the church, and also restrictions imposed by civil law have never been applied to baptized Jews on the part of the church.[6]

Noting that the church may have "spots and wrinkles" in its earthly weakness (Ephesians 5:27), the Marburg theologians continued:

But intentionally to disfigure the church is a sin against the Holy Spirit which is given to her. To tolerate any imperfection in the church other than for the sake of the weak—and no one claims that depriving Christians of Jewish background of their rights in the German Evangelical Church is so intended—means to make a lack of faith and love into a virtue and to abolish the Gospel of God's rule and of the justification of the sinner by grace through faith.[7]

---

5 "Die Kirche vor der Judenfrage," in *Bonhoeffer*, 12:351–52 (*Bonhoeffer's emphasis*).

6 Schmidt, *Bekenntnisse*, 1:180.

7 Schmidt, *Bekenntnisse*, 1:181.

Next, the Marburgers sought to counter the attempt to validate concepts of racism and *Volkstum* on the basis of the order of creation. They granted that perhaps the church has neglected these concepts in past times,

> but the true Order of Creation [*sic*] is nothing else than God's own lordship over all that he has created, and his redemptive judgment over sin, under which all things are concluded. But the cultivation of race and *Volkstum* in the church as gifts of creation is not possible in any way other than that it [the church] brings these together in itself and that it proclaims to each person how he has been called in those matters where he is different, as well as his indebtedness for that in which he is different. Otherwise, reverence for that which is created usurps the place of reverence due to the Creator.[8]

The Marburg Opinion pointed to the fact that converts from Judaism had brought great blessings to Christianity and that no one suggested that there was an un-German quality in the theological writings of August Neander, the church hymns of Philipp Spitta, or the paintings of Wilhelm Steinhausen, all of whom were Christians from a Jewish background. "Instead, they are all representatives of the peculiar German stamp of evangelical piety and they prove that their talented and consecrated nature has in no way endangered the preservation of Christian unity in faith and love."[9] The Marburg Opinion is dated September 19, 1933, and signed by the dean of the theological faculty, Hans Freiherr von Soden, a man who took a decisive position against the Nazis in the church struggle.

THE ERLANGEN OPINION

A September 12, 1933, letter from Sasse to Bonhoeffer discloses that a critique of the Aryan Paragraph by the Erlangen theological faculty was already underway before they received the request from the Kur-Hesse conference. (This is not surprising, considering the Erlangen professors were opposed to the Prussian Union.) Sasse wrote that the anti-Jewish statement of the Prussian Union "means that also the apostles of Jesus Christ, yes, the Lord himself, who was a son of David according to the flesh, would have to resign from the preaching office of the Prussian Church. This new decree separates the Prussian Church from all Christianity."[10]

---

8 Schmidt, *Bekenntnisse*, 1:181.

9 Schmidt, *Bekenntnisse*, 1:182.

10 From Sasse's letter in *Bonhoeffer*, 12:129. In the same letter, Sasse criticized Elert's pamphlet in the series *Ecclesia militans*. Sasse wrote: "Elert doesn't know the German-Christians at all, just as the other people living here [in Erlangen] live in a touching ignorance [*in einer rührenden Ahnungslosigkeit*] over against what is really going on" (*Bonhoeffer*, 12:130).

The Erlangen professors have been roundly criticized for their "Opinion on the Aryan Paragraph," and the Erlangen Opinion has widely been misinterpreted as an acceptance of the teaching of the Prussian Union. It seems clear that the professors of Erlangen, writing on September 25, 1933, were without a clue regarding the dreadful racism that was about to break out in Germany. Although their statement rejected the Aryan Paragraph of the Prussian Church and insisted that men could not be dismissed from their calls as Lutheran pastors because of Jewish descent, it obviously was not intended as a comprehensive statement refuting Nazi racism. The path that National Socialism would take during the next twelve years was as yet unknown, and the Erlangen Opinion shows a certain indecisiveness toward the new government. Some past writers have actually claimed that the Erlangen Opinion supported the Aryan Paragraph. For example, Berndt Hamm insists that the Erlangen Opinion supported the GDC and the Nazi Party.[11] In most cases, critics have not examined the Erlangen Opinion as a whole but have seized a few sentences out of context. Therefore the present study will investigate the complete document. Previous critics have generally overlooked the statement of paragraph 7 in which the Erlangen professors clearly reject discrimination against pastors of Jewish descent on ethnic grounds: "In particular, it offends the very substance of the pastoral office, ordination and the call, if the church as a general practice should dismiss pastors of Jewish or half-Jewish descent, who have proved themselves in service, merely because of their descent."[12]

Historians would do well to make a more adequate examination of the original documents and their origin. Some have described the Erlangen Opinion as solely the work of Werner Elert and Paul Althaus.[13] However, the document opens with the express statement that it was written as a digest of what had been said at a meeting of all the theological professors at which the Aryan Paragraph had been fully discussed. This opening statement further claims that the opinion registered was a consensus of the faculty: "The theological faculty, after an extensive consultation that resulted in a total agreement regarding the matters under debate, delegated the professors of systematic theology to answer the petition [submitted by the Union Church of Kur-Hesse]."[14] Therefore, though Elert and Althaus might have played a leading role in faculty deliberations, as well as in preparing the final draft, what was presented was not their own position but the opinion of the faculty as a whole, including Sasse[15] and Hermann Strathmann.

---

11 See Hamm, 32–33. Hamm's claims will be addressed in greater detail below.

12 Schmidt, *Bekenntnisse*, 1:186.

13 Schmidt, *Bekenntnisse*, 1:182.

14 Schmidt, *Bekenntnisse*, 1:183.

15 See the statement to this effect made by Sasse to Bonhoeffer in *Bonhoeffer*, 12:129.

As was characteristic of the other opinions on the Aryan Paragraph, the Erlangen writers distinguished between church and state, saying that the state had the right to determine qualifications for civil service but insisting that the church's standards were taken from the Bible and must therefore differ from those of the state.[16] The first part of the document seems to be written with great caution, but the writers become increasingly bolder. Finally, in paragraph 7 they firmly oppose discrimination against any pastor because of Jewish or part-Jewish blood.[17]

Because the Erlangen Opinion had been commissioned as an evaluation of the Aryan Paragraph of the Prussian Union, it included large extracts from that unfortunate document.[18] In a preliminary statement, the Erlangen professors observed that the church had always set certain personal standards for its pastors. The professors noted that besides German citizenship, certain biological characteristics, such as age, gender, and bodily capabilities, were required: "To the above qualifications has now been added the demand of Aryan descent." It would be the task of the faculty in the following lines to evaluate this demand.[19] This assignment was carried out in eight parts.

In paragraph 1, after noting that the Christian faith is founded on the death and resurrection of Jesus Christ, the professors referred to the words of 1 Timothy 2:4, which state that God wills all people to be helped:

> From the universal validity of this Gospel no human being, and least of all no entire *Volk*, is excluded. . . . In the fellowship with Christ there is, before God, no difference between Jew and non-Jew. But the relationship as children of God among all Christians does not remove the biological and social differences, but binds everyone to the estate in which he was called (1 Cor. 7:20). The biological bond with a particular *Volk* must be recognized by the Christian in thought and deed.[20]

In paragraph 2, the professors of Erlangen noted that "according to the teaching of the Reformation and in distinction from Roman Catholic doctrine, the Christian church must take into account not only the universality of the Gospel but also the historic nationality of Christian people [*der historisch-völkischen*

---

16 The distinction between a civil and churchly approach to non-Aryans is held by most respondents, including Bonhoeffer and Künneth, and was not a mark of *völkisch* theology. See the elaborate distinction between church and state on this matter in Künneth, "Das Judenproblem und die Kirche," in Künneth and Schreiner, *Die Nation*, 91–99.

17 Schmidt, *Bekenntnisse*, 1:186–87.

18 Schmidt, *Bekenntnisse*, 1:183.

19 Schmidt, *Bekenntnisse*, 1:184.

20 Schmidt, *Bekenntnisse*, 1:184.

Gliederung der christlichen Menschen]." This is followed by a citation from Article VII of the Augsburg Confession, stating that the sole criterion for unity in the church is the pure doctrine of Word and Sacrament. The opinion also referenced the Apology of the Augsburg Confession, Article VII 42ff., which notes that the church order followed by the Jewish Christians in the ancient church differed from that followed by the Gentile Christians.[21] What were the professors trying to say? In light of the situation in the German churches of 1933, a consideration of "the historic nationality of Christian people" meant a Wendish pastor for the Wends, a Low German pastor for the East Frisians, a Swabian pietist for those in Württemberg, or a Bavarian—by no means a Prussian—for the regionally minded Bavarians. The Erlangen Opinion notes that the sixteenth-century reformers respected local traditions and that the nineteenth-century foreign missionary movement sought, in establishing new churches, to embrace local customs and to avoid forcing European customs upon aboriginal converts to Christianity.[22] In view of the fact that there were no all-Jewish congregations, however, where did a pastor of Jewish descent belong?

Paragraph 3 continues the argument that the ethnic (*völkische*) nature of the congregation should be reflected in the appointment of a pastor: "The bearer of the pastoral office must be bound with his congregation in its earthly existence in such a way that the bonds that grow out of the congregation are also his bonds. The bond to the same *Volkstum* belongs here."[23]

In paragraph 4, the question of whether Christians of Jewish descent belong to the German *Volk* is discussed. The professors think that this question cannot be decided from religious criteria but the decision belongs to the state:

> For the church, the Jewish *Volk* of today is not a *Volk* like others: it remains in its election and its curse the *Volk* of salvation history, the *Volk* of Jesus and the apostles according to the flesh, a *Volk* being preserved for the final history of Jesus Christ with that *Volk* (Matt. 23:39; Rom. 11). In its dispersion among the nations without its own country, it reminds one of the limitations of all ethnic [*völkischen*] exclusiveness, of the temporariness of the separation of the nations, and of that one Kingdom of God which will come through the Christ who was promised to Israel. . . . Neither can the church give a universally valid answer to this question in regard to Jewish Christians, perhaps with respect to the Sacrament of Baptism. The confession of the church regarding the significance of baptism for salvation does not include, e.g., an answer to the question whether marriages between Germans and baptized, believing

---

21 All texts of the Erlangen Opinion that I have seen, including Schmidt, *Bekenntnisse*, 1:184, mistakenly give the citation as Ap IV 42ff. The correct citation is Ap VII 42ff.

22 Schmidt, *Bekenntnisse*, 1:184.

23 Schmidt, *Bekenntnisse*, 1:184.

Christian Jews as a whole are desired or advised against. The question regarding the ethnic [*völkisch*] relation between what is German and what is Jewish is of a biological and historical nature. It can only be answered by our *Volk*, as by every other *Volk*, in view of its special biological-historical situation.[24]

One might prematurely jump to the conclusion that the Erlangen Opinion intended to say that the Sacrament of Holy Baptism did not place Christians of Jewish descent on the same level as Christians of Gentile descent. However, in paragraph 6 it is said clearly that baptized Jewish people are part of the German *Volk*. One must wait patiently until the Erlangen theologians arrive at that point.

In paragraph 5, the Erlangen professors drew a distinction between the civil and the religious understanding of the racial problem.

The German *Volk* today, more than ever before, feels as though the Jews in its midst were a foreign people [*fremdes Volkstum*]. The German *Volk* has recognized the threats placed upon its own life by an emancipated Judaism and arms itself against this danger with legal exclusions. In struggling for the renewal of our *Volk*, the new state has excluded men of Jewish or half-Jewish descent from the leading civil offices. The church must recognize the basic right of the state to take such statutory measures. It knows itself in the present situation to be called to a new consideration of its task to be the *Volk*-church of the Germans. To this belongs the need to establish the basis of the ethnic [*völkischen*] bond of the pastor with his congregation and to apply this also to Christians of Jewish descent. For the position of the church in the life of the *Volk* and for the fulfilling of its task, it would place a serious burden and hindrance under the present situation to use men of Jewish stem to fill its pastoral offices. Therefore, the church must ask for Jews to refrain from the offices. Their full membership in the German Evangelical Church [DEK] is not thereby denied or limited any more than that of other members of our church who in some way or other do not fulfill the requirements for admission to the vocational offices of the church.[25]

What shall be said about the above? That final sentence sounds like requests made in the United States during the 1960s that black Christians remain in the background to avoid needless conflict in the church. How would the Erlangen professors, or their counterparts in the United States, justify such an attitude when compared with the parable of the Good Samaritan (Luke 10:25–37), in which Christ taught the Jewish people of his day tolerance toward a hated minority in their midst?

An examination of paragraphs 1–5 of the Erlangen Opinion impresses one the most by its ambivalence. One need not try to justify but must try to understand

---

24 Schmidt, *Bekenntnisse*, 1:184–85.

25 Schmidt, *Bekenntnisse*, 1:185.

the hesitancy found in the Erlangen Opinion by considering the emotional turmoil of 1933. After years of unpopular and floundering rule under the Weimar Republic, a decisive leader had finally emerged in the person of Hitler. To thoughtful Germans in 1933 it appeared that his program contained much that was good alongside much that was questionable. His program seemed to offer strong medicine for a weak patient. Much of what Hitler said seemed to make sense. But what about Hitler's rabid anti-Semitism? In 1933, the typical German church leader simply did not take the racial threats seriously. For example, on April 26, 1933, Wilhelm Freiherr von Pechmann, a prominent Lutheran layman from Bavaria, introduced a resolution to the German Evangelical Church Federation (*Deutscher evangelische Kirchen Bund* [DEKB]) that strongly affirmed the rights of Christians of Jewish descent. However, the Prussian Union-dominated DEKB accorded his resolution only one vote, dismissing the resolution as serving no purpose.[26]

The ambiguity of paragraphs 1–5 of the Erlangen Opinion seems to have been intended partly as a smoke screen to deflect the attention of the careless reader from the clear statements that were yet to come. This maneuver, and the words of the following statement, were typical of Elert's manner. Paragraph 6 of the Erlangen Opinion at last takes a cautious stand, and paragraph 7 takes a firm stand against the Aryan Paragraph. Paragraph 6 advances the concept of exceptions to the rule. The civil Aryan Paragraph, which had spurred the Prussian Union to promulgate its own decree, had allowed exceptions that were missing in the version adopted by the church. The Erlangen Opinion, and it can be thought that also Elert, pleads like an attorney for Christians of Jewish background:

> The state's "Decree for the Restoration of the Professional Civil Service" recognized, in its exceptions from the rule, that Jews might be included within the German *Volk*, e.g., by their readiness to offer up their lives for Germany. Thereby the concession is given that the boundary between the Jews and the German people [*dem deutschen Volke*] is not rigid but flexible. The church itself knows that also and that, especially in the genuine conversion to Jesus Christ, a Jew, by taking root in the church, can be led from a foreign status into membership in the German *Volk* [*aus der Fremdheit zur Gliedschaft am deutschen Volke*].[27]

This clear answer rejected the position that the Jews must remain a foreign people (*ein Gastvolk*) and maintained that they could be regarded as fully German. This was similar to the position taken by Paul Leo, a pastor of Jewish descent. One might object that Jews should be allowed to practice their own religion and should not have to convert to Christianity for protection. However, the

---

26 Helmreich, 145.

27 Schmidt, *Bekenntnisse*, 1:185.

Erlangen Opinion did not address that issue but only the question raised by the Prussian Union's Aryan Paragraph, that is, whether people of Jewish descent who had become Christians could enjoy full membership in the church. And the Erlangen Opinion answered that question in the affirmative. Ordination into the ministry was not a "human right" but a divinely ordered privilege. For example, women could be full members of the church, but the New Testament did not extend to them the privilege of ordination. The Erlangen Opinion did not forbid the ordination of Jewish men, but it recommended caution and due regard for the feelings of local congregations. Regardless of ethnic background, the church has always sought, in placing candidates, to provide pastors whom the members of the church would accept. The Erlangen Opinion stated: "In accordance with all this, the church in its order explicitly leaves a place for the exception, so that Christians of Jewish or partly Jewish origin shall be admitted to its offices. The filling of church offices by those of Jewish descent has always been a rarity and it should remain an exception in the future; but as such it must remain possible in special circumstances."[28]

For all the hysteria in the Prussian Union, this was an almost moot problem. In 1933 there were barely two dozen pastors of Jewish descent in all Germany. In the Land Church of Hanover, one of the largest Lutheran churches in Germany, their number increased from three to four (including Leo) when Hanover annexed the small territorial church of Schaumburg-Lippe in 1938.

Paragraph 7 is where the Erlangen professors took a stand firmly in support of the retention of pastors of Jewish descent in the church. The professors insisted:

> In particular, it offends the very substance of the pastoral office, ordination and the call, if the church as a general practice should dismiss pastors of Jewish or half-Jewish descent, who have proved themselves in service, merely because of their descent. It's not—as in Paragraph 3 of the Prussian Church law [Aryan Paragraph]—that special justification is required for leaving Jews in office, but rather, for dismissing them from office. Cases in which difficulties that cannot be overcome arise between the pastor and the congregation, on account of Jewish descent, should be handled according to the rules that apply also for all other cases where trust is destroyed between pastor and congregation. The church here cannot merely take over the decisions of the civil statutes [that is, the "Decree for the Restoration of the Professional Civil Service"], but must follow rules that come out of her essence as the church.[29]

Because of the evident knowledge of church law, these appear to be Elert's words. In this statement, the professors of Erlangen, and particularly Elert and

---

28 Schmidt, *Bekenntnisse*, 1:185.

29 Schmidt, *Bekenntnisse*, 1:185–86.

Althaus, openly contradicted the racist ideology and practice of the Nazi Party, the GDC, and the Prussian Union. The closing statement of paragraph 8 went still further when it asserted that the church would have to plan for future cases of admitting men of Jewish blood to the pastoral ministry and that, besides preparing itself for "such exceptions" by developing measures "of a churchly nature," these cases would be left to the judgment of the bishops. As shall be seen, Strathmann soon published a separate statement in which he was less favorable to accepting Jewish men for the study of theology and eventual candidacy to the pastoral office.[30]

Despite the fact that the Erlangen Opinion stated unequivocally that there could be no rejection of men for the ministry on the basis of their Jewish ancestry, and despite the fact that the University of Erlangen continually accepted a number of theological students of full or partial Jewish descent, Elert and Althaus have been routinely denounced for accepting the Aryan Paragraph.[31] It is hard to see how such conclusions can be sustained in view of the findings reported above. When Hamm attacks this wise counsel of Elert and Althaus, his strong personal assault on these men shows both a lack of knowledge of the facts that have been drawn from the primary sources and a lack of understanding of the qualifications needed for placing pastors. As will be shown, the church has always taken personal qualities into account when determining where to place its pastors.[32]

There are many examples in which ethnicity was considered during placement of pastors in U.S. Lutheran churches. It was once customary to seek pastors of East Frisian extraction to serve East Frisian congregations in Illinois or German-Russian pastors to serve German-Russian congregations in North or South Dakota. In both cases, this was not only because of language considerations but also because of folk temperaments. Some pastors of Reich-German background felt they lacked the skills to serve the immigrants from Russia. Some of the same concerns continue to influence pastoral leadership choices in predominantly African American

---

30 Interestingly, Strathmann differed from his Erlangen colleagues in favoring both the Union church and the Barmen Declaration.

31 Thus Bettina Simon erroneously claims that the Erlangen Opinion approved the Aryan Paragraph of the Prussian Union (Simon, 22). Her citations from the original text of the Erlangen Opinion are limited to twenty-one lines from three scattered pages, and her interpretation is determined by two writers who are unknown to me and whom she cites as E. Röhm and J. Thierfelder (Simon, 23).

32 Elert and Althaus are roundly denounced for the Erlangen Opinion in Hamm, 32–33. Space restrictions forbid a thorough debate with this writer, especially because it has been shown in the preceding presentation that his arguments do not agree with the facts.

churches or communities even in today's ostensibly pluralistic society in which racial integration is considered a priority.[33]

How much harder it must have been to get a German congregation to accept a pastor of Jewish descent at a time when the nation's political leadership was feverishly fostering racial hatred and forbidding people to associate with Jews. Within such a political and social environment, how could church members associate with a pastor of Jewish parentage? Furthermore, there is no basis in the text of the Erlangen Opinion for Hamm's claim that "racial unity with their congregations was more binding than the unity in Christ . . . with the Jewish Christians."[34] While commenting on a remark in the Apology of the Augsburg Confession (VII, 42ff.), it can be stated that the first-century Jewish Christians had church orders that were different from those in Gentile churches. The Erlangen Opinion concludes: "The being one in Christ is, for the Lutheran Confessions, not a question of external organization but one of faith."[35] The Lutheran view that church orders are not divinely inspired differed from the Reformed position. As noted previously, in contrast with Nazi ideology that regarded Jews as foreigners, the Erlangen Opinion asserted that a true conversion to Jesus Christ must mean full membership in the German *Volk* (paragraph 6). Although a Jewish person of the synagogue might not have said it the same way, this position cannot be called racism.

Almost immediately after the fall of the Third Reich, Elert and Althaus found themselves blamed for the Erlangen Opinion. In 1947 Althaus was discharged from his position at the university as part of the U.S. military's denazification process. At that time, three of Althaus's colleagues—Künneth, Hans Liermann, and Walther von Loewenich—made statements in his defense and commented on these words of the Erlangen Opinion, paragraph 7: "The church here cannot merely take over the decisions of the civil statutes [that is, the "Decree for the Restoration of the Professional Civil Service"], but must follow rules that come out of her essence as the church." Althaus's three defenders were correct when they stated in their votum: "This was a sharp and fundamental rejection of a coordination of the statutes of the Evangelical Church to those of National Socialism."[36]

---

33 As stated previously, I do not regard Caucasians, Jews, or blacks as distinct races but as ethnic variations of the single human race.

34 Hamm, 33.

35 Schmidt, *Bekenntnisse*, 1:186.

36 From Künneth, Liermann, and Loewenich, "Sachverständigengutachten," commissioned October 13, 1947, and completed in November 1947, p. 4, from Althaus Papers, file "Entlaßung 1947," in the possession of Gerhard Althaus.

The Erlangen Opinion's discussion of the place of Jewish people in the church was not an isolated response to the Aryan Paragraph of the Prussian Union. It was remarkably similar to the stated positions of Bonhoeffer, Künneth, and Niemöller.[37] All these writers registered a distinction between the positions of the state and of the church regarding the Jewish people. They avoided denouncing the anti-Jewish discrimination of the state but rejected discrimination within the church.[38] Künneth and Bonhoeffer tried to accommodate themselves to the distinction between Aryan and non-Aryan church leaders. The statement by Niemöller also dealt with this distinction and was in other respects almost identical with the opinion of Elert and Althaus.[39] Bultmann, who as a member of the faculty took part in the Marburg Opinion, issued another statement in which he agreed with the Erlangen Opinion that pastors of non-Aryan descent should not be sent where their ethnicity might become a hindrance to the work of the church.[40] This leads to the conclusion that to be historically sound any discussion

---

37 Five weeks after the publication of the Erlangen Opinion, Niemöller published "Sätze zur Arierfrage" (repr. in Schmidt, *Bekenntnisse*, 1:96–98). This statement was similar to that of Elert and Althaus. Niemöller began with a discussion of the concepts of *Volk, Volkstum,* and *Volkskirche* as supplying the context of the missionary task of the church (§ 1). He continued:

> Since, according to Rom. 11:25–26, there will be only scattered instances of Jews converted to Christianity, they cannot be expected to be placed in a separate church and should remain in Gentile congregations [§§ 2–3]. Therefore, excluding Jews from the "communion of saints" would contradict the Third Article of the Creed, and in the case of the Jews, the German churches must show that they have a fellowship that surpasses natural relationships [§ 4]. However, pastors of Jewish descent must practice great restraint to avoid giving offense in the work of the *Volksmission* because of the "weakness" of its members.

Niemöller opined that pastors of non-Aryan descent should not be placed in church government or in places where they would be prominent among the people. Nevertheless, these matters cannot be regulated by laws because they must remain under Christian liberty (§ 5).

38 Simon faults Künneth for recognizing a distinction between the policies of the state in hiring for civil service and those of the church in dealing with its called pastors, a distinction that was also present in Bonhoeffer. Her opinion of Künneth (see Simon, 25) was borrowed from two previous writers whom she names as M. Smid and H. E. Tödt, whereas she quoted Bonhoeffer's own writings (see Simon, 26–29). Had Simon read Künneth more carefully, she might have reported differently.

39 See p. 141 n. 33.

40 In *Theologische Blätter* (1933), col. 367, as cited in Beyschlag, 165 n. 321. Bultmann had written: "As the Erlangen Opinion rightly pointed out, the Christian churches have for a long time required certain presuppositions which were not of a fundamental char-

of the Erlangen Opinion must consider it within the context of other statements opposing the Aryan Paragraph. Taken in that context, it becomes clear that the Erlangen Opinion should not be singled out for abuse or denunciation.

Strathmann, professor of New Testament at the University of Erlangen, published an article in *Theologische Blätter* (1933) that, though it did not differ greatly in content, was more incisive in language but weaker in substance than the official Erlangen Opinion.[41] Strathmann distanced himself from the folk-jargon:

> The church as such is not grounded in *Volkstum* but in faith in the one Lord Jesus Christ as the Savior of all people. This faith establishes fellowship which reaches over and above all human differences of estate, gender, and peoples [*Völker*]. This fellowship of faith establishes also a fellowship of love. Thus it becomes clearly impossible to do that which the newly awakened self-feeling of our people [*des Volkes*] demands otherwise.[42]

Strathmann next took up the question whether men of Jewish heritage could become pastors. He said this must be decided on the basis of whether it could be beneficial to the church. In the case of old and established congregations, he advised that the pastor should be of the same ethnic group as the people whom he served. Times change, and when he wrote those lines, Strathmann thought that public opinion had been turned so much against Jews that it would be unwise to impose a clergyman of Jewish descent upon a typical congregation.[43] But this did not mean that non-Aryans could not serve as pastors. For example, men from a Jewish background who were already serving effectively should be allowed to remain in office. Nevertheless, Strathmann cautioned against opening wide the doors to the ordination of men of Jewish descent, lest this hinder the missionary program of the church.[44] Strathmann did not hold a close relationship with his

---

acter but of an expedient character for vesting in a churchly office. Can the Aryan question be handled from this position? I do not hesitate to answer this question in the affirmative, within certain limitations. . . . It seems to me to be self-understood that a church government must examine and decide in each individual case whether the non-Aryan descent of a candidate for the pastoral office might hinder a fruitful accomplishment in some congregation or not." Thereby Bultmann placed himself in substantial agreement with Elert and Althaus. Nevertheless, Simon praises the Marburg Opinion and criticizes the Erlangen Opinion for the same position (see Simon, 23). She also condemns Künneth for the same argument (see Simon, 24). It seems that Simon does not realize that pastors are placed according to their suitability for the local situation to which they are sent.

41 Quoted in Schmidt, *Bekenntnisse*, 1:186–89.

42 Schmidt, *Bekenntnisse*, 1:187.

43 Schmidt, *Bekenntnisse*, 1:188.

44 Schmidt, *Bekenntnisse*, 1:188–89.

Erlangen colleagues, with whom he differed in favoring the Barmen Declaration. Particularly Sasse and Elert regarded Strathmann as a weak Lutheran at best, and because his political activities resulted in his absenteeism in the classroom, they considered him to be derelict in his teaching duties.

When Strathmann's essay is compared with the Erlangen Opinion, striking parallels can be noted. Strathmann's comments in the faculty meetings had been heard, but there were two notable differences. Strathmann's warning against *völkisch* talk separated him from Elert and particularly Althaus. Also, rather paradoxically, these two colleagues were much more open than Strathmann to preparing men of Jewish background for the ministry. As is seen elsewhere, Althaus was regarded as the special ally of Jewish students at Erlangen, and Elert, as dean of the theological faculty, shielded non-Aryan students from the secret police and found financial aid for them, despite the illegality and risk involved in doing so.

To help Jewish students became especially dangerous after September 15, 1935, when Hitler's government issued the Nuremberg Racial Decree, which brought the principles of the Aryan Paragraph to bear upon almost all vocations and restricted nearly every aspect of Jewish life. This "Racial Statute for the Protection of German Blood and German Honor" forbade mixed marriages, as well as other relationships between Jewish and non-Jewish people. For example, it forbade the employment of non-Jewish women under the age of 45 in Jewish homes or businesses. Kurt Meier writes that the Nuremberg Racial Decree "served to legalize the increasing measures against Jews and removed all means of a livelihood from the German Jews in the following years."[45]

ACTIONS OF GERMAN PROTESTANTS WHO OPPOSED JEWISH OPPRESSION

Although men such as Althaus felt that some "greedy" Jews exerted a destructive influence on the German economy and culture and that certain measures needed to be taken to control such predators, whether Jews or Gentiles, he was uneasy about the gathering cloud of hatred toward all Jewish people. In a prominent Lutheran church paper, Wilhelm Laible reported on a presentation made by Althaus at a conference of pastors at Riederau am Ammersee, April 7–9, 1931. Althaus spoke on the attitude of Christianity toward "*Volk*, Race, and Judaism, National Socialism, and the Position of the Church toward National Socialism," which presentation and subsequent discussion Laible summarized as follows:

> The church in its relation to Judaism should let itself be led from salvation history as given in the Old and the New Testament. It sees both the curse resting

---

45 Meier, *Kirche und Judentum*, 12.

upon the Jews for their rejection of God's Son as well as the divine promises that still avail for the Jewish people today. The church rejects all hateful and prideful judgments against the Jews as well as against all other men and recognizes God as the only Judge over all people, and therefore also over the Jewish people.[46]

In the following some anecdotal evidence relating to the attitudes of Christians toward Jewish people will be surveyed.

THE CAUSE CÉLÈBRE OF JOHANN GERHARD BEHRENS

In 1935, Johann Gerhard Behrens, a Lutheran pastor, was harassed by Nazi sympathizers because of his opposition to anti-Semitism. As a pastor in Stade, a small city southwest of Hamburg in the northernmost reaches of the Lutheran Land Church of Hanover, Behrens belonged to the Confessional Fellowship and was active in the Confessing Church. The National Socialist leader Julius Streicher, who edited the anti-Jewish newspaper *Der Stürmer*, had run a piece in which he denounced Jews by citing Jesus' words in John 8:44: "You are of your father, the devil, and you desire to do according to your father's desire. He is a murderer from the beginning and has not stood in the truth, for the truth is not in him. When he speaks lies, he speaks of his own nature, for he is a liar and the father of lies." Streicher's interpretation and use of this passage was based on the claims advanced by members of the radical German-Faith Movement faction that Jesus was not a Jew but an Aryan and that Jesus was a racist who hated Jews.

Behrens faithfully taught his confirmation class the teachings of the Bible, but several of the children, under the influence of Holste, their schoolteacher, who was a Nazi, derided their pastor as "a bondsman of the Jews" (*judenhörig*). On September 13, 1935, some members of the confirmation class referred to the article in Streicher's paper and claimed that Jesus was a denouncer of Jews. The pastor replied that Jesus did not call the Jews "children of the devil" because of their race but because they were sinners and enemies of God. Behrens was said to have called *Der Stürmer* a "filthy tabloid" (*Schmutzblatt*). Behrens also was accused of preaching a sermon in which he warned his people against the myth of blood, soil, and race.

Several days later, Behrens was attacked on the street by the Nazi elite guard (*Schutzstaffel* [SS]), then, accompanied by Nazi storm troopers (*Sturmabteilung*), he was paraded through the streets of Stade under a hail of ridicule and abuse.

---

46 Editorial summary by Wilhelm Laible in *AELKZ* 64, no. 17 (April 24, 1931): 403. Scholder mentioned this event and added the following comment: "There was general agreement that one should work with the people [*völkischen Arbeit*] connected with an emphatic warning against racial anti-Semitism" (Scholder, *Kirchen*, 1:174).

Finally, the group reached the police station, where Behrens was incarcerated. He was set free by the presiding officer of the community.[47]

It soon became clear that this mob action directed against a Lutheran pastor concerned with the anti-Jewish actions of others had produced an unpleasant fallout that was embarrassing to the Reich, the Nazi Party, the city of Stade, and the church. The presiding officer who had rescued Behrens could not shield him from the clamor that he be removed from his position, and it was obvious that the beleaguered pastor could not return to his difficult confirmation class or deal with the parents of the pupils. Bishop August Marahrens provided a haven for Behrens in Loccum Abbey. There, Behrens, who was an internationally recognized astronomer, was able to carry on discussions with fellow scientists until he received a call to the parish at Detern in East Friesland, where he served peacefully until his retirement after World War II.[48]

But the common folk of the region around Stade had been deeply shocked by the scandalous way in which Behrens had been treated. It was whispered that the ringleader, who had painfully pinned Behrens's arms as he paraded the pastor through the city, had the later misfortune of having a child born without arms. This seemed like a divine punishment upon the infant's father. Noting the significance of this event in terms of those who (in the mid-1930s) were not afraid to stand up against National Socialism and in terms of the tensions in the state, the community, and the Nazi Party that such actions exposed, Eberhard Klügel supplies massive documentation so future researchers may investigate "the Behrens Affair."[49]

Combatting Jewish Persecution in Bavaria

Jewish persecution reached a new extreme on the "Night of Broken Glass" (*Kristallnacht*), November 9, 1938, when unruly mobs were incited by the Nazis to smash the windows of Jewish shops and dwellings and to destroy synagogues.

What did Christians think about this attack against Jewish people? Elert related after the war that he had been so horrified by the violence of *Kristallnacht* that he became totally convinced that no good was to be expected from National Socialism. *Kristallnacht* opened his eyes to the depths of evil in the Nazi movement. Julius Schieder, a leading Lutheran pastor who at that time was director of the Preaching Seminary at Nuremberg, expressed his regret that he had not come out more strongly against these racist actions. Shortly before his death in 1964, Schieder said: "It still troubles me that I did not protest against the *Kristallnacht* of

---

47 Klügel, *Landeskirche*, 280–83.

48 Klügel, *Landeskirche*, 281.

49 Klügel, *Landeskirche*, 283 n. 27. These events are chronicled in Klügel.

1938 in some form or other. I have to accept reproach for that, and I have to reproach myself. . . . We all failed, but God did not fail."[50] Marahrens wrote in 1945: "It weighs especially heavy upon me—I have said this many times already—that the church did not find the saving word during the first storm of persecution that broke out over the German Jews. . . . They should never have been attacked in this inhuman manner."[51]

Some people, such as Friedrich Wilhelm Hopf, pastor at Mühlhausen in Franconia, publicly denounced *Kristallnacht*. The Jewish people of Mühlhausen had suffered tremendously from this "volcanic outburst of Jewish hatred," and Hopf preached a stirring sermon in St. Mary Lutheran Church on November 13, 1938, based on James 5:9b: "Behold, the Judge is at the door!" Hopf was a close friend of Sasse, who had also repudiated Nazi racism.[52] Sadly, both Hopf and Sasse found themselves ostracized after World War II. Both men vigorously opposed the entry of the Lutheran Land Church of Bavaria into the EKD because it was unionism, that is, outward union where there was no doctrinal agreement. Their voices were not heard, and eventually both men withdrew from the Bavarian church and joined the Free Lutheran Church.

COURAGEOUS ACTIONS BY CARL GOERDELER

The fulminations of Hitler and the Nazi Party had steadily increased after they came to power in 1933. Jewish people were systematically deprived of their economic, civil, and personal rights. Carl Goerdeler, a Lutheran layman who served as the mayor of Leipzig, became involved in resistance to Nazism over the "Jewish question." When the Nazis staged a boycott of Jewish shops, Goerdeler donned his black dress suit and top hat and ostentatiously visited several Jewish fur shops to express his outrage at anti-Semitism. In November 1936, while Goerdeler was away from Leipzig, the Nazis demolished the Felix Mendelssohn monument in front of the Gewandhaus, the famous concert hall where Mendelssohn, who was a Lutheran of Jewish descent, had once presided. In protest, Goerdeler resigned as mayor of Leipzig. Goerdeler's daughter, Marianne Meyer-Krahmer, later said: "When Goerdeler shortly after his resignation entered the Gewandhaus to attend one of its regular Thursday concerts, the enthusiasm

---

50 Schieder, "Wir alle hatten verzagte Stunden," in *ZwKK*, 79–80.

51 Marahrens, "Wochenbrief an die Pfarrerschaft," August 15, 1945; cited in Simon, 117.

52 Hopf's bravery is related by Hans Siegfried Huß, "Friedrich Wilhelm Hopf—Evangelisch-lutherischer Pfarrer zu Mühlhausen (Oberfranken) (1936–1951)," in *Unter einem Christus sein und streiten: Festschrift zum 70. Geburtstag von Friedrich Wilhelm Hopf,* ed. Jobst Schöne and Volker Stolle (Erlangen: Verlag der Ev.-Luth. Mission, 1980), 206. On the stalwart position of Bishop Theophil Wurm in neighboring Württemberg, see Schäfer, *Wurm*, 153–58.

and applause of Leipzig's citizenry [for him] was boundless. This was one of the most embarrassing acts for Leipzig's National Socialists."[53]

From this time forward, Goerdeler became involved in efforts to remove Hitler from power. In these efforts he was financed by the wealthy Stuttgart industrialist Robert Bosch. Uwe Siemon-Netto writes: "Bosch is one of the unsung heroes of the German resistance. That his important role is almost unknown in Germany and abroad must again be attributed to cliché thinking."[54] Bosch was a practicing Lutheran layman who assisted the opposition movement by providing contacts with his business associates in other countries. Especially important was Bosch's enlistment of Arthur Primrose Young in England, whose notes of his meetings with Goerdeler are a crucial historical source. With the aid of Bosch, Goerdeler traveled to the United States, Canada, England, and France to warn foreign leaders of the threat Hitler posed. However, when Goerdeler warned the leaders of the free world in 1937 not to make concessions to Hitler, Édouard Daladier, the prime minister of France, and Neville Chamberlain, the prime minister of Great Britain, refused to listen. They continued on their course of appeasement in which they betrayed Czechoslovakia to Hitler. Goerdeler told Young: "If the British Government decided to assemble Parliament and decided to make an announcement [of firmness] . . . there would be no war. Either of two things would happen: (a) Hitler himself would abandon his present plan and hold the peace; (b) if Hitler was still determined on war, then the generals would stop him from putting his plan into action."[55]

Correspondence of Arthur Primrose Young with Carl Goerdeler

An important source of information on the German resistance movement is found in Young's papers. In these documents, Young used an "X" to refer to Goerdeler and a "Y" to refer to Bosch to conceal and protect their identities. In contrast to the people in Germany and in other countries who thought at that time that Hitler was a decent man and that others were responsible for the tyranny and oppression, Goerdeler insisted that Hitler himself had ordered the *Kristallnacht* pogrom of November 9–10 and the other atrocities perpetrated against the Jews. Young gave the following report:

> X spoke with great feeling of the way in which many German citizens, at great risk to themselves and their dependents, had given individual assistance to the Jews in their terrible plight. He spoke with burning indignation of two terrible

---

53 Uwe Siemon-Netto, *The Fabricated Luther: The Rise and Fall of the Shirer Myth* (St. Louis: Concordia, 1995), 141.

54 Siemon-Netto, *Fabricated Luther*, 141.

55 Cited in Siemon-Netto, *Fabricated Luther*, 142.

features of this pogrom. Little children were driven from their homes, clad only in thin nightshirts into the streets, to suffer the agonies of hunger and cold. Jewish virgins were violated by young Nazi gangsters who carried out the pogrom. He cited the case of a Jewish virgin, known to him, who only escaped this terrible fate by telling those that would violate her that she was suffering from syphilis.[56]

From his death cell in prison, Goerdeler wrote the following words concerning the persecution of the Jewish people:

> Hitler personally ordered all these cruelties, murders and tauntings. He approved all these measures in every detail, and prohibited any form of criticism. He ordered that the synagogues be set on fire, that Jewish morgues be desecrated, Jewish shops be looted, and Jewish property of any kind be handed over to the mob and the most brutal among the Hitler youth leaders. . . . These orders were phrased in such a way that perverted people even drove naked children from Jewish orphanages into the cold of the night, until Christians took them in. It is important to know that in the face of this infamy many German families displayed a powerful spirit of neighborly love, protecting their persecuted fellow-citizens and giving them shelter.[57]

RESCUE EFFORTS AT THE UNIVERSITY OF ERLANGEN

Meanwhile, the professors at Erlangen covertly did what they could to support people of Jewish descent. Elert later told how he had shielded forty or fifty students who were being pursued by the Gestapo, some because of Jewish parentage and others because of political activism.[58] After the war, Fritz Fraenkel of Göttingen and Rolf Neumann of Schürbitz, two Jewish students whom Elert had supported, testified in legal depositions that Elert had shielded them from Nazi persecution during the Third Reich. Neumann declared that Elert had even bent the rules and twice secured financial aid for him from the Zahn-Stipendium.[59] Regarding Althaus, an anonymous person writes in 1947: "Althaus was regarded as the special confidant of non-Aryan theological students and of theological students who were politically denounced and persecuted because of their position against the church politics of the Third Reich." This writer also referred to Fraenkel and Neumann as Jewish students who were helped by Althaus.[60]

---

56 Siemon-Netto, *Fabricated Luther*, 116.

57 Siemon-Netto, *Fabricated Luther*, 142–43.

58 Document in Beyschlag, 279–80.

59 These two depositions, dated April 26, 1947, and November 23, 1947, are in the Werner Elert Papers, ATF.

60 "Althaus galt als besonderer Vetrauensmann der nichtarischen Theologiestudenten

During the Third Reich, church services were monitored by Nazi observers. As a result, many courageous preachers ended up in jail. Nevertheless, as university preacher, Althaus made some rather bold remarks in his sermons. In 1942, on the Tenth Sunday after Trinity, he preached on Matthew 23:34–39, the text that speaks of the destruction of Jerusalem. In his introduction Althaus said: "Frederick the Great once asked a pastor, 'Can you give me a single proof for the existence of God?' The pastor replied, 'Your Majesty, the Jews!' " Althaus then went on to say that one cannot understand Jews on the basis of racial biology alone but that there is a divine mystery surrounding their survival through history. Jews had suffered much after they rejected Christ, but God had preserved them through the centuries: "This is a testimony that the God of the Bible is alive; that his Word spoken by the prophets is the truth in Jesus; that God lives and that he cannot be mocked; a proof for the truth of the Bible!"[61]

Althaus, who had known Paul Leo at Göttingen where the fathers of both men were professors at the same university, tried to shield Leo's Jewish relatives in Erlangen. Leo's uncle, *Geheimrat* Paul Hensel, was the noted professor of philosophy at the University of Erlangen. Hensel died in 1930, leaving his widow, Elisabeth, and two daughters, Fanny and Cecilia. In a November 1952 conversation, the Hensels told me that Althaus had defied the Nazi rule requiring the ostracism of Jews to visit them in their home, help provide them with food, and, as university preacher, offer them spiritual support. Althaus's son, Gerhard, told me in July 1998 that his father had expected him to disregard the rules against fraternization with non-Aryans and to be friendly with the Jewish children at school.

ALTHAUS AND THE 1941 BREMEN/OLDENBURG CASE

At the 1941 Reformation Festival Service held by St. Stephan's of Bremen, three non-Aryan members (marked by the Jewish star) received the Lord's Supper from Pastor Gustav Greiffenhagen. Herr Fischer, a German-Christian clergyman who had been installed as a pastor at St. Stephan's against the will of the congre-

---

und der Theologen, die wegen ihrer Haltung gegen die Kirchenpolitik des dritten Reiches politisch verdächtig und verfolgt waren" (from the "Nachlaß Althaus," file "Entlaßung, 1947"). Unfortunately the document is incomplete and the last page with the name of the writer, who was obviously present at the events that he describes, is lost. A parallel testimony states: "Ferner gehört in diesen Zusammenhang, daß Althaus Vertrauensmann der nichtarischen Studenten der Theologie gewesen ist . . ." (from Künneth, Liermann, and Loewenich, "Sachverständigengutachten," commissioned October 13, 1947, and completed in November 1947, from Althaus Papers, file "Entlaßung 1947," in the possession of Gerhard Althaus).

61 From a 1942 unpublished sermon found among Althaus's papers in possession of Gerhard Althaus.

gation, reported this to the Gestapo, which consequently arrested a number of church members. Although some were released, four schoolteachers remained in jail. On November 7, 1941, Greiffenhagen wrote a letter of protest to Reich Minister for Church Affairs Hanns Kerrl and to the DEK Church Chancellery in Berlin. In this letter Grieffenhagen stated his case and demanded the liberation of those who were still imprisoned. Apparently, he received no response. Meanwhile, Kerrl died unexpectedly in Paris on December 12, 1941.[62]

On May 12, 1942, Heinz Kloppenburg, a pastor in neighboring Oldenburg, wrote to Althaus and asked him to prepare a theological opinion to help in the defense of three of the Lutheran teachers from St. Stephan's: Hedwig Baudert, Anneliese Dittrich,[63] and Maria Schröder. One of the teachers had explicitly stated to the Gestapo that she had not been a personal friend but had found one of the (Jewish) women to be disagreeable, and all three said that they had provided aid only as their Christian duty. Nevertheless, the teachers had been imprisoned since November and steps had been considered for transporting them to a concentration camp in Warthegau. Kloppenburg pointed out in his letter that this political action was in violation of the legal commitment given by the Nazi government not to interfere with the churches in the DEK in matters of doctrine and worship.

In his May 16 reply, Althaus expressed his concern and agreed with Kloppenburg's position that the women had only done their Christian duty, but he questioned whether a theological opinion would be respected by the court because the action against the teachers was a matter of civil law. He advised Kloppenburg to find a "churchly" lawyer to pursue the case.[64] Although several intervening letters are missing, Kloppenburg took Althaus's advice and retained Karl Mensing as attorney for the women. Mensing sought and obtained a theological opinion from Althaus in the matter. Although the text of this opinion seems to be lost, its content is quoted in a later document from Mensing. When Althaus was accused of Nazism and suspended by a U.S. tribunal during the 1947 denazification proceedings, Mensing wrote a letter to support the beleaguered professor with extensive quotations from Althaus's 1942 theological opinion. Mensing noted that at a time when it was dangerous to disagree with Hitler, Althaus, despite the attendant risks, had sent a strong opinion repudiating this form of anti-Semitism,

---

62 Greiffenhagen's letter is included among the documents in Meier, *Kirche und Judentum*, 114–15.

63 Dittrich was the daughter of a Lutheran pastor and the sister of Eva Dittrich, who married Paul Leo; see p. 121 n. 65.

64 Kloppenburg's May 12, 1942, letter and the prompt reply from Althaus (dated May 16), together with the 1947 deposition of Karl Mensing and other pertinent papers, of which I have photocopies, are in Althaus Papers, file "Entlaßung 1947," in the possession of Gerhard Althaus.

denouncing the proceedings against the teachers, and upholding the action of the pastor and his attorney.[65] In referring to the opinion, Mensing gave the following statements by Althaus in defense of the teachers:

> The accused teachers are members of the German Evangelical Church, which is recognized as such by the law of the Reich [*Reichsgesetz*] of July 14, 1933, as in conformance with national law [*reichsrechtlich*]. In Article I of its constitution, which as such was recognized by the Reich, it is declared that "the inviolable basis of the DEK is the Gospel of Jesus Christ, as it is testified to us in the Holy Scriptures and as it was newly brought to light in the Confessions of the Reformation."[66]

Despite the danger of angering the Nazi authorities, Althaus did not mince words as he continued his apology for the Jews:

> Paul writes in Galatians 3:28: "There is neither Jew nor Greek, there is neither bondsman nor freeman, there is neither male nor female, for you are all one in Christ Jesus." . . . But in spite of the undeniable and basic importance of the differences of the races and the *Völker,* faith in Jesus Christ establishes a fellowship that reaches over these differences and across these lines. . . . As with other *Völker* and races, thus also the Jews, who in faith confess Jesus Christ and are baptized, are members of the Christian Church.[67]

What was the end of the story? Mensing writes in his deposition that though the Nazi court had insisted that the teachers had committed a crime, he was able to argue against that position. Thus "it was possible for me [Mensing] . . . to achieve a very substantial mitigation of the sentence, whereby their salaries were reduced by only 1/5 for a period of three years," thanks to Althaus's expert opinion [*Gutachten*].[68] Therefore the teachers were allowed to keep their positions.

THE CASE OF JOCHEN KLEPPER

As measures against Jewish people were tightened, their lives were increasingly restricted. Severe penalties were leveled against Germans who married non-Aryans. The case of Jochen Klepper, a brilliant young journalist, poet, and hymn writer who was married to a Christian woman of Jewish descent, was one such

---

65 Deposition of Karl Mensing of Wuppertal-Elberfeld, August 19, 1947, in Althaus Papers, file "Entlaßung 1947," in the possession of Gerhard Althaus.

66 Deposition of Karl Mensing of Wuppertal-Elberfeld, August 19, 1947, in Althaus Papers, file "Entlaßung 1947," in the possession of Gerhard Althaus.

67 Deposition of Karl Mensing of Wuppertal-Elberfeld, August 19, 1947, in Althaus Papers, file "Entlaßung 1947," in the possession of Gerhard Althaus.

68 Deposition of Karl Mensing of Wuppertal-Elberfeld, August 19, 1947, in Althaus Papers, file "Entlaßung 1947," in the possession of Gerhard Althaus.

tragic example. Klepper was a strong Lutheran layman who had attended the University of Erlangen to study theology in 1922. The following year he had continued his studies at the University of Breslau. Despite the persecution he experienced from the Nazi government, Klepper adhered to his strong Lutheran convictions and refused to join the Dahlem Front of the Confessing Church because he thought it did not heed the words of Romans 13:1: "The powers that be are ordained of God." In view of his popularity with the general public, the Nazis avoided a direct confrontation with Klepper.

Klepper maintained that anti-Semitism came only from the Nazi Party; he did not think that the common people hated Jews. The November 7, 1938, assassination of a German diplomat in Paris by a Jewish man upset with the deportation of his family was used by the Nazis as the pretext for a new outbreak of violence against Jewish people in Germany. The Nazi propaganda spoke of "the fury of the people [*Volkswut*]" against all Jews, thus the Nazis unleashed the violence of *Kristallnacht*. Writing in his journal, Klepper doubted that the German people were angry with the Jews and gave some significant evidence for his position. On Thursday, November 17, 1938, his wife, Hanni, had to register as a Jew. Klepper commented: "And that is the characteristic thing about the 'folk's outrage' [*Volkswut*] in Berlin: after supplying this information, people are more polite, more interested, more kindly."[69]

Regarding the Nazi attacks on *Kristallnacht* (November 9, 1938) and the days of rioting and looting that followed, Klepper wrote in his journal that the Nazis tried to claim that the German people wanted Jews suppressed, but he noted that the common people did not really feel that way. Instead, many were angry about the way Jews were being misused. "Yes, the [German] people are angry, but against whom!"[70] During the following days, Klepper made a number of entries in his journal that afford an inside view of the gradually mounting suffering of the Jewish population:

> *On November 10, 1938:* Out of the various "Jewish" neighborhoods of the city we hear that the populace does not stand behind the violence. From various neighborhoods of the city we hear how the populace repudiates such organized actions. It's almost as though the anti-Semitism which was so widely

---

69 Jochen Klepper, *Unter dem Schatten deiner Flügel: Aus den Tagebüchern der Jahre 1932–1942*, ed. Hildegard Klepper (Stuttgart: Deutsche Verlags-Anstalt, 1955), 679.

70 Klepper, *Unter dem Schatten deiner Flügel*, 677. For additional evidence of a nationwide revulsion toward Nazi measures against Jews, see William Sheridan Allen, "Die deutsche Öffentlichkeit und die 'Reichskristallnacht'—Konflikte zwischen Werthierarchie und Propaganda im Dritten Reich," in *Die Reihen fast geschlossen: Beiträge zur Geschichte des Alltags unterm Nationalsozialismus*, ed. Detlev Peukert and Jürgen Reulecke (Wuppertal: Hammer, 1981), 397–411.

present in 1933 had very, very much dwindled since the exaggeration of the Nuremberg Race Laws of 1935. But it is otherwise with the Hitler Youth organization, which encompasses all the German young people. I don't know how far the parental homes can still exercise a counterweight.[71]

On November 11, 1938: Also that which Hanni heard people say today and observed from the demeanor even of the National Socialist people from the south end and from Steglitz, from the wives of marine officers to the women in the bakeries, from the men at the newsstand to the closest neighbor.[72]

On November 12, 1938: In the evening paper it said: "Jews may no longer attend cultural productions. An order of Dr. Goebbels prohibits admission to theaters, movies, concerts, lectures, and expositions."[73]

On November 13, 1938: All the [*Kristallnacht*] damage that came through the anger of the people over the aggression of international Jewry against National Socialist Germany on September 8 and November 10–11, 1938, must be immediately compensated for by the Jewish owners.[74]

Beginning in 1942, the forces of hell were unleashed against the remaining Jewish people in Germany. They were sent to the death camps by the hundreds of thousands. On December 11, 1942, when his wife and stepdaughter were to have been deported to the death camp, Klepper and his family chose to die together. They committed suicide by turning on the gas jet in their house in Berlin. Their housekeeper found them the next morning, lying on a quilt on the kitchen floor. Above them they had placed a picture of Christ. It is said that Hitler, who enjoyed reading Klepper, was furious when he heard of Klepper's death. He berated Adolf Eichmann for allowing the destruction of this talented and popular writer.[75]

THE CASE OF WILHELM GROSS

Wilhelm Gross, a promising young Christian sculptor of Jewish heritage, belonged to a group of artists, including Käthe Kollwitz and Ernst Barlach, who were producing religious works marked by honesty and integrity. In 1931 Gross hailed the approaching Third Reich as a solution for the events following Ger-

---

71 Klepper, *Unter dem Schatten deiner Flügel*, 675.

72 Klepper, *Unter dem Schatten deiner Flügel*, 676.

73 Klepper, *Unter dem Schatten deiner Flügel*, 676.

74 Klepper, *Unter dem Schatten deiner Flügel*, 677.

75 Joel Herl comments on Klepper and one of his hymns in *Hymnal Supplement 98 Handbook* (St. Louis: LCMS Commission on Worship, 1998), 60. Herl draws from Günter Wirth, *Jochen Klepper* (Berlin: Union, 1972), and Ernst G. Riemenschneider, *Der Fall Klepper: Eine Dokumentation* (Stuttgart: Deutsche Verlags-Anstalt, 1975).

many's humiliation in the Versailles Treaty. By 1933 he had sculpted "Christ in Gethsemane," an outstanding work that Max von Schilling displayed in his gallery at Berlin's Parisier Platz (near the Brandenburg Gate).[76]

One of Gross's art students was Eva Dittrich, a talented young woman,[77] who related the following story. Gross had entered an exhibition for artists in Frankfurt am Main. One of his pieces had been given a first-place award and declared the best work in the exhibit. However, when the as-yet undisclosed artist was asked to come forward to receive his award, the judges, perceiving that Gross was Jewish, held a hurried consultation and declared there had been a mistake. They awarded the prize to an Aryan artist instead.

Oppression quickly spread against Jewish artists, and Gross was forced to go underground. As a Christian of Jewish background, he became a member of the Confessing Church, served on its board of directors for the Berlin-Brandenburg Church, and joined in the struggle against the Reich bishop. Because he could no longer execute large sculpture projects, Gross began to produce woodcuts. One of these is a portrayal of the Old Testament prophet Amos, the prophet of social justice.[78] The facial features are identical to those of Otto Dibelius, the ousted superintendent in Brandenburg. This portrait became a symbol of the resistance movement and was displayed in underground centers of the Confessing Church. Gross survived World War II. He remained in Potsdam under Soviet rule and continued to produce woodcuts, which were smuggled out of East Germany. Eva Dittrich Leo sold these works in the United States and sent the proceeds to Gross in Potsdam to aid in his struggle for existence under the Communist regime.[79]

THE RESCUE WORK OF HEINRICH GRÜBER

The Evangelical Place for Assistance of Non-Aryan Christians (*Evangelische Hilfsstelle für nichtarische Christen* or *Büro=Grüber*) was operated by Heinrich

---

76 Related by Martin Fischer, "Wilhelm Gross, sein Werk und sein Auftrag," in *Der Fels der Mitfolge: Christus im Alten Testamen. 18 Kohleskizzen von Wilhelm Gross* (Berlin: Lettner, 1953), 6.

77 Eva was a sister of Anneliese Dittrich, one of the four teachers of St. Stephan's in Bremen who had been arrested for helping Jews. Eventually Eva married Paul Leo. See pp. 121 (esp. n. 65), 150–52.

78 This woodcut is in my possession.

79 Much of this information about Gross was related to me by Eva Dittrich Leo, who, after studying under Gross, established her own church art studio in Hildesheim. For more information on Gross, see Meier, *EKK*, 1:282, 590 n. 990. In 1956, when I was pastor of Peace Lutheran Church, Herreid, South Dakota, Paul and Eva Leo helped commission a carved wooden crucifix by Gross to be placed in the church. Such gracious actions were typical of the Leos.

Grüber, a pastor in Berlin. This office was established by the second Provisional Church Leadership (*Vorläufige Kirchenleitung* [VKL]) in the autumn of 1938. By July 1939, Grüber operated with a staff of thirty-five people. The work was divided among five departments: (1) emigration, (2) homes for the aged, (3) evacuation of children, (4) welfare, and (5) school and spiritual care.[80] The most renowned work of Grüber's office was the operation of an "underground railway" that rescued beleaguered Jewish people, smuggled them out of Germany, and transported them to a safe haven in Lutheran Sweden. His work continued for only a couple of years. Grüber was arrested during Christmas 1940 and spent nearly three years in concentration camps at Sachsenhausen and Dachau. After the war, Grüber was a prominent leader in church circles in Berlin.[81]

THE FINAL MOVES OF THE DEK AGAINST NON-ARYAN CHRISTIANS

The Nazi state had ostracized Jews, requiring them to wear a yellow ribbon and place a Star of David on their outer garments. The churches dominated by German-Christians followed suit. On December 17, 1941, church leaders Johannes Klotzsche of Saxony, Paul Kipper of Nassau-Hesse, Walther Schultz of Mecklenburg, Christian Kinder of Schleswig-Holstein, Rudolf Wilkendorf of Anhalt, Johannes Sievers of Lübeck, and Dr. Hans Volz of Thuringia announced an action against "the Jews as the born enemies of the world and of Germany."[82] On December 22, 1941, Günther Fürle, director of the DEK Church Chancellery in Berlin, issued a decree that in the DEK "baptized non-Aryans are to be kept away from church life in the German congregation. Baptized non-Aryans must find means and ways to create arrangements that can provide for their own church services and spiritual care."[83] On December 28 a similar decree was promulgated by Martin Sasse, the German-Christian bishop for Thuringia.[84]

A sharp protest against Fürle's statement was written by Bishop Theophil Wurm of Württemberg. Wurm took issue with Fürle's statement that "the Evangelical churches in their service of the eternal Gospel are directed to the German

---

80 Niemöller, *Evangelische Kirche*, 387. A list of Grüber's representatives throughout Germany is given in Meier, *Kirche und Judentum*, 110–11.

81 Grüber was sent to Dubuque, Iowa, by the Federal Republic of Germany to present the Commander's Cross of the Order of Merit to Julius Bodensieck at his retirement dinner in 1965. I was invited to the dinner as a representative of Bodensieck's former students and was honored to be seated at the head table next to Grüber, which provided a good opportunity to talk with this courageous man.

82 *KJahr 1933–1944*, 481.

83 *KJahr 1933–1944*, 482; also in Meier, *Kirche und Judentum*, 116–17.

84 *KJahr 1933–1944*, 482.

people." Wurm asserted that it should say that "the churches in their service to our people are directed to the eternal Gospel" and that the Gospel is directed to all people. Wurm asked: "If we cast out those who have been received in our church through baptism and with whom we have carried on church fellowship, how can we still at Christmas speak of the joy that is meant for all people [Luke 2:10]?"[85]

Nathan A. Stoltzfus points out that the only Jews to survive the Third Reich while living legally inside Nazi Germany were the Jewish husbands of non-Jewish wives.[86] One major reason for this was that the public protest of the wives in early 1943 embarrassed the regime; another reason was that the Nazis were afraid of a public repudiation for attacking the integrity of marriage.[87]

It may well be that the protest of Marahrens also contributed to the survival of the remaining Jewish people. Marahrens wrote a letter to the minister of the interior on December 19, 1943, in which he spoke against the state policy that forced divorces in the case of marriages between Jews and non-Jews, warning that recent actions of the Nazi government "had sorely troubled the Christian conscience of broad circles of the population." Against these wrongful measures the bishop insisted that God's commandments are valid under all conditions: "When the sanctity of life is not regarded, when marriages are destroyed, and wrong and violence are perpetrated against the innocent, such things conflict with the most elementary commandments of God." Marahrens said it was not his duty to determine how widespread such happenings had become, "[b]ut we hold it for our duty to bring up these matters to the leaders of the state."[88]

---

85 Wurm's words are given in an abridged form in Meier, *Kirche und Judentum*, 117–18; the unabridged text is in *KJahr 1933–1944*, 482–84.

86 William Sheridan Allen asserts that in the year 1933 more than half the marriages that German Jews entered into were with non-Jews. This was a clear sign that the age-old policy of ethnic segregation was breaking down among the Jewish population (personal communication with the author).

87 I am indebted to William Sheridan Allen for referring me to the book by Nathan A. Stoltzfus, based on his doctoral dissertation, *Resistance of the Heart: Intermarriage and the Rosenstrasse Protest in Nazi Germany* (New York: Norton, 1996).

88 The quotations from Marahrens are in Klügel, *Landeskirche*, 498–99.

CHAPTER SEVEN

THE 1933 BETHEL CONFESSION

A LUTHERAN CRITICISM OF NAZISM

The Bethel Confession was the first extensive manifesto written to evaluate the goals of the German-Christians in light of Christian doctrine, particularly as taught in the Sacred Scriptures and the Lutheran Confessions. Especially noteworthy was its courageous support of Jews in its discussion of the racial question. No other "confession" surpassed the Bethel Confession in this regard. Its most celebrated authors were Hermann Sasse, Dietrich Bonhoeffer, and Georg Merz, but they were assisted by several other noted theologians: Hans Fischer, Wilhelm Vischer, and Gerhard Stratenwerth.

WHAT IS A CONFESSION OF FAITH?

The Lutheran Church is a confessional church, that is, it is guided in theology and practice by certain written symbols or confessions that were prepared in the sixteenth century. These confessions were written by Martin Luther, Philip Melanchthon, Martin Chemnitz, Nicholas Selnecker, David Chytraeus, Christopher Körner, and Andreas Musculus. The documents were collected in 1580 and printed as *The Book of Concord*, a volume synonymous with the phrase "the Lutheran Confessions."

The *Oxford English Dictionary* (OED) defines a *confession* as "a formulary in which a church or body of Christians sets forth the religious doctrines which it considers essential; an authoritative declaration of the articles of belief; a creed."

The OED then notes that there were a number of Reformational and post-Reformational creeds among Protestants, the first of which was the 1530 Augsburg Confession.[1] The Augsburg Confession was prepared for the Imperial Diet of Augsburg, which was held in the spring and summer of 1530. This confession was an irenical document that tried to show that Lutheran teaching and practice were truly catholic and in line with the universal Christian church through the ages. Often called "the Augustana," this document was spurned by the Roman Catholic emperor and his ecclesial advisors. However, in 1555, during the Religious Peace of Augsburg, it was given legal sanction. This allowed churches that professed the 1530 Augsburg Confession to enjoy religious toleration in the Holy Roman Empire. This edict excluded the Reformed or Calvinist churches. Finally, in 1648, the Peace of Westphalia granted the Reformed churches similar toleration in the empire.

Between 1555 and 1648, some Calvinists, in a search for tolerance, claimed to accept the Augsburg Confession despite their doctrinal differences with the Lutherans, particularly the disavowal of the Lutheran teaching of the real presence in the Lord's Supper.[2] Wilhelm Niesel, the editor of a recent collection of the Reformed Confessions, writes as follows: "There is no such thing as a conclusive formulation of Reformed confessions and there is not a single confessional writing that is valid for all the Reformed churches."[3]

In Lutheran circles, confessions or symbols played a much more important role. During the formation of Lutheran territorial churches between 1530 and 1918, the confessions as contained in the 1580 *Book of Concord* had achieved the status of legal as well as religious documents and had become the basis for church-state relations. Although the Weimar Republic disestablished the territorial churches, the Lutheran Confessions continued to hold legal status, a situation that also prevailed during the Third Reich. It is striking to today's reader to see how often one of the Lutheran land bishops was able to prevail over the Nazi government by quoting from the Lutheran Confessions. Although the Union churches were by definition doctrinally ambivalent and ambiguous, they also learned to use the word *confession* in their struggles against National Socialism.

---

1 The statement of the OED is not completely accurate. The first of several documents that have come to be known collectively as the Lutheran Confessions were Luther's Large and Small Catechisms, which were written in 1529.

2 Accordingly, the new edition of the Confessions for the Evangelical Church of the Union (EKU) presents both the 1530 Unaltered Augsburg Confession and the 1540 *Augustana variata*; see *Evangelische Bekenntnisse: Bekenntnisschriften der Reformation und neuere Theologische Erklärungen: Im Auftrag des Rates der Evangelischen Kirche der Union*, ed. by Rudolf Mau (Bielefeld: Luther Verlag, 1997), 23–97.

3 *BSKO*, 333.

After all, every Union church had a plurality of Lutherans, though they were not permitted to express themselves as such.

The word *confession* experienced an inflation of meaning in the 1930s. During the Third Reich, many incidental doctrinal opinions were described as "confessions." For example, Karl Barth wrote some recommendations and called them his "Confession for the Church Election" of 1933,[4] and several German-Christians wrote their own "confessions." When employed by adherents of the Confessing Church, the gerund form of *confession* was used, implying that confession was an existential action of speaking out today rather than an adherence to the Lutheran Confessions of the sixteenth century. It almost seemed as if everything written by a member of the Confessing Church became *eo ipso* a new "confession." Thus from 1934 to 1936, Kurt Dietrich Schmidt was able to publish 700 pages of *Bekenntnisse*, or "confessions," from the *Kirchenkampf,* and many more "confessions" were written in the following decade. Obviously, the meaning of the word had been changed and the importance of the historical confessions of the sixteenth century had thereby been reduced and marginalized.

Could a new "confession" be formulated that might win the same reception as the old symbols? During the early years of the Third Reich, such attempts were made in meetings held at Bethel and Barmen. Eberhard Bethge, Dietrich Bonhoeffer's biographer, writes: "Someday the special task of clarifying the history of the Bethel Confession will be required. This would explain in a nutshell the powers, currents, and countercurrents which would later constitute the tragically divergent groups with and alongside the Confessing Church."[5] In his 1987 doctoral dissertation, Guy Christopher Carter undertook this task. Carter's work will be consulted in the present study of the genesis, course, and silencing of the 1933 Bethel Confession.[6]

WRITING THE BETHEL CONFESSION

The Bethel Confession took its name from the place where it was written. Located near Bielefeld (a city of several hundred thousand in northern Westphalia), Bethel was a famous institution of mercy that was founded in 1867. From 1872 until his death, Friedrich von Bodelschwingh (1831–1910) was its leader. After World War II, Bethel cared for more than 20,000 people. It provided a hospice; care for epileptics, the handicapped, those incapacitated by injury, and the mentally disabled; and a home for orphans and the aged. Bethel also sponsored a foreign

---

4 Schmidt, *Bekenntnisse*, 1:47.

5 Eberhard Bethge writes as the editor of *Gesammelte Schriften: Dietrich Bonhoeffer* (Munich: Kaiser, 1965), 2:80.

6 See p. 16 for bibliographic details.

mission station in Tanzania, offered programs to help the local poor, and conducted educational institutions, including the well-known Theologische Schule Bethel, a theological seminary. Bodelschwingh, the founder of "work therapy," believed that work was the best medicine and required that all the sick and handicapped people in his institutions be given worthwhile work according to their ability.[7] The stately Zion Church of Bethel employed outstanding musicians and was an important center of church music. The founder's son, also named Friedrich (1877–1946), succeeded him as head of the Bethel institutions in 1910. (After the second Friedrich's death in 1946, a third Friedrich, a cousin, succeeded as director of the Bethel institutions.)

The second Bodelschwingh was a highly respected theologian and church leader. As the choice of leading German churchmen for the position of Reich bishop, Bodelschwingh had assumed the office, though he was forced by the Nazis to resign and make way for Ludwig Müller, Adolf Hitler's choice. After his resignation, Bodelschwingh directed his activities toward preparing a new statement to meet the challenges of the time. He called a preliminary meeting at Bethel on August 5 with Bonhoeffer and Merz. (The latter was a young Lutheran theology professor at Bethel.) The need was expressed for a new Lutheran declaration that would answer the challenges coming from the German-Christians. The result of the meeting was summarized by Bodelschwingh in a letter written the same day to Pastor Georg Schultz at Barmen, the leader of the Sydowa Brotherhood:

> Over and over the wish was expressed that from the Lutheran Confession there might be a witness-type [*zeugnishaft*] response to today's problems, in order to provide a firm basis for the controversies, to which the isolated combatants might refer . . . . We united ourselves in the wish that a small circle of theologians might meet here and open this project.[8]

Immediately, steps were taken to provide that statement, which became known as the Bethel Confession.

There are several textual problems in discussing the Bethel Confession. In its original form, the document was circulated only in a hectographed copy. Both a preliminary draft and the final text (August 1933) of the Bethel Confession are given in the collected works of Dietrich Bonhoeffer.[9] After Sasse, Bonhoeffer, and their associates had completed their work, which came to be known as the August Confession, Bodelschwingh sent copies to a number of church leaders and theologians for comment. However, this effort to distribute a Lutheran confession to

---

7 On the elder Friedrich von Bodelschwingh, see the article by Gerhard Jaspers in *EKL*, 1:540–42.

8 *Bonhoeffer*, 12:503–4.

9 *Bonhoeffer*, 12:362ff.

a broad spectrum of Lutheran, Reformed, and Union spokesmen, including Barth and Adolf Schlatter, yielded only dissension. Barth branded the Bethel Confession as "too Lutheran"; Schlatter considered it too Barthian. Martin Niemöller was appointed to take stock of these contradictory votums and to edit the Bethel Confession for publication. His revision—called the November Text, the only one given in the widely used collection of documents from the *Kirchenkampf* compiled by Kurt Dietrich Schmidt—did not give a true picture of the original Bethel Confession, and Bonhoeffer repudiated it.

Niemöller made many substantive changes to the August Confession. In discussing the Reformation, where the August Confession had spoken of the renewal of the Gospel through Luther, Niemöller added "the second reformation" of Zwingli and Calvin. Niemöller stated that these men agreed with Luther on "the pure and unadulterated Gospel of Jesus Christ" but that their differences on Law and Gospel, the Lord's Supper, justification, and predestination presented "very grave and deep doctrinal differences" that made a union of the two evangelical churches impossible in the sixteenth century.[10] In the doctrine of the church's ministry, Niemöller gave the following statement from the August Confession: "We reject the attempt to transfer out of the natural world the modern *Führer* thoughts upon the Office of Preaching."[11] Niemöller almost immediately employed the "*Führer* word" again: "The bishop shall be the shepherd of the shepherds and a *Führer* to those who lead [*den Führenden ein Führer sein*]."[12]

Undoubtedly, Niemöller had been given an impossible task. He had been asked to reconcile the widely disparate amendments proposed by various writers, including those from the two archopponents Barth and Schlatter, both of whom were not Lutheran but Reformed.[13] The changes to the confession that resulted under the editorship of Niemöller yielded a document that pleased no one. Thus both principal writers of the original text, Bonhoeffer and Sasse, refused to endorse the November Text. Consequently, an important opportunity was lost for involving the large Lutheran majority in a united stand against the German-Christians and National Socialism, but that belongs to the subsequent history. For the purposes of the present study, our attention will be devoted primarily to the August Confession.

The suppression of the Bethel Confession is one of the greatest tragedies of the DEK in the Third Reich. Although the writers were all members of the Prussian

---

10 Schmidt, *Bekenntnisse*, 1:108.

11 *Bonhoeffer*, 12:398.

12 Schmidt, *Bekenntnisse*, 1:124.

13 On the opposing tactics of Barth and Schlatter concerning the Bethel Confession, see Carter, esp. 208–11.

Union (except for Sasse, who had grown up in the Prussian Union but had joined the Lutheran Land Church of Bavaria several months earlier upon his move to Erlangen), this confession could have been accepted by the overwhelming Lutheran majority both in the Lutheran churches and in the Union churches. Such action could have provided the solidarity that was so sorely lacking later in the Confessing Church. Not only did the Bethel Confession not receive serious consideration, it actually was suppressed by those with other theological agendas. Barth could not forgive the Bethel formulators for not adopting his opposition to the Lutheran doctrine of orders, and he succeeded in having the Bethel Confession replaced by a document that reflected his own personal theology, the 1934 Barmen Declaration. Thus Barmen rejected the Lutheran distinction between Law and Gospel and the two governances.

Barth's triumph at Barmen was a costly victory that would bring dire consequences for the church's impending resistance against Nazism. The Barthian theology of the Barmen Declaration hindered Lutherans from supporting it and from participating wholeheartedly in the Confessing Church. The dissension caused by these unresolved problems came to a head in the Fourth Confessing Synod of the DEK at Bad Oeynhausen in February 1936. There, the Confessing Church split into factions that were for or against Barmen. Whereas the Brethren Councils (*Brüder-Räte*) were to have spoken for all the churches of the DEK, the dissension at Bad Oeynhausen prompted the Lutheran land churches to establish their own Luther Councils (*Luther-Räte*) that accepted the Lutheran Confessions.

If the Bethel Confession had been adopted instead of the Barmen Declaration, these tragic developments might have been avoided. After all, Lutherans made up more than 80 percent of German Protestants, both within and outside of the Prussian Union. Carter notes that "on 28 November 1933, Bonhoeffer addressed a group of pastors in Bradford, Yorkshire. In his report on the heresy of the German-Christians, Bonhoeffer mentioned the confession which he, 'Merz und Sasse' had prepared but that had been 'frustrated' by Bodelschwingh and 'thwarted' by 'a couple of pastors.' "[14]

The August 1933 Bethel Confession was probably the best of all the doctrinal statements written during the Third Reich, but it was sentenced to a quiet death and to the forgetfulness of history. The Bethel Confession is not discussed at all in the important histories by Ernst Christian Helmreich, Heinrich Hermelink, Eberhard Klügel, or Kurt Meier.[15]

---

14 Carter, 266; Bonhoeffer quotation from Bethge, *Gesammelte Schriften: Dietrich Bonhoeffer,* 2:87.

15 A brief description of the Bethel Confession is given in Scholder, *Kirchen,* 1:578–82 (English ed., 1:455–58).

The Content of the Bethel Confession

The original August 1933 form of the Bethel Confession had the following contents:

I. Regarding the Holy Scriptures

II. What Is Reformation?

III. On the Trinity of God

IV. On Creation and Sin

    1. Faith in the Creator and Natural Knowledge

    2. The Orders

    3. The Law

    4. Sin

V. Concerning Christ

VI. On the Holy Spirit and the Church

    1. Regarding the Holy Spirit

    2. On Justification and Faith

    3. a) On the Church

       b) The Ministry and Confession

    4. Church and *Volk*

    5. Church and State

    6. The Church and the Jews

    7. On the End of All Things

According to marginal notations written on a copy of the November Text by Gerhard Stratenwerth, who was present at the meetings, Bonhoeffer and Sasse wrote part I, Merz authored part II, Bonhoeffer authored part III, part IV.1 to VI.2 was written by Bonhoeffer and Hans Fischer, Stratenwerth wrote part VI.3a, Merz authored part VI.3b, parts VI.4–5 were written by Stratenwerth, Wilhelm Vischer and Merz wrote part VI.6, and Stratenwerth wrote part VI.7.

Let us turn to a brief analysis of this document. The first article declares: "The Sacred Scriptures of the Old and New Testaments are the only source and norm of the church's teaching." This comes from the Prologue of the Formula of Concord (1577) and is not, in itself, an affirmation of the biblicism of Barth. The first article continues in a remarkable statement that asserts that the church itself is a part of divine revelation:

The Holy Scriptures are the only witness of the divine revelation. This has taken place in the unique, unrepeatable, and completed history, which has come to pass in the promise given to the fallen Adam and completed in the founding of the church. This history proclaims that the church is God's deed of revelation that is valid for us. In that the Scriptures testify to these deeds, it is the Word of God directed to us. Only in the exposition of the Scriptures can the church proclaim the revelation of God.[16]

Schlatter, the legendary New Testament scholar at the University of Tübingen, faulted the August Confession for what he perceived to be several negative qualities. Carter characterized Schlatter as one who

steadfastly defends natural theology versus the Bethel Confession's dialectical insistence on a single source of revelation in Christ. He does not care for the anti-*volkisch* tone of the Confession and seems to accuse the Bethel confessors of caring more about their bond with the Jewish Christians than they do about their kinship with other Germans.[17]

Merz later recalled that Schlatter had objected to the condemnation of other viewpoints and had added that "if any *damnamus* is to be pronounced, it ought to be against the 'Bonn heresy' [i.e., against Barth's rejection of all natural theology]."[18] Schlatter, who had been one of Althaus's teachers, offered the criticism that the August "Confession was 'fettered à la Barth' [*Barthisch gefesselt*]." Stratenwerth recalls his own fruitless efforts to disabuse Schlatter of his firmly held conviction that Barth was "a dreadful person [*ein schrecklicher Mensch*]."[19]

In view of the distortions of Christology by many German-Christians, the Bethel Confession makes strong statements concerning the death and resurrection of Christ. Part I, composed by Bonhoeffer and Sasse, staunchly attacks the German-Christian repudiation of the Old Testament.[20]

In part II, Merz discusses the question *What is Reformation?* In an obvious rejection of German-Christian teaching, he distinguishes the Reformation movement "from every Protestantism that identifies the church with some national, cultural, or religious movement." Merz insists: "The Reformation in its innermost being is the reflection upon the Holy Scriptures, submission to the Holy

---

16 The Bethel Confession has been translated into English from vol. 12 of *Bonhoeffer* (quotation *Bonhoeffer*, 12:363) with the permission of Augsburg Fortress. The Bethel Confession is a remarkable formulation of the Lutheran distinction between the Scriptures and the preached Word.

17 Carter, 117–18.

18 Carter, 117.

19 Carter, 118. Schlatter was not the only elderly theologian who had found Barth impertinent. Carl Stange remembered Barth as an arrogant and conceited younger colleague during the latter's four-year sojourn at Göttingen. Stange told me how, when the instructors of systematic theology were planning a mutual colloquium to discuss theological problems, Barth insisted that they discuss the Barthian system first. Stange regarded this as a serious departure from decorum and deference toward Barth's older colleagues. Carl Stange, interview with the author, in Göttingen, July 1957.

20 *Bonhoeffer*, 12:367.

Scriptures." In the church, Luther is "the teacher who is obedient to the Word of the Sacred Scriptures."[21] In the November Confession, Niemöller broadened this into a criticism of the Union churches:

> The attempts of later times to establish unity by artificially evading the truth and setting up unions that did not take the truth seriously enough proved unable, also in those cases where evangelical Union churches of various kinds came to pass, to establish a true unity of evangelical Christendom. . . . Out of this comes the painful fact that in present-day Germany the evangelical Christians are unable to give clear answers to the questions that are now placed before them.[22]

Many pastors and laypeople devoutly willed the dismantling of the Union churches and the restoration of the Lutheran and Reformed denominations. Even Barth saw a problem here. Carter writes: "Barth had stated, in his general observations, that the old problem of Lutherans and Reformed was going to have to be dealt with at some point."[23] Nevertheless, Barth approved the unionism expressed in the later Barmen Declaration, and his personal magnetism tended to draw men such as Martin Niemöller and Hans Asmussen away from their Lutheran roots and into positions that equivocated concerning the Lutheran and Reformed confessions.

Part III, "On the Trinity of God," is ascribed to Bonhoeffer. He supports the traditional doctrine of the Trinity with references to Luther's Smalcald Articles and Articles II and VIII of the Formula of Concord. He concludes: "We reject every attempt to tear asunder the revelation of the triune God and thus to try to conceive the creation, atonement, or redemption out of itself. Rather the triune God makes himself known to us alone in Christ."[24] This passage follows Luther's teaching that the *Deus absconditus* (the hidden God) has become the *Deus revelatus* (the revealed God) in Jesus Christ.

Bonhoeffer and Fischer are attributed to be the authors of parts IV to VI,2 in the August Confession. Part IV presents a lengthy discussion of creation and sin. It begins with the statement that God created the world at its beginning out of nothing and that we can learn this only by divine revelation of the triune God as the church teaches it on the basis of the Holy Scriptures. The attempt to know the

---

21 *Bonhoeffer*, 12:369.

22 Schmidt, *Bekenntnisse*, 1:108.

23 Carter, 192. When the Barmen Declaration was criticized as pointing to a new Union Church, Barth declared: "We do not want any Union" (Gerhard Niemöller, *Die erste Bekenntnissynode der Deutschen Evangelischen Kirche zu Barmen,* AGK 5 [Göttingen: Vandenhoeck & Ruprecht, 1959], 96). What Barth meant is a matter for the reader to decide.

24 *Bonhoeffer*, 12:370.

Creator from the contemplation of creation can only lead back to the *Deus absconditus*: "Faith and natural knowledge are therefore no longer one, since we live in a fallen world, that is, because the world is no longer the unambiguous and visible Word of God."[25] Because of the great fall, God is hidden from view: "In the fallen creation both God and the devil work in every happening." The Bethel Confession at this point insists that we can know God only through the Bible as it is proclaimed in the preaching of the church: "Solely from obedience toward the Word of God out of the Scriptures do we know the Creator, not out of some sort of interpretation of happenings in the world."[26]

Thinking to represent Luther's *Deus absconditus*, the August Confession calls this hidden God a *despot* or *tyrant*, a word that does not correspond with Luther's terminology.[27] For Luther, the *Deus absconditus* is not a tyrant or despot; he is unknown until he manifests himself in his plan of salvation. It is seen that his true nature has been hidden until it can be made known in divine revelation in Christ, who is *Deus revelatus*.

The Bethel Confession next presents a number of condemnations. Its writers rejected as false doctrine the opinion that the world of today expresses the creative will of God as it was before the fall and that, therefore, the world of today must be affirmed. However, though the world is fallen, this does not contradict the Lutheran concept that God still rules the world through the order of creation, despite sin. More to the point was an attack on the philosophical notion that life is a struggle for existence. The German-Christians were following the Nazi Party view that struggle and violence was the ground rule of creation, a concept that had more in common with Social Darwinism than with the Bible. The August Confession spoke out against this as follows: "We reject the false teaching that the fundamental law of the original creation is combat [*Kampf*] and that a combative behavior [*kämpferische Haltung*] is an established command of God from the original creation."[28] As we have seen, this position leads to a caution concerning, but not a rejection of, the concept of the order of creation. Before we consider this, let us turn to the concept of kairological time.

In chapter 5, the concept of the "historic hour" and decisionism is discussed. Carter observes: "Germany's 'historic hour' was constantly appealed to by NSDAP and GDC leaders alike, so much a part of the Nazi lingo that it is virtually impossible to associate the Bethel Confession's attack on the implications of this phrase with a particular figure."[29] It is noteworthy that the DEK constitution began with

---

25 *Bonhoeffer*, 12:371–72.

26 *Bonhoeffer*, 12:372.

27 *Bonhoeffer*, 12:373.

28 *Bonhoeffer*, 12:373.

these words: "In the hour in which God has let our German *Volk* experience a great historical turning point . . . ." The writers at Bethel replied: "We reject the false teaching that God out of a certain 'historical hour' speaks immediately to us and reveals himself in his creation by an immediate action, for it is enthusiasm [*Schwärmerei*] to want to learn the will of God without the external word of the Holy Scriptures, to which God has bound himself."[30] This example is cited: "God spoke, Let there be *Volk*! and there was *Volk* (Hossenfelder)."[31] The statement continues: "We reject as an enthusiastic interpretation of history the false doctrine that the voice of the *Volk* is the voice of God. The voice of the *Volk* shouted 'Hosanna' and 'Crucify him!' Then they all shouted: 'Not this one but Barabbas!' "[32]

In the second portion of part IV, the Bethel authors present a teaching on the order of creation that is rather critical of much that was being written at that time. Carter is not correct, however, when he writes that "the Bethel confessors [Bonhoeffer and Fischer ?] steadfastly rejected the orders of creation doctrine in any form."[33] Instead, the Bethel confessors criticized a distortion of the orders. Indeed, it must not be overlooked that Bonhoeffer taught the existence of the orders under his chosen term, "the mandates of creation," which he developed in his book on ethics. There Bonhoeffer lists the "mandates" as civil government, the church, marriage, and employment or labor.[34] The August Confession states that these "are not orders of the original creation" but orders of a fallen world. It lists the following orders: the sexes, marriage, the family, the *Volk*, property (employment and industry), and civil rule.[35] The unity of the human race has unfolded in the course of history in a plurality of tribes and peoples (*Völkern*): "Neither the Bible nor the Lutheran Confessions speak concerning an order of race." Of course, the Old Testament spoke of the presence of "the strangers within thy gates," for it specified, "He shall be treated by you as one of your native-born (Lev. 19:34)." These words, cited in the Bethel Confession, were obviously intended to apply to the presence of Jews among the Germans and to serve as a corrective for Nazi racism.[36]

---

29 Carter, 199. See the discussion of decisionism in chapter 5.

30 *Bonhoeffer*, 12:374.

31 Hossenfelder cited in *Bonhoeffer*, 12:374.

32 *Bonhoeffer*, 12:374.

33 Carter, 205.

34 Bonhoeffer, *Ethics*, ed. Eberhard Bethge, trans. Neville Horton Smith (New York: Macmillan, 1955), 207.

35 *Bonhoeffer*, 12:375.

36 *Bonhoeffer*, 12:376.

The following words seemed to be aimed against the doctrine of orders as believed by a Lutheran theologian such as Friedrich Gogarten: "We reject the false teaching that there are somehow permanent orders in this fallen world which were not placed under God's curse through the fall and that they may be recognized and affirmed as undamaged Orders of Creation in their original form." The Bethel confessors continued: "We reject the false teaching that a certain order of estates [*ständische Ordnung*, or class system] may be designated as God's Order of Creation," and they noted that in Luther's teaching the same person might simultaneously belong to several of the various orders or estates (domestic, political, and ecclesial).[37] As will be seen later in the chapter on the orders of creation (chapter 9), the theologians of the University of Erlangen confined natural knowledge to the Law. Since Barth rejected a Law distinct from the Gospel, he had no place for any knowledge of God's Law from nature. Within these parameters, the position of Sasse and Bonhoeffer did not differ greatly from that of Althaus and Elert. All these men differed fundamentally from Barth in recognizing an independent concept of the Law, together with the distinction of Law and Gospel.

Part IV,3 is devoted to "The Law." The Law is related to the orders as follows: "In the orders, the world is preserved according to God's will until the end. These orders are known equally among heathen and Christians. It is the Law which distinguishes among them. The Law is the personal address to mankind by God in his revelation." The Law is not something to be determined by the individual—it is the authoritative voice of God as given in the Bible. The same is true of the orders: "The Christian learns the Law of God only in the scriptural proclamation of the church. He therefore understands also the orders in which he lives as God's Law, only from the Holy Scriptures."[38] The Old Testament must not be relativized, as by way of a comparison; it must be allowed to stand alone as the subject of the church's proclamation. The discussion of the Law ends with a resounding rejection of *Volk*-law enthusiasm as it was held by men such as Wilhelm Stapel and Gogarten: "We reject the false teaching that the orders of God are one and the same as the law of the people [*der Völker*]." This is implied in the First Commandment of the Decalogue: "Its uniqueness consists in this: that in the First Commandment, every attempt is contradicted by which one might appeal to any orders as to laws of God." Because the first and second tables of the Decalogue are an indissoluble unity, "the Christian who would live obediently in the orders as in God's Law can do this only on the basis of the proclamation of the biblical Law."[39]

---

37 *Bonhoeffer*, 12:378. Thus there might be a personal union when one man was a husband and father, a citizen, and a pastor.

38 *Bonhoeffer*, 12:380.

39 *Bonhoeffer*, 12:381.

In the ensuing discussion of sin (part IV,4), the traditional doctrine of inherited lust (*Erbsünde*) and total depravity of every human being is presented. The numerous citations from the Formula of Concord highlight the distinctively Confessional Lutheran orientation of Bonhoeffer and Fischer, the authors. One can hear Bonhoeffer specifically in the following pithy statement: "The gnostic attempt to handle sin as a necessary thing gives an excuse for sin, makes white out of black, enables a person to justify himself, and thereby cancels the atonement by the crucificial death, removes the final seriousness from the contradiction of good and evil, and leads to the destruction of discipline."[40]

Part V of the Bethel Confession is devoted to the doctrine of Christ. After a statement of orthodox Christology, which concludes by quoting the famous explanation of the Second Article from Luther's Small Catechism, the confessors take direct issue with a statement by August Jäger, the Nazi *kommissar* for churches: "We reject the false teaching that the appearance of Jesus was a blaze of glory of a Nordic type in the midst of a tortured world suffering from the manifestations of decay." In opposition to the German-Christian penchant for Christ as a hero, the Bethel confessors declared: "We reject it as a false teaching that we have to confess ourselves to Jesus as Lord on account of his heroic piety. Alone, the one who was sent by the Father, the Son and Savior who for us was crucified and resurrected, is our Lord."[41] The article continues with a refutation of the German-Christian generalization of the cross as a symbol for the sacrifice of the German *Volk* for National Socialism. The article closes with a criticism of those who tried to make Jews solely responsible for the death of Jesus: "We reject the false teaching as though the crucifixion of Christ was the sole guilt of the Jewish *Volk*, as if other peoples [*Völker*] and races had not crucified him. All peoples and races, also the highly advanced, share the guilt for his death and increase their guilt daily if they despise the Spirit of grace (Heb. 10:29)."[42]

At the end of this treatise on Christology, the writers quote the words of Paul Gerhardt's Passion hymn: "What Thou, O Lord, hast suffered, I should myself have borne, For truly I am guilty Of all Thy grief and scorn."[43] This is an expression of Confessional Lutheran theology, which teaches both universal guilt and universal atonement. Accordingly, the guilt of all people, including Jews, was expiated by the death of Jesus, and Jews must not be singled out to receive all the blame for his crucifixion. Thus in Lutheran Sweden, where Nazi ideology was

---

40 *Bonhoeffer*, 12:383.

41 *Bonhoeffer*, 12:385.

42 *Bonhoeffer*, 12:386.

43 See *Lutheran Service Book* (St. Louis: Concordia, 2006), 450:3.

rejected and the doctrine of the universal atonement was upheld, Jews found a safe haven.

Part VI, which is devoted to the doctrine of the Holy Spirit and the church, rejects the enthusiasm of the German-Christians. Paragraph 1 voices the Confessional Lutheran position that the Spirit is given "only through the external Word [preaching] and Sacrament in the church." This is followed by an important restriction on the orders: "We reject the false teaching that the Holy Spirit is intelligible without Christ in creation and its orders; for the Holy Spirit always comes through the Son, in whom this fallen world is judged."[44] The folkish rebellion (*völkische Auflehnung*) against the doctrine that the Holy Spirit comes only through Christ is buttressed with this statement from Article I of the Augsburg Confession: "We reject all heresies which say that the Holy Ghost is a created impulse in creatures." Luther's Smalcald Articles (III, VIII) are further cited to oppose an enthusiastic view of orders: "God never gives his Spirit or grace except through or with the preceding external Word [preaching], so that we may guard ourselves against the enthusiasts, that is, the spirits who boast that they have the Holy Spirit without and before the [external] Word."[45]

In the presentation "On Justification and Faith," the writers contrast the Christian understanding of faith (*Glaube*) with the "God trustfulness" (*Gottvertrauen*) of Nazism as religious truth. The writers at Bethel affirmed:

> Against this, Christian faith is completely bound to Christ as the Word of God who goes with us into judgment, who lets us die before God, and who again calls us into life out of unseeable grace and power. Christian faith knows the wrath of God, remains in repentance, fears God, and receives his grace as the great miracle that the world cannot comprehend. Christian faith is therefore directed toward the end of the world.[46]

Here, the difference between Christian faith and German-Christian paganism had been made as clear as possible. In a statement aimed against a formulation of Reich Bishop Müller, the Bethel Confession stated: "We reject, as Israelitic thinking, the teaching that God in the last judgment will question a person only according to his 'decency' [*Anständigkeit*]." Müller's original statement had been: "On the judgment day the Lord God will not ask whether we were Catholic or Evangelical, but whether we have done our duty."[47] Although one might wince at this labeling

---

44 *Bonhoeffer*, 12:387. A critical theologian might object to subordinating the Holy Spirit to Christ as Barthian and might insist that the Spirit blows where he pleases (John 3:8).

45 *Bonhoeffer*, 12:387–88.

46 *Bonhoeffer*, 12:389.

47 The first statement is given in *Bonhoeffer*, 12:390; the second is given in *Bonhoeffer*, 12:390 n. 57.

of Müller's formulation as an "Israelitic" notion, one can scarcely suppress a smile over the poetic justice in relating the Reich bishop's comparison to the Judaism that he so cruelly persecuted. For the Bethel writers, such virtues as trust in God or a sense of duty may not be traced back to faith: "Faith, which is totally the work of God, does not look at its own fruits but alone upon its Lord."[48]

Next the writers take up the doctrine of church and ministry. The church cannot be understood by the eyes of the world but only by the eyes of faith. The church is the body of Jesus Christ and the communion of saints. They are saintly not because they are without sin, but because they are part of God's activating call: "Therefore, the church is a fellowship of the ungodly, that is, a fellowship of people who are lost. Through God's activation in his forgiving justification, that is, from the direction of God alone, the ungodly become children of God."[49]

Bonhoeffer, who had authored part III of the August Confession, prepared a revised form a few weeks later in which he added the following problematic statement: "[The church] stands under the killing and the vivifying Word of God—under his judgment, which is always simultaneously grace."[50] A bit of Barth's Reformed theology crept in at this point. Barth denied the Lutheran position that Law and Gospel could be distinguished, and he taught that the Law was only the "needful form" of the Gospel. The very fact that God speaks to us, even in judgment, is grace, according to Barth. The Lutheran position is very different, however. It teaches that the Law always kills and only the Gospel bestows mercy. Therefore judgment is not simultaneously grace. However, it must be remembered that Bonhoeffer, the systematician, was only 27 years old in 1933 and that, though he tried to be independent of Barth, he had been powerfully influenced by the Swiss theologian. Did Sasse know that Bonhoeffer had made such a change? If so, it must be remembered that Sasse, the church historian, was only 38 years of age and might have overlooked this alteration. At any rate, had the Bethel Confession received the discussion it deserved, Sasse's Erlangen colleagues, the systematicians Elert and Althaus, would certainly have pointed out this discrepancy.

Next, the doctrine of the church's ministry is discussed. In accord with the Lutheran Confessions, it is stated that the ministry was instituted by Christ to provide the preached Word and the Sacraments: "The ministry is not the property of any individual or any fellowship, but it is a fief of the divine Word, ordered by the commission of the Christian congregation." It is the task of the congregation to confess God's Word over against every distortion that arises. This duty of testing doctrine is the norm for the office of the ministry in the congregation.[51] Any

---

48 *Bonhoeffer*, 12:391.

49 *Bonhoeffer*, 12:391.

50 *Bonhoeffer*, 12:392.

attempt to base the authority of the ministry upon the Führer concept must be rejected: "The Office of Preaching is service in the Word of reconciliation, and therefore it stands in opposition to every kind of *Führer*-magic."[52]

The Bethel Confession denies that the church should conform to any particular outward norm: "According to the example of the apostles, it becomes 'a Jew to the Jews, a Greek to the Greeks,' a German to the German, a Chinaman [*sic*] to the Chinese, 'in order that some might be won.' "[53] The confession insists that "the boundaries of the church are never the same as those of the *Volk*."[54] At this point, the confession speaks against the words of Emanuel Hirsch, who had written in the sense of the German-Christians: "We have no inner right to try to prevent it that the Evangelical Church might become 'Church in the National Socialist State,' or Reich Church." Hirsch called for the incorporation of the Evangelical Church into the Nazi government and advocated implementing the Führer principle in church leadership to conform with the state.[55] The Bethel Confession retorts: "The church can never be dissolved within the state, which means it can never be 'built into' the state. It always remains opposite every worldly government because of the content of its proclamation."[56] There follows a bold statement of the role of the church in a totalitarian state, in which one seems to hear an echo of Sasse's critical view of Nazism:

> The ties of the worldly government with the church consist in this alone, that by the right proclamation of the church it is kept within the bounds of its own order and thereby will not become a tool of the devil, who in the end seeks only disorder, so that all life may be destroyed. Worldly government must expect only this service from the church. With this service, the church protects people who are under the government from the deceit of the devil, who would have them worship an unbounded government as giver of life and bringer of salvation.[57]

These, and the ensuing words, were a disclaimer of any theocratic function of the church in the secular state, a position that must have cut Barth to the quick. The church must never become "a state within the state." A blunt assertion is made: "We reject the false teaching of a Christian state in every form."[58] The

---

51 *Bonhoeffer*, 12:397–98.

52 *Bonhoeffer*, 12:398.

53 *Bonhoeffer*, 12:398–99.

54 *Bonhoeffer*, 12:399.

55 Emanuel Hirsch, "Die wirkliche Lage unserer Kirche," *Pastoraltheologie* 29 (1933): 182–85; cited in *Bonhoeffer*, 12:440 n. 71.

56 *Bonhoeffer*, 12:400.

57 *Bonhoeffer*, 12:401.

Bethel Confession declares: "The state cannot misuse the church as its moral religious foundation. It is an error that the church is the soul or conscience of the state."[59] The last traces of theocracy are rejected as follows: "We reject every attempt at establishing a visible kingship of God on earth by the church as an encroachment upon the order of government."[60] This was a sharp rejection of Barth's socialistic opinion that the state must become the agent in bringing into fruition the kingdom of God on earth.[61]

In section six came an important discussion of the sensitive issue of the relation of the church to Jewish people.[62] According to Eberhard Bethge, the first sketch for this section was written by Vischer.[63] Most of the opposition to anti-Semitism in this section was removed by Niemöller in his November version.[64] The original Bethel Confession affirmed that the Israelites were the chosen people of God. The Sanhedrin and the Jewish people had rejected Christ. They wanted a national Messiah who would free them politically and lead them to rule the world. But by his crucifixion and resurrection, Christ Jesus had removed the wall between Jews and Gentiles. The place of the covenant people of the Old Testament had now been taken by the Christian church, which is drawn "out of, and is in, all the nations."[65] Although most Jews had rejected Christ, God had not given them up but willed their redemption. The confessors at Bethel wrote:

> Therefore, God kept a holy remnant out of Israel according to the flesh, which would neither be dissolved by emancipation nor by assimilation into another nation, nor through a Zionistic or similar efforts to become one nation among others, nor could it be destroyed by the means of a Pharaoh. This holy remnant bears the indestructible character of the chosen people. The church has received the commission from her Lord to call the Jews to conversion and to baptize those who believe unto the forgiveness of their sins (Mt. 10:4f.; Acts 2:39ff.; 3:19–26). A Jewish mission which out of cultural or political considerations refuses to carry out Jewish baptisms refuses to obey its Lord.[66]

---

58 *Bonhoeffer*, 12:401. Hossenfelder, the leader of the GDC, had claimed that the church is "the soul of the nation" (*Bonhoeffer*, 12:402 n. 73).

59 *Bonhoeffer*, 12:401.

60 *Bonhoeffer*, 12:402.

61 On Barth's political theology, see the reference in chapter 1 to George Hunsinger, ed. and trans., *Karl Barth and Radical Politics* (Philadelphia: Westminster, 1976).

62 *Bonhoeffer*, 12:402–6.

63 Bethge, *Gesammelte Schriften: Dietrich Bonhoeffer*, 2:356.

64 Schmidt, *Bekenntnisse*, 1:127–28.

65 *Bonhoeffer*, 12:402–3.

66 *Bonhoeffer*, 12:403. Niemöller removed this entire paragraph in his November version.

The German-Christians had stated on May 6, 1933, that "the Evangelical Reich Church is the church of the German-Christians, that is, of Christians of Aryan race."[67] The Bethel Confession contradicts this position as follows: "The fellowship of those who belong to the church is not decided by blood and also not by race, but by the Holy Spirit." It continues in its repudiation of the notion that the DEK should be an Aryan church:

> We stand against the enterprise of turning the German Evangelical Church into a Reich Church of Christians of the Aryan race, and thereby to rob it of its promise. For thereby a law regarding race would be erected before the entrance to the church, and thereby such a church would itself be turned into a congregation of legalistic Judaizing Christians. . . . What is special about Jewish Christians is not based on their race or manner or history, but solely in the special faithfulness of God over against Israel according to the flesh. Thereby, in that the Jewish Christian is not directly placed in the church in some legalistic manner, he is a living monument in the church to the faithfulness of God and a sign for the fact that the wall between Jews and Gentiles has been torn down, and that the faith of Christ dare not be falsified in the direction of a national religion or a racially oriented Christianity. Christians who come from the Gentile world would sooner subject themselves to persecution than to give up, voluntarily or compulsorily, the churchly brotherhood with the Jewish Christians, which has been given through Word and Sacrament.[68]

The Bethel Confession closes with part VII, "On the End of All Things." The teaching here is traditional but marked by the modern emphasis upon eschatology as an event that is already underway: "Because the historical, the present, and the coming Christ is one and the same, therefore the end and judgment are also both present, and still to come, in him."[69]

The Bethel Confession clearly rejected anti-Semitic racism. One would seek in vain for such a statement in the vaunted Barmen Declaration, which contained little that spoke against the anti-Jewish stance of Nazism. In this respect, Barmen was a sorry substitute for Bethel.[70]

---

67 *Bonhoeffer*, 12:404 n. 80.

68 *Bonhoeffer*, 12:404–5.

69 *Bonhoeffer*, 12:404–6.

70 On the failure of the Barmen Declaration to speak against anti-Semitism, compare Simon, 31, who refers to this observation in two writers whom she identifies only as Röhm and Thiefelder.

CHAPTER EIGHT

THE 1934 BARMEN DECLARATION

A BARTHIAN CRITICISM OF NAZISM

L utheran church leaders wrote the Bethel Confession to overthrow the teach-ings of the German-Christians, but Karl Barth regarded the Bethel statement as "too Lutheran." Barth was an influential scholar whose theology in the 1920s had been widely beneficial in overcoming liberalism and leading people back to the Bible. Under Barth's leadership, a document called the Barmen Declaration was produced to supersede the Bethel Confession. Much has been written about the Barmen Declaration; it is not the purpose of this present study to repeat the familiar facts. Instead, the succeeding pages will focus on the controversies evoked by Barmen, why it was unacceptable to Confessional Lutherans, and how it damaged church resistance to the German-Christians and the Nazi Party.

THE FIRST BARMEN DECLARATION (JANUARY 3–4, 1934)

The city of Barmen was historically a strong center of the German Reformed Church. In 1929, the city merged with Elberfeld and Vohwinkel to form the new city of Wuppertal. There were two Barmen declarations issued in early 1934; both expressed the distinctive theology of Barth. The first was a purely Reformed statement; the second was a union declaration by Lutheran, Reformed, and Union church leaders. In these declarations Barth was proposing a unique doctrine of revelation to German theologians, a view that rejected all natural knowledge of

God and permitted a knowledge of God only from the Bible. He was successful in having his viewpoint accepted in both Barmen declarations.

The First Barmen Synod was a gathering of Reformed churches on January 3–4, 1934. To avoid controversy at the meeting, only those who were ready to declare, with Barth, that "the only source of revelation of our faith is the Word of God of the Old and New Testaments"[1] could attend. Following a paper by Barth, the delegates approved the first Barmen Declaration, which bore the following title: "Declaration over the Right Understanding of the Reformational Confessions in the German Evangelical Church of the Present."[2] The content of this statement differs from Lutheran thinking in that the Bible, rather than Christ, is seen as the source of revelation. This point would soon be modified in the second Barmen Declaration to read: "Jesus Christ, as he is witnessed to in the Holy Scriptures, is the one Word of God that we must hear . . . trust, and obey."[3] The first Barmen Declaration clearly confessed the theology of Barth when the synod declared:

> The 320 Reformed elders and preachers from 167 Evangelical congregations of Germany, assembled to a free Reformed Synod, proclaim that the paper that they have heard over the right understanding of the Reformational Confessions in the German Evangelical Church of today, written by Herr Professor D[r]. Barth, witnesses to the truth of the Holy Scriptures, and they gratefully receive it as their own responsibility.[4]

The first Barmen Declaration tried to counteract the German-Christians. In so doing, it called upon all the congregations of the Reich Church, regardless of their Lutheran, Reformed, or Union background, to affirm an essential unity "of their proclamation through preaching and sacrament, of their confession and of their tasks."[5] The Lutherans would be unable to ignore the significant doctrinal differences in these matters, however, particularly concerning the Lord's Supper. These were factors that raised the inevitable question whether such a unity did, in fact, exist. The demands of this Reformed document went even further: "Thereby is rejected the view that the justifiable representation of Lutheran, Reformed, or Union 'concerns' might be or must be elevated above the requirements of a common evangelical confession and action against error and for truth."[6] This prompts

---

1 *BSKO*, 328.

2 *BSKO*, 328.

3 *BSKO*, 335.

4 *BSKO*, 328.

5 *BSKO*, 329:25–32.

6 *BSKO*, 329:33–36.

the question: How could representatives from 167 Reformed congregations imagine that they could set the policies for tens of thousands of Lutheran congregations, thereby demanding that they set aside their own Lutheran doctrine and accept Reformed propositions? Nevertheless, the stage had been set for the second Barmen Declaration, which was to cause serious discord among the representatives of the Lutheran, Reformed, and Union churches for years to come. However, despite the objectionable features of the first Barmen Declaration, it must be recognized that it also spoke courageously against the biblical relativism and dangerous racism of the GDC.

THE SECOND BARMEN DECLARATION (MAY 29–31, 1934)

Preparations for the First Confessing Synod, which was to meet May 29–31, 1934, at Barmen, had been made by a hastily summoned committee of Barth, Hans Asmussen, Thomas Breit, and Hermann Sasse. One hundred thirty-eight delegates came to the First Confessing Synod from the Protestant land or provincial churches of Anhalt, Baden, Bavaria, Braunschweig, Bremen, Danzig (now Gdansk), Hamburg, the Lutheran Church of Hanover, the Reformed Church of Hanover, electoral Hesse, Lippe-Detmold, Mecklenburg, Hesse-Nassau, Oldenburg, Prussia with Pomerania, Rhineland, Saxony, Silesia, Wesphalia, the Free State of Saxony, Schleswig-Holstein, Thuringia, and Württemberg.[7] Those who came to Barmen bore a deep concern that the DEK was being taken over by the German-Christians and that the German-Christian program of seizing control of the separate land churches and incorporating them into the Reich Church (*Gleichschaltung*) threatened to destroy the independence and integrity of all the German Protestant churches. This set the stage for the First Confessing Synod at Barmen and for the promulgation of the Barmen Declaration.

This second Barmen Declaration also was built on the theology of Barth, who had an aversion to Lutherans.[8] The *Confessio Barmensis*, as Werner Elert dubbed

---

7 List in Hermelink, 114.

8 Barth's unreasoned hostility against Lutherans came out in a December 17, 1949, letter to Sylvester P. Michelfelder in which Barth gave his reasons for refusing to participate in the *Festschrift* for Anders Nygrén, noted Lutheran theologian and bishop of Lund, Sweden. Barth wrote: "I have so much against the German Lutherans (from Meiser to Schlink, from Althaus to Asmussen, from Gogarten to my old friend George Merz—with the exception of a few individuals like [Hans-Joachim] Iwand, Ernst Wolf, and Heinrich Vogel); their stubborn confessional romanticism, their obstinate connection with political reaction, their unenlightened ritual Romanising [i.e., Lutheran liturgy, church art, and church music], their poor showing in the Church Struggle, and now last of all their sabotage of the unity of the EKD through their separation into the

it, disregarded the Lutheran doctrine of Law and Gospel.[9] The confessional ambiguity of the Barmen Declaration, which recognized both Lutheran and Reformed symbols, was a further worry and fueled Lutheran concerns that a new Union church was being fostered. The declaration purported to give a single "confessional" statement that represented both Lutheran and Reformed, as well as Union, churches, with opposing theologies lumped together within a single statement.

The second Barmen Declaration consisted of six articles, each preceded by Bible verses. It incited significant controversy among the representatives of the Lutheran, Reformed, and Union churches, who might instead have worked together in combating Nazism. Many of the leading Confessional Lutherans, especially at Erlangen, rejected the Barmen Declaration. This document is well known, and we shall analyze it only in respect to the criticisms that it provoked. Of special significance is Elert's incisive essay "*Confessio Barmensis* [The Confession of Barmen]," which appeared in the June 29, 1934, issue of *AELKZ*.

The Barmen Declaration had stated: "Article 1: Jesus Christ, as he is witnessed for us in the Holy Scriptures, is the sole Word of God which we have to hear, and which we have to trust and to obey in life and in death."[10] Although this sounded like a brave battle cry against the enemies of the church, it contained several doctrinal aberrations. For example, in positing revelation solely in Christ, it rejected the theological concept of a natural revelation and a theology of creation, as well as the distinction between Law and Gospel. It replaced these Lutheran positions with a theocratic concept, which Paul Althaus dubbed a "Christocracy." This offended Lutheran theology, which, unlike Roman Catholic and Reformed teaching, rejects the concept of Christ as the "giver of a new Law." Elert objected: "The statement that no truth is to be recognized as God's revelation apart from Christ is the repudiation of the authority of the divine Law over against that of the Gospel."[11] Article 1 apparently identified both the Law and the Gospel with Christ.

VELKD." In this letter, Barth does not mention his deep aversion to the Lutheran office of bishop, which Nygrén happened to fill. The statement of Barth is from the papers of Anders Nygrén in Lund; copy in LWF Archives, Geneva. It is cited here from Jens H. Schjorring et al., ed., *From Federation to Communion: The History of the Lutheran World Federation* (Minneapolis: Fortress, 1997), 25–26.

9 The bitter animosity of Barth against the Lutheran distinction of Law and Gospel was expressed as follows: "Lutheranism created the atmosphere for German heathenism, and, with its separation of the Law from the Gospel, pointed it to its own sacred space" (cited by Horst Stephan, *Luther in den Wandlungen seiner Kirche*, 2d ed. [Berlin: A. Töpelmann: 1951], 92).

10 The Barmen Declaration appeared under the following title: "Theologische Erklärung zur gegenwärtige Lage der DEK 1934" (*BSKO,* 335–37; here, 335).

11 Elert, "*Confessio Barmensis,*" *AELKZ* 67 (June 29, 1934): 603.

THE 1934 BARMEN DECLARATION

When taken in the light of another statement by Barth—that "the Law is only the needful form of the Gospel"—these words moved toward antinomianism, that is, the abandonment of the Law in the proclamation of the church. It seemed to the Confessional Lutherans that if the Law is only a form of the Gospel that the Gospel is virtually identified with the Law, and both Law and Gospel are ultimately destroyed. This concern, which was voiced by the Lutherans, was not taken seriously enough by Barth and the supporters of Barmen. Thus Asmussen wrote in support of Barmen that the great fear was "to seek God without Christ," whereby Asmussen replaced a trinitarian concept with "Christomonism": "What we fear . . . is the fact that the creatures of God and the events of history will lead us into the temptation . . . to seek God, without Christ, out of them and in them. Always [!] where this takes place . . . one's own wisdom, one's own righteousness, one's own sanctification, and one's own redemption is carried out."[12]

Asmussen seems to be saying that whoever does not agree with the version of theology held by Barth and himself is guilty of a theology of human reason and good works. Asmussen, in the footsteps of Barth, is supporting a theology restricted to the Second Article of the Apostles' Creed on Christ and redemption. This refusal to deal with the First Article (the Father and creation) and with the Third Article (the Spirit and sanctification) seemed to reduce the Holy Trinity to the Second Person of the Godhead and to rob the adherents of Barmen of powerful tools against the ideologies of the German-Christians regarding *Volk*, race, and blood. Confessional Lutherans regarded these Nazi concepts as distortions of the article of creation and thought they could be corrected only by an authentic doctrine based upon the First Article. However, the supporters of Barmen vociferously rejected a theology of creation. It was declared at Barmen:

> Article 2: Just as Jesus Christ is God's promise of the forgiveness of all our sins, so with the same seriousness he is also God's powerful claim upon our whole life; through him we experience the joyful liberation from the godless ties of this world to free, thankful service to his creatures. We therefore reject the false teaching as though there are realms of our life in which we belong not to Jesus Christ but to other lords, realms in which we do not need justification and sanctification through him.[13]

Confessional Lutherans faulted Barmen for overlooking the doctrine of the two governances, for the declaration seems to have no place for God's kingdom of the left hand, or secular rule. Political power is described in Barmen as "godless

---

12 Cited by Ernst Wolf, "Königsherrschaft Christi und lutherische Zwei-Reiche-Lehre," in *Peregrinatio* (Munich: Christian Kaiser, 1965), 2:213.

13 *BSKO*, 335.

ties." Are not politicians thereby freed from all accountability? Lutherans held instead that political ethics should be placed under divine rule.

Elert presented two trenchant criticisms of Article 2. First, he noted its ambiguous language when it is described that Jesus Christ is "God's powerful claim on our lives." Pondering that this statement might be meant differently in relation to Ephesians 1:14; Galatians 5:24; or Matthew 16:24, Elert pointed out that in the context of Article 1, those words suggested that Christ was a new Law-giver, a Calvinist concept that is explicitly rejected in the Lutheran Confessions. Elert then examined the term "godless ties" to this world: "Are all ties to this world godless? Or only a few? Is the tie to every civil order godless? Or only to this one or that one, for example, the German one of today? Is every marital tie god-less, or only this one or that one?" Elert continued: "When it says here, 'liberation from the godless ties of this world to a free, thankful service to his creatures,' this can only have been meant in the sense of self-excluding opposites." Elert con-trasted this with the position of the Lutheran Confessions:

> If the word "godless" had not been there, one might think of the statements in the Lutheran Confessions according to which the believing Christian cannot, as a sinner, accomplish the demands of the Law, but fulfills them as a believer, "out of a free and joyful heart." But then the ties would have to be understood as ties from the Law of God and could not therefore be called "godless ties."[14]

Nevertheless, Ernst Wolf, the noted historian and follower of Barth, simply ignored Elert's brilliant criticism years later and defended this antipolitical article when he insisted that the totalitarian claims of the Third Reich conflicted with the totalitarian claims of Jesus Christ. Writing as late as 1965, Wolf lashed out against his Lutheran opponents as follows: "The Lutheran criticism of the formulation, 'godless ties,' signifies against this background the conscious or unconscious attempt to dilute the uncompromising sharpness of the contrast of the two con-flicting totalitarian demands; this is, however, possible at the expense of a privati-zation of the Christian life."[15]

The Confessional Lutherans objected that Wolf was making Christ a totalitar-ian tyrant by claiming that there are two opposing totalitarian systems and com-paring Christ and his totalitarian claims with those of Hitler. Wolf's statement dis-solves the distinction between the two governances and replaces it with the concept of a theocratic totalitarianism that, in overlooking the God-given respon-sibility of sound government, could hardly have dealt adequately with the Nazi

---

14 Elert, "*Confessio Barmensis*," 604.

15 Wolf, "Königsherrschaft Christi," 214. Normally a sharp and incisive thinker, Wolf was not at his best here. For a more balanced criticism of Elert's "*Confessio Barmensis*," see Meier, *EKK*, 1:194–96.

threat. The reader may well be surprised that these words were written by Wolf, a brilliant scholar, many years after the fall of National Socialism.

Elert also strongly objected to the Reformed doctrine of the church as presented in Article 3 of the Barmen Declaration: "We reject the false doctrine as though the form of her proclamation and of her Church Order [i.e., polity] had been left to be determined by the church according to prevailing ideological and political convictions."[16] Elert noted that this thesis conformed to the Calvinist teaching that the Bible commanded a certain form of church polity and labeled Lutheran practice a "false doctrine." Elert pointed out that the Lutheran Confessions (the Augsburg Confession and the Treatise on the Power and Primacy of the Pope) had left matters of polity and constitution to human discretion (*jus humanum*) and had assigned divine authority only to Word and Sacrament (*jus divinum*). Elert asserted that any Lutheran who signed the Barmen Declaration placed himself in contradiction to the Lutheran Confessions and historical facts.[17]

Elert remarked that the refusal of the Barmen group to relate its declaration to the important political changes that had taken place in the Nazi takeover of Germany belied the title of their work: "Theological Declaration to the *Present* Situation of the German Evangelical Church."[18] The framers of the Barmen Declaration, in discussing the new church order, had refrained from comparing it to the new civil order and had only referred to the latter as a "a change of political conviction [*Wechsel der politischen Überzeugung*]." Elert reminded his readers that one has to deal with church law and that church law stands in some relation to civil law. Just as the independent congregations that characterize American Protestantism are incorporated under the laws of their respective states—and must therefore adjust their local constitutions to meet the requirements of the civil government (for example, concerning the fiscal policies of a nonprofit organization)—so it was incumbent upon the German churches to adjust their statutes to meet the new legal standards. Of course, when these words were written in June 1934, neither Elert nor anyone else could envision the bumpy road over which the Nazi state would lead the churches in the eleven years to come.

> Article 4: The various offices in the church do not establish any authority of one above the other, but the exercise of the ministry entrusted and committed by the entire congregation. We reject the false doctrine as if the church, aside from this ministry, can give or allow to be given special ministries of leaders [*Führer*] that are equipped with authority to rule.[19]

---

16 *BSKO*, 336.

17 Elert, "*Confessio Barmensis*," 604.

18 Elert, "*Confessio Barmensis*," 604–5 (*Green's emphasis*).

19 *BSKO*, 336.

This article follows the Reformed tradition that claims certain forms of church polity are stipulated in the Bible. It seems to be leveled against the office of land bishop, which was developing among the Lutherans. Elsewhere in this work, it is pointed out that the democratic forms of polity advocated by Barth made the churches susceptible to political takeovers by the German-Christians and that the only large land churches that avoided incorporation into Hitler's Reich Church were those headed by the three strong bishops: Hans Meiser, Theophil Wurm, and August Marahrens.

Although Article 1 had limited the testimony of the Scriptures to the proposition that Jesus Christ is the only Word of God, the Barmen Declaration still had to come to terms with the place of civil authority. It continued:

> Article 5: The Scriptures tell us that the state, according to a divine arrangement, has the task in this unredeemed world, in which the church also stands, according to its measure of human insight and ability, to provide for justice and peace by means of the threat and exercise of force. The church recognizes, in thanks and reverence toward God, the benefit of this arrangement. The church reminds the people of God's Kingdom and of God's commandments and righteousness, and thereby of the responsibility of those who rule and those who are ruled. The church trusts and obeys the power of the Word, through which God supports all things.[20]

Elert applauded this felicitous inconsistency (*Beata, sancta inconsequentia!*) of Article 5 with Article 1, but added this comment:

> Here could and must be said in all clarity, in a "Theological Declaration Regarding the Present Situation of the DEK," that the church obligates its members to obedience toward the civil order. Instead of this[, the declaration] says that the divine arrangement of the state "reminds concerning God's Kingdom, God's commandment and righteousness, and thereby on the responsibility of those who rule and those who are ruled."[21]

Elert presses regarding the weak verb *reminds*: "The state 'reminds' of God's commandment. Why so diplomatic? Why is only the word 'arrangement' taken over from Romans 13? Why not also the phrase 'that the civil power is the minister of God'? If the civil power is also this, then it not only reminds of God's commandment but it also tells it to us."[22]

Barmen stated:

> Article 6: The commission of the church, upon which its freedom is grounded, consists in delivering the message of the free grace of God for all people, in the

---

20 *BSKO*, 336.

21 Elert, "*Confessio Barmensis*," 606.

22 Elert, "*Confessio Barmensis*," 606.

stead of Christ, and therefore in the ministry of his own Word and work, through preaching and sacraments. We reject the false teaching as if the church in human self-pride might place the word and work of the Lord at the service of its own desires, purposes, and plans.[23]

Elert remarks that Article 6 is irrefutable, but he mentions one further short-coming: "Unfortunately, one misses any instruction regarding the distinguishing marks by which the beginning and end of such human high-handedness is to be recognized in the church, as, for example, in regard to synods."[24] The last state-ment was likely intended as an attack upon the authoritative claims of the Con-fessing Synod of Barmen.

In his sharp rebuttal against the criticisms of the Barmen Declaration offered by Elert and Althaus, Wolf did not really deal with the problem of antinomianism but instead indulged in attacks upon the Lutheran distinction between Law and Gospel and the two governances. Wolf's essay seems to have been aimed at "dam-age control" in defense of the position of Barth and Barmen. It would have been more helpful had the supporters of the Barmen Declaration listened carefully to the Lutheran criticisms and responded to them constructively. Many Confes-sional Lutherans subsequently protested that though the Lutheran churches later found themselves pressured into adding subscription of the Barmen Declaration to their ordination pledges, from a Lutheran standpoint the Barmen Declaration stands in conflict with the teachings of the Lutheran Confessions that the ordi-nand pledges to uphold.

Two stalwart Lutherans who registered such complaints were Eberhard Klügel and Heinz Brunotte. Klügel published the following criticism of Barmen in 1964: "The question of truth was not solved in Barmen, but in some respects, first raised there. The actual problem of Barmen is the phenomenon of hearing the brethren one after another and then moving on together despite the deep, unre-solved dissent. The factuality of this dissent was artificially bridged over in the Declaration but not overcome."[25] Brunotte deplored the unwillingness to consider the Lutheran position on the part of the more strident Barmen supporters and wrote: "There seems to be an unwillingness on the part of some theologians to concede that the Lutherans offered genuinely theological arguments."[26]

The Barmen Declaration persisted long after the dangers of National Social-ism had ended in 1945. From a Confessional Lutheran perspective, Barmen seemed to reject any viable theology of creation and offered no provision for

---

23 *BSKO*, 337–37.

24 Elert, "*Confessio Barmensis*," 606.

25 Klügel, *Landeskirche*, 170.

26 Heinz Brunotte, "Barmen Declaration," in *ELC*, 1:194.

protecting the natural environment from the abuses of a technological society. Furthermore, by denying the ethics of the two governances, theologians consigned the German churches to developing a program of political activism out of Christology, that is, out of the Gospel instead of out of the Law. In the end, a theology of creation was replaced by an antinomianism that could offer no constructive arguments for the ecological problems of the twentieth century. It had lost the sense that "the earth is the Lord's and the fulness thereof" (Psalm 24:1) and the imperative for ecological concern and enviromental protection.

The radical position of Martin Niemöller and his Dahlem Front in the Confessing Church, especially their insistence that everybody must subscribe the Barmen Declaration, troubled many sober Lutherans. Martin Stallmann, a leader in the Conference of Evangelical Lutheran Theologians in Westphalia, wrote Asmussen on June 29, 1934: "Above all else, do not let the negotiations fall into the hands of Niemöller or the Berlin circle, for, if we follow their 'all or nothing' politics, everything will be lost."[27]

ALTERCATIONS BETWEEN CONFESSIONAL LUTHERANS AND UNION CHURCHES LEAD TO SCHISM IN THE CONFESSING CHURCH

The existence of the Union churches was a neuralgic issue for Confessional Lutherans. In 1935 there was an acrimonious exchange between defenders of the Prussian Union, on the one hand, and Confessional Lutherans, on the other. In February of that year, a document was published entitled "A Theological Consideration of the Conflict over the Union" ("*Theologische Bedenken zum Kampf um die Union*"). It bore the signatures of Wilhelm Lütgert, Barth, Friedrich Horst, Otto Weber, Ernst Wolf, Kurt Deißner, Rudolf Hermann, Erdmann Schott, Hans Wilhelm Hertzberg, Hans Freiherr von Soden, Friedrich Büchsel, Georg Wehrung, and Professor Otto Frommel of Heidelberg. All these men were either Reformed or were somehow connected with the Prussian Union.

The "Theological Consideration" excoriated theologians and church leaders who wrote critically of the Prussian Union and, in its own way, pleaded that past history be forgotten and that the Union churches be given more recognition and acceptance. For example, one thesis stated: "[8]. Is it rightly done when one emphasizes the theological problem of confessionalism, but hinders making the confessional heritage fruitful theologically, in consequence of a legalistic-rationalistic style of confessional subscription?"[28] This was apparently a slap at Luther-

---

27 Meier, *EKK*, 1:202. The controversies over Barmen were seemingly endless; see Meier, *EKK*, 1:192–203.

ans for expecting all pastors to affirm acceptance of the Lutheran Confessions because (*quia*) they agreed with biblical teachings. Many in the Union churches were willing to accept the Lutheran Confessions only "insofar as" (*quatenus*) they agreed with the Scriptures, an unacceptable position to Confessional Lutherans.

Friedrich Ulmer of Erlangen saw this "Theological Consideration" as an attack upon Confessional Lutherans and issued a sturdy reply: "7. It is not rightly done when one construes a possible case of a legalistic-rationalistic style of confessional subscription as the pattern in a church that after 1817 as well as before 1817 had committed itself to measure and still measures its confessional obligation on nothing else than the Holy Scriptures and the confessions of the church." Ulmer here was repudiating the accusations of some men in the Prussian Union that Confessional Lutherans were legalistic because they insisted upon doctrinal integrity and loyalty to the Confessions. In opposition to the tendency to call for a "German" evangelical church embracing all Protestants, placing nationalism above ecumenism, regardless of confessional differences, Ulmer emphasized the worldwide character of the church: "5. It is not rightly done when one sees the Evangelical Lutheran Church on German territory in an isolated sense and not as belonging to the Evangelical Lutheran Church in the whole world. Such a view is only possible from the isolated standpoint of the German Union church."[29] Ulmer saw some form of nationalism to be the unavoidable plight of the Prussian Union, which differed from the international nature of Confessional Lutheranism. After all, there was no Prussian Union outside Germany.

The plight of Lutheran congregations and pastors within the Prussian Union presented an awkward situation when plans were made for holding the German Lutheran Diet at Hanover in July 1935. At this meeting, Lutheran representatives from Prussia constituted a special Union Church Committee. One of the most noteworthy of the attendees was Detlev von Arnim-Kröchlendorff, a strong Lutheran layman, who said that in the struggle against the German-Christians "we need the sharp and cutting Luther-Confession, as it cannot be present in the Union. Confessional clarity cannot be born in a spirit that is filled with the atmosphere of the Union."[30] The Prussian Lutherans presented three resolutions. The

---

28 Schmidt, *Bekenntnisse*, 3:69.

29 Ulmer is quoted in Schmidt, *Bekenntnisse*, 3:86. It is worth noting that even Hans Ehrenberg, a pastor of Jewish descent in the Union Church of Westphalia, advocated a national church rather than a Confessional Lutheran church with ecumenical ties to other countries, thereby unconsciously supporting the goals of the GDC. See § 62: "Both sides in the conflict [that is, both for inclusion and exclusion of Jews in the DEK] desire a National Church" (Schmidt, *Bekenntnisse*, 1:72).

30 "The Basis for the Propositions of the Old Prussian Lutherans through the Chairman of the Old Prussian Committee," in Reese, 442 n. 57.

first was: "The representatives from the Old Prussian Union regard the continuation of the Union as neither desirable nor tolerable." The resolutions went on to call for "a grouping of the Brethren Councils [*Brüder-Räte*] in the Old Prussian Union according to the confessions as called for by the resolutions of Dahlem." In the second resolution, they insisted that the Lutheran congregations and synods within the Prussian Union must be represented in its council "by a Lutheran who accounts for the will of the Lutheran Church, just as the corresponding representation is guaranteed the Reformed." As long as this representation is missing, the Lutherans must be directed to the Lutheran member of the Provisional Church Leadership, High Church Counsellor Thomas Breit. Third, "the continuation committee of the German Lutheran Diet must set up directives for the arrangement of a confessionally bound church government for the Lutheran congregations in the Old Prussian Union and discuss its implementation with the Provisional Church Leadership." Hans-Jörg Reese finds it noteworthy that the initiative for a closer relationship between the Prussian Lutherans and the rest of German Lutheranism came from the Prussians themselves.[31]

In February 1936, at the Fourth Confessing Synod meeting at Bad Oeynhausen, the disagreements going back to Barmen came to a head. Julius Schieder of Bavaria made an impassioned plea to participants for an understanding of the Confessional Lutheran position,[32] but his entreaty seemed to fall on deaf ears. At Bad Oeynhausen, the Confessing Church split into many factions; consequently, the church's resistance to National Socialism was fragmented and lost its urgency. Brunotte, himself a leading member of the Confessing Church, in a rebuttal to the pledge of loyalty to the Barmen Declaration that was demanded by people of the Confessing Church, strongly warned the Osnabrück Circle against an exaggerated and unrestricted commitment to Barmen.[33] After the war, Brunotte commented that the Barmen group had never been willing to give serious attention to the valid problems concerning its declaration, which had been discussed by thoughtful Lutherans.[34] Lutherans had been asked to comment, and their suggestions should have been considered in a constructive manner. Instead, Brunotte noted that the side defending Barmen continually denounced their comments, as if Lutherans did not have the right to raise questions about the

---

31 Reese, 443.

32 See "Rede von *Oberkirchenrat* Schieder, Nürnberg," in *Zeugnisse der Bekennenden Kirche,* ed. Erik Wolf (Tübingen: Furche-Verlag, 1946), 58–62.

33 Heinz Brunotte, "Antwort auf die Osnabrücker Erklärung vom 29. November 1935," cited in Klügel, *Landeskirche,* 208–9, and nn. 197–99. See also Gerhard Niemöller, *Die erste Bekenntnissynode der Deutschen Evangelischen Kirche zu Barmen,* AGK 5 (Göttingen: Vandenhoeck & Ruprecht, 1959), 220–21.

34 Brunotte, "Barmen Declaration," in *ELC,* 1:193.

Barmen Declaration.[35] It is tragic that the Barmen supporters refused to acknowledge that some of the criticisms raised by the Council of the Evangelical Lutheran Church in Germany needed to be addressed and disdained the official response of the Lutheran Council.[36]

Little attention was paid at Barmen to the Bethel Confession of the previous year. Instead of providing a basis for united action against the common foe of National Socialism, Barmen divided those who might have worked together. The advocates of Barmen refused to listen to Lutheran objections that their declaration confounded Law and Gospel, rejected the two governances, and held "Christocratic enthusiasm." Instead, they condemned their Lutheran colleagues.

What led to the schism at Bad Oeynhausen? Wilhelm Maurer, a member of the Confessing Church, relates that "the First Provisional Church Leadership [*Vorläufige Kirchenleitung* (VKL)], presided over by Land Bishop August Marahrens, had admonished the leaders of the Confessing Church to confine themselves to the inward upbuilding of the congregations and land churches on the basis of the Scriptures and the confessions, and to wait to see what the Reich Church Commissions [*Kirchenausschüsse*] might accomplish."[37] However, this was not the way it was to go. More radical voices in the Brethren Councils declared the VKL incompetent because it "had cast aside" the decrees of the Dahlem Synod that established the Emergency Church Government (*das notrechtliche Kirchenregiment*) and, in so doing, "no longer stood on the

---

35 On July 16, 1936, a statement from the second VKL [*Vorläufige Kirchenleitung*] (Provisional Church Leadership) of the DEK denounced any who rejected the Barmen Declaration in the following statement: "Where the doctrinal decision of Barmen is not recognized, there one is abandoning the Reformational confessions" (Document 308 in Schmidt, *Dokumente*, 886). Unlike the moderates who constituted the first VKL, the people in the second VKL were members of the militant Dahlem Front. In their misplaced ardor, they overlooked the fact that they were making Barmen the arbiter, or *norma normans*, that declared how the Lutheran Confessions were to be interpreted. Lutherans have always rejected the possibility of such a "paper pope" and have held that the Bible is the sole norm for doctrinal statements.

36 The council of the Evangelical Lutheran Church in Germany, at a February 17, 1937, meeting in Berlin, formulated its position toward the Barmen Declaration. In its concluding paragraph, it said: "We deny that the fact that Lutherans, Reformed, and United people together wrote the 'Theological Declaration,' means that thereby a new Confession has arisen as the foundation for a new church. But we say with thanks that through the 'Theological Declaration,' every church of the Lutheran Reformation is also admonished thereby to take her Confessions really seriously, to let her doctrine, form, and order be determined by the Sacred Scriptures and the Lutheran Confessions, and thereby to testify that she is called at all times by her Confession to make a confession" (Klügel, *Dokumente*, 132).

37 Maurer, "Ausklang und Folgen des Kirchenkampfes," in *Tutzing*, 1:238.

foundation of Barmen [the Barmen Declaration]."[38] At a January 3, 1936, meeting in Berlin, a resolution was passed that "whoever cannot agree that the church must pronounce and carry out the repudiation of false doctrine in the sense of the Barmen Declaration" could not be allowed to speak or act on behalf of the Confessing Synod. Although this resolution was approved by seventeen voices—including Asmussen, Gerhard Jacobi, Heinz Kloppenburg, Wilhelm Link, Martin Niemöller, Reinold von Thadden-Trieglaff, and Gotthild Weber—eleven people opposed the resolution, including Karl Koch, Breit, Wilhelm Flor, Hugo Hahn, and Hans Freiherr von Soden. Soden protested that the resolution "implied a dogmatic condemnation or even an excommunication of those members of the- Provisional Leadership (*Vorläufige Leitung*) and the Reich Brethren Council (*Reichsbruder-Rat*) who might think differently regarding the way the Confessing Church should counter the measures of the state's Church Commissions."[39] It is evident that Soden presented a compelling argument. Had he been listened to, and had the Confessional Lutherans thereby been spared the accusations of the majority at Berlin, the ensuing breakup of the Confessing Church might have been avoided.[40]

THREE TENDENCIES
WITHIN THE CONFESSING CHURCH MOVEMENT

Although he had been one of the founders of the Confessing Church Movement, Walter Künneth was capable of a critical review of its history, and in his later years he gave an incisive description of three separate groups within the Confessing Church in the 1930s.

THE DAHLEM FRONT

First, Künneth discusses the Dahlem Front of the Brethren Councils (*Brüder- Räte*), which was largely present in the areas of the Prussian Union. This group, which emerged from the PNB, began with 2,000 pastors and increased to more than 7,000 members in 1934. Künneth noted that "these were the picked troops of inexorable opposition against the use of force by the German-Christians, the Nazi

---

38 Maurer, "Ausklang und Folgen des Kirchenkampfes," in *Tutzing*, 1:238.

39 The documents in Hermelink, 313–14. See the interpretation of this episode by Maurer, in *Tutzing*, 1:238–39. The list of participants is given in Meier, *EKK*, 2:405. An account of the January 3, 1936, Berlin meeting is also given in Reese, 380–84.

40 Bonhoeffer, who was usually balanced in his thinking, once remarked in a vein similar to the opponents of Soden that "whoever knowingly separated himself [from the Confessing Church] thereby separates himself from eternal salvation" (Meier, *Kirche und Judentum*, 23). Apparently Bonhoeffer was not present at this meeting.

Party, and the state." This group consummated the break with the puppet governments of the destroyed churches and replaced them with an Emergency Church Government and a Reich Brethren Council.[41] This circle educated theological students in its own underground seminary, maintained an illegal commission for the examination of its theological students (which included Künneth), and ordained its own candidates into the ministry. The Dahlem Front tended to make extreme judgments, so even Jochen Klepper, a man married to a Jewish woman and in constant conflict with the Nazi state, refused to work with the Confessing Church because of what he regarded as extremism in its leaders, including Niemöller, Bonhoeffer, and Helmut Gollwitzer. Klepper stated: "The 'confessing people' are also wrong when they too quickly and forcefully make themselves out to be martyrs instead of being thankful that preaching can still be done in Germany."[42] Klepper excoriated those "confessing people" who insisted that there must be no intercessory prayers for the Führer.[43] As we shall see, Friedrich Hauck, a schoolteacher in Erlangen, was ousted in the denazification process for offering the prayer "God bless the Führer" in those days.

THE LUTHER COUNCILS

The second group Künneth described were the Luther Councils (*Luther-Räte*) of the land churches of Bavaria, Württemberg, Hanover, Saxony, and Braunschweig, as well as Lutherans from the Union Church of Silesia under the leadership of Bishop Otto Zänker. After the abortive attempt to seize the Lutheran land churches of Bavaria, Wurttemberg, and Hanover, Hitler had formally received Bishops Hans Meiser, Theophil Wurm, and August Marahrens. August Jäger was forced to resign; Ludwig Müller, who refused to resign, was sidetracked; and the three land bishops set up a Provisional Church Government (*Vorläufiges Kirchenregiment*) that was carried on by the Brethren Council of the Confessing Churches and the Luther Council of the Confessional Lutheran land churches.

The chief leader of the Luther Council was Breit, a High Church Councillor (*Oberkirchenrat*) of the Bavarian Lutheran Church. The other Brethren Councils hurled harsh criticisms at the Luther Council and the intact land churches, claiming that they did not cooperate with them sufficiently. In defense of the bishops of the intact land churches, however, it must be said that conditions were different in the various regions, and the bishops of the land churches of Bavaria, Hanover, and Württemberg bore a primary responsibility to their own

---

41 Künneth, *Lebensführungen*, 118.

42 Künneth, *Lebensführungen*, 119.

43 Künneth, *Lebensführungen*, 119.

constituencies. Moreover, the confessional ambiguity of the Union churches placed grave obstacles before the Confessional churches because these Confessional churches needed to meet the requirements of their constitutions, which required fidelity to the Lutheran Confessions.

THE MIDDLE GROUND

Künneth identifies a third group that tried to stand in the middle between the Confessing Church and the DEK. This group insisted that whatever concerned the internal life of the church—its doctrine, proclamation, and diaconate—must be independent and free from interference from the government, but this group was willing to allow the state to take over matters of polity and external affairs. They were unable to make the decision to engage in the *Kirchenkampf* against the state, but they were totally against the German-Christians and their machinations.

Characteristic of this position was the October 1, 1935, inauguration of the Reich Church Commission (*Reichskirchenausschuß* [RKA]). Two important Lutherans who supported the new commission were Wilhelm Zoellner of Westphalia, who served as president of the RKA, and Theodor Heckel, leader of the Office for Foreign Affairs of the church. Both Zoellner and Heckel were roundly denounced by members of Niemöller's Dahlem Front as traitors to the Confessing Church. Künneth offers the following defense of Heckel: "As a member of the Young Reformation Movement he was no less against the German-Christians than the 'Dahlemites'; but the growing tragedy in his Berlin period was his great talent and readiness for diplomatic compromise," which overshadowed Heckel's theological gifts and his confessional loyalty. After the war, the more radical Confessing Church people continued to harass Heckel, but Künneth interceded for him with Meiser, who made Heckel dean of Munich. "There, with superior organizational talent and mighty labor, he brought about an outstanding and widely reaching reconstruction" of the church in the destroyed metropolis.[44]

Künneth concludes his sketch of the three groups of the Confessing Church with the observation that the intention toward compromise was a big mistake. One cannot make such a distinction between form and content or between organization and proclamation. In the end, all three groups were seriously impeded when the Nazi government seized control of church finances and thereby began to strangle the churches.

---

44 Künneth, *Lebensführungen*, 123–25.

THE FATEFUL SECOND SESSION
OF THE FOURTH CONFESSING SYNOD
OF THE PRUSSIAN UNION AT HALLE: MAY 9–12, 1937

It has been noted that the Prussian Lutherans, headed by the nobleman Detlev von Arnim-Kröchlendorff, had complained at the German Lutheran Diet at Hanover in July 1935 about being suppressed in the Prussian Union and had asked the assistance of other German Lutherans to help them find a hearing in their own church body. At the May 9–12, 1937, synod of the Prussian Union at Halle, Arnim-Kröchlendorff protested that the Lutheran congregations in the Prussian Union "are under the impression, and for a hundred years have been subjected to a legal policy, that their [Lutheran] confession is an unimportant matter, a matter which must be leveled off." He continued: "The Lutheran congregations say, 'We are Lutheran congregations, but no one gives us this legal right; and why should we struggle in a Confessing Church when no one gives us such a legal right that we might follow our claim?' "[45]

Obviously, many members of the Prussian Union within the Confessing Church were displeased by such a declaration and were unwilling to support the confessional rights of Lutherans who were willing to speak up. Actions taken by the Halle Synod greatly increased Lutheran distrust of the Prussian Union. In the past, the Prussian Union had been expressly an "administrative union" composed of discretely Lutheran and Reformed congregations that had retained their respective confessional identities, though Lutherans were not allowed to speak with a united voice. At that time, the Prussian Union stood in contrast to the "consensus union" found in other places, such as the land churches of the Palatinate or Baden, which were said to have merged Lutheran and Reformed doctrines. Confessional Lutherans had deplored that development, which they saw as the rejection of sound teaching and the espousal of doctrinal indifference.

It was acknowledged prior to the meeting at Halle that the Prussian Union did not have a satisfactory theology of the confessions when it accepted all the symbols of the Protestant Reformation, some of which contradicted others. The "Halle Resolutions" recognized three confessional positions. Lutheran congregations should confess the Unaltered Augsburg Confession, the Apology of the Augsburg Confession, Luther's Large and Small Catechisms, and the Smalcald Articles (ignoring the 1577 Formula of Concord, which had been aimed against the Reformed). Reformed congregations should confess the Heidelberg

---

45 Arnim-Kröchlendorff's statement is given in Gerhard Niemöller, ed., *Die Synode zu Halle 1937: Die zweite Tagung der vierten Bekenntnissynode der Evangelischen Kirche der altpreußischen Union. Text—Dokumente—Berichte,* AGK 11 (Göttingen: Vandenhoeck & Ruprecht, 1963), 267–68.

Catechism and, among the French Reformed congregations in Germany, the Confession de Foi. United congregations, if they were not inclined to one of these distinct positions, were to accept all the named symbols without understanding any of them exclusively of the others.[46]

During the church struggle, the tendency to gloss over confessional differences began to spread. Doctrinal distinctions came to be viewed as unnecessary and divisive. In 1937 Asmussen declared in a statement preparatory to the Halle Synod: "The division of the one church into different confessions is a work of the flesh which humans have accomplished under the seduction of the devil."[47] Asmussen demanded that the churches overcome their doctrinal differences and achieve an outward unity. A fateful step in this direction was taken by the Prussian Union in its May 9–12, 1937, synod at Halle. Steps were taken there that proved a serious hindrance to gaining the understanding needed between the destroyed churches in the Confessing Church and the intact Lutheran land churches.

The "Consensus on the Doctrine of the Gospel" that was adopted by the Halle Synod was based upon the preparatory paper given by Asmussen. The Consensus began with the claim that the Barmen Declaration "bears witness to the indispensable presupposition without which the confessions that are valid among us cannot be rightly taught and truly confessed."[48] This meant that the Lutheran Confessions should be reinterpreted to make them agree with the Barmen Declaration, which strict Confessional Lutherans rejected. It was added that because the Prussian Union was made up of congregations with differing "Reformational" confessional statements, this consensus was presented as a guide for collaboration among those who held diverging confessional positions.

In discussing the question of the confessions, the essayist began by noting that the confessions of Lutheran, Union, and Reformed congregations called the Holy Scriptures "the only rule and norm by which all doctrine and teachers are to be judged," a quotation from the prologue to the 1577 Formula of Concord. Almost immediately, the Formula of Concord, which had been directed against the Reformed, was shunned by the synod. The consensus stated that the Confessions of the Lutheran Church were "the Unaltered Augsburg Confession, the Apology, the Small and Large Catechisms of Luther, and the Schmalkald Articles." The Formula of Concord was intentionally omitted. For the Reformed, confessions were limited to the Heidelberg Catechism and, among the French Reformed congregations in Germany, the Confession de Foi. As to the Union congregations, it was stated that they followed the already named "Reformational confes-

---

46 See the insightful comments of Reu in *KZ* 61 (1937): 441.

47 Cited in Niemöller, *Die Synode zu Halle 1937*, 171.

48 Report of Reu in *KZ* 61 (1937): 440.

sions," insofar as they did not expressly accept one or the other confessional position.[49] Other confessions not named here, which might be held by some congregations, had to be reported within six months to the Brethren Council of the Prussian Union, which would then decide whether the confession could still be adhered to.

This claim of parity among contradictory Reformational confessions raised a serious problem already at the catechetical level. Luther's catechisms teach that the bread is the body of Christ; the Heidelberg Catechism teaches that the bread is not the body of Christ. The Halle Consensus said that Union congregations were to accept both the Lutheran and the Reformed catechisms "without understanding any of them exclusively of the others." So the official position was that the bread is the body and the bread is not the body of Christ. How was a layperson to understand this kind of double-talk? But such confusion had been going on in various forms since the founding of the Prussian Union, and this position would find official recognition after the war in the Leuenberg Concord.[50]

The Halle Consensus added that where confessional agreement as taught in the Barmen Declaration is not recognized, the validity of a Reformational confession cannot rightly be maintained. These words appear to make Barmen the arbiter of what the Lutheran Confessions are allowed to say and, beyond that, of what the Bible is allowed to teach.[51] According to the resolutions made at Halle, if a congregation in the Prussian Union wished to be called "Evangelical Lutheran," "Evangelical Reformed," or "Evangelical United," it must submit its request within a month to the Provincial Brethren Council, which would decide whether it was appropriate. Moreover, in the paragraph "Regarding Ordination," Lutherans were bound not only to all the Lutheran symbols except the Formula of Concord but also to the interpretations of the Barmen Declaration.[52] However, the following safeguard was given for Lutheran (as well as Reformed and Union) candidates: "At ordination, the candidate has the right to deliver his ordination vows before an

---

49 Report of Reu in *KZ* 61 (1937): 441.

50 Luther's Small Catechism: "Es ist der wahre Leib und Blut unsers Herrn Jesu Christi, unter dem Brot und Wein uns Christen zu essen und zu trinken von Christo selbs eingesetzt" (*BSLK*, 519–20). The Heidelberg Catechism questions whether the body and blood of Christ are present and replies in the negative: "Nein: sonder wie das wasser in dem Tauff/ nicht in das blut Christi verwandlet/ oder die abwaschung der sünden selbst wird/ deren es allein ein Göttlich warzeichen vnd versicherung ist (a) also wirdt auch das heilig brodt im Abendmal nit der leib Christ selbst (b)/ wiewol es nach art vnd brauch der Sacramenten (c)/ der leib Christi genennet wird" (*BSKO*, 168). For many in the Union churches, these contradictions seemed unimportant.

51 *KZ* 61 (1937): 441–42.

52 *KZ* 61 (1937): 443.

ordinator of his own confession; likewise, no ordinator can be required to ordain the candidate of another confession."[53]

The Halle Consensus dismissed the Formula of Concord as a case of theological bickering. It stated: "Where other confessions are in force [scil., the Formula of Concord], this must be reported by the pastors to the Brethren Council of the Evangelical Church of the Old Prussian Union within a half year. In case any objections are raised out of the Holy Scriptures against such confessions, the decision whether they may be retained any longer must be obtained from the Confessing Synod."[54] This allowed the Brethren Council of the Union Church to decide which confessions any Lutheran congregation might be allowed to retain. It was not hard to predict how this council—composed of Lutheran, Reformed, and Union members—would react to the Formula of Concord, which contains many criticisms of Reformed teaching and, by implication, forbids the Union Church. After all, the Prussian Union attempted to be a "confessing church" on the basis of Lutheran and Reformed symbols that contradict each other. With such a lack of doctrinal certainty, is it any wonder that the members of the Union churches lacked the strength to stand up to the Nazis and instead fell under their sway?[55]

The Formula of Concord teaches that no creeds or confessions but only the Sacred Scriptures are to be the "rule and norm" for judging doctrine. This later gave rise to the teaching in seventeenth-century Lutheran Orthodoxy that the Scriptures were the *norma normans*, the norm by which all doctrine is to be judged, and that creeds and confessions were only *norma normata*, that is, they held only a derived norm. No man-made creeds, not even the Lutheran Confessions, could hold any authority above that of the Bible.

However, the Halle Consensus declared: "The Confessing Synod of Barmen of the DEK (German Evangelical Church) bore witness in its 'Theological Declara-

---

53 *KZ* 61 (1937): 444.

54 *KZ* 61 (1937): 441.

55 Künneth was a pastor in the Prussian Union at the time of the 1937 Halle Synod. After the fall of National Socialism, he commented regarding the dire consequences of the doctrinal weakness of the Union church as follows: "The first blow from National Socialism was directed against the Evangelical Church in Prussia which, because of the lack of a unanimously bound and confessional character in its disunited institutional church, and because of the lack of churchliness of the population in Brandenburg and Vorpommern, seemed to be the least secure and the most susceptible to new ideas. In fact, the church bureaucracy and church leadership of the Old Prussian Union was not capable over against the onslaught of the German Christians" (*Abfall*, 208). Perhaps the lack of interest on the part of the people was partly the result of the arrogant bureaucracy of the Prussian Union, with its cavalier attitude and its repression of Lutheran doctrine as displayed at Halle.

tion' to the unavoidable presupposition without which the confessions that are valid among us cannot be rightly taught and cannot be truthfully confessed."[56] Therefore the Barmen Declaration seemed to replace the Bible as the normative norm (*norma normans*) in deciding the validity of the confessions that, according to Lutheran teaching, are the derived norm (*norma normata*). This implied that only the Barmen Declaration could determine the correct interpretation of the Sacred Scriptures or of the Confessions of the Lutheran Church. It appears that the Barmen Declaration had become a "paper pope" or legitimizer of doctrine.

The justification for this new norm was elaborated as follows: "Where the adherence to the Holy Scriptures and the confessions of the church, as they are attested in the 'Theological Declaration' of the Confessing Synod of the German Evangelical Church at Barmen for the warding off of contemporary false teachings is not recognized, there the validity of a Reformational confession cannot rightly be claimed."[57] Here, the authority of the Sacred Scriptures was subjected to the interpretations of Barmen. Interpretations by Confessional Lutherans who rejected the Barmen Declaration were declared invalid, regardless of the arguments presented. Had not the men of the Confessing Church seriously overreached themselves?[58]

Johann Michael Reu, writing from Wartburg Seminary in Dubuque, Iowa, noted that at Halle there had been a much more earnest spirit than was previously seen in the Prussian Union, but he objected that not only was the Barmen Declaration made equal at Halle to the Lutheran Confessions but also that the consensus claimed that nobody could rightly interpret the Lutheran Confessions unless the Barmen Declaration was followed. Reu concluded that "it is impossible for a Lutheran to go along with this."[59]

Nevertheless, the guidelines of the Halle Consensus were not forgotten. The DEK, which had fallen so miserably to Hitler's German-Christians, was rehabilitated after World War II as the EKD, which resurrected the concept of open Communion expressed at Halle and presented this position in the Arnoldshain Theses and the Leuenberg Concord. Under extreme pressure after 1945, the Lutherans who had resisted merger (*Gleichschaltung*) in the DEK came into the EKD and soon found themselves pressured into accepting statements that laid aside doctrinal differences and insisted upon intercommunion among Lutheran, Reformed, and Union churches.[60]

---

56 *KZ* 61 (1937): 440.

57 *KZ* 61 (1937): 441–42.

58 For an account of the mixed reactions to the conclusions of the Synod of Halle, see Reese, 470–75.

59 *KZ* 61 (1937): 445.

60 For a defense of the resolutions of the Synod of the Confessing Church at Halle by an avowed supporter of Barth and the Barmen Declaration, see Ernst Wolf in *EKL* 2:8–9.

Fig. 6: Karl Barth
(photo courtesy of Karlmann Beyschlag)

Fig. 7: Hans Asmussen
(photo courtesy of Karlmann Beyschlag)

CHAPTER NINE

THE DEBATE CONCERNING THE ORDERS OF CREATION

Bitter controversies occurred between Lutheran theologians and the group sur-rounding Karl Barth concerning the doctrine of creation and the place for nat-ural things in Christian thought. Lutherans affirmed the world of nature as part of God's creation and the consequent importance of sound environmental planning. Because God had created the earth, it stood to reason that traces of the Maker could be found in his creation. Lutheran theologians spoke of a natural knowledge of God. They believed that the Creator had made himself evident in nature and in human history. A love of nature was characteristic in Lutheranism since the days of Martin Luther and had been expressed in the great hymns of nature written by Paul Gerhardt and others. However, Barth's beliefs engendered from a postplatonic dualism, which accounted material things as inferior and only spiritual things as good. Barth and his followers blamed Lutherans for their view of a natural knowl-edge of God and claimed that the Lutheran concept of orders, as well as the writ-ings of Luther, provided support for the German-Christians and the Nazis.[1]

Confessional Lutheran theologians during the Third Reich held that they represented Luther's thought when they spoke about the three natural orders of creation: marriage and the family, the civil government, and the church and its ministry. Thoughtful dicussions on the natural orders, sometimes substituting

---

1 Barth was joined in his denunciations of Luther by other writers, such as William Inge and William Shirer, who claimed that Luther was responsible for the rise of National Socialism and its atrocities. For a scholarly reply to some of these insinuations against Luther, see Uwe Siemon-Netto, *The Fabricated Luther: The Rise and Fall of the Shirer Myth* (St. Louis: Concordia, 1995).

other terms, were published by men such as Friedrich Gogarten, Emanuel Hirsch, Dietrich Bonhoeffer, Franz Lau, Paul Althaus, Werner Elert, Emil Brunner, Walter Künneth, and Hermann Sasse. To the previously named orders, Bonhoeffer added economic production and labor, and he seriously pondered whether "race and blood" should also be included.[2] In the vigorous debates that ensued, all sides appealed to the authority of Luther. But where did Luther really stand in these matters? This chapter explores to what extent such a theology of orders can really be ascribed to Luther, as well as how much of the twentieth-century theology of orders might have been an invention of the times or even a distortion of Luther. It will be evident that Lau presented a sober picture of Luther, which differed from the common perception of that time, and that some of the prominent writers distorted Luther in their teaching on the orders of creation.

LUTHER AND THE ORDERS OF CREATION

The debate over Luther's position regarding the orders of creation is meaningless if it is not placed within the larger context of his teaching as a whole. This means that it must be related to his dialectical distinctions between Law and Gospel, between the hidden and revealed God, and between the absolute and ordained power of God. An important part of Luther's consideration of these matters has come to be known as the doctrine of the two kingdoms. However, Luther did not speak of two kingdoms but of two regiments or governances.

The terminology of "two kingdoms," which was introduced into the discussions during the twentieth century, can be misleading for two reasons: first, because it has been twisted by some to make it appear there are two separate kingdoms with God in control only of the spiritual realm and with the civil governance operating autonomously and independent of divine control; and, second, because the concept of "kingdom" is susceptible to theocratic distortions. The notion of two independent kingdoms is wrong not only because of the way Luther's thought was distorted in the Nazi conception of an autonomous state that was independent of God but also because it violates Luther's cardinal rule as it was especially brought out in *Bondage of the Will:* that God works all in all. This means that any view that makes civil government independent of divine jurisdiction falls far short of Luther's understanding.[3] For a presentation on the power of God (as absolute and ordained power) in Luther, the discussion can be turned to the exposition of Lau.

---

2 *Bonhoeffer*, 12:410.

3 Bernhard Rust, the Prussian Minister for Cultural Affairs, excused the June 1933 takeover of the Evangelical Church of the (Old) Prussian Union on the ground that the state assumed control only of "matters of the earthly organization" of the church and

In 1933 Lau published the book *"Outward Order" and "Worldly Thing" in Luther's Theology.*[4] Lau was an independent and impeccable scholar who in this book produced one of the finest recent works about Luther. When one reads Lau, one has the sense that he does not describe the orders in Luther's work to meet some political agenda of 1933 but presents sober and impartial scholarship that serves as a corrective to the writings of his more subjective fellow scholars. Noting that Luther did not use the term "orders of creation" at all, Lau steadfastly refuses to put words into Luther's mouth. Instead, Lau bases the title of his book on two concepts of Luther that related to the concept of the orders: external orders and worldly things.

Lau shows how Luther had distinguished between the absolute power of God (*potentia Dei absoluta*), under which God is almighty and is remote from humankind, and the ordained power of God (*potentia Dei ordinata*), by which God enters human affairs, saves his people from their sin, and works through his creatures in maintaining and governing the earth.[5] In this ordained or transferred power given to men, God works in the external orders, or, as Althaus called them, the orders of creation. The prime example of God's working through human agency was in the incarnation of the Son, Jesus Christ, when God became man, born of the Virgin. According to Luther, "the ordained power is fulfilled in the incarnate Son."[6] God's ordained power currently extends to his creation by the agency of pastors, parents, and civil magistrates (the three estates of Luther). The gift of salvation won by the incarnate Son is made available in the church through the pastors. When the means of grace are presented through pastors, God is working salvation through human instrumentality; for example, the ordained power of God works salvation for humankind through Holy Baptism. Luther states: "It is his will for us to operate according to his ordained power."[7] This is how the ordained power of God is carried out by men in the church. Other or similar cases

---

did not interfere with the actual life of the church, its "faith and confession." Here we are confronted with the false dichotomy or dualism that has distorted Luther's distinction of the two governances. In Luther's understanding, both governances were subject to the Law of God, and there was no outward aspect of the "spiritual kingdom" that was placed under the "secular kingdom" in the sense in which Rust interpreted matters. This false interpretation of the two-kingdoms concept was actually closer to Reformed theology, with its divorce of the finite and the infinite (*finitum non capax infiniti*). This Reformed position was held by Barth and was rejected by Lutheran writers such as Elert, Althaus, and Lau.

4 Original German title *"Äußerliche Ordnung" und "weltlich Ding" in Luthers Theologie*; see p. 18 for bibliographic details.

5 Lau refers to Luther, *Lectures on Genesis*, WA 43:71.7–16.

6 WA 43:73.3–4.

are given in the order of marriage—through which God carries on procreation through a man and a woman—and the rule of God exercised through the civil authorities. All civil power is an ordered or ordained power derived from God's absolute power and is granted by God alone to the government.[8] Any civil ruler who claims to hold absolute authority is in conflict with God, according to Luther.

Luther gives the following axiom in his *Lectures on Genesis* (1535–1545):

> The rule therefore remains, concerning which I spoke above, that God no longer wishes to work according to extraordinary things or, as the sophists express it, his absolute power. But he wishes to work through his creatures, whom he does not wish to become idle. Thus he gives food, not as when he gave manna from heaven to the Jews in the wilderness, but he gives it through labor, when we diligently carry out the work of our vocation. Nor does he wish to make more men out of clay as he did with Adam, but by the union of a male and a female, whom he blesses. This they call the ordained power of God, namely, when he employs angels or men in his work.[9]

Luther adds one of his scintillating axioms: *Quae supra nos: nihil ad nos*, that is, "The things that are beyond us are of no concern to us." This means that we are not to seek God outside his revelation in the incarnate Son and in the Scriptures. For God does not deal with us according to his majesty (*potentia absoluta*), but he condescends to meet with us in earthly forms, such as Word and Sacrament in the church. And God meets us in the earthly orders of family, government, and church (*potentia ordinata*).[10] Lau gives the following picture of the orders of civil government, marriage, and spiritual authority in Luther:

> Under temporal gifts, civil government is the greatest of all. With almost offensive language, Luther established the validity of worldly forms of community living simply because of their need for the continuance of life and their indispensability. And this constant speaking about the indispensability of civil authority, of marriage, and so forth, is not something preliminary, after which he will come to speak of the godliness of these establishments in another sense. No—the statements about the timeliness, bodily character, and indispensability of the Life Orders are already completed descriptions of that which was said in the first part. Thereby stands the exclusive working of God in his creatures, in that he provides temporal peace and outward order for them in the most outward sense possible.[11]

---

7 WA 43:71.27–28.

8 Citation of WA 18:275.16–28 in Lau, *"Äußerliche Ordnung,"* 26–27.

9 WA 43:71.7–13.

10 WA 43:71.18.

Lau asserts here that marriage or civil government, as physical arrangements and in their own right, are divine gifts, without any added spiritual embellishment.

However, the orders of marriage, government, and church are also subject to misuse. This occurs when a person who holds power in one of these orders imagines that he has absolute power, which belongs only to God, rather than ordained power, which God has entrusted to humanity in the order of creation. Such misuse of power is idolatry. Lau discusses such demonizing of earthly power, the misuse by men of the powers ordained by God when they begin pridefully to disregard God and to regard the power entrusted to them by God as being by their own authority.[12]

A misuse of the orders occurs when one confuses the human order (*ordinatio humana*), which is based on natural law, with the divine order (*ordinatio divina*), which rests upon divine Law. Both divine Law and natural law are from God, but divine Law represents the *potentia divina absoluta* and is not accessible to men. To usurp what God has kept for himself is an act of revolt against God and is reprehensible. However, God has reached out to his creation in his *potentia divina ordinata*, and it is here, in the orders, that God has placed man the creature. Man does not have any jurisdiction related to divine Law, but God has empowered man to work within the orders, which fall under natural law. Men are to attempt only to work within the orders that have been entrusted into their hands and to disavow any usurpation of the authority God has reserved for himself.[13]

---

11 Lau, *"Äußerliche Ordnung,"* 26–27. One of Lau's pupils makes a statement that is perplexing when she writes: "With Lau, the Kingdom of God on the left hand and the Kingdom of God on the right hand are relatively independent—in this he stands close to Ernst Troeltsch. [Martin] Schmidt draws from this the conclusion that thereby the modern secularization of the state and of the world are made understandable" (Ingetraut Ludolphy, "Franz Lau (1907–1973): Kirchenhistoriker und Anwalt evangelischer Diaspora," *JMLB* 48 [2001]: 205–18; this citation, 211). Surely neither Lau nor Schmidt meant to infer that the civil government was autonomous from God's Law. Instead, Schmidt's comment seems to be aimed against theocratic enthusiasm.

12 Lau, *"Äußerliche Ordnung,"* 72–73. One might note, parenthetically, that this could be the man who abuses his wife or children, the ruler who becomes a tyrant, or the pastor who corrupts his office by false doctrine.

13 Lau discusses these matters with generous citations from Luther; see *"Äußerliche Ordnung,"* 72–73. It might be added that the matters discussed in church law in the Lutheran sense belong to the *potentia ordinata,* under which one distinguishes between *jus humanum* (matters in which the human members of the church are free to make their own rules according to the law of love) and *jus divinum* (matters that God alone decrees, such as Word and Sacrament), in which God himself works through human agency and concerning that which man does not have the right to change.

As we shall see, critics of Confessional Lutheran theologians objected that they taught an autonomy (*Eigengesetzlichkeit*) of the orders without God, that is, that the people who set up the specific orders wrote their own rules and then claimed divine sanction for the rules they had written. Actually, some misguided Lutherans during the 1930s did teach that the Nazi understanding of *Volk* was an order of divine creation and that laws decreed by men regarding *Volk* bore the authority of God's Law. In other words, some claimed that the questionable decrees of the Nazis held divine authority. Nonetheless, it was a grave error when this misunderstanding was ascribed by some to Luther.

We have just learned from Lau that Luther's distinction between the absolute and the ordained power of God forbade man to confuse divine and human authority. For man to claim for his laws the aura of divine authority was blasphemous. Luther stated in his *Lectures on Genesis:* "They call it the ordained power of God when, namely, he uses the service of angels or of men." Luther adds: "Thus it is the ordained power of God when water moistens, fire burns, etc. But in Babylon, the friends of Daniel lived unscathed in the middle of the fire. This was the absolute power of God, according to which he did it, but he has not commanded us according to this. He wants us to do according to his ordained power."[14]

One concept of Luther that was later reflected in the modern theology of orders was his understanding of the "three estates": the spiritual, the political, and the marital.[15] But he also spoke of only *two* estates. In his discussion of Baptism in the Large Catechism, Luther named two divinely instituted estates: parenthood and temporal authority.[16] In his expositions of the First Article of the Creed and the Fourth Petition of the Lord's Prayer and in both the Large and Small Catechism, Luther discussed further how God provides for his people by means of *three* estates. These estates, or *Stände* ("standing places"), were not exclusive. They did not comprise a rigid caste system, as in the Hindu religion. The housefather not only begat his children and provided for their needs (economic estate), but he also ruled his family (civil estate) and taught them from the catechism (spiritual estate). In his *Lectures on the Psalms of Ascent,* delivered around 1533 but first published in 1540, Luther named *two* authorities, the civil and the economic (family), but he also noted that God made man "in his own image." Luther concluded: "This text clearly shows that God divinely implanted in man both law and science, agriculture, medicine, and other arts."[17] Nevertheless, Luther did not employ the term "orders of creation," and one must be careful not to impute later concepts to him.

---

14 These references are from WA 43:70.13–14, 71.25–28, respectively.

15 "Great Confession on the Lord's Supper (1528)," WA 26:504–5.

16 *BSLK,* 694.

17 WA 40/3:222.22–23.

When the orders of creation were elaborated upon during the Third Reich, and even augmented by the addition of controversial new "orders" such as *Volk* and race, the danger was real that Luther's views on the orders might be severed from the theonomous laws of the Creator and replaced by autonomous human laws, such as the corrupt laws of the Nazi state (a so-called *Eigengesetzlichkeit*). In all candor it must be said that not only writers such as Gogarten and Hirsch, who were more open to German-Christian notions of race and blood, but even men who were strongly opposed to German-Christian positions, such as Bonhoeffer and Elert, spoke of race and blood as orders of the Creator. For example, Bonhoeffer wrote in his 1933 "Theses on the Aryan Paragraph": "Race and blood are one among the orders in which the church enters, but they dare never become the criterion for belonging to the church: that is only the Word of God and faith."[18] Obviously at this time in his career the young Bonhoeffer was relatively unaffected by the theology of Barth, who lashed out vehemently against any suggestion of a theology of orders. And Elert carefully differentiated a sound view of race and blood from the strange teachings of the German-Christians, as is seen in his book *Bekenntnis, Blut und Boden* (*Confession, Blood and Soil*).[19]

Why did the debate on the orders of creation become so acrimonious during and after the Third Reich? The disagreement rested partly upon the doctrinal differences between Lutheran and Reformed teachings. The Neoplatonic rule *finitum non capax infiniti*, that is, "the finite cannot contain the infinite," had been prominent for centuries among the writings of some Reformed spokesmen. This dictum manifests itself in a strong tendency to downgrade earthly things and to exalt what is invisible. This philosophical presupposition was implicit when Zwingli taught that an earthly element cannot convey a heavenly gift, thus rejecting Luther's insistence that the consecrated bread in the Supper is the very body of Christ. Calvin inveighed against any teaching that would degrade the body of Christ by enclosing it in sacramental bread. One suspects that behind all this lay the doubt whether one could really say concerning the incarnation of Christ that "the Word *became* flesh" (John 1:14) or whether one should instead alter the words to say that "the Word *assumed* flesh." Such dualism, in which the material is evil and the immaterial is good, seems to underlie much of the thought of Barth and some other representatives of Reformed theology, and it made them unable to deal with a theology of creation.

Lutherans have emphasized that the Word *became* flesh, that the bread in the Supper *is* Christ's body, that the incarnation and the Sacrament have given dignity to the material creation, and that the pursuit of natural science is the study of the

18 *Bonhoeffer*, 12:410.

19 See p. 16 for bibliographic details.

things that God has made, a walk in the steps of the Creator. It is not surprising that out of the strong interest among Lutherans for natural science as the study of divine creation a whole theology of creation and natural orders should have developed. This chapter investigates these matters, particularly as they were developed by the Erlangen theologians during the first half of the twentieth century.

A Theology of Orders as the Rejection of Neoplatonic Dualism and as an Expression of the Theology of Creation

The First Article of the Apostles' Creed declares: "I believe in God the Father Almighty, Maker of heaven and earth." Therefore the theology of creation is often called the "theology of the First Article," which has been characteristic of Protestant theology for centuries. Lutheran theology at its best has held a positive view of the "Article of Creation" and the natural orders, often called the orders of creation. Among Reformed theologians, Emil Brunner strongly affirmed the orders of creation, whereas Barth vehemently rejected every form of a theology of nature. Lutherans argued that if God (the Creator) had indeed created the world (his creation), it would follow that one could learn about the Creator by studying nature (natural science; natural knowledge of God) and that if God still controlled the course of history (divine providence), one could find traces of God's providence in the pages of history as well.

Under the twin concepts of the Law-Gospel distinction and the dialectic of the two governances, Lutheran theologians categorized natural theology under the "Law" knowledge gained by human reason, in contrast to the "Gospel" truth that can only be learned by divine revelation in the incarnate Christ. This placed the study of natural science under natural law, or the temporal realm, and thereby freed scientific studies from the theological strictures of the spiritual realm. As Sachiko Kusukawa has convincingly demonstrated, this Law-Gospel distinction gave early Lutheranism free course for the study of natural science, so places such as the Universities of Wittenberg and Tübingen became spawning grounds for emerging new concepts, such as the Copernican theory. Scholars such as Philip Melanchthon, Georg Rheticus, Erasmus Reinhold, Leonhard Fuchs, Michael Maestlin, Tycho de Brahe, and Johann Kepler flourished under the intellectual freedom provided by the two-governances ideology of the Lutheran Reformation, and they paved the way for the so-called scientific revolution of modern times.[20]

---

20 Sachiko Kusukawa, *The Transformation of Natural Philosophy: The Case of Philip Melanchthon*, Ideas in Context (Cambridge: Cambridge University Press, 1995).

One finds First Article thought not only in the doctrine of natural revelation among the older dogmaticians but also in Lutheran devotional materials, in hymnody, and even in church music; see, for example, the poetry of Paul Gerhardt, Matthias Claudius, Jochen Klepper, and Rudolf Alexander Schröder, and the musical compositions of Johann Sebastian Bach.[21] This consciousness of the presence of God in creation also underlies the understanding of history among Lutheran writers such as Georg Hegel and Leopold von Ranke in the dictum "History is the passing of God through the world."

What became known as an organic view of history could also lead to a wrong direction, of course, as in the case of Social Darwinism and National Socialism, which maintained doctrines of history as a biological struggle in which the strong must overcome the weak, insisted that the survival of the "fittest" would lead to the emergence of a master race, were prejudiced against non-Aryan peoples, and advocacated eugenics and "ethnic cleansing"—notions that burgeoned in the Third Reich. But this danger might appear in any worldview in which an excessive homage is paid to biology.

As was suggested above, Lutheran writers from 1528 to 1842 continued to consider ethical matters under these three orders or estates.[22] However, one does not find a fully developed doctrine of orders before the Erlangen theologian Adolf Harless (1806–1879). In his epochal 1842 *Christian Ethics*, Harless introduced a concept of the divine orders imbedded in creation. He wrote that not only the orders of God in creation but also certain human orders are embraced in the divine will. For scriptural basis, he cited 1 Peter 2:13 as it was interpreted in Luther's translation and in the 1611 Authorized Version.[23] Harless defined the orders as marriage and the family, the political entity, and the church.[24]

---

21 In their hymns, Gerhardt, Claudius, and Schröder all expound the beauties of nature; see also Johann Sebastian Bach, Cantata 17, "Wer Dank opfert, der preiset mich," which is an exposition of the Lutheran doctrine of the First Article. See also the first recitative: "The whole world must become a silent witness of God's lofty majesty; Air, water, firmament and earth When their Order is held as in ropes . . . ." See also the first aria: "Lord . . . If I did not otherwise know how gloriously great Thou art, I could easily perceive it in Thy works. How could one but ever be praising Thee? Thou who also dost show us the way to salvation." All of this is strikingly un-Barthian.

22 I have found a number of works espousing the three estates or orders written by sixteenth-century Lutheran writers whose works are collected in the Herzog-August Library in Wolfenbüttel, Germany. See, for example, Johann Spangenberg, *Des Ehelichen Ordens Spiegel und Regel . . .* (Nordhausen, 1544), and Hieronymus Weller, *Pius et eruditus libellus, De Officio ecclesiastico, politico, et oeconomico* (Nuremberg, 1552).

23 Harless, as well as Elert, *BBB*, 28–29, appealed to 1 Peter 2:13 as an important proof text for the theology of orders. Luther translated this in the 1544 edition of the German Bible as follows: "Seid unterthan aller menschlichen Ordnung um des Herrn-

LUTHERAN REJECTION OF THE GERMAN-CHRISTIAN INTERPRETATIONS OF THE THEOLOGY OF ORDERS

Certain German-Christians developed their own version of the orders of creation in a way that supported the teachings of National Socialism. Their interpretations were challenged by Elert in an August 26, 1939, address in Vienna in which he cited these words from Article XVI of the Augsburg Confession: "Regarding political matters and civil government, it is taught among us that all authority in the world, and orderly government and laws, are good order, created and established by God." Elert continued: "From these words, the expression 'orders' has taken its place in the terminology of our theological schools, which in recent years has brought on an inflation of investigations over the 'Orders' of God, Orders of Creation, and the like." Noting that it was understandable that this problem had occupied people's thoughts since "the great political change" of 1933, Elert nevertheless issued this caution: "It is a question whether and in which sense we are supposed to use the term 'orders' in our situation."[25] Elert was pointing to the fact that the German-Christians had all too eagerly borrowed the concept of orders of creation. In their "inflation" of the doctrine, they sought to provide theological support for the Nazi ideology of *Volk* and race. Elert and Althaus cautiously discussed the proposed new "orders" in writings that were rather skeptical but that also recognized that *Volk* and race were in some way connected with humanity and its Creator, as Bonhoeffer also admitted. Although one's people and one's nationality are a part of how one was created by God, these factors are hardly a legitimate part of the orders of creation, and their inclusion soon raised serious problems and stirred a heated controversy.

One of the principal men who supported German-Christian thinking and who was involved in developing the biological concept of *Volk,* thereby asserting an autonomous *Volk* law, was Wilhelm Stapel (1882–1954). Stapel was born in Salzwedel in the Altmark and came out of a Lutheran church within the Prussian Union. A layman, he was a philosopher, art historian, religious writer, and journalist who pursued a rather tragic professional course. Stapel should not be called a theologian because he never undertook the formal study of theology and he lacked a systematic structure in his spiritual thought, but he had by his own read-

---

willen." The 1611 Authorized Version of the Bible followed Luther: "Submit yourselves to every ordinance of man for the Lord's sake." Some recent New Testament scholars have rejected this interpretation.

24 Gottlieb Christoph Adolph von Harless, *Christliche Ethik,* 7th ed. (Gütersloh: Carl Bertelsmann, 1875), 490–92 et seq.

25 Elert, *Stand und Stände nach lutherischer Auffassung* (Berlin: Verlag des Evangelischen Bundes, 1940), 8.

ing amassed considerable knowledge of religious matters. Stapel's exceptional competency in the history of German art represented his vocational specialty, but he also was a specialist in Germanic linguistics, which he combined with a mixture of religious liberalism, a romantic concept of "German *Volkstum*," a vehement German nationalism, and a popular religious activism unconnected with the church. Beginning in 1912 with his writings on Johann Gottlieb Fichte (1762–1814), Stapel promoted nationalism until he had become an important supporter of National Socialism.

Did this make Stapel a "political theologian"? The term "political theologian" has been used rather carelessly to decry leading Lutherans during the Third Reich. They might better have taken a hint from Elert, who wrote in a typically wry formulation, that "political theology—or antipolitical theology, which is the same thing—and theological politics—or antitheological politics, which is also the same thing—lie together in today's struggle." His was the sage observation that both the Barmen group and the German-Christians were essentially political theologians.[26] Nevertheless, partisan historians have singled out certain individuals as political theologians while overlooking others and notably omitting the most political theologian of them all, Karl Barth. Accordingly, Klaus Scholder lumps together Stapel, Hirsch, Gogarten, and Althaus and dubs them "political theologians" as if they all shared the same position, which is, of course, misleading. This is not a sound historical procedure.[27] Hirsch, Gogarten, and Althaus had widely differing approaches; moreover, as we have already noted, Stapel was a layman, not a theologian at all. However, theologians felt challenged by Stapel and constrained to respond to his radical positions. Althaus reacted negatively to Stapel, whereas Hirsch and Gogarten replied more positively. Hirsch and Gogarten wrote on *Volk* and race as early as 1914. In August 1916, Althaus delivered a paper at a pastoral conference in Lodz, Poland, in which he lamented the loss of a German identity among the clergy and laity in the Lutheran churches in Poland and advocated that a sense of their belonging to the German *Volk* be inculcated in the congregations.[28] Eleven years later, in June 1927, Althaus presented his much-discussed paper entitled "Church and *Volkstum*" at Königsberg.

Stapel tended toward extreme and one-sided positions. In 1915 he published an essay entitled "Why I Do Not Pray to God But to the German God."[29] In the

---

26 Elert, *BBB*, 7.

27 Scholder, *Kirchen*, 1:125–26, 130–32, 134–35, 140–42, 149–50, etc.

28 "Die Stellung der Kirche im Volksleben," in Althaus, *Stunde*, 55–60. The notion that an immigrant Lutheran congregation in another country must retain its German character would not be popular in the modern United States.

29 From the journal *Christliche Welt*, vol. 4 (1915), cited in Wolfgang Tilgner, *Volks-*

1920s Stapel was calling for the annexation of Austria, the eastward expansion of Germany, steps to control the influence of Jewish people, and the rejection of Western democratic ideas.[30] One of his most dangerous teachings was that the Law of God is identical with the law of the *Volk*, that moral instruction as a part of *Volk* law should be carried on not by the church but only by the state, and that the church should avoid teaching the Law and stick to the Gospel alone.

Althaus carried on a courteous but critical dialogue with Stapel in which Althaus displayed his gentle humor:

> W. Stapel has set up a formula for peace, of Solomonic wisdom: "morality is the concern of the *Volk* and of the state"; "the state has the right to assume the moral education of the *Volk* in its full totality"; to the church belongs "all that has to do with its confession to Jesus in word and work." "Thereby there is no conflict between state and church. A conflict can arise only where one of these powers invades the territory of the other."[31]

Althaus refuted this with the observation that the teaching of both Law and Gospel belonged to the church and that the church could not abdicate its responsibility to proclaim the whole counsel of God by handing over the teaching of the Law to the civil authorities.

Gogarten had started out in the dialectical group of theologians surrounding Barth, but like Brunner, he later moved away from Barth. Gogarten was a much more balanced person than Stapel, with whom, however, he was briefly associated. Althaus presented this account of Gogarten's position, with which he then sharply differed: "Gogarten has declared: 'The law is given to us in our *Volkstum*' and emphasized that in this he 'simply agrees' with Stapel. According to this, the perception of the law is the concern of the state."[32] Althaus protested that

> the demands on the people by the state and the church do not agree so smoothly and obviously as it would appear in Gogarten. Gogarten presents a peace without struggle by materially turning the law over completely to the state and entrusting to the church merely the testimony concerning the radicality of the Law as it witnesses to the Gospel. . . . I do not believe that one serves the present hour when one conceals the ever new task of the relation of church and state with overly simplified theories.[33]

---

nomostheologie und Schöpfungsglaube, AGK 16 (Göttingen: Vandenhoeck & Ruprecht, 1966), 92 n. 13.

30 From the journal *Christliche Welt*, vol. 4 (1915), cited in Tilgner, *Volksnomostheologie und Schöpfungsglaube*, 95–96.

31 Althaus in *Luthertum* 1, no. 1 (1934): 24; quotations from Wilhelm Stapel, *Die Kirche Christi und der Staat Hitlers* (Hamburg: Hanseatische Verlagsanstalt, 1933), 63–64.

32 Althaus in *Luthertum* 1, no. 1 (1934): 22.

33 Althaus in *Luthertum* 1, no. 1 (1934): 25.

Althaus was making the point that any claim for folk *nomos* to represent the divine Law must be tested against the Law as given in the Sacred Scriptures. In other words, an autonomous law was not acceptable and the theonomous orientation of the law must be maintained. Of course, this refutes the charge against Althaus of teaching the autonomy (*Eigengesetzlichkeit*) of the orders of creation. Althaus showed how the church can teach only a theonomous law in his 1935 book *Theology of Orders*:

> It is not self-understood that *Volk* law always respects the established norms in God's revelation: the holiness of life, also in its embryonic stages, the holiness of lifelong monogamy, and the sovereignty of the Creator, who alone establishes for our life its goal and limits and who forbids suicide as well as euthanasia and the destruction of so-called worthless life. Human reason might here, under certain conditions, consider the opposite to be meaningful and advisable. It requires the criticism that comes from God's Word. Therefore, Christian criticism of the orders is necessary and possible.[34]

Althaus explicitly warned "that we must not allow the orders to be yielded to a secular autonomousness without God [*Eigengesetzlichkeit*]."[35] Eight years after the fall of Hitler, Althaus warned in his book on ethics that the "world orders" might, "under the life of a sinful humanity," be robbed of their connection with creation and be "corrupted from being the means of life into becoming idols and tyrants."[36]

A few words must be said about the "racism" of Stapel. Although in the 1920s Stapel was advocating steps to control the influence of Jewish people, he was not really an anti-Semite. Concerned by what he regarded as an excess of Jewish political and financial power, which he thought was detrimental to Germany, he called for the supremacy of German *Volkstum* and advocated sending the Jewish people out of Germany and establishing a new Zionist state for Jews. Later, when he saw his arguments used by the Nazis to justify persecution of the Jewish people, Stapel was horrified and denounced such anti-Semitism. The National Socialists then turned against Stapel, and in 1938 they shut down his periodical, *Deutsches Volkstum*. After he was ostracized by the Nazis and until his death in 1954, Stapel had little following. However, he published several books on other topics in his final years, which Elert recognized rather cordially.[37]

---

34 Althaus, *Th. Ord.*, 39; see p. 15 for bibliographic details.

35 Althaus, *Th. Ord.*, 44.

36 Althaus, *Grundriss der Ethik*, 2d. ed. (Gütersloh: Carl Bertelsmann, 1953), 111.

37 In a review of Stapel's *Über das Christentum* (Hamburg: Agentur des Rauhen Hauses,

CONFESSION, BLOOD, AND SOIL:
ELERT'S REJECTION OF THE TEACHINGS OF BOTH BARMEN
AND THE GERMAN-CHRISTIANS

In 1934 Elert published a pamphlet under the arresting title of *Bekenntnis, Blut und Boden* (*Confession, Blood and Soil*). In the vilification of Elert since 1945, this small book has been widely cited as an example of Elert's accommodation to the Nazis and the German-Christians. Many critics of this book seem not to have read Elert carefully enough. *Bekenntnis, Blut und Boden* is directed against two targets: (1) the writers of the Barmen Declaration (the *Bekenntnis* or *Confession* component) and (2) the German-Christians (the *Blut und Boden* or *Blood and Soil* components). It is a book about confession, on which subject Elert speaks against those who misuse the confession of the church, and about the authentic meaning of blood and soil against the German-Christians, who misuse those concepts. Under *blood*, Elert discusses the true meaning of family and blood relationships, and under *soil*, Elert means the earth as God's creation. Essentially, *blood* and *soil* stand for heredity and environment. Elert's presentation is a strong repudiation of the fanatical prating about blood and soil by many German-Christians.

The first chapter bears the title "Die Schicksalsbindung an Blut und Boden." *Schicksal* in this context might be interpreted as follows: "our being bound to blood and soil by those circumstances that were given us." The word *Schicksal* is difficult to translate into English; some have misinterpreted it to mean "blind fate," which is completely wrong. A much closer translation comes from the fifth definition of *ordinance* in the *Oxford English Dictionary*: "That which is ordained or decreed by the Deity . . . a dispensation, decree, or appointment of Providence or of Destiny." In Elert's theology, the word *Schicksal* is derived from the word *schicken* and means what God has given us before and after our life began—we might say, colloquially, "our giv'ns." Compare the hymn "Herr, wie du willst, so schick's mit mir" ("Lord, as thou wilt, deal thou with me").[38] *Schicksal* includes the "giv'ns" of stature and weight, sex, race, nationality, health, mind and intellect, talents, degree of wealth, and the time in which one lives. To translate this into American thought categories, we might use the terms of heredity and environment to get the sense of Elert's "blood and soil."

Let us examine *Bekenntnis, Blut und Boden* more thoroughly. Observing that everybody is setting up battlefronts against others, Elert calls it demonic and

---

1951), Elert praises this layman for his knowledge of theology, history of religion, and German linguistics. Elert's review is in *Lutherische Rundschau* 2 (1952): 38–39.

38 *The Lutheran Hymnal* (St. Louis: Concordia, 1941), 406:1. Cf. "Der Krieg ist Schicksal, Schickung von dem, der über uns allen ist" (Schäfer, *Württemberg*, 6:840).

adds: "Over against this it is the task of theology to uncover the demonism of such battlefronts and to lead back again to the point."[39] Regarding *Bekenntnis*, or confession, Elert states that this is the main concern of theology, which prompts the question "But what has it to do with blood and soil?" Elert says that revelation is "the appeal of God from another world into this our world, which is characterized by 'Blood' and 'Soil.'" Our speech about revelation is "speech regarding people in whom earthly Blood circulates and who stand upon earthly Soil, and therefore all theological talk must carry the earthly scent of this world of Blood and Soil."[40] Having now defused these rather electrifying terms, the rest of the pamphlet is a refutation of the claims of the German-Christians, and where he talks about confession, Elert rejects the Barmen Declaration and the Confessing Church circle that supports it.

The reality of a natural revelation of God was accepted by both Althaus and Elert. However, whereas Althaus taught that not only a negative revelation (Law) but also a positive knowledge of God from nature and reason may serve as a preparation for the Gospel, Elert accepted only a negative service of natural knowledge prior to faith, for faith is grounded in the revelation in Christ or in the Scriptures. Through blood we inherit sin and the soil becomes the place where we carry out our sin, which is enmity against God. Original sin means "that our existence as sinners is set together with our dependence upon those preexistent powers."[41] In other words, natural revelation can only be negative, that is, the message of the Law, and never positive, that is, the message of the Gospel.[42] Having rejected a preparation from nature and reason for salvation in Christ, Elert writes: "Our being bound to flesh and blood, to Blood and Soil, does not mean reconciliation but conflict with God; it does not mean life but corruption."[43] These were certainly unwelcome words to the German-Christians. Elert believed that not until the Gospel has been experienced and one has thrown oneself, poor and without any conditions, into the arms of God has one learned that God is his or her Father. Elert writes: "Here is now the place for a new natural theology,

---

39 Elert, *BBB*, 7–8.

40 Elert, *BBB*, 8. Hans Ehrenberg, a Christian of Jewish descent, warned against a certain jealousy in which the blood relationships within Judaism might lead to a blood enthusiasm among nationalistically minded Gentile Christians (Schmidt, *Bekenntnisse*, 1:71). Of course, such enthusiasm developed in the teachings of the GDC, against which Elert also polemicized.

41 Elert, *BBB*, 15.

42 Elert was certainly aware of Sasse's 1932 statement that National Socialism and Christianity stood in radical opposition to each other because of the biblical doctrine of original sin.

43 Elert, *BBB*, 17.

which is no longer prior to the revelation of God in Christ and faith, but which is borne by this revelation and this faith. This natural theology . . . comes not before faith but after faith and out of faith, and from no other faith than that which justifies us before God for the sake of Christ."[44] A surprising demonstration of natural theology indeed! Elert continues: "It is precisely out of faith that we confess our being bound to Blood and Soil, because the same things apply to them which Luther said regarding the First Article of the Creed."[45]

Elert maintains that there are two things about the Law that are indisputable: "It tells us the will of God, and it shows that there is no part of our earthly existence, not a single moment, not any relationship, where we are not subjected to its will or in which we are free from the Law."[46] Elert continues:

> This order . . . consists therein, that I am a concrete man of the blood relationship of my *Volk* and that I am assigned a place in its living space. It is a token of my earthly existence and applies, insofar as it consists in blood relationship, for my entire life. Insofar as it consists in the commonality of living space it can be abolished as, for example, by emigration to another country. . . .[47]

Speaking of the orders, Elert writes: "These [orders] are subordinated also to the revealed will of God, which is spoken to us here in the Word and is therefore law. Through the revealed law, the natural orders are expressly placed under the guarantee of God." He goes on: "This is of momentous practical significance. If we are to be subject to the civil authority, parents, and masters, not only by virtue of natural order but also by virtue of the divine law, then the law of God meets us directly also in the separate requirements which these direct toward us."[48] Elert first illustrates this with our parents, whom we are obliged to obey not only by virtue of natural order but also by virtue of divine Law:

> We are obliged to obey our parents. My father tells me what I have to do in a concrete case within the order of the family. Because he is authorized by God, his concrete task announces directly the will of God. All the natural orders to which I am subjected step beneath the authority of divine law and step simultaneously in his service. That applies of course also to that civil order under which I live.[49]

---

44 Note the long citation from Luther's exposition of the Second Article in the Small Catechism (*BBB*, 19).

45 Elert, *BBB*, 21.

46 Elert, *BBB*, 24. This counters several U.S. interpreters who have found antinomianism in Elert.

47 Elert, *BBB*, 26.

48 Elert, *BBB*, 29. Elert refutes here certain German-Christian notions of an autonomous *Volksethos* that imply that the voice of the *Volk* is the will of God.

If God has made himself known to us both by the Christ revelation in the biblical revelation and by natural revelation in creation, how does natural revelation work? Elert asserts that the orders are to be interpreted by means of human reason: "Under reason one understands everything that is not revelation in the theological sense. This means not only the powers of reason but includes also custom, justice, civil law, history, sense of honor, human assignment, what is functional, political purpose, and so forth."[50] What should a Christian do when an evil government commands him to do something that is against God's Law? Or what if the state orders a citizen to do something that is against the legal basis upon which that state stands? Here is where the Christian is to employ his God-given reason, which will counsel him to disobey the wicked demand of the state or even to take part in a revolution. Elert makes this rather surprising statement:

> Even so [one is to disobey] when a secular authority commands something that conflicts with the civil order from which it derives its right for obedience. Or when another, which derives its authority out of the will of a *Volk* association, commands actions that destroy that same *Volk* association. . . . Also the question of the right of revolution can only be answered within these perimeters. Thereby we remain formally within the perimeters of divine law, which points us to the natural orders with their immanent rationality.[51]

Elert also differed fundamentally from Stapel and the German-Christians regarding the doctrine of the Law. In fact, Elert's greatest criticism of Barth was that he destroyed the Law when he merged it with the Gospel as its "needful form." For Elert, the distinction of Law and Gospel was the most important element in theology, and one cannot distinguish Law and Gospel if one is an antinomian and rejects the Law. Elert held that in a theological doctrine the Law is not fulfilled by meeting certain external requirements:

> The Gospel and faith generate and shape the new man, the eternal man in his beginning. But this beginning is consummated only in the simultaneous destruction of the old man. These are two sides of the same act. For the destruction of the old man, the believing sinner needs the continuous conviction by the Law of God until the very end of his earthly existence as it is given in the natural orders.[52]

He added: "If the believing sinners remain earthly, i.e., still bound to Blood and Soil, then the church must preach the Law until the Judgment Day. If she does not do this, then also the Gospel will be spoken by her into empty air."[53]

---

49 Elert, *BBB*, 29.

50 Elert, *BBB*, 33.

51 Elert, *BBB*, 33.

52 Elert, *BBB*, 35–36, 37.

As we ponder Elert's insistence that the church must continue to preach the Law as well as the Gospel, we should remember that he taught that only Christ could fulfill the Law and that he fulfilled the Law on the sinner's behalf. The Law cannot be fulfilled at all by the believer's good works. The Apology of the Augsburg Confession teaches *Lex semper accusat* ("The Law always accuses"). Elert taught not a casuistic but a theological function of the Law. He pointed by contrast to the Calvinists who taught the Law casuistically, even to the point of setting up a theocracy in which all the details of personal, familial, and civil life were regulated.

According to Lutheran teaching, the ethical life of a Christian is carried out exclusively within the natural orders. The "freedom of the church" does not mean the surrender of certain ethical areas on the part of the civil order nor the voluntary self-limitation of the state in these areas to the benefit of the rule of the church, but only freedom of the churchly confession, that is, churchly proclamation.[54]

How did Elert formulate his position during the war years? In an August 23, 1939, address delivered in Vienna, Elert connected the concept of the orders with a person's *Stand*, or station in life, on the one hand, and with the concept of *Beruf*, or one's calling, on the other. One's station in life is where God has placed one. The orders are not a system of rules or requirements, but they deal with facts, with things the way they are. For example, Elert wrote: "Marriage is a station or an order. And not marriage as a general concept, but every concrete separate marriage. It is an order of God. . . . The order of marriage consists in this, that one partner is a man and the other is a woman, and that both are ordered together. This is in order because the relation between both cannot be reversed."[55]

After the terrible Nazi experience and World War II, Elert returns to the orders in *The Christian Ethos* (*Das christliche Ethos*).[56] Here, Elert speaks of "the natural orders" and uses the term "orders of creation" rather sparingly; this was also characteristic of his earlier writings on the subject, where he preferred to speak, like Luther, of the estates of mankind and generally avoided entangling phrases.

Rather little has been written in the United States concerning the orders of creation.[57] One of the few U.S. treatises on the natural orders during the 1930s is

---

53 Elert, *BBB*, 38. Here Elert is refuting the notion that the church preaches only the Gospel and leaves the Law to the state. See this notion in Stapel, *Die Kirche Christi und der Staat Hitlers*, 63–64.

54 Elert, *BBB*, 46.

55 Elert, *Stand und Stände*, 8–9.

56 Elert, *Christian Ethos*, 77–139 (*Ethos*, 11–187).

57 A short article by William Lazareth, "Orders of Creation and Preservation," is given in *Baker's Dictionary of Christian Ethics*, ed. Carl F. H. Henry (Grand Rapids: Baker,

the volume *Christian Ethics* by Johann Michael Reu and Paul H. Buehring, two Confessional Lutherans.[58] A section written by Buehring discussed "relationships" rather than orders but followed the three orders commonly listed: the family, the church, and the state. Buehring added a fourth relationship, roughly corresponding to Bonhoeffer's fourth order of vocation. Buehring called these "purely human relationships," dealing with the brotherhood of men, including the racial problems of the United States, social intercourse, labor and property, and the occupations. Rue prepared the bibliography for this section, which included Althaus's *Theologie der Ordnungen* (1934), Brunner's *Das Gebot und die Ordnungen* (1933), and volume 2 of Elert's *Morphologie des Luthertums* (1932).[59]

VIEWS OF OTHER THEOLOGIANS
ON THE ORDERS OF CREATION

Although the position of Althaus and Elert on the orders of creation have been widely read, the views of others must also be noted. Here, we turn to Brunner, Lau, Bonhoeffer, Sasse, and Künneth.

The Swiss Reformed theologian Emil Brunner esteemed highly the doctrine of the orders of creation. In fact, the title of his scholarly system of ethics may be translated into English as *The Commandment and the Orders: The Sketch of a Protestant Ethics.*[60] Brunner wrote in his dialectical manner as follows: "God as Creator demands the recognition of his orders and one's participation in them, as the first part. God as Redeemer simultaneously demands, as the second part, the non-recognition of the given orders and a new action in view of the coming Kingdom of God."[61] Brunner went on to say that we meet our neighbor as the bearer of God's orders, the most important of which is the ordering together of man and woman in marriage: "The husband, in order to be a man, is pointed to the woman; the wife, in order to be a woman, is directed to the husband. This being directed to live together, to a fellowship, consists in the natural attraction of both to each other that was laid in creation."[62] Brunner added that the mark of the

---

1973), 475. Lazareth presents the issues incorrectly when he tries to distinguish between "theonomous ordinance" and "autonomous order," ascribing the former to Luther and the latter to Althaus and Elert.

58 Reu and Buehring, *Christian Ethics* (Columbus: Lutheran Book Concern, 1935), 256–396.

59 Elert, *Morphologie des Luthertums*, 2 vols. (Munich: C. H. Beck, 1931; 2d ed., 1952).

60 Brunner, *Das Gebot und die Ordnungen: Entwurf einer protestantisch-theologischen Ethik* (Zürich: Zwingli, 1939).

61 Brunner, *Das Gebot und die Ordnungen*, 192.

62 Brunner, *Das Gebot und die Ordnungen*, 192.

orders of creation is that our actions are all fulfilled in our relations to others: "Giving is proud and makes one proud; receiving is humbling and makes one humble . . . . True love is the knowledge of being dependent on another; it is the renunciation of self-sufficiency, the destruction of ego pride." Brunner goes on to remark that the orders of creation show an inborn inequality by which one person needs the other, "whether it is the relation of young and old, child and father, leader and those led, productive and receptive . . ." These differences are implicit in creation, which has required that we should depend upon one another.[63]

Some Lutherans were uncomfortable with the term "orders of creation" and presented their own distinctive positions. Bonhoeffer spoke in early years of the "preservation orders of God." In later years, particularly in his ethics, Bonhoeffer spoke of the "mandates of creation," under which he numbered four: work, marriage, civil authority, and church. In the 1933 summer semester, Bonhoeffer wrote:

> The [church] has neither to praise nor to blame the laws of the state, but rather to affirm the state as the Preservation Order of God in the godless world. [The church] has to recognize its Creation of Orders—whether good or bad, when seen from a humanitarian point of view—and to understand them as established in the preserving will of God in the midst of the chaotic godlessness of the world. This judging of the actions of the state stands beyond every moralism and distinguishes itself from humanitarianism of every shade through the radicality of separating the place of the Glad Tidings and the Place of the Law. The actions of the state remain free from churchly interference.[64]

Sasse[65] and Künneth both questioned the validity of the expression "orders of creation" and sought different terminology that would ensure divine control (theonomy) and exclude any human machinations (autonomy). Sasse preferred to speak of the "orders of the Creator," thereby protecting their divine character, and Künneth used the term the "orders of preservation," thereby limiting their scope to the work that God performs.

One of the most thorough discussions of the orders is given by Künneth in his large monograph *Politik zwischen Dämon und Gott* (*Politics between Demon and God).*[66] Künneth notes that the concept of natural law or divine Law was tam-

---

63 Brunner, *Das Gebot und die Ordnungen*, 196.

64 *Bonhoeffer*, 12:350.

65 Despite his hedging at the terminology, Sasse presented a spirited defense of the Lutheran teaching and a refutation of Barth in his book *Here We Stand: Nature and Character of the Lutheran Faith* (New York: Harper & Bros., 1938; repr., Minneapolis: Augsburg, 1946), 163–64, especially n. 158.

66 In Künneth, *Politik*, the second part is devoted to the orders (pp. 115–253). See p. 17 for bibliographic details.

pered with during the period of the Enlightenment and was replaced by the concept of the free or autonomous man. Künneth declares that the vacuum created by the rejection of natural law was filled by the concept of state sovereignty. Although this might sound democratic, it was this placing of Law underneath state sovereignty that prepared the way for the absolutism of eighteenth-century France and for the unbounded totalitarianism of the Hitler state.[67] Although one may personally favor "human rights," freedom, and equal opportunity for all, one must still distinguish between what comes from human ideologies and what comes from divine Law. Künneth points out that many of these ideas have stemmed from philosophers and political writers and cannot be directly ascribed to God.[68]

THE THEOLOGY OF CREATION AS THE BASIS FOR OPPOSITION TO CRIMES AGAINST HUMANITY

In the explanation of the First Article of the Creed in Luther's Small Catechism, the believer confesses: "I believe that God has made me and all creatures." All people have come from the creative hand of God. Therefore it follows that all human life is sacred and that to take life arbitrarily is a grave sin against the Creator. This conviction was mirrored in Lutheran opposition to the Nazi crimes against humanity. In his refusal to acknowledge a natural knowledge of God, Barth had no room for such a theology of creation, and because of his rejection of Christian ethics as a separate theological discipline, Barth was unable to offer adequate arguments against the Nazi atrocities. In chapter 6, it was demonstrated that Lutheran theologians opposed the Aryan Paragraph and other discrimination against Jews because the Jewish people had also come from God the Creator. This section will be restricted to Lutheran opposition to the National Socialist concept of "useless life" and the Nazi practice of genocide, abortion, and euthanasia, particularly in the liquidation of handicapped and afflicted people.

A clandestine bill called the "Secret Reich Matter" (*Geheime Reichssache*) was signed into law by Adolf Hitler on September 1, 1939. This bill read: "Reich leader Bouhler and Dr. Brandt have been made responsible for broadening the authority of certain physicians so that they can, by a human assessment based upon a critical judgment of the patients' physical condition, deem them incurably sick and

---

67 Künneth, *Politik*, 124; see also Künneth, *Politik*, 135.

68 Künneth, *Politik*, 126–27. Lau writes that in Luther's thinking the relation between *jus naturale* and *jus positivum* is that natural law comes from God directly and that positive law is also binding indirectly because the lawgiver has authority from God. Lau writes: "And God speaks to me through this positive law. For me it is divine law (*jus divinum*); its claim is God's immediate claim upon me" (*"Äußerliche Ordnung,"* 36).

suited for a mercy death."[69] This bill became the legal basis for the large-scale extermination of the weak. The hidden purpose of this barbarous and inhumane program was, evidently, to save food and financial resources for the war effort, as Hitler was about to provoke World War II. Such focus on resources was part of Hitler's total plan for victory.

Seven sites were selected as places of annihilation: Hadamar in Hesse, Hartheim in Austria, Brandenburg, Sonnenstein near Pirna, Irrsee by Kaufbeuren, Bernburg on the Saale, and Grafeneck in Württemberg. A shocking description of the events instigated by this decree was given by Pastor Paul Gerhard Braune, leader of the Hoffnungstal Institution at Lobetal, Württemberg. Braune described how tens of thousands of mentally disabled, epileptic, crippled, deaf and blind, and other afflicted and handicapped people were rounded up from church or state institutions, placed in gray transport buses, and moved to one of the extermination centers.

Ironically, these centers were called health and nursing care facilities (*Heil- und Pflegeanstalten*), but their weak victims were mistreated and starved to death. Anecdotal information relates how the afflicted were placed on floor mats in overcrowded facilities, how food was withdrawn, how the patients could be heard moaning, "Hunger, hunger, hunger!" Perhaps most dramatic were the stories of how the more able were punished if they shared food with the weakest. When death finally relieved the pain of the tormented, relatives would receive a letter that stated their loved one had died of a weak heart, pneumonia, or the like. The letter would also state that the danger of contagion had necessitated cremation of the deceased with any clothing, but the ashes were available to the family.[70]

Things looked suspicious as identical stories began to accumulate in a given community. The populace became increasingly aware of the enormity of the Nazi crime of euthanasia, and their outcries reached the ears of Bishop Theophil Wurm in Württemberg. Indeed, perhaps the most notable protests against this destruction of the weak came from Wurm. In a July 19, 1940, letter addressed to the Reich Minister of the Interior in Berlin, Wurm recounted how hundreds of afflicted people had been rounded up and sent to particular places, from which they were reported dead in a few weeks. Wurm continued:

> Moved by the numerous queries from the very different circles out of city and countryside, I hold it to be my duty to make the Reich Government aware of the fact that this matter has aroused a very great sensation in our small province. First of all, this is because one of these places, to which the patients

---

69 Schäfer, *Wurm*, 115.

70 Hermelink, 520–32; *KJahr 1933–1944*, 415–23.

are brought and where there is a crematory and an office of death records, is located in Schloss Grafeneck, situated here in Württemberg.[71]

Wurm remarked that because of excessive intermarriage in the more remote areas, the number of "degenerated" people was especially high in Württemberg and that therefore many families were affected by the annihilation of the afflicted.[72] Wurm repudiated the concept that government could choose who should live and who should be killed, and he stoutly insisted: "The decision over when an end shall be given to the life of a suffering person belongs to Almighty God, who in his unsearchable will at times allows a completely healthy and productive person to be snatched away before his time and, on the other hand, allows one who is unfit to live to linger on in poor health."[73]

High Consistorial Counselor Reinhold Sautter, who served under Wurm in the Land Church of Württemberg, wrote the following protest to the chairman of the special court at Stuttgart:

> In an objective consideration the question always arises immediately whether "useless life" may not be destroyed. The black tribes in inner Africa at earlier times regularly carried their elderly and sick people into the jungle and, leaving them with a little food, exposed them to the wild animals. The Christian missionaries opposed this practice and taught their congregations that Christians, in thankfulness for the many healthy people, must also care for the sick, because God has given us this task and because a *Volk* develops some very definite and indispensable qualities in the work for the healthy as also in the work for the sick.[74]

Wurm was likely thinking of the killing of the insane when he wrote a letter to the Council on National Defense, a letter received by the most influential people in the government and the Nazi Party. In this letter, Wurm stated: "At a time such as this, one should not cause such an offense to large parts of the citizenry in regard to questions of the inner heart and of the conscience, as it has occurred repeatedly since the beginning of the war and has now reached an almost unbearable extent."[75]

There are other anecdotes of heroism. Hilmar Ratz, the *Konrector* of the Lutheran school for mentally disabled children at Neuendettelsau, received word from the Nazis that they wanted to perform a visitation on a particular date. Surmising that they intended to seize the children, Ratz decided to send the pupils

---

71 Schäfer, *Wurm*, 119.

72 Schäfer, *Wurm*, 119–20.

73 Schäfer, *Wurm*, 121.

74 Schäfer, *Wurm*, 118.

75 Schäfer, *Wurm*, 143.

back to their parents. On each child he placed a badge with his or her name and address, took the youngsters to the railroad station, and sent them all home. When the commission arrived to collect the children, Ratz told them: "I'm so sorry. There are no children here. They've all gone home on holiday." Thus a tragic outcome was averted, at great personal risk to Ratz, though he was not arrested for this act of defiance.[76] Friedrich von Bodelschwingh, superintendent of the Bethel Institution at Bielefeld, simply defied the Nazis, refusing to turn over any of his handicapped individuals. He, too, went unpunished.

At a time when Europeans and Americans are considering legalizing euthanasia, when abortion is already legalized in many countries, and when racial cleansing atrocities continue to surface from around the world, one could learn from the arguments of people such as Wurm, Braune, and Sautter, who rejected the measures of the Nazis against "worthless life." Were they alive today, they would certainly argue that a government must never again be allowed to determine who shall live and who shall die nor to carry out actions to dispose of people it no longer wants. Opponents might point to the word of the Scriptures: "Whoso sheds man's blood, by man shall his blood be shed. For in the image of God created he man" (Genesis 9:6). They might find that these biblical words were fulfilled literally in the fall of National Socialism in 1945.

Relevance of the Lutheran Theology of Creation for Today

At the beginning of the third millennium, there is much public concern about the deterioration of our earthly environment, including global warming and the "greenhouse effect," as well as an alarming increase in violent weather disturbances. Theological solutions to these concerns might be found in the theology of creation as it was presented by Confessional Lutheran writers during the 1930s and 1940s. Such a theology of creation emphasizes that the earth is God's and that people are human beings created by God in his own image. We might turn to the words of Franz Lau:

> In spite of all the violent objections which in contemporary theology have been made against speaking of orders of creation, it is impossible to dispense with this term and instead speak only perhaps of orders of preservation. To be noted in this regard is that God is creating unceasingly (*creatio continua*). On the other hand, Luther's concept of creation would be false, if one were to subsume all of God's acts under a doctrine of creation, without discerning the fact

---

76 This anecdote was related to me while in Erlangen in 1954 by Ratz's son, Erhard. The opportunity to hear the story came during an unforgettable visit with the Ratz family at Neuendettelsau.

that creation has as its object the finite world (against an understanding of a theology of creation in Luther which abolishes the distinction between the First and Second Article—Löfgren).[77]

Much modern theology, following in the steps of Barth, has abandoned the theology of creation and has turned over First Article concerns to the social sciences or to political activism. These concerns include such matters as world hunger and sickness, the fear of overpopulation, abortion and euthanasia, genocide and ethnic cleansing, environmental concerns, atomic and germ warfare, relations between the genders, heterosexuality and homosexuality, feminism and the role of women in society, women in the church and specifically in the clergy, minority rights, race relations, and so forth. Problems such as these might best be clarified by returning to a theology of creation (divine orders) and observing the principle of the two governances, whereby the church follows God's Word and the state exercises political power. Had they lived, men such as Elert, Althaus, and Sasse might have thought that the political activism that was advocated by religious leaders since World War II was a form of theocratic enthusiasm, which both undermined the state (Law) and destroyed the proclamation of the church (Gospel).

German theology lost its world leadership after 1965. According to Lau, matters would not get better until theologians returned to the whole counsel of God as reflected in a theology of both Law and Gospel. Lau writes: "The world of creation with its tasks is larger and broader than that which God revealed to us in the Gospel. There are problems in which the revelation of God lets us completely drift and we are left to ourselves, to our considerations and experiments, to our reason and our daring."[78] This comment reminds one of Luther's dictum that it is not pious to seek in the Scriptures for that which God has made manifest in creation and to reason. Not until we develop a serious doctrine of creation will we be able to deal with some serious modern problems, and that will be by the application of sanctified human reason. But a return to the theology of creation can be greatly helped by a reconsideration of the thought of Elert, Althaus, Sasse, and Künneth.

In the United States, issues such as conscientious objection and civil disobedience, patriotism and love for country, or whether the state should foster prayer or religion in the public schools cannot be dealt with coherently until the theocratic enthusiasm inherited from the Pilgrims and the Puritans is acknowledged and dealt with. This can only be done by one who knows the distinction of the two governances. The lingering emotional ills that stem from the Vietnam War cannot be healed except by a theological ethic that is acquainted with the

---

77 Lau, "Two Kingdoms," 367.

78 Lau, "Two Kingdoms," 372.

distinction of Law and Gospel. "*This* kingdom stuff" (Law) must not be allowed to replace "the *other* kingdom stuff" (Gospel). Here is the contribution that Confessional Lutheran theology from the past can make toward overcoming the contemporary theological confusion in Europe, the United States, and the Third World.

CHAPTER TEN

Theocratic Enthusiasm

History and Its Place in the Thought
of Karl Barth and National Socialism

The much-maligned Lutheran concept of the two governances (inaccurately called the two-kingdoms doctrine) ties in with modern views of the separation of church and state. The concept of a totalitarian state is impossible when terms in the two governances are properly balanced. Conversely, single-governance views tend toward some form of totalitarianism: either a theocratic or religious rule (seizure of civil affairs by the religious) or a caesaropapistic form of government (dictation of church affairs by civil powers). Proponents of both theocratic as well as caesaropapistic rule oppose the doctrine of the two governances and insist upon a single-governance doctrine. A theocratic concept supposes that God himself, or some religious institution, should govern the secular affairs of society. A caesaropapistic view is that the secular authority should control the whole society in religious as well as civil affairs. The two theories are essentially one. Karl Barth wanted his religion to control the civil realm and Adolf Hitler wanted his political system to control the church. From the Lutheran standpoint, both are wrong because both are a deformation of the Law-Gospel distinction; both positions confuse the rule of God from his left hand with his rule from the right hand. In terms of U.S. political ideology, this becomes the mingling of church and state. Nevertheless, despite nervousness regarding separation of church and state in the United States, there has been much intermingling of the two in theocratic notions since the time of the founding fathers of the United States.[1]

THEOCRATIC IDEAS IN WORLD HISTORY

Theocratic notions have pervaded societies in Europe, Asia, Africa, and North America throughout history. In the early fourth century, Constantine the Great made Christianity the state religion of the Roman Empire. Two centuries later, Justinian the Great completed the marriage of throne and altar by uniting the Byzantine state with the Greek Orthodox Church. Under him, Greek Orthodox theology moved from Christ as Savior to Christ as *Pantocrator* or king. Because Christ had said, "All power is given to me" (Matthew 28:18), and because Christ had delegated all authority to Justinian, the emperor assumed totalitarian rule over church and state. This was depicted in the famous mosaic at Ravenna, which shows Christ as παντόχρατορ (*Pantocrator*) in the apse and Justinian as αὐτόχρατορ (*Autocrator*) on the wall below.[2]

In the Roman Catholic Church of the West, the theocratic accomplishments of Justinian were reflected in the rise of papal ambitions to civil power. Theocratic enthusiasm appeared in the medieval crusades when European armies fought "in the name of Christ" for a variety of causes. Particularly, the Investiture Controversy of the eleventh century revealed a struggle between the emperor's attempt to control the church (caesaropapism) and the pope's machinations to block the

---

1 Typical of postwar criticism of the Confessional Lutheran separation of the two governances is Bettina Simon's criticism of Paul Leo's views in 1933: "A general criticism of the civil measures [against Jews] remained unavailable to him in view of his problematical (as seen today) expounding of the two kingdoms doctrine, which included a basic affirmation of the National Socialist state" (Simon, 121–22). Others, including me, would argue that the two-governance position, rightly explained, is the only valid solution.

2 The mosaics are presented in Santi Muratori, *I Mosaici Ravennati della chiesa di S. Vitale* (Bergamo: Istituto Italiano d'arti Grafiche, 1945), plate 1, 31–33. On their interpretation, see Elert, "Der durch den irdischen Autokrator vertretene Große Gott und Erlöser," and "Der politische Christus in der bildenden Kunst," in Elert, *Ausgang*, especially 165–67, 170–71. See also Elert's earlier booklet *Die Herrschaft Christi und die Herrschaft von Menschen,* Theologia Militans 6 (Leipzig: A. Deichert, 1936), 4. Elert also discussed Christ-the-King enthusiasm in "Regnum Christi: Das Reich Christi als Thema der christlichen Mission," in Elert, *Zwischen Gnade,* especially 83–85. Elert's impressive knowledge of Russia and its Orthodox Church is manifested in his article "Theokratie und Bolschewismus," in Elert, *Zwischen Gnade,* 17–37. See also Lowell C. Green, *Adventures in Law and Gospel: Lectures in Lutheran Dogmatics* (Fort Wayne, IN: Concordia Theological Seminary Press, 1993), 156–60, on how Christ-the-King is related to Law or Gospel in a Lutheran doctrinal paradigm.

emperor and seize temporal as well as ecclesial control of society (the *Corpus Christianum*). In either case, the problem was a single-governance view. Even in Augustine's conception, which differentiated "two cities," only the church was God's city (*civitas Dei*) and the state was man's sinful city (*civitas diaboli*). As we shall see, Luther differed from Augustine when he placed both governances, the spiritual and the secular, under God and recognized the dignity of temporal government. But during the Middle Ages, some of the most regrettable episodes of history resulted from the interference in temporal government by the Catholic Church. The mismanagement of temporal rule by the church in the Italian papal states, the pope's interference in temporal government, and the rule by the prince-bishops in medieval Germany all exposed the fallacies in a theocracy in which religious authorities assume political power.

On a worldwide basis, theocratic concepts have caused much unrest. For example, extremist groups arising from Islamic societies carry out terrorist acts in various parts of the world, all in the name of Allah. A notable case is the September 11, 2001, hijacking of four U.S. passenger airplanes that resulted in the destruction of the World Trade Center in New York, damage to the Pentagon in Washington DC, and a tragic crash in rural Pennsylvania. Theocratic trends also appear in Hindu countries, where a rigid caste system, originating with white invaders, has suppressed the native people in the name of religion and robbed them of social and economic rights for thousands of years. Several tragic examples of the confusion of religious and political power have also occurred in places such as Jonestown, Guyana; Rwanda; Waco, Texas; and Ruby Ridge, Idaho, as well as in the religious massacres in Uganda at the turn of the millennium. Recent history teems with the excesses of theocratic enthusiasm.

THEOCRATIC VIEWS IN PROTESTANTISM

Theocratic views reappeared in the Protestant churches following the Reformation, pervading the political writings of the Anabaptists, Zwinglians, Calvinists, and, eventually, the Puritans. Thus when Calvin returned to Geneva in 1541, the city accepted a theocratic reform based upon his *Ecclesiastical Ordinances*. Although the ecclesial and political powers were said to be separate, in practice they always spoke in unison. Religious leaders dictated to the civil powers, and the citizens of Geneva were subjected to a system of "Blue Laws" that tried to legislate morality.[3]

---

3 On the "repressive discipline, harsh laws, and paternalistic controls" in Calvin's Geneva, see John T. McNeill, *The History and Character of Calvinism* (Oxford: Oxford University Press, 1970), 190. Preserved Smith writes: "During the years 1542–46 there were, in this little town of 16,000 people, no less than fifty-eight executions and seventy-six banishments" (*The Reformation in Europe* [New York: Collier-Macmillan, 1962], 136).

Building upon elements from the thought of Zwingli, Heinrich Bullinger, Martin Bucer, Melanchthon, and Calvin, the seventeenth-century Reformed theologian Johannes Coccejus attempted to ameliorate the severity of Calvinism by developing the concept of federalism (from the Latin *foedus,* a league or treaty), often called "covenant theology." As a point of departure, Coccejus used the idea of the Old Testament "covenant," an agreement between God and his people in which both sides bound themselves together. The covenant had visible signs (sacraments) and was built upon the command and the promise. Covenant notions spread in England and Scotland before, during, and after the reign of Oliver Cromwell and the Puritan Revolution. The federalism of Coccejus was to issue a new form of theocracy in the New World.[4]

THEOCRATIC ENTHUSIASM IN THE UNITED STATES

The North American colonies were being settled at the very time that Coccejus promulgated his thinking, and these covenant ideas came to have a decisive impact on the history of the United States. The religious word *federal,* as well as its cognate *confederate,* became a cliche in political jargon in the American colonies. The *Oxford English Dictionary* defines *federal* as "of or pertaining to a covenant, compact, or treaty" (s.v.). The first constitution after the secession of the American colonies from England was called the Articles of Confederation (1781). A conservative group in the early American republic, which worked toward the adoption of the subsequent constitution of 1789, called itself the Federalist Party; significantly, this party was especially strong in New England, the home of Puritan covenant ideology. During the Civil War, those who seceded called themselves the Confederate States of America, while the abolitionists used religious arguments against slavery. In the late nineteenth-century in the United States, theocratic enthusiasm was to change much Protestant theology into the "Social Gospel," an activist program that sought to carry out the teachings of the Sermon on the Mount in the political and social arenas of the day. Among supporters of this new ideology, the image of Christ as the Savior from sin dwindled in favor of the concept of Christ as the Teacher of social activism. The "political Christ" of Justinian had returned in a new form.

---

4 For a scientific word study of *covenant* in the Bible by two eminent scholars, see the presentation on διαθήκη and בְּרִית in the Old Testament by Gottfried Quell and the investigation of διαθήκη in the Septuagint, rabbinics, and the New Testament by Johannes Behm (*Theologisches Wörterbuch zum Neuen Testament,* ed. Gerhard Kittel [Stuttgart: W. Kohlhammer, 1935], 2:106–37). For a short summary of covenant thinking, see Julius Bodensieck, "Covenant," *ELC,* 1:627–28. See also the presentation on Coccejus, federal theology, and Puritanism in histories of theology or in reference works.

For centuries, Americans have cherished the Puritan myth that there is a unique covenant between God and the American nation. Schoolchildren were taught that Americans were the chosen people of God. Linked to this were notions that the white Anglo-Saxon Protestants were a superior race, provided with a "manifest destiny" to practice imperialism. It was the "white man's burden" to rule over the inferior races, particularly blacks, lest the evolutionary process be stalled or reversed by inferior racial strains. American wars were God's wars. In World War I, U.S. soldiers, true to the national covenant with God, fought a holy war to make the world safe for democracy. Of course, God was on the side of the United States; thus Germany, which was on the wrong side, was defeated. Germany's evil monarchy was dismantled, together with its territorial churches, and in the Weimar Republic, the Germans received a form of government that exhibited at least a few of the virtues of U.S. democracy.[5]

Another example of theocratic enthusiasm was the temperance movement led by many Protestant churches in the United States. Reminiscent of the forced morality in Calvin's Geneva, religious teetotalers exerted enough pressure to bring about an amendment to the U.S. Constitution that prohibited the sale and consumption of alcoholic beverages. The belief that one can legislate conduct, or even moral conduct, rests upon an assumption that there are two categories of people: those who are morally superior and make the rules and those who are morally inferior, for whom the rules are made. It includes the theological assumption that sin consists of outward actions that can be improved by some power other than the Gospel, that is, by legislation and the enforcement of laws. Therefore theocratic concepts stand in great tension not only with New Testament theology but also with democratic ideals.[6]

THEOCRATIC ENTHUSIASM IN GERMANY

The rise of the modern Prussian state began with the conversion of Elector Johann Sigismund of Brandenburg from Lutheranism to Calvinism in 1613. He

---

5 The notion that Americans as God's covenant people were ministers of God for bringing justice into the world, and the conviction that the United States must win every war, was strengthened by patriotic songs, such as "America the Beautiful," "God of Our Fathers," and Rudyard Kipling's "God of Our Fathers, Known of Old," found in most Protestant hymnbooks and sung in church services. National flags hanging in nearly every church also point to the concept of the U.S. covenant with God.

6 Something went wrong in the Vietnam War. Many Americans believed the United States was in the right, but God seemed to think differently. The United States lost. In the process, the country also lost its exaggerated self-esteem. Nevertheless, some Americans still have not recognized the role of a specious covenant ideology nor the danger of U.S. theocratic enthusiasm, which has been cherished since the age of Puritanism.

saw this as a window of opportunity to develop his country in Western-style absolutism. However, Johann Sigismund also absorbed Reformed theocratic notions and developed what one current historian calls the "National Protestant View of History." Berndt Hamm presents a picture that is strangely similar to U.S. beliefs of a special covenant with God:

> German history was raised to a revelatory history of God, who leads his chosen German people. The wars of the Germans are therefore holy wars, and the service of Kaiser, *Volk*, and fatherland is Divine Service. The national state with a great *Führer*-personality at the top appears as God's order and a moral task, which must be attended to by the churches, strengthening the bonds of "throne and altar" with total devotion.[7]

Hamm fails to see where Reformed and Lutheran thought diverge in the question of theocracy, and he overlooks the logical conclusions when he adds: "The two-kingdoms thinking lamed the [Lutheran] church, at least in the first years, over against everything that took place outside its own sphere."[8] Hamm insists that men such as Hermann Sasse and Werner Elert should have accepted the theological premises and the unionism that he himself believes to be correct.[9] This in turn implies that Lutherans should follow the theocratic doctrines of Barth, though Hamm himself has demonstrated the speciousness of such teachings.

BARTH'S ATTEMPTS TO SOLVE THE PROBLEMS OF CHURCH AND STATE

In approaching the problem of the church in a hostile state, Barth worked from two principles that reflected his personal beliefs and his Reformed theology: the replacement of the *Volkskirche* with conventicles of true believers (Confessing Church groups) and the concept of theocracy, with the state as an agent of the church.

BARTH'S DISLIKE FOR THE *VOLK* CHURCHES

Barth lashed out in angry attacks against the Lutheran *Volk* churches because he wanted to replace the traditional *Volk* churches with churches of true believers, or conventicles. Barth was annoyed with the Lutherans for not recognizing his Barmen Declaration and for remaining aloof from the Confessing Church, and he classified the Lutherans as "neutrals" in their attempt to maintain their tradi-

---

7 Hamm, 27.

8 Hamm, 38.

9 Hamm, 41. In his attacks against Sasse and Elert, Hamm seems to step over the line that marks scientific scholarship.

tional entities. Barth seemed oblivious to the fact that the three intact churches were *Volk* churches and were the only ones to avoid annexation by the Reich Church. Barth could never understand why Lutherans were committed to their Confessions and wanted to avoid his Confessing Church with its implicit unionism. He thought that the old differences in doctrine and practice had lost their meaning in view of the threat from Hitler and National Socialism.[10] He also lamented that stubborn Lutherans in the Confessing Church still expressed their doctrinal concerns, to the detriment of a common confession and action.[11] However, for Confessional Lutherans, the theological issues, such as the doctrine of Christ and the Sacrament, were not as easily negotiable as they were for Barth. Men such as Elert, Althaus, Sasse, Friedrich Ulmer, and Otto Procksch could not simply barter their beliefs so they might bask in the warmth of Barthian approval. This would have required giving up the *theologia crucis* for the *theologia gloriae*.[12]

Barth describes the German church as being under trial and asks: "Can we speak of a true church if it is not tested, if it is not a church that is moved by these questions? Can the church be present if these are not living questions? And if they are not living questions, are our churches then true churches?"[13] For the Confessional Lutheran, the *notae ecclesiae* are the gifts of God in Word and Sacrament. For the Reformed Barth, the *notae ecclesiae* that determine the true church do not consist in some divine action but in human actions: suffering under trial and afflictions. Understanding the church as a conventicle, or as the gathering of the "elect," makes it in practice the gathering of the religious elite, a gathering of those who are morally and spiritually superior.

Years later, Wilhelm Maurer pointed out the danger as well as the foolishness in Barth's argument against the *Volk* churches as follows:

---

10 Barth wrote: "The old controversies, but also the old things held in common in the church, the cohesiveness of Lutherans, the Reformed, and the positive and liberals, had all become meaningless or unimportant in view of the newly established question" (*Not und Verheißung im Deutscher Kirchenkampf* [Bern: Buchhandlung der Evangelischen Gesellschaft, 1938], 8).

11 "There was and still is the almost unbelievable confessional narrowness on the part of some of the Lutherans who were involved in the Confessing Church who are ever intent on new trouble in the church" (Barth, *Not und Verheißung*, 18).

12 In his 1518 Heidelberg Disputation, Luther had distinguished between a theology of glory and a theology of the cross (WA 1:353–74). A theology of glory sought the approval of men or yearned for the wealth and honor of this world and was opposed to Christ. A theology of the cross focused on Christ and readily bore the disapproval of the world and the reproach of the cross. The mark of the *theologia gloriae* was pride; the mark of the *theologia crucis* was humility, with the willingness to face the disapproval of the world.

13 Barth, *Not und Verheißung*, 10–11.

In an anti-Christian state such as National Socialism, the renunciation of the breadth of the *Volk* church, and thereby of its public significance, would have led to the rapid de-Christianization of our people. The church would thereby have helped the National Socialist leadership to have reached its goal, which was the destruction of Christianity and the church in Germany. The *Volk* church would thereby have denied its own history and have abandoned its mission to the German *Volk*.[14]

BARTH'S ESPOUSAL OF THEOCRATIC NOTIONS

Barth's political theology, with its theocratic tendencies and its interference in political matters, became apparent in 1966 when he belittled Walter Künneth's battle against theological liberalism as follows:

Are you willing and ready to start and to attend a similar "movement" and "demonstration" that is against the rearmament of the West German army with atomic weapons? Against the war and the warfare in Vietnam by the American allies of West Germany? Against the ever recurring outbreaks of wild anti-Semitism in West Germany? For a peace agreement of West Germany with the states of Eastern Europe with the recognition of the 1945 boundaries? Only when a confession that is right according to the testimony of the Holy Scriptures regarding the crucified and resurrected Jesus Christ includes and expresses these [political] matters, only then is it a right, precious, and fruitful confession. But if it does not include and express these things, then, in all its correctness, it is not a right confession, but a dead and cheap one, a Pharisaical confession that strains at gnats while swallowing camels.[15]

It sounds as if Barth is calling Künneth a hypocrite and insisting that he should be concerned with issues from the political sphere rather than with the teachings of the Bible. But for Künneth, religious faith could not be more promiscuously mixed with political expediency than it is in these unfriendly lines by the Swiss theologian. It is difficult to see how the supporters of Barth could excoriate their opponents for being "political theologians."

Barth rejoices in 1938 that many Christians are keeping the faith. Were these the ones who followed Barth's own personal line? Those who opposed Barth were also strong and faithful witnesses. Among the Confessional Lutherans, one thinks of names such as Künneth, Jochen Klepper, Sasse, Hanns Lilje, Ernst Kinder, the Confessional Lutheran bishops, and the regular *Volk* in the Lutheran provincial

---

14 Maurer, "Ausklang und Folgen des Kirchenkampfes," in *Tutzing*, 1:243. Extremely similar is the comment of Künneth: "The evangelical church cannot and wishes not to distance itself from the folk to whom she has been called by God to serve" (*Abfall*, 242).

15 Künneth, *Lebensführungen*, 261–62.

churches who staunchly backed their imprisoned bishops by mass demonstrations until they had secured the release of these men and the overthrow of the oppressors, August Jäger and Ludwig Müller.[16]

Not to be forgotten is the courageous protest by the theological faculty at the University of Erlangen against the German-Christian takeover of the Bavarian Church. On October 13, 1934, the faculty declared: "These measures offend against love for one's brother, faithfulness, and truthfulness, divine commandments which the church of Christ must obey." The statement was signed by all the full professors: Elert, Althaus, Hermann Strathmann, Procksch, Hans Preuß, and Ulmer, as well as Sasse.[17] In reporting this protest, Max Tratz comments: "This declaration, as well as the protest of thirty professors in Munich who were not theologians, could at that time have cost every one his permission to teach and perhaps also his personal freedom."[18] Moreover, mention should be made of Elert, who, as dean of the theological faculty at Erlangen, steered his ship in a steady but inconspicuous course, which avoided the opposite dangers of National Socialism and Barthian theology (see chapter 15).

THEOCRACY AS BARTH'S SOLUTION

Barth's program to have the state serve as the instrument for bringing the kingdom of God into fruition on earth has been noted previously.[19] Hitler's state did not fulfill that expectation, and Barth wrote as follows concerning the church struggle as a crusade of the church against the state:

> In time to come, the Church Struggle will give scholars much to think about and say. These scholars will have to show how it all came to pass, how the two great opponents in this struggle, the church of Jesus Christ and the National Socialist state of Adolf Hitler, confronted each other, how in this meeting at first neither side understood the other, and how then both the church and the state revealed themselves in their true nature, how they got into conflict and what, in the end, on the part of both sides, became the final result of the controversy.[20]

---

16 See Eduard Putz and Max Tratz, "Bauern kämpfen für ihren Bischof," in *ZwKK*, 9–23, and Julius Schieder, "Wir alle hatten verzagte Stunden," in *ZwKK*, 75–80. See also other eyewitness accounts in this collection of essays; bibliographic details are on p. 19.

17 Schmidt, *Bekenntnisse*, 2:155.

18 *ZwKK*, 19.

19 See the presentation on Barth in chapter 1; the discussion of the Bethel Confession, Art. VI, §§ 4–5, in chapter 7; and the references to George Hunsinger, ed. and trans., *Karl Barth and Radical Politics* (Philadelphia: Westminster Press, 1976) in both places.

20 Barth, *Not und Verheißung*, 3.

Accordingly, Barth understood the *Kirchenkampf* as the conflict between the church of Jesus Christ and the Nazi state, as a holy war, a crusade on the part of the church against the state.[21]

Künneth, who was deposed from his office at the Seminar for Apologetics in Berlin and brought before the Gestapo for his books against Alfred Rosenberg, later found himself confronting the attacks of Barth, who was safe, secure, and prosperous in his Swiss professorship at Basel. Writing in a socialist newspaper, Barth criticized people in the Confessing Church such as Künneth for not confronting Hitler and the Nazi Party more fiercely. Barth also criticized the intact Lutheran churches of Hanover, Bavaria, and Württemberg for concentrating on Word and Sacrament rather than political involvement.[22]

In scolding the Lutherans for not carrying out his theocratic, political agenda, Barth never faced the dangers of those he was ridiculing, least of all the dangers faced by men such as Künneth, Lilje, Bonhoeffer, Sasse, or Elert. Barth's primary problem was that Lutherans had different beliefs from his own and he was intolerant of such divergences. Künneth defended the Lutheran rejection of a theocratic position, stating that the church had not lost its soul in politics but had concentrated upon preaching the Gospel. He pointed out that contrary to the opinion of Barth, the mistake of the German-Christians had consisted in allowing the church to be caught up in politics. Instead, as a Lutheran, Künneth insisted that the church receives its strength by the presence of its risen Lord, Jesus Christ. Künneth added that "the more the church becomes a truly confessing church, the more it will help the religious policies of the state to a new understanding of churchly reality."[23]

---

21 Barth, *Not und Verheißung*, 3.

22 Künneth protested: "Barth wrote in the Swiss Marxist weekly, *Die Nation*, in March 1936, as follows: 'The Confessing Church has not as yet come to bring the National Socialist state to an accounting also for the other fields of its activity . . . It has until now on the whole satisfied itself with the struggle for its own purity and freedom. This is its limitation and its weakness.' He [Barth] complained that the church had simply not drawn the breath to approach the 'completely immense task as the guardian of the spirit, of law and of freedom also in other areas than its own . . .' In agreement with these demands that the Confessing Church engage in political fighting, Barth accused the Lutheran bishops and the 'intact' churches, in another article in the *Neue Zürcher Zeitung* from February 14–15, 1937, of 'inertia and opportunism' in such a way that, through their readiness to compromise, the true face of National Socialist church politics is covered up and excused" (*Lebensführungen*, 128).

23 Künneth wrote: "The German-Christian Movement provides rich illustration of what demonism can do in political affairs. So soon as one has seen through this danger of a politicization of the church, the limitation is set against methods that can never be allowed within the church without corrupting its very nature. The church of Jesus

Coming out of a Calvinist and Reformed background, Barth rejected the Lutheran distinction between Law and Gospel and replaced it with his concept of Gospel and Law, in which the Law was only a form of the Gospel. Paradoxically, this destroyed the Gospel by setting up nomism, and it destroyed the Law by creating antinomianism. It is significant that when Barth spoke of the Word of God as that which upholds the persecuted faithful in Germany, he used a word about transcendence—the "*majesty* of the Word of God" ("*die Herrlichkeit des Wortes Gottes*")—and spoke of a biblical totalitarianism (*biblischer Totalitätsanspruch*) that resonated with claims for an absolutist state instead of a Christian faith. Hitler's totalitarianism was replaced here not by evangelical liberty but by a totalitarianism of the Law as it was understood by Barth. In terms of Lutheran thinking, however, one would avoid such a concept derived from the Law and replace it with an assertion of gracious divine intervention.[24]

Elert strongly criticized the theocratic tendencies of Barth. In a short article from 1938, Elert also accused Barth of duplicity as he cited the following promise to Czech soldiers made by Barth: "Every Czech soldier who then fights and suffers will do it also for us and also for the church of Jesus Christ." As he roundly criticized Barth for his theocratic tendencies, Elert compared this pronouncement of the Swiss theologian with the indulgence proclaimed in 1095 by Pope Urban II in favor of all who took part in the First Crusade. Elert asserted that Barth's movement was built squarely upon the Prussian Union and was antagonistic toward the Confessional Lutheran Church.[25] Elert's Confessional Lutheran heritage supplied him with the stabilizing force of the dialectic of Law and Gospel, and in the time of National Socialist hysteria, Elert could see more clearly than Barth the pitfalls of theocratic enthusiasm. Elert noted that in the medieval Holy Roman Empire, one

---

Christ possesses its strength not in the politics of religion; its invincibleness rests upon the command and the power of the risen Lord. The setting of political goals stands in open contradiction to the nature and task of the church. This is the responsibility of the hour, that the heritage of the Reformation that has been given the German people shall not be destroyed by thoughtless hands" (*Lebensführungen*, 133–34).

24 Barth uses all law words—words that demand some action of the individual—in the three biblical verses that he cites: "I am the LORD your God, who brought you out of Egypt, out of the land of slavery. You shall have no other gods beside me" (Exodus 20:2–3); "Whoever shall confess me before men, him I will also confess before my Father in heaven" (Matthew 10:32); "Blessed are they who are persecuted for righteousness' sake, for theirs is the kingdom of heaven" (Matthew 5:10). See Barth, *Not und Verheißung*, 17.

25 The original words of Barth were as follows: "Jeder tschechische Soldat, der dann streitet und leidet, wird es auch für uns—und, ich sage es heute ohne Vorbehalt: er wird es auch für die Kirche Jesus Christi tun" (cited in Werner Elert, "Randbemerkungen," *Luthertum* 49, no. 12 [1938]: 372–73).

spoke of society as a unified *Corpus Christianum*, with both political and ecclesial instances merged within a single unity. Elert comments that that fateful power was broken when Luther undermined it with theological arguments.[26] Luther's rejection of papal domination had emancipated the political powers of the state. The church was also set free, but it had a different purpose. Elert stated firmly: "The Word that is proclaimed by the church can only be an evangelical witness,"[27] thereby rejecting any political agenda for the church.

There were uncomfortable similarities between Hitler and Barth. Hitler followed a one-kingdom doctrine under which he was also marketing a religion. Hitler presented himself as the priest of a new religion, the religion of racism, blood, and soil. In fact, his policy in 1933 was to gain control of the churches by uniting them in an official *Reichskirche* or imperial church. This was to be realized through his German-Christian Movement.[28] Whereas Barth made a Law out of the Christian faith and issued his totalitarian summons in the name of Jesus Christ, Hitler propounded the religion of nation, *Volk*, and race and issued a totalitarian summons in his own name. Therefore despite his courageous words and deeds, the enthusiastic ideology of Barth was not capable of overthrowing the enthusiastic ideology of Hitler. In both forms of theocracy—whether held by Barth or Hitler—the result was a monarchistic divine rule without checks and balances and without any real restraints or control on the one who exercised the power. The respective ideologies of both Hitler and Barth were a form of philosophical dualism issuing into theocratic enthusiasm. Barth identified the social order with the kingdom (*Reich*) of Christ; Hitler identified it with the kingdom (*Reich*) of National Socialism. Some critics of Barth and Barmen have observed that the Confessing Church was likewise a totalitarian movement, demanding total acceptance of its concepts and denouncing people who differed with it, such as Sasse.

In Lutheran thought, the worldly and the spiritual powers relate to each other like Law and Gospel: "The divergence of the two realms of God's rule is identical with the divergence of Law and Gospel."[29] In attempting to deal with the charge

---

26 "Luther first smashed the idea of the Holy Roman Empire, i.e., the teaching that Christianity as a whole must be both a political and an ecclesiastical unity, under one spiritual and one political head, the emperor. Others had previously jolted it. But its fateful power was first broken when the ground under it was removed by the theological arguments of Luther" (Werner Elert, "Die Lutherische Kirche im neuen Reich," *Luthertum* 48, no. 2 [1937]: 38–39).

27 Elert, "Die Lutherische Kirche im neuen Reich," 42.

28 The religious aspects of Hitler are discussed in detail in Künneth, *Abfall*, 69–165. Hitler never officially left the Roman Catholic Church.

29 Elert, *Ethos*, 534.

that Lutherans teach a double standard (*Doppelgeleisigkeit*), Elert observed that this is valid only inasmuch as each Christian has a twofold character to his deeds: as a *private* person and Christian believer, on the one hand, and as an *official* person in his relations to others (ruler, teacher, spouse, parent, child, servant, etc.), on the other hand. These are done in "personal union" by the same person; nevertheless, they come under different aspects of Law and Gospel. In every case, there is no such thing as an autonomous ethic in Christian theology.

Elert noted that political actions differed when they were done by a Christian because in this case they were done out of love.[30] However, a non-Christian could serve in political office, but in this case without the love of Christ. Elert insisted that whether led by believers or unbelievers, political actions must be in accord with the Law of God. No leader was exempt from following the divine Law: "Every political happening is a legal happening, and the highest praise that one can give is to acknowledge that it has taken place in accord with the Law of God."[31]

---

30 Elert, *Ethos*, 537.

31 Elert, *Ethos*, 531.

CHAPTER ELEVEN

THE ANSBACH MEMORANDUM

For Confessional Lutherans, the involvement of Werner Elert and Paul Althaus in the 1934 *Ansbacher Ratschlag*, generally translated as the Ansbach Memorandum or Ansbach Counsel, was one of the most neuralgic issues of the whole *Kirchenkampf*. It might seem strange to the reader to devote an entire chapter to this issue, but there are two reasons for doing so. First, the Ansbach Memorandum receives frequent mention, but it has not been examined carefully within its historical and ideological context. Second, the Ansbach Memorandum is frequently cited as a black mark against the Confessional Lutherans and against their opposition to the Barmen Declaration and the theology of Karl Barth. It has become much like a macro on the computer: One simply presses the "Ansbach" button, and *causa finita est,* particularly when condemning Elert and Althaus. Charitable writers such as Sigurjón Arni Eyjólfsson and Wolfgang Trillhaas treat this uncomfortable incident with extreme delicacy, while aggressive writers such as Gerhard Niemöller and Berndt Hamm seemingly cannot draw enough blood over the "guilt" of the two Erlangen professors in the matter.

This macro must be traced back to its component parts to achieve more scholarly conclusions. Upon further review, one finds that, in light of subsequent events, it was a big mistake for Elert and Althaus to have signed the Ansbach Memorandum. However, on the basis of the limited knowledge of Adolf Hitler and National Socialism that they possessed at the time, and in light of their perception of the twin perils of Barthianism and the GDC, their choice was reasonable. The good reputation of Elert and Althaus was damaged, however, and the complaint has been frequently raised that the memorandum resulted in grave confusion within the German church.

EVENTS THAT LED TO THE ANSBACH MEMORANDUM

On June 11, 1934, nine Lutherans met in the quaint city of Ansbach in Middle Franconia. Dr. Hans Sommerer, director of the Deaconess Nursing Home at Bruckberg (near Ansbach), organized the meeting with the assistance of Dr. Ludwig Beer, pastor at Nuremberg-Eibach. Pastors Gottfried Fuchs (Ansbach), Heinrich Griessbach (Ansbach), Christian Seiler (Wildenholz), and Karl Werlin (Kleinhaslach); schoolteacher Ernst Fikenscher (Ansbach);[1] and professors Werner Elert and Paul Althaus completed the gathering.

The Ansbach Memorandum was intended as a response to a twofold danger: the GDC on the right and the Barmen Declaration on the left. The two men of Erlangen regarded the GDC as a great danger but thought the Barmen Declaration was both erroneous in its theology and unable to cope with the threat from the GDC. Systematic theology was customarily divided into dogmatics (doctrine) and ethics (life), but Barth had eliminated ethics from the theological system. Additionally, though Barth was completely political in his outlook in a theocratic sense, he pontificated against those who wrote about problems of political ethics. This did not seem to be a reasonable solution for Confessional Lutherans. Thus Elert explained his short-term involvement with the Ansbach Circle in an essay of October 1934: "The suspension of the ethical has been represented by a completely different theology for ten years. The Ansbach Memorandum has sought to work against the catastrophic effects which permanently result from the ethical sterility of this theology."[2]

Who wrote the Ansbach Memorandum? I believe it was written by Hans Sommerer (b. 1892). Writers routinely ascribe its authorship to Elert and its revisions to Althaus, but there is no evidence that it was written by either one of them.[3] Furthermore, Althaus and Elert, in depositions written in 1947 and 1948 respectively, each declared that he had not authored the document but that it already was complete upon its presentation to the group in Ansbach on June 11, 1934. Each man also said that his participation was restricted to a few revisions. Hans Rössler calls Sommerer the "initiator" of the document. Because Sommerer had called the meeting and was its chairman, he likely did not come empty-handed.

---

1 The most complete list of names is given in Meier, *EKK*, 1:193. Meier errs in regarding Elert as the principle author of the memorandum. Meier's list also omits Ludwig Beer.

2 Elert, "Der 'Ansbacher Ratschlag von 1934' und die kirchliche Lage in Bayern," *Korblatt* 59 (October 29, 1934): 479, second column.

3 Gerhard Niemöller claims that Elert was the author of the Ansbach Memorandum in *Die erste Bekenntnissynode der Deutschen Evangelischen Kirche zu Barmen,* AGK 5 (Göttingen: Vandenhoeck & Ruprecht, 1959), 143; see also Carter, 102. In fact, the allegation of Elert's authorship is widespread in the historical literature.

Instead, Sommerer would have brought along the first draft of the memorandum, which he himself must have written.[4] Anxious to win the support of the famous Erlangen professors and well-acquainted with their writings, Sommerer seems to have couched it in language similar to theirs. It was this first draft upon which the participants debated and which was then revised and, in its final form, presented for their signatures and then published. The framing of the introduction to the published memorandum is generally attributed to Sommerer.[5]

OVERVIEW OF THE ANSBACH MEMORANDUM

The Ansbach Memorandum should be examined within its historical context.[6] It was a short statement consisting of two parts: first, the doctrinal character of the church and, second, the current task of the church. The doctrinal basis of the church was defined as the Word of God, in which "God speaks to us in Law and Gospel." In the second part of the memorandum, the church, according to its outward character, was regarded as adhering to the orders of creation, such as the language of the people (§ 6). The memorandum stipulated that the duty of the church is to proclaim this Word and administer the Sacraments and the power of the keys (§ 7).

---

4 Rössler, "Das Ende einer Freundschaft—Rektor D. Hans Lauerer und Pfarrer Hans Sommerer im bayerischen Kirchenkampf (1934)," *Zeitschrift für bayerische Kirchengeschichte* 57 (1988): 77. See also the suggestion that Sommerer was the author of the Ansbach Memorandum in Elert, "Der 'Ansbacher Ratschlag,' " 478, column 2: "daß 'Herr Sommerer im Ansbacher Ratschlag eine Sittenlehre vorgelegt hat . . . .' "

5 There does seem to be an incongruity that Sommerer, an ardent German-Christian and member of the Nazi Party, should have written this memorandum, which Elert and Althaus regarded as a refutation of the positions of the GDC as well as those of Barth and Barmen. The memorandum was congenial to Sommerer, however, because it affirmed the orders of creation and stated allegiance to Hitler. In the Ansbach Circle, Sommerer evidently was posturing to win over the group from Erlangen, and he did not show his true colors until he connived in the *Gleichschaltung* of the Lutheran Land Church of Bavaria into the DEK in October 1934. At that time Sommerer was appointed bishop of Franconia (northern Bavaria) by Ludwig Müller and August Jäger. Sommerer replaced Hans Meiser. This unwelcome surprise for Elert and Althaus caused them (and three others) to denounce the Ansbach Circle and withdraw from it in autumn 1934. This action also prompted the Erlangen theology professors to sign a statement repudiating the *Gleichschaltung* and the deposing of Meiser. Sommerer's duplicity becomes clear in Rössler's characterization of him in "Das Ende einer Freundschaft" (see n. 4 above).

6 The text of the Ansbach Memorandum is given in Schmidt, *Bekenntnisse*, 2:102–4. It is also supplied to English readers by Reu in *KZ* 58 (August 1934): 506–8. Reu did not include Sommerer's prologue.

The first part, on the doctrinal foundation of the church, was focused on counteracting the teachings of the Barmen Declaration, which recognized only the Gospel of Christ, thereby neglecting the Law. In § 2, the Ansbach Memorandum stated: "The Word of God speaks to us as Law and Gospel. The proclamation of the church must orient itself accordingly. The Gospel is the message of the Lord Jesus Christ who died for our sins and rose again for our justification." In § 3, the writer continues with the observation that the Law, "the unchangeable will of God" (FC Ep VI 6), "meets us in the total reality of our life . . . It binds us to the estate in which God has called us and obligates us to the natural orders, under which we have been placed, such as family, *Volk*, and race (i.e., blood relationships). . . . In that the will of God further meets us today and in our place, it binds us also to a certain moment of the family, the *Volk*, the race, i.e., a certain moment of history."[7] With such a firm statement on the Law, one can understand Elert's willingness to try to work with the men at Ansbach.[8]

In § 4, the Ansbach Memorandum points out that the orders not only place us before the imperative will of God but also before the gubernatorial divine will. In asserting that the Christian accepts government—whether kind or harsh, healthy or deformed—as a God-given order, the memorandum alludes to 1 Peter 2:18: "Be subject to your masters with all fear; not only to the good and gentle, but also to the forward."

The most controversial part of the Ansbach Memorandum was § 5, which ventured to endorse Hitler's new government: "In this knowledge, we, as believing Christians, thank God the Lord that he has given our people in its need a leader [*Führer*] as a 'pious and faithful lord' and that, in the National Socialistic Constitution, he wants to give us 'good government,' a government with 'order and honor.' "[9] One may note the allusions to the Fourth Petition in Luther's Small Catechism. We might compare this with another statement from that time by Elert in which he asserts that the state is only a "natural order" and that if the state transgresses against this characteristic in such a way that forbids the Gospel, it forfeits the obedience of its people, in accordance with the *clausula Petri* of Acts 5:29.[10]

---

7 Schmidt, *Bekenntnisse*, 2:103.

8 In his theology, Elert distinguished three aspects of the Law: a creational aspect, expressed in the orders; an imperative aspect (the Decalogue), commanding what should be done and left undone; and a judicatory aspect, exposing sin. For an investigation of these three functions of the Law in Elert, see Eyjólfsson, 45, 113, 119.

9 Schmidt, *Bekenntnisse*, 2:103.

10 Elert wrote that not Peter but the authorities had broken the civil law when they forbade preaching the Gospel. "The *clausula Petri* of Acts 5:29 is not a stipulation regarding the duty to obey, but rather the simple reminder that the government is a natural order, not less, but also not more" (*BBB*, 34–35).

THE HISTORICAL CONTEXT OF THE ANSBACH MEMORANDUM

It must be asked: How could the two professors from the University of Erlangen have declared their allegiance to such a corrupt man as Hitler? The answer to this question lies in the fact that the Ansbach Memorandum can only be accurately interpreted when it is considered within its historical context. For this to be done, one must compare a series of pledges of allegiance to the new government that were given in its first year not only by Elert and Althaus but by men such as Martin Niemöller, Walter Künneth, Hanns Lilje, and even Hermann Sasse.[11] As we have seen before, the ill-fated Ansbach Memorandum had a twofold target: It was aimed against the theology behind the Barmen Declaration and against the ideology of the German-Christians, which had not been adequately addressed by the Barmen Declaration.[12]

Regarding the historical context, it is important to realize that the Ansbach Memorandum was written during the early part of the new government. During the first two years after Hitler's election in March 1933, the new chancellor, who had won only 43 percent of the vote, proceeded cautiously. At the start, Hitler did not introduce a full-fledged National Socialist state, only a nationalistic regime. This tended to blind the Germans to Hitler's true intentions. After he was firmly established, he gradually introduced a totalitarian dictatorship, which became increasingly repressive.[13] During the first two years of Hitler's government, a number of statements of support for the new political order were given by church leaders from all sides.[14] Previous considerations of the Ansbach Memorandum have neglected to compare it with other pledges of loyalty from that time. There are several kindred statements backing Hitler that deserve attention.

For example, in the May 1933 Appeal of the Young Reformation Movement (*Der Aufruf der Jungreformatorischen Bewegung*), Künneth, Niemöller, and Lilje, who were all later known for their vehement opposition to National Socialism,

---

11 A pledge of allegiance is not unknown in the United States. In fact, this continues to be a daily practice in most, if not all, schools.

12 See Althaus's critique of Barmen, "Bedenken zur 'Theologischen Erklärung' der Barmer Bekenntnissynode," repr. in Beyschlag, 258–63; allusion here to 261.

13 Concerning the unawareness of church leaders in 1934 regarding the deceptiveness of Hitler, Erich Beyreuther writes: "Hitler knew how to bring about, in a masterful way, a 'national uprising,' a 'national revolution,' of the whole German nation. He set up a nationalistic, but not a National Socialistic government [during 1933 and 1934]. The black-red-gold flag of the Weimar Republic disappeared, the swastika did not yet appear, but instead the black-white-red flag of the pre-war [World War I] period was raised on the flagpoles" (*Die Geschichte des Kirchenkampfes in Dokumenten 1933/45* [Wuppertal: R. Brockhaus, 1966], 21).

14 Beyreuther, *Die Geschichte des Kirchenkampfes*, 23.

signed a similar pledge: "§ 11: We demand that the Evangelical Church, *in a joyful affirmation of the new German state*, fulfill its God-given task in full freedom from all political influence and simultaneously bind itself to an indissoluble commitment of service to the German *Volk*."[15] On October 15, 1933, the day after Germany declared its withdrawal from the League of Nations, a group of pastors from Niemöller's circle gave this public pledge of loyalty in a telegram sent to Hitler: "In this hour, which is so decisive for *Volk* and fatherland, we greet you as our Führer. We thank you for the manly deed and the clear word which guards German honor. In the name of more than 2,500 evangelical pastors who do not belong to the German-Christian Movement, *we pledge you our loyal following* and our prayerful thoughts."[16] This statement was written by Wilhelm Harnisch of Berlin and signed by Werner Messow of Steglitz and by Fritz Müller, Niemöller, and Eberhard Röhricht, all of Dahlem.

Moreover, an important parallel to the doctrine of orders in the Ansbach Memorandum is found in an essay written a year earlier by Dietrich Bonhoeffer in which he, too, spoke of good and poor orders as stemming from God's creation:

> The Reformational church . . . does not praise or reprimand the laws of the state. But rather the church affirms the state as God's order of preservation in the godless world. The church recognizes its creation of orders, whether good or poor from the humanitarian viewpoint, as based in the preservative will of God amidst the chaotic godlessness of the world. This evaluation of the state's actions through the church stands beyond all moralism and distinguishes itself from humanitarianism of every shading by the radicalness of the separation of the place of the Glad Tidings and the place of the Law. The actions of the state remain free from the intervention of the church.[17]

---

15 The original German: "Wir fordern, daß die evangelische Kirche in freudigem Ja zum neuen deutschen Staat den ihr von Gott gegebenen Auftrag in voller Freiheit von aller politischen Beeinflussung erfüllt und sich zugleich in unlöslichem Dienst an das deutsche Volk bindet" (Schmidt, *Bekenntnisse*, 1:146; *Green's emphasis added to the English translation*). This document and its origin are described by one of its authors, Künneth, in *Lebensführungen*, 106ff., esp. 111.

16 The original German: "In dieser für Volk und Vaterland entscheidenden Stunde grüßen wir unseren Führer. Wir danken für die mannhafte Tat und das klare Wort, die Deutschlands Ehre wahren. Im Namen von mehr als 2500 evangelischen Pfarrern, die der Glaubensbewegung Deutscher Christen nicht angehören, geloben wir treue Gefolgshaft und fürbittenden Gedenken. Harnisch, Berlin; Messow, Steglitz; Müller, Dahlem; Niemöller, Dahlem; Röhricht, Dahlem" (*Junge Kirche* 1 [1933]: 252; *Green's emphasis added to the English translation*). See the comments by Scholder, *Kirchen*, 1:638 and n. 41, 847. Scholder glosses over this statement as an example of a general disillusion with the League of Nations and overlooks its profession of loyalty to Hitler.

By April 28, 1934, a month before the Synod of Barmen and six weeks before the adoption of the Ansbach Memorandum, Bonhoeffer complained in a letter to a Swiss friend that Niemöller still thought he could advance the objectives of the church by working with Hitler's Third Reich.[18] It would be a safe generalization to say that most intellectual Germans lacked a prophetic vision of political events, but this did not mean that they had evil intentions.

OPPOSITION TO THE ANSBACH MEMORANDUM

In 1934 and thereafter, the Ansbach Memorandum encountered fierce opposition from the supporters of the Barmen Declaration and the Confessing Church. Moreover, only four months after the meeting at Ansbach, Bishop Hans Meiser was apprehended by the Nazis and placed under house arrest. Kurt Frör called the Ansbach Memorandum "a dagger's stab" in the bishop's back. Barth and his circle of followers denounced the memorandum ferociously.

The Ansbach Memorandum had been intended as a moderate position on the political situation, but German-Christian members of the Ansbach Circle misused it to support concepts that neither Elert nor Althaus could endorse. Thus on September 9, 1934, Hans Sommerer published a summons under the title "Peace in the Church!" He appealed for the incorporation of the Bavarian Land Church within the DEK, a position neither Elert nor Althaus could support. Therefore both professors from the University of Erlangen publicly withdrew from the Ansbach Circle without, however, repudiating the theological content of the Ansbach Memorandum itself.[19] Elert made this clear in a September 19, 1934, letter to Meiser in which he wrote: "Of course, after I received a copy of the 'Declaration' by the members of the 'Ansbach Circle,' I immediately renounced this group."[20]

---

17 Bonhoeffer, "Die Kirche vor der Judenfrage," in *Bonhoeffer*, 12:350. This statement from June 1933, shortly before the writing of the Bethel Confession, shows Bonhoeffer at a time when he was relatively free of Barthian influence and still embraced the Lutheran doctrine of creation, which was spurned by Barth. Several years later, Barth wrote to Bonhoeffer that he should leave the safety of his position in England to return to Germany and engage in the church struggle. Sasse remarked that he should not have listened to Barth, who afterward found himself a safe position in Switzerland whereas Bonhoeffer, hearkening to Barth, pursued a course that led to his death at the hands of the Nazis.

18 April 28, 1934, letter to Erwin Sutz in Eberhard Bethge, ed., *Gesammelte Schriften: Dietrich Bonhoeffer* (Munich: Kaiser, 1958ff.), 1:39–40; cited also in Friedrich Baumgärtel, *Wider die Kirchenkampf-Legenden* (Neuendettelsau: Freimund, 1976), 39.

19 Rössler, "Das Ende einer Freundschaft," 77.

20 Letter to Meiser in ATF, file "Elert."

During the time Meiser was under house arrest by the Nazis, Elert spoke out in a October 29, 1934, article that appeared in the church paper for Bavarian pastors. Elert objected that an anonymous writer in a circular letter had claimed that "the theology of the Ansbach Memorandum was at work" in the circumstances behind the seizure of the land church by the German-Christians. It was asserted in the circular: "If there are only temporal orders and no unconditionally valid, divine commands that are permanent according to their content, then the iniquity will take place over which we must lament." The critic had also written: "Mr. Sommerer presented a morality in the Ansbach Memorandum that makes the divine commandments dependent upon the *volkische* situation of a particular time and thereby completely relativizes morality." Elert puzzles over the motivation of the writer, saying: "It cannot be unknown to the writer that following the latest church developments in Bavaria, five of the eight signers of the Ansbach Memorandum have announced their withdrawal from the Ansbach Circle. Dr. Althaus and I have added to our public cancellation of membership the assurance of our abiding assent to the Ansbach Memorandum."[21]

Elert goes on to add that the author of those anonymous lines must have been aware that the entire theological faculty of Erlangen had denounced the aggression of the Reich Church leadership against the church of Bavaria, a statement that, Elert points out, was signed by Althaus and himself.[22] Writes Elert: "He might have come thereby to the conclusion that the 'theology of the Ansbach Memorandum' must lead to completely different conclusions than those he himself has suggested."[23] Elert goes on to discuss the underlying problem with which the Ansbach Memorandum had attempted to cope:

> Over against the teaching of the other side, that the church does not recognize anything else as a "source of her proclamation" aside from the one word Jesus Christ [Barmen Declaration], the memorandum presents with considerable emphasis the teaching of the Lutheran Confessions that the proclamation of the church must give an accounting that God's Word speaks to us not only as Gospel but also as Law. The Law is characterized there, with the words of the Formula of Concord, as the "unchangeable will of God."[24]

Elert's words are significant because they were delivered during a time when it was important to appear friendly to the Nazi cause, though he nevertheless took a

---

21 Elert, "Der 'Ansbacher Ratschlag,' " 478.

22 Elert is referring here to the "Stellungnahme des Theologischen Fakultät Erlangen," which had been propagated on October 13, 1934 (Schmidt, *Bekenntnisse*, 2:154–55).

23 Elert, "Der 'Ansbacher Ratschlag,' " 478.

24 Elert, "Der 'Ansbacher Ratschlag,' " 478.

critical stance against the machinations of the GDC. Elert reported to Rector Fritz Specht of the University of Erlangen on November 17, 1937, as follows:

> Our relationship with the "Ansbach Circle," which stood behind the "Ansbach Memorandum," fell into pieces when their leaders took part with Jäger in breaking into the Land Church Office in Munich, and two of them made themselves into bishops for Bavaria and Franconia. We could not consent to this violence on churchly territory. The liberation and restoration of Meiser which followed by the personal intervention of the Führer showed that we were right.[25]

Many years later, Elert wrote the following concerning the Ansbach Memorandum:

> The Ansbach Memorandum of June 11, 1934, came out of a time when one still made the attempt to hold the new powers to their own promises. Together with Dr. Althaus, I was asked by a circle of pastors who were previously unknown to me to place my name under the statement. Subsequently I had neither a further conversation with this circle nor any further meeting with them.

> The draft of the declaration was already completed when it was placed before us. Althaus and I suggested only a few corrections. I viewed this as nothing else than a statement of loyalty which I, as a state employee, had already been required to give by the oath to Hitler. The expressions, "pious and faithful lords," "good government," "discipline and honor," were placed within quotation marks to remind the reader that they were taken out of Luther's Catechism.[26]

There is a similar statement by Althaus. In 1947, Althaus's subscription of the Ansbach Memorandum was one of the charges brought against him by the U.S. occupation forces that led to his suspension. Althaus wrote a significant statement to explain his part in the matter:

1. I was not the author of the Ansbach Memorandum. In that one and only session of the "Ansbach Circle" which I attended at the request of Dr. Elert, the text was presented already in basically the very form in which it was later published.

2. I remember with real certainty that in that session, upon my recommendation (partly in common with Dr. Elert) revisions in the text were still undertaken. . . . There where it originally said: "God *has prepared* his *Volk* a governance with discipline and honor, . . ." at the wish of Elert and myself it was changed to read: "God *wills to prepare* his *Volk.* . . ." I do not

---

25 "Report to the Rector," ATF, file "Elert Papers," 10.

26 "Preliminary Examination," ATF, file "Elert Papers," 1–2.

need to clarify the meaning of this recommendation; its significance is self-evident.

3. I acceded to the wishes of the Ansbach Circle to join them, and I signed the memorandum because, in the situation at the beginning of June 1934, I was deeply concerned that the necessary struggle against the power of the German-Christians, in the wake of the Barmen meeting and Declaration, might be carried on with the weapons of Barthian theology as the land churches represented at Barmen had accepted it. I saw therein a real danger for the church. For if this theology determined the action of the church and its theological pronouncements, in that case, in my judgment, unsurrenderable truths of Lutheran political ethics, as the German-Christians misused them, would fall under the table. That would have meant that one had not really overcome the German-Christians.[27]

Althaus then closed with a reference to his June 1934 article "Concerns about the 'Theological Declaration of the Barmen Confessing Synod.' "

At the beginning of this chapter, the Ansbach Memorandum was compared to the macro button on a computer. There are other such macros used by some historians to achieve their purposes, buttons that are never adequately examined but that, when pressed, are thought to achieve a desired emotional result. This discussion of the Ansbach affair was intended to guide the reader to develop less-biased conclusions regarding the matter and to a more moderate consideration of history "as it actually happened." After World War II, the Ansbach Memorandum was also used by some people from the former Confessing Church as a tool of manipulation against the Confessional Lutherans. Therefore the above clarification is urgently needed.

There can be no question that Elert and Althaus lacked a thorough knowledge of what Hitler and Sommerer were up to when they worked with the Ansbach Circle in June 1934. Future events revealed the mistake made by the Erlangen professors. However, it was not a mistake to have insisted firmly upon the distinction between Law and Gospel. This distinction is the heart of all Lutheran theology, and despite its opponents, one cannot simply write off the theology of the world's largest Protestant faith. The theology of Elert and Althaus at this point was in accord with the Lutheran Confessions, and in the ensuing fifty years, the failure to pursue that theology more consistently became the cause of many theological, political, and social dysfunctions. The mistake of Elert and Althaus was that they

---

27 The above is from a typewritten statement by Althaus in the file "Entlaßung 1947 P. Althaus," from Althaus Papers, in the possession of Gerhard Althaus. In this 1947 statement, Althaus also refers to his 1934 paper "Bedenken zur 'Theologische Erklaerung' der Barmer Bekenntnissynode," which originally appeared in several church papers and was reprinted in Beyschlag, appendix 7, 258–63.

carried on a conversation with a group that was headed by Sommerer, a German-Christian and a Nazi with unscrupulous political ambitions. They recognized their blunder as early as September 1934 and publicly acknowledged it in October of that year. Despite the fulminations of Barth and Barmen, Elert and Althaus continually insisted that the church must proclaim not only the Gospel but also the Law as the unchanging will of God. It was precisely the antinomianism of their opponents that, albeit unknowingly, supported the lawless course that Hitler would soon pursue.

Elert and Althaus had pointed out that not even National Socialism had the right to stand above God's Law, and it is difficult to understand why Barth opposed that position. If we might speak of a certain blindness on his part, it was likely Barth's rejection of the distinction between Law and Gospel that misled him into antinomianism. One could not countermand Hitler by saying it wasn't nice to kill the Jews (Barth's Gospel-Law dialectic); instead, one had to thunder out with the force of God's Law on Mount Sinai: "Thou shalt not kill." It was their near-desperation at the blunders of the Barmen Declaration that drove Elert and Althaus into the arms of the Ansbach Circle. Scholars must not handle this unfortunate episode without appropriate attention to its historical and theological context.

CHAPTER TWELVE

ENDEAVORS TO ACHIEVE LUTHERAN UNITY IN GERMANY

In 1932 there were fifteen Confessional Lutheran land churches in Germany. Most Lutherans wanted to overcome the historical divisions that had placed them in separate territorial churches and combine into one United Evangelical Lutheran Church in Germany that could work with other Lutheran churches worldwide and participate in the ecumenical movement. But there were strong nationalistic voices in Germany that called upon Lutherans to give up their confessional identity and work instead toward a nationalistic German Protestant Church. These individuals wanted national rather than ecumenical ties. Often these voices came from the Prussian Union, but Karl Barth also spoke in favor of such unity. On April 20–21, 1927, Barth had spoken differently before Thuringian Lutheran pastors at the Rudolstadt Free Pastoral Conference. His position was described by a witness as follows:

> Barth also acknowledged repeatedly in his conclusion that a deep inward penetration into the final questions is only possible where the minds have neither been weakened by liberalism nor blunted by Union Church tendencies. In other words, this can happen only where there is still understanding for the great questions that moved our fathers in the sixteenth and seventeenth centuries. Lutheranism and Calvinism still show themselves as precisely today's types of evangelical Christianity, which do not avoid the deepest problems but instead understand how to address them and know how to solve them.[1]

---

1 Reported by Krohn of Rudolstadt in *AELKZ* 60 (1927): 448.

For the present, we shall not try to account for the change in Barth's favorable attitude toward Lutheran solidarity in 1927 and his later insistence that the differences between Lutheran, Reformed, and Union doctrine no longer mattered, so Lutherans should give up their autonomy and join in the nationalistic German Protestant movement.[2] This meant that the Confessional Lutherans who strove to bring about one United Evangelical Lutheran Church in Germany faced raucous opposition from other Protestant entities, such as the followers of Barth and the Dahlem Front.

It has been previously noted that many Lutherans hoped the DEK might unite all German Lutherans into a Confessional Lutheran Reich Church. But their hopes faded as they saw the DEK become an extension of the Prussian Union and Hitler's Reich Church. Lutherans soon found themselves fighting against the incorporation (*Gleichschaltung*) program of Reich Bishop Ludwig Müller. Those churches that were unsuccessful in evading incorporation found that they had become puppet churches under the Reich bishop. Therefore Lutheran leaders looked in other directions to achieve Lutheran unification in Germany. Their goal of one united Lutheran Church would not occur until after World War II, but important steps toward Lutheran unity were taken throughout the years of the Third Reich.

WILHELM ZOELLNER'S SUMMONS FOR LUTHERAN UNITY

Wilhelm Zoellner issued an appeal to German Lutherans to work together, an appealed entitled "The Church at the Rebirth of the Nation: An Appeal for the Coming Together of the Lutherans."[3] Writing in April 1933, Zoellner was a plucky Confessional Lutheran within the Union Church who was concerned that the devastating measures of the Prussian Union might be applied to the Confessional Lutheran churches as they prepared for the formation of the DEK (see chapter 3). His appeal sounded the warning for Lutherans to guard their confessional integrity during the debates over the projected DEK. Regarding Zoellner, Georg Merz commented that he was one of those men "who had authority and who did not waste it." Guy Christopher Carter writes:

> President of the Reich Church Committee, General Superintendent of the Westphalian Province of the Evangelical Church of the Old Prussian Union, Zoellner was firmly behind the move toward a new Reich Protestant church and was determined that that church would bear an unmistakably Lutheran

---

2 For Barth's changed position in this regard, see Karl Barth, *Not und Verheißung im Deutscher Kirchenkampf* (Bern: Buchhandlung der Evangelischen Gesellschaft, 1938), 8.

3 Title in Meiser, *Verantwortung*, 1:1 n. 1. Text without title in Schmidt, *Bekentnnisse*, 1:140–41. For a more detailed discussion of Zoellner's appeal, see chapter 3.

stamp. In the person of Wilhelm Zoellner, the new political regime and the GDC [German-Christians] found themselves confronted by the full weight of Prussian civic and church tradition which would not tolerate the obliteration of traditional ecclesiastical prerogatives and protocol, not even and particularly in the name of "revolution."[4]

The Lutheran Meeting at Würzburg on May 14, 1933

The most direct response to Zoellner's summons occured when representatives of all the Lutheran land churches came to a meeting at Würzburg on May 14, 1933, to discuss cooperation among Lutherans. The meeting had been called by the new bishop of the Lutheran Land Church of Bavaria, Hans Meiser, who was concerned that the projected founding of the Reich Church would endanger the position of the Lutheran Confessions in the churches.[5] Representatives attended from the churches of Bavaria, Württemberg, Saxony, Thuringia, Hanover, Mecklenburg, Schleswig-Holstein, Braunschweig, and Oldenburg.[6] Men such as Meiser hoped for a future United Lutheran Church of Germany that would be firmly grounded in Confessional Lutheran principles. The role of the Lutheran churches within the future DEK was discussed by the participants, and they affirmed the following resolution: "The Lutheran land churches of Germany unite together as a Lutheran branch within the forthcoming German Evangelical Church for the preservation and representation of their common Lutheran Confession and for the promotion of the resultant common tasks, under the reservation that the individual churches shall remain in charge of their own affairs."[7]

At the conclusion of the meeting, the following resolution was released regarding the uncertain situation that the churches faced following the accession of Hitler as German chancellor:

> We wrestle and pray that the new beginning of the nation will mean also a new breakthrough to God. Therefore, we see ourselves obligated to speak to our people the message of the Lutheran Reformation: It is God who has ordered the nation [*Volkstum*] and the civil authorities. It is God who in his judgment and in his grace leads to forgiveness of sins and only by this to true freedom. It is God who brings to realization true fellowship and discipline in his church.[8]

---

4 Carter, 129–30.

5 See Meiser, *Verantwortung*, 1:1; Helmreich, 134. Cf. Meier, *EKK*, 2:110.

6 Meier, *EKK*, 2:110.

7 Hermelink, 36.

8 Klügel, *Landeskirche*, 43.

They added: "We demand that in the forthcoming German Evangelical Church the faith of Luther and the confession of our fathers be given free course; . . . that this church be organized according to its own rules and thereby all foreign things that are remnants of parliamentary forms be excluded."[9]

The conference at Würzburg was significant. But Lutheran unity was impeded by Nazi interference and repression of the churches during the Third Reich. At the same time, the church struggles taught people to work together against a common foe. The United Evangelical Lutheran Church of Germany (*Vereinigte evangelische-lutherische Kirche in deutschland* [VELKD]) was successfully organized after World War II. Unfortunately, it had to deal with the resentment of Union church leaders against Lutherans and the competition from the EKD, as Hermann Dietzfelbinger has pointed out.[10]

FURTHER STEPS TOWARD LUTHERAN UNITY IN GERMANY

The Würzburg Resolutions from the previous year had a direct influence on the organization of the Lutheran Council (*Lutherischer Rat*) when representatives of the various Lutheran land churches gathered at Hanover on August 25, 1934.

Several weeks earlier, on August 9, the disgraceful National Synod of the DEK had taken place in Berlin. Reich Bishop Müller had despotically removed a number of church leaders with whom he felt uncomfortable and had arbitrarily issued decrees that overturned important measures of the DEK Constitution. On August 14, Meiser, in the name of the Evangelical Lutheran Land Church Council in Munich, sent a stiff protest to Wilhelm Frick, Reich Minister of the Interior, who dealt with church affairs. Meiser protested:

> The Reich Church government has added to its previous open violations of the constitution a new breach of the law . . . in that it, by a decree of July 7, 1934, arbitrarily set forth certain requirements for belonging to the National Synod and, in a likewise arbitrary application of these rules, removed from their office certain irreproachable and respected members of the National Synod and replaced them by others. . . . The actual course of the National Synod was unworthy of a synod. . . . We are, by virtue of our office and by our conscience, obligated to unmask this perversion of an evangelical synod from its false appearance, and all the more so as the Reich Church government will doubtless exploit this misleading representation in its well-known tendency to deceive.[11]

---

9 Hermelink, 36.

10 Discussed in Klügel, *Landeskirche*, 43–44; see also the account of his own experiences in Dietzfelbinger, 219–23.

11 Reported by Reu in *KZ* 58 (1934): 632–33.

It was this crisis in the DEK that provided the tone for the organizational meeting of the Lutheran Council at Hanover. Among the representatives present were four Lutheran land bishops: Meiser, August Marahrens, Theophil Wurm, and Otto Zänker (Breslau). Others present included Zoellner (Düsseldorf), Heinz Kloppenburg (Wilhelmshaven), and Paul Althaus and Friedrich Ulmer (Erlangen).[12] It was a time of great peril. Marahrens was engaged in a mortal struggle with the GDC to keep his church intact, and at the very time the council met, August Jäger and Müller were plotting to seize control of the intact land churches of Württemberg and Bavaria and to suppress permanently the doctrinal positions held by Confessional Lutherans. At that meeting, the new Lutheran Council declared: "Instead of taking seriously the critical issues raised ever and again by the Lutheran Confessions, one went ahead with incorporating the Lutheran churches into the German Evangelical Church in such a way that we, before and after, must recognize an injury to their mettle [*Charakter*] as Lutheran churches."[13]

Klügel speaks of the steamroller effect of the church merger politics (*Gleichschaltung*) that attempted to level off the confessional differences among the churches. He summarizes the significance of of the Lutheran Council as follows: "If resistance had not been exerted at this point, the Lutheran Church in Germany would have had to give itself up."[14]

On February 13, 1935, three Lutheran land bishops—Meiser, Wurm, and Marahrens—entered an agreement that would result in better coordination of the work of their respective land churches. It was called the Lutheran Pact (*Lutherischer Pakt*). Six objectives were listed:

1. To promote close cooperation in administrative matters among the land churches that joined the pact.

2. To provide uniformity concerning the church year with its calendar of festivals and to establish consistency in liturgical practices and in the Scripture selections read in the church services, as well as to standardize religious instruction among the churches (insofar as this could be carried out within the school laws of the state) and to establish uniform guidelines for youth programs and for the work of inner missions (*Volkmission*).

3. To develop compatible principles in educating men for the ministry, theological examinations, and ordination.

---

12 Hermelink, 134–35; cf. Meier, *EKK*, 2:111.

13 Klügel, *Landeskirche*, 254.

14 Klügel, *Landeskirche*, 254.

4. To set up a commission to unify as much as possible the legislation among the land churches, the gathering of church taxes, the changing of territorial lines between churches, and so forth.

5. To trust the leadership of common matters to Land Bishop August Marahrens until further notice.

6. To allow other land churches to join this pact so long as they shared its confessional stance and procedures.[15]

The three bishops also expressed their confidence in the work of the Provisional Church Leadership (*Vorläufige Kirchenleitung* [VKL]), which consisted of five men of ecclesiastical repute and was headed by Marahrens.

These three intact churches had an important task in maintaining their own freedom from Nazi attempts at seizure; they also used their independence to succor the destroyed land churches, especially those of the Lutheran confession.[16] The pact was a source of stability during the upheavals of the Third Reich, but it did not fulfill all expectations, for it had only limited powers, and it could not overcome the age-old cultural differences among the Lower Saxons, the Bavarians, and the people in the Swabish church.[17]

Another key event in Lutheran cooperation was the German Lutheran Diet (*Deutscher Lutherischer Tag*), which was held July 2–5, 1935, in Hanover. Representatives from the various land churches attended this meeting, which built upon the May 1933 Würzburg Resolutions. At the Confessing Synod in Dahlem it had been decided that the leadership branches within the Confessing Church should be set up according to confession; therefore the German Lutheran Diet chose leaders for the Lutheran branches. It was also decided that a continuation committee for the Diet would be arranged in concert with the Lutheran Council to continue this task in the future.[18]

Especially important for Lutheran unity was the formation of the Commission for Lower-German Lutheranism (*Ausschuß für das niederdeutsche Luthertum*). Since the Reformation, Northern (Lower) Germany had been predominately Lutheran, but this area had suffered from political fragmentation into many small states. Thus the church also went through ecclesiastical fragmentation into many small Lutheran land churches. According to Eberhard Klügel, this fragmentation helped the German-Christians to seize control and subjugate these

---

15 Document in Hermelink, 264–66. Also given in Schmidt, *Bekenntnisse*, 3:59–61. See also the presentation on the Lutheran Pact in Meier, *EKK*, 2:112–13.

16 Meier, *EKK*, 2:112.

17 Klügel, *Landeskirche*, 258–59.

18 Klügel, *Landeskirche*, 259–63; Meier, *EKK*, 2:113.

churches under the Third Reich. The Commission for Lower-German Lutheranism endeavored to unite these churches. This occurred when the *Brüder-Rate* (Brethren Councils) of eight North German Lutheran land churches met in Lüneburg on October 7, 1935, and signed the Lüneburg Agreement (*Lüneburger Abkommen*).[19] The churches who signed, in addition to Hanover, included Schleswig-Holstein, Hamburg, Lübeck, Mecklenburg, Braunschweig, Oldenburg, and Schaumburg-Lippe.[20] Marahrens was given the clerical leadership of this commission.

During the conflict between the Lübeck pastors and their land church council, which was controlled by Nazis, the pastors were guided by the Lüneburg Agreement. This agreement also guided the efforts of the pastors in Mecklenburg in their troubles with the High Church Council in Schwerin, as well as the pastors in Hamburg in their struggle against the insurgent Bishop Franz Tügel.[21] It was also this continual struggle against the German-Christians and the Nazi authorities that prevented the commission from carrying out the hoped-for unification of German Lutherans in the north. All the Lower German churches except Hanover and Schaumburg-Lippe were under GDC control. Although Hamburg and Braunschweig joined the Luther Council, the German-Christian presence in these two churches prevented the full development of the possibilities for Lutheran unity in the north.[22] It wasn't until some years after World War II that the North German churches could finally form a single Lutheran land church.

THE FOUNDING OF THE VELKD

The single most important factor in the drive toward Lutheran unity was the founding of the Luther Council (*Luther-Rat*). Following the virtual collapse of the Confessing Church at Bad Oeynhausen, the Luther Council was founded on March 18, 1936, by Meiser, Wurm, and Marahrens. This was the permanent alliance that eventually led to the founding of the VELKD.[23] The Luther Council was patterned somewhat after the Brethren Council (*Brüder-Rat*), which the Confessing Church had set up for its destroyed churches.

The Brethren Council of the Confessing Church was represented by additional Brethren Councils in the various land churches. The objectives of these

---

19 Klügel, *Landeskirche*, 71 n. 28.

20 Text in Hermelink, 266; see also Klügel, *Landeskirche*, 263–66.

21 On the situation in Schwerin, see Niklot Beste, *Der Kirchenkampf in Mecklenburg von 1933 bis 1945: Geschichte, Dokumente, Erinnerungen* (Göttingen: Vandenhoeck & Ruprecht, 1975).

22 Klügel, *Landeskirche*, 265.

23 Documents in Hermelink, 331–36.

local councils, adapted to the situation in the Union church and often aligned with the Dahlem Front, did not correspond fully with needs in the destroyed Lutheran churches. The intact Lutheran land churches worked toward the formation of organizations analogous to the local Brethren Councils, which would serve the needs of the destroyed Lutheran churches; these groups within the various land churches came to be known as Luther Councils.

The Luther Council was established at the national level as a step toward the unification of all German Lutheranism. The leadership of the Luther Council was vested in the three land bishops: Marahrens, Meiser, and Wurm. Additional leadership came from Thomas Breit, Hanns Lilje, and Niklot Beste.[24] Later, Paul Fleisch took the place of Lilje, who had to resign because of his heavy commitments to the ecumenical movement. To avoid the danger of the Luther Council being pushed aside by busy bishops, a separate secretariat was established, which was administered by a commission headed by Breit, a good administrator and a strongly Confessional Lutheran theologian from Bavaria. Fleisch, an excellent theologian and administrator, represented the church of Hanover on the Luther Council.

Unlike the Dahlem Front, which had a negative attitude toward the Reich Church Commission (*Reichskircheausschuß* [RKA]), the Luther Council tried to cooperate with Hanns Kerrl to establish church commissions in the destroyed churches. These land church commissions under Kerrl helped to provide ecclesiastical governance that was out of reach of the German-Christians.[25] In fact, in the case of Lübeck, the RKA tried to protect the Confessing Church pastors during their confrontation with the German-Christian Church Council. Zoellner, a member of the RKA, was to visit Lübeck to investigate the conflict. When the Gestapo prevented his visit, Zoellner resigned in protest. When the other members of the commission followed suit, the RKA fell apart, much to the chagrin of Kerrl.

Beste related how the Luther Council assisted his own destroyed church of Mecklenburg, and he described how Breit traveled to Schwerin and negotiated with the German-Christian High Consistorial Council in an attempt to ameliorate conditions for the persecuted Lutheran pastors of Mecklenburg. Moreover, Marahrens, from the neighboring Land Church of Hanover, took a keen interest in matters in Mecklenburg and was a source of strength to Beste and his fellow pastors.[26]

---

24 Klügel, *Landeskirche*, 266.

25 Meier, *EKK*, 2:115; Klügel, *Landeskirche*, 270–71.

26 Beste, *Der Kirchenkampf in Mecklenburg*, 158–59. The Church Commission in Mecklenburg challenged the German-Christian High Consistorial Council of Schwerin,

The Luther Council could have been the venue for full Lutheran unity in Germany. However, occasionally the bishops placed restrictions upon the work allotted to the council, so Lutheran unity had to be deferred until after the war.[27] The full influence of the Luther Council finally came to fruition when the VELKD was founded at Eisenach, July 6–8, 1948.[28]

A NEW LUTHERAN JOURNAL: *LUTHERTUM*

A new theological journal, *Luthertum* (*Lutheranism*) was founded in 1934 to serve as a sounding board for Confessional Lutheran writers. It was edited by Johannes Bergdolt, pastor for students in Würzburg, and the following men were members of the editorial committee: Elert, Althaus, Meiser, Marahrens, and Simon Schöffel, land bishop of Hamburg. It was described as the new series of the longtime voice of Lutheranism *Neue kirchliche Zeitschrift*, which had been published since 1890.[29] Germany seemed to be experiencing a breath of new life in 1933 after the fifteen years of depression, hunger, unemployment, and international scorn that followed World War I. With the global community intent upon appeasing Hitler between 1933 and 1939, it is not surprising that German theologians wanted to make their theology relevant to the current trends and that they sought to accommodate their scholarship to Nazi ideology (e.g., Emanuel Hirsch and Friedrich Gogarten), or at least to seek points of harmony between that ideology and Christian theology (e.g., Althaus and Elert). The outlook of men such as Althaus and Elert found expression in the early pages of *Luthertum.*

In "German Lutheranism at the Turning Point of Time," the opening editorial of *Luthertum*, Simon Schöffel reminds his readers that the first complete edition of Luther's translation of the Bible had been published exactly 400 years previously in 1534 and adds: "Lutheranism stands before great decisions, especially in Germany. But the first one is this, that it once more recognizes its own *Volk*, the German people." Schöffel laments that Luther's idea of *Volk* was lost in the mystic

---

which had exerted a heavy hand over Confessing Church pastors. The reaction of this consistory to the efforts of the RKA to improve matters in Mecklenburg, as well as the hostility of other German-Christians against the Church Commission, is related by Beste, *Der Kirchenkampf in Mecklenburg*, 148–56. In the end, the RKA was unable to settle the conflicts between German-Christians and the Confessing Church in Mecklenburg.

27 Klügel, *Landeskirche*, 268–70.

28 Paul Fleisch, *ELC*, 2:1,419.

29 After World War II, the periodical resumed as an occasional serial, with a sequence of pamphlets written by leading Lutheran theologians published under the title *Luthertum.*

individualism of the Renaissance, the Enlightenment, and idealism. Schöffel states: "The phenomenon of *Volk* is present today in an incomprehensible, infinite, indescribable, but clearly active mystery of Creation, and demands our 'Yes.' "[30] The same issue included an article by Kurt Frör, who would become a determined opponent of National Socialism and, after the war, professor for catechetics at the University of Erlangen. Frör characterizes the years 1918–1933 as a bleak period and adds: "The cultural, philosophical, ethical and political chaos created as its necessary result a crisis in education."[31]

Althaus wrote the next article, "Theological Responsibility," in which he described a crisis in the church: "Our church is torn apart. Fellowship and trust have been widely shattered."[32] In this crisis, *Luthertum* would point a way for the church to go. Theology at this time must serve only the Lord of the church, but it accomplishes this service only "when it serves the present hour. . . . One is only true to this living Lord when one is completely open to the present hour."[33] Althaus now continues in a spirit of self-criticism: "We were very proud of the renewal of theology out of the spirit of the Reformation as it was given to us in the last fifteen years. But we unquestionably fell into a theological inbreeding in the sense that we did not take the concrete reality of the man of nature and the man of history seriously enough."[34] It was this neglect that had given rise to the "antitheological, heretical, heathen" teachings of the German-Christians. Althaus now announces a new program:

> We need a new Christian understanding of natural life, of history, of the orders and of their movement. We need a new Christian message concerning the actions of God with us and in the history of the peoples, a new word about the relationship of human honor, worth, power, and dedication to sin and death, grace and the Holy Spirit. We can overcome the new idolization of the historical and the human only by means of a new theology of history and of man.[35]

These words show that Althaus saw the danger in the ideology of National Socialism and asserted that it was the duty of the church to provide theological answers to "the historical" and "the human" questions. Unfortunately, it soon became clear that National Socialism was not so open as Althaus had hoped to the prob-

---

30 *Luthertum* 1, no. 1 (1934): 2. For a more accurate assessment of *Volk*, see chapter 5, esp. pp. 109–11.

31 Frör, "Evangelische Erziehung im Dritten Reich," *Luthertum* 1, no. 3 (1934): 63.

32 *Luthertum* 1, no. 1 (1934): 13.

33 *Luthertum* 1, no. 1 (1934): 12.

34 *Luthertum* 1, no. 1 (1934): 14.

35 *Luthertum* 1, no. 1 (1934): 14.

lem solving attempted by the theologians; instead, National Socialism wanted to follow its own "idolizations."

Actually, Lutherans had not been idle. Previously, we devoted attention to Althaus's 1927 address at Königsberg on the relationship of *Volk*, the state, and theology; to the impact of his small book *Theologie der Ordnungen* (*Theology of Orders*), which went through two editions (one in 1934–1935); and to the larger study on the orders that had been published in 1933 by Franz Lau under the title *"Äußerliche Ordnung" und "weltlich Ding" in Luthers Theologie* (*"Outward Order" and "Worldly Thing" in Luther's Theology*).[36] This program stood in opposition to the tenets of the Barmen Declaration and it soon drew enemy fire from Barth. The stage was set for the response of Confessional Lutheran theology to the ideology of National Socialism and the German-Christians.

In the essay "Politisches und kirchliches Führertum" ("Political and Ecclesial Leadership"), which appeared in 1934 in *Luthertum*, Elert discussed the concept of "Führer" as meaningful for both state and church.[37] Besides Hitler, Elert had a new ecclesial leader in Hans Meiser, the first bishop of the Lutheran Land Church of Bavaria. Meiser's predecessor, Friedrich Veit, had been president of the Bavarian Land Church from 1921 to 1933. In replacing the church president with a land bishop, the church was altering its polity by giving unprecedented power and authority to its leader. In writing on the concept of "Führer," Elert showed his approval for the new office of land bishop; his respect for its first incumbent, Meiser; and his expectations of Hitler. Elert opined that the new political Führer (Hitler) would eschew the methods of Machiavelli, would lead the people instead of driving them, and would carefully ascertain the wishes of his people and then seek to carry them out. Elert's good intentions are shown not only in his overly optimistic evaluation of Hitler but also in his application of the same model to the ecclesial leader, who was to be a bishop rather than a church president. Elert noted that in the Russian military, the leaders followed their men and drove them, but among the older generations of Germans, the leader rode before his soldiers. Elert continued:

> A *Führer* is someone who goes ahead. This is applicable in the church as well as in politics. The *Führer* is distinguished from him who drives others, and therefore goes behind in order to watch that no one breaks away. But the *Führer* can reckon that the others will follow him when he is of one mind and will with them. . . . If the confession of a bishop is really the confession of the church, he will also have his church behind him. But if the situation is other-

---

36 For bibliographic details on Lau, *"Äußerliche Ordnung,"* see p. 18. For a discussion of Lau's book, see chapter 9. Regarding Lau, see "In Memoriam D. Franz Lau," *Luther-Jahrbuch* 42 (1975): 7–10, with photo.

37 *Luthertum* 1, no. 4 (1934): 102–17.

wise, not only does he cause a division but also an offense. What he then merits, Christ has said in Matt. 18:6 [Whoso shall offend one of these little ones which believe in me, it were better for him that a millstone were hanged about his neck, and that he were drowned in the depth of the sea].[38]

Conversely, Elert was saying that he was unwilling to support a Führer in either state or church who used compulsion or ruled contrary to the ethical persuasions of those who were being governed.[39] Was Elert's understanding of the word *Führer* naive? Meiser, the new bishop, was to become the stalwart and faithful leader, the spiritual Führer whom Elert had advocated. However, Elert's hopes for an ideal political Führer were dashed by the violent seizure and arrest of the land bishops of Bavaria and Württemberg in October 1934. Similarly, Müller, the new Reich bishop, who had engineered the coup against Wurm and Meiser, had become a most disappointing Führer. As early as October 1934, Elert joined his fellow professors in signing a strongly worded statement against the attempt of Müller and his German-Christian followers to "incorporate" the church of Bavaria into the Reich Church of the Nazi state.[40]

On March 15, 1935, Elert delivered a lecture at Berlin in which he further distanced himself from the word *Führer*. He clearly differentiated between what he had intended by *Führer* and the distortions of the office of bishop in the DEK under Reich Bishop Müller. Elert criticized the July 11, 1933, DEK Constitution, which lacked proper safeguards. He said that Müller's primary jurisdiction should have been restricted to a normal bishopric; instead, Müller had been given the powers of a pope, which he had then abused.[41] The second error was in choosing Müller at all, for he was the wrong person and, said Elert, he lacked the qualifications necessary for a simple village pastor.[42] The third error was that Müller had violated the teachings of the Lutheran Confessions.[43] In contrast, Elert noted the example of Adalbert Paulsen, bishop of Schleswig-Holstein, who, though he had been a German-Christian until November 1934, had supported a pastor opposed to the German-Christians by citing a passage from the Lutheran Confessions.[44]

---

38 Elert, "Politisches und kirchliches Führertum," 117.

39 Elert, "Politisches und kirchliches Führertum," 117.

40 See the October 13, 1934, "Protest of the Erlangen Theological Faculty to the Governor of Bavaria," in Hermelink, 176.

41 "Lutherische Grundsätze für die Kirchenverfassung," in Elert, *Ein Lehrer*, 122. This pregnant lecture, edited by Elert's pupil Max Keller-Hüschemenger, was not published during Elert's lifetime.

42 Elert, *Ein Lehrer*, 122–23.

43 Elert, *Ein Lehrer*, 123–24.

44 Elert, *Ein Lehrer*, 125.

By 1937 Elert was fully aware that the German Führer was not the beneficent leader he had praised in glowing terms earlier. In that year, the beleaguered students of theology at Leipzig were faced with an expected conscription into the German army, and they asked Elert to visit Leipzig to speak on the topic "The Christian and the *Völkisch* Will for Armament." In his March 4, 1948, report for a denazification procedure, Elert gave the following account of that lecture:

> The whole situation gave my lecture the character of a defense, not for myself nor for National Socialism nor for the military, but for the beleaguered theological students, who had appealed to me for help. . . . [I said that the use of military equipment] must be by the will of the *Volk* . . . so that it can be called the *volkisch* will. It is therefore not the will of an individual, also not the will of a powerful individual . . . No listener could be in doubt regarding which "powerful individual" I was thinking of. . . . I do not think that anything was spoken more clearly against the Führer principle [*Führerprinzip*] anywhere else at that time.[45]

In 1946, Elert again expressed his disappointments in the Führer in his essay "Paul and Nero." This essay was an inexorable indictment of Hitler's ruthlessness and faithlessness, as only the irrepressible Elert could frame it.[46] In any case, Elert's words of 1934 already contained a hidden warning for Hitler, as well as for any religious leader who would attempt the use of illegitimate force.[47]

---

45 This statement is from "An den Vorprüfungsausschuß im Berichte des Staatsminister für Unterricht und Kirche für die Universität Erlangen," in ATF, March 4, 1948. Elert's Leipzig lecture was published under the title *Der Christ und der völkische Wehrwille*, Theologia militans 15 (Leipzig: A. Deichert, 1937).

46 "Paulus und Nero," in Elert, *Zwischen Gnade*, 38–71. See also the essay "Philologie der Heimsuchung," in Elert, *Zwischen Gnade*, 9–16, which is a personal statement of Elert's disillusionment with Hitler's Third Reich.

47 Elert, "Politisches und kirchliches Führertum," 117. Elert's timing here was poor. Evidently, he sent this article on the Führer to press shortly before publication of "Kundgebung der bayerischen Landeskirche über das kirchliche Amt" (March 17, 1934), in which the criticism was given that "in the church, the Führer-principle must finally end in a new papacy where a single person has control over the teaching and practice of the church" (Hermelink, 78). As early as 1932, a strong criticism of the concept of *Führertum* had been published by Hermann Sasse under the title "Die Kirche und die politischen Mächte der Zeit," which appeared in *KJahr 1932*, 30ff. (repr. Sasse, *In Statu Confessionis*, 1:251–64). Sasse wrote: "Over against this philosophy of revolution (which is humanly understandable in Hitler due to his emergence out of a totally shaken state and the course of his life), the church must disagree and point out that that which is here called authority is not authority at all, since such a popular power becomes authority in the first place in that it yields to an authority that stands above it [scil., of God], and not to some law that comes from a human will. Thus, the modern leadership (*Führerschaft*) idea is the reverse side of collapsed genuine authority, part of

Debates over Issues of Church Governance

From 1933 to 1934, Confessional Lutherans, as all the other Protestants in Germany, were groping for a suitable and effective place in the new structure of the Third Reich. No one knew which way things were going to go, but Confessional Lutherans were wary of the DEK, which was dominated by the Prussian Union. This was disconcerting for two reasons: (1) the vacillating doctrinal stance of the Union churches, which made them easy targets for assimilation into the DEK; and (2) the Prussian Union's aggressive efforts to destroy the confessional integrity of the Lutheran churches it had previously seized and incorporated. This latter effort had included, at one time or another, not only the churches that remained in the Evangelical Church of the (Old) Prussian Union in 1934 but also Lutheran land churches that had been for a time in the Prussian Union and later had freed themselves from its tentacles, such as those of Hanover and Schleswig-Holstein. Both of these churches still bore the scars of their previous *Gleichschaltung*. The Universities of Kiel, Göttingen, and Marburg had lost their Lutheran character when they were placed under the Prussian Ministry for Culture in Berlin, which had no interest in maintaining a faculty that supported Confessional Lutheran theology. The theological faculty at the University of Göttingen became a haven for Nazis and German-Christians during the Third Reich (e.g., Hirsch and Otto Weber).[48]

For one hundred years, many efforts had been devoted toward the achievement of Lutheran unity in Germany. Lutherans tried to avoid entanglements with the more radical elements of the Confessing Church, contrasted their theology with the position of the Barmen Declaration, and differentiated their church polity from the parliamentary systems of the Reformed.[49] Because of this, Lutherans were frequently misunderstood and denounced as standoffish. As has been seen, some Lutherans, in grappling with questions of church polity, played with

---

it real collapse and part of it the lack of understanding with which people of the present, including the theologians, face this basic fact of human life" (Sasse, *In Statu Confessionis*, 1:252–53 n. 1).

48 On the effects of the Prussian Union upon previously Lutheran theological faculties, see "Zur Lage des Luthertums nach dem Zweiten Weltkrieg" (1945), in Sasse, *In Statu Confessionis*, 1:293.

49 See the February 17, 1937, "Position of the Evangelical Lutheran Church of Germany to the Theological Declaration of the Confessing Synod of Barmen, 1934." This document noted: "Since the Barmen statements intentionally made no choice between the truth of the Lutheran or of the Reformed confessions, and also refrained from attacking either the one or the other confession, they are themselves in need of a fundamental exposition on the basis of the confessions of those churches" (Klügel, *Dokumente*, 132).

the Führer concept. In expounding their theology of the First Article (theology of orders), some theologians fell into the trap of embracing German-Christian notions of blood, *Volk*, race, and soil (Hirsch and Gogarten), while others presented their positions in a strongly profiled contrast against those of the German-Faithful (*Deutschgläubige*), as well as the German-Christians (e.g., the work of Althaus, Elert, Sasse, Bonhoeffer, Künneth). As bishop of Hanover, Marahrens commented in his January 1, 1935, "Memorandum at the Turn of the Year":

> We dare not hide from ourselves the fact that it would mean a terrible damage for the Lutheran line of the German Reformation if insights that are very basic to Lutheranism, such as a positive evaluation of the natural possessions of blood and soil, were to be enlivened by perceptions from outside of Christianity and were to be overpowered by an un-Christian politics of violence which would destroy its credit and its effectiveness. . . . If everything that was respectable and tolerable in the program of the German-Christians might be presented as Lutheran heritage, the failures of the German-Christian church leadership would also endanger the Lutheran position as such within the circles of those in evangelical Germany who are confessionally loyal, and would suppress it into the background.[50]

Various local meetings of Lutherans were held to discuss the political and confessional problems faced by their churches. Thus Lutheran pastors within the Union Church of Westphalia met in April 1934 to organize the Conference of Evangelical Lutheran Theologians in Westphalia. Present were Zoellner, Georg Merz, Heinrich Quistorp, Karl Leutiger, Wilhelm Bartelheimer, Martin Berthold, and Martin Stallmann, among others. The group discussed the problems raised by the German-Christians and criticized the "Twenty-Eight Theses of the *Volk* Church of Saxony Regarding the Internal Structure of DEK."[51]

---

50 Niemöller, *Evangelische Kirche*, 193.

51 See Meier, *EKK*, 1:201–2; theses in Schmidt, *Bekenntnisse*, 1:98–102.

CHAPTER THIRTEEN

THE FATE OF THE EVANGELICAL LAND CHURCHES DURING THE THIRD REICH

From its founding in September 1933 until its fall at the end of World War II, the DEK experienced a rocky history. Ludwig Müller, with Adolf Hitler's blessing, had pushed himself foward as Reich bishop and as leader of the GDC in the summer of 1933. However, after a year of recurrent tumults, ending in the unsuccessful attempts by August Jäger and Müller to seize the Lutheran land churches of Bavaria, Württemberg, and Hanover, Hitler fired Jäger and quietly dropped Müller.

MERGERS OF LAND CHURCHES
INTO THE REICH CHURCH IN 1934

During the summer of 1934, the German-Christians were successful in the take-over or merger (*Gleichschaltung*) of a number of land churches. The most notorious was the March 2, 1934, seizure of the largest German Protestant denomination, the Evangelical Church of the (Old) Prussian Union. The Prussian Union was especially vulnerable to a hostile takeover. Because of its ambivalence to the Lutheran Confessions, it lacked a clear-cut position in doctrine and practice. Hermann Sasse, who had moved from a position as pastor in the Prussian Union (St. Mary's Lutheran Church, Berlin) to a theological chair at the University of Erlangen, was vehement in denouncing the Prussian Union for its doctrinal vacillation. Sasse insisted that there must be a clear and firm doctrinal position in any sort of church merger.

After the takeover of the Prussian Union, the following mergers incorporated most of the German land churches into the DEK:

Church	Date of Incorporation
Hesse-Nassau	April 27, 1934
Sachsen	May 4, 1934
Schleswig-Holstein	May 8, 1934
Thuringia	May 14, 1934
Hamburg	May 24, 1934 (Bishop Simon Schöffel deposed March 5)
Braunschweig	June 1, 1934
Oldenburg	June 11, 1934
Bremen	June 13, 1934
Pfalz	June 28, 1934
Lübeck and Eutin	July 13 and 17, 1934
Hesse-Kassel with Waldeck	July 16, 1934
Mecklenburg	July 20, 1934

The Prussian Union became the means for further seizures of churches through the following mergers: Lippe joined the Provincial Church of Westphalia on June 27, Birkenfeld-Oldenburg joined the Provincial Church of Rhineland on July 3, and Anhalt joined the Church of the Province of Saxony on July 4. Besides these incorporations, the Land Church of Hanover was temporarily taken over by the German-Christians on May 15, 1934, but this action was surmounted by the courageous leadership of Bishop August Marahrens, who managed to circumvent the German-Christians and block the takeover. As a result, the Land Church of Hanover can be said to have remained "intact" until the fall of the Nazis in 1945.[1]

The relation of the intact churches to the Reich Church became a serious problem because though these churches had joined the DEK, which had passed into the Reich Church, they avoided being annexed by the Reich Church. This is actually the story of the "big three" Lutheran churches and their resistance to the Reich Church and, ultimately, to National Socialism and its evil manifestations.

THE "DESTROYED" LUTHERAN LAND CHURCHES

The Union churches were not the only ones to fall prey to the Reich Church. A number of Lutheran land churches also proved susceptible. Before focusing on the

---

1 Hermelink, 91–92.

intact churches of Hanover, Württemberg, and Bavaria, the discussion will focus on the destroyed churches and their fate after incorporation into the Reich Church.

The Lutheran Land Church in the Free State of Saxony

The Free State of Saxony was the fragment of the former powerful Electorate of Saxony that remained intact after Prussia annexed its northern areas into the Province of Saxony, a region that contained important sites associated with the life of Luther, such as Eisleben, Mansfeld, Wittenberg, Halle, and Magdeburg. The churches in these cities had lost their specifically Lutheran character in the nineteenth century when, after their territory was annexed by Prussia, they were subjected to merger (*Gleichschaltung*) into the Prussian Union. However, in the Free State of Saxony, which included important cities such as Leipzig, Dresden, Chemnitz, Zittau, Bautzen, Meissen, Freiburg, and Zwickau, the church remained a Confessional Lutheran land church. Despite the loss of its territory to Prussia, in which there were nearly 3,000,000 Lutherans in 1932, the Lutheran Land Church of the Free State of Saxony still had 4,465,880 members in 1932, making it by far the largest Lutheran church in Germany.[2]

Ludwig Ihmels, a noted systematic theologian from the Erlangen School, was land bishop of Saxony from 1922 until his death in 1933. After the difficult years of the Weimar Republic following World War I, Ihmels, like many other Germans, welcomed the rise of Hitler. Ihmels prepared an announcement to be read from the pulpits of all his churches on March 26, 1933, from which several excerpts are presented:

> The church can only admonish: Joyfully, bravely forward, so that the old Gospel will become a new power in the life of the *Volk*. In fact it is an hour of highest decision which we are experiencing. Coming generations will want to hear of us and how we experienced this hour. We speak of wasted hours in world history, of wasted hours also in the history of the church. This hour must not come in vain. We are responsible for it. . . . I want to beg with great earnestness that all the members of our *Volk* put our church to the test at this point. It can and must be experienced by all the people: In the holy fellowship of the church there is a genuine togetherness with one another. With this message, the church steps out into the times. The church must do it in the certainty that the truth will overcome at last. The church calls its members to the joyful, courageous faith that God would lead us to a new time and that he only waits for us. May he not wait in vain![3]

---

2 Church statistics of the principle land churches supplied by Sasse in *KJahr 1932*, 558–85.

3 Cited by Reu in *KZ* 57 (May 1933): 316–17.

The modern reader is almost incredulous at the absence of misgivings toward National Socialism in the spring of 1933. The 74-year-old Ihmels harbored such an unsuspecting enthusiasm less than three months before his death, and it led him to trust men such as Friedrich Coch and to place them in positions from which they could do irremediable damage to the land churches. Ihmels's unexpected death on June 7, 1933, prevented him from experiencing the dark side of Hitler's regime. Had he lived a little longer, the great expectations that Ihmels had placed in Hitler would have been cruelly dashed.

The noted Heidelberg historian Martin Schmidt had been a parish pastor in Saxony at the time the German-Christians seized control. In an interview in Boone, North Carolina, in September 1971, Schmidt related his view of the takeover, which preceded and followed the June 7, 1933, death of Ihmels. Schmidt said that Ihmels should have retired earlier and that for years he had discussed his retirement. His loyal friends, unmindful of the gathering storm, had prevailed upon Ihmels to remain in office.[4]

Meanwhile, Coch, an ambitious cleric who was also a member of the Nazi Party, was rising to power during the final months of Ihmels's administration—with the approval of the aged bishop. On June 26, during the vacancy following Ihmel's death, Coch demanded that he be made a *Kommissar* bishop, but on June 29 the Standing Synodic Commission and the Council of Elders of the Land Synod unanimously rejected Coch's candidacy. At this point, Nazi officials intervened and reinforced Coch's bid as *Kommissar* bishop. In the confusion that followed, Saxony Minister for the Interior Karl Fritsch intervened with an "Order for Removing the Emergency Situation in the Church Life of the Evangelical Lutheran Land Church of Saxony." As a result, Coch was given dictatorial powers over the Saxon church.

Coch used his new powers to throw out those who were opposed to him and to bring in his supporters. In the Brown Synod of August 11, 1933, at which nearly all the representatives wore Nazi uniforms, Coch was elected unanimously as land bishop. The newly elected bishop was endowed with full powers to suspend the constitution and rule by decree. The Lutheran Land Church of Saxony had been overpowered by the GDC.[5]

Coch proved to be an unscrupulous leader. His policies and deeds provoked opposition from the PNB, which led to the formation of a rival Confessing Church in Saxony. Its head was Hugo Hahn, pastor at the celebrated baroque Frauenkirche in Dresden and the valiant superintendent of the Dresden Confer-

---

4 Ihmels's death came three weeks before the retirement date upon which he had finally decided. Meiser, *Verantwortung*, 1:6 n. 1.

5 Chronicled in Meier, *EKK*, 1:479–81.

ence of the Saxon land church.[6] Hahn and his followers declared their Confessing Church movement to be "the legally valid continuation of the Lutheran Church in Saxony."[7]

However, a large group of pastors did not align themselves with either the GDC or the Confessing Church. This neutral group remained in the land church and thereby in Coch's camp.[8] Later efforts toward unity among all the Lutheran land churches in Germany led to the March 18, 1936, formation of the Luther Council. Hahn became its leader in Saxony, and the Luther Council helped to unite the Saxon Lutherans who were opposed to Coch.[9] These steps toward more complete Lutheran cooperation drew bitter denunciations from members of the Confessing Church who belonged to the Union churches and wanted the Saxons to support their own Brethren Council instead of the Luther Council.[10]

Hahn became a legendary figure for his personal integrity and for his unshakable courage in taking a stand for the things in which he believed. Obviously, he was not Hitler's man. Hahn was banned from Saxony by Reich-Governor Martin Mutschmann in 1938. The DEK also joined the condemnations of Hahn with the following denunciation in 1942:

> He has shown himself to be so unteachable and self-willed, and to be so obsessed with the notion of his own unconditionally absolute authority as bearer of an office in the legal fellowship of his land church, in regard to his obligations over against the order of law, that he, if for only this reason, has shown himself as incapable and unwilling to accept his place within the external legal organism of his land church and to fit himself into a church regiment that is not agreeable to him.[11]

---

6 Regarding the famous Bishop Hugo Hahn, see Gottfried Fuss, "Gruß an Altbischof D. Hahn," *AELKZ* 10 (September 15, 1956): 373–75; and Wilhelm Hahn, "Zum Heimgang von Altbischof D. Hugo Hahn," *AELKZ* 11 (December 15, 1957): 430. Hahn was born in 1886 in Reval, Estonia, the son of Traugott Hahn, pastor at the prestigious St. Olai Lutheran Church. Hahn's brother, also named Traugott, a professor at Dorpat, was murdered there by the Communists in 1919. Driven from Estonia by the Communist takeover, Hahn went to Germany, where he became pastor at Worbis near Göttingen in 1919 and at St. Thomas in Leipzig in 1927. In 1930 he was called as superintendent and pastor at the Frauenkirche, Dresden.

7 Hermelink, 94. See the documents in Joachim Fischer, *Die sächsische Landeskirche im Kirchenkampf 1933–1937*, AGK 8 (Göttingen: Vandenhoeck & Ruprecht, 1972), 187–266, esp. documents 15–17 (pp. 195–97), which relate to Hahn's courageous actions.

8 Hermelink, 94.

9 Meier, *EKK*, 3:565.

10 On the formation of the Luther Council, see Helmreich, 198, and especially Meier, *EKK*, 2:108–15.

11 Fuss, "Gruß an Altbischof D. Hahn," 373–76.

After his ousting from Saxony, Hahn came to Bishop Theophil Wurm in Württemberg as a refugee. Wurm provided Hahn with a new home and put this talented man to work in the pastoral ministry. During his years in Württemberg, Hahn was struck by two blows: News arrived that his beloved Frauenkirche in Dresden was destroyed in the incendiary bombing of the city (February 13, 1945), and his faithful wife died. In 1947 Hahn was called back to Dresden as bishop of the Lutheran Land Church of Saxony. Although he was weak and knew he could only serve for a few years, he accepted and was installed at a service in the historic cathedral of Meissen. Hahn retired in 1953. A word of greeting at Hahn's seventieth birthday characterized him as "no diplomat, no bureaucrat, and no autocrat" ("*kein Diplomat, kein Bürokrat und kein Autokrat*").[12]

MECKLENBURG

The end of World War I and the Treaty of Versailles brought years of depression, hunger, and unemployment to Mecklenburg, as to other parts of Germany. The churches suffered with their people. When the German state-church system was abolished in 1919, there were two separate Lutheran land churches in Mecklenburg: Mecklenburg-Schwerin, with 653,972 members, and Mecklenburg-Strelitz, with 107,603 members. In both parts of the region, Lutherans constituted more than 93 percent of the population. During the preceding years, the population had not shown a deep interest in church matters. From 1922 until 1930, the land bishop of the larger church had been Heinrich Behm, who had shown great wisdom in his endeavors to increase the involvement of the laity, to provide for continuing theological education of the pastors, and to enhance mission activity in the church.[13]

In 1930, Heinrich Rendtorff, professor of practical theology at the University of Kiel, became bishop of Mecklenburg-Schwerin. Rendtorff was both a noted theologian and a gifted speaker, and he devoted all his talents to improving the conditions in his church. Thus he arranged a Church Conference at Güstrow for June 19, 1932, which attracted 20,000 people who wanted to see the church prosper.[14] Although Lutheran ministers could join political parties, they were not allowed to influence their parishioners on political issues or actions. However,

---

12 Fuss, "Gruß an Altbischof D. Hahn," 375.

13 See the description in Niklot Beste, *Der Kirchenkampf in Mecklenburg von 1933 bis 1945: Geschichte, Dokumente, Erinnerungen* (Göttingen: Vandenhoeck & Ruprecht, 1975), 13. This book is not only a gold mine of information concerning the Lutheran Land Church of Mecklenburg under both National Socialism and Communism, but it is also a primary source of history because it was written by one of the chief players during those turbulent years. Beste was a pastor during the Third Reich and served as bishop of Mecklenburg from 1946 to 1971.

14 Beste, *Der Kirchenkampf in Mecklenburg*, 19.

Rendtorff was personally interested in such matters, and he joined the moderate CDB (see chapter 1). Because this group refused to favor any single party, it disbanded in late summer 1933 after the National Socialists had established themselves as the only party in Germany. Because there were approximately fifteen pastors in his land church who were members of the Nazi Party, Rendtorff turned a cautious ear to the blandishments of the Nazi Party and the GDC. He was searching for ways to gain the attention of his Lutheran population and bring new life into his church. Perhaps he should have listened more critically when the German-Christians issued a call on December 11, 1932, that included the demand that half-Jews as well as Free Masons should be thrown out of the land synod and their voices should be stifled in the church press.[15] But who could foresee the inherent dangers at that time?

The goodwill toward these new movements on the part of Rendtorff was sharply betrayed in the first takeover of his land church on April 18, 1933. On that date, the Nazi minister-president of Mecklenburg-Schwerin, Walter Granzow, installed a radical Nazi, Walter Bohm of Hamburg, as state *Kommissar* administrator over the land church. Bohm usurped control, discharged the high church councillors (*Oberkirchenräte*), and stripped Rendtorff of most of his powers as bishop, reducing his authority to caring for the souls of individuals and conducting church services. This seizure of power was only temporary. Rendtorff appealed to Reich Minister for the Interior Wilhelm Frick, who summoned both Granzow and Rendtorff to a meeting in Berlin, where the radical steps taken by Granzow were reversed.[16]

Despite such an experience, Rendtorff allowed himself to be further duped in a series of acts during which, on the basis of deceitful promises by German-Christian leaders, he applied for membership in the Nazi Party on May 2, 1933. Rendtorff received a temporary membership number, but his membership was never completed by the NSDAP. Evidently, the Nazis really didn't want the bishop to become one of their number.[17] The bishop also lent his support at this time to the GDC, but Rendtorff was to learn that he could not do business with the Nazis. Things fell apart for him after a pastoral conference at Bad Kleinen on May 29, 1933. At that time, pastors who belonged to the Nazi Party gave him their support and "welcomed with joy the cooperation of the Faith Movement of German-Christians within the church." In response, Rendtorff rejected the plan to elect Friedrich von Bodelschwingh as Reich bishop and declared his support for the candidacy of Hitler's choice, Ludwig Müller.

---

15 Beste, *Der Kirchenkampf in Mecklenburg*, 20.

16 Beste, *Der Kirchenkampf in Mecklenburg*, 25–28.

17 Meier, *EKK*, 1:340.

Nevertheless, Rendtorff's measures were to prove his undoing in two ways. First, his espousal of Nazism only strengthened the position of the real leader of the Nazi pastors, Walther Schultz. On September 12, a new land synod dominated by German-Christians established Schultz in the position of "Leader of the Land Church" (*Landeskirche-Führer*). This act placed most of a bishop's powers in Schultz's hands and divested Rendtorff of all his jurisdiction except preaching and the care of souls (*Seelsorge*).[18] This was in line with the Nazi teaching that the "temporal affairs" of the churches should be managed by the National Socialist government and that the bishops and preachers had jurisdiction only in "spiritual matters." Second, Rendtorff's rejection of Bodelschwingh provoked a group of pastors and theological professors at Rostock (including Helmuth Schreiner) to contest him and to found the Federation of German Lutherans (*Bund deutscher Lutheraner* [BDL]). The BDL had loose ties to Walter Künneth's Young Reformation Movement and bucked Rendtorff's support for the Nazi Party and the GDC.[19]

The unification of the land churches of Mecklenburg-Schwerin and Mecklenburg-Strelitz was an unfulfilled desideratum. To expedite this merger and the choice of a new bishop for all Mecklenburg, Rendtorff resigned as bishop on January 6, 1934, saying gallantly, "I will hereby perform my last service to the Land Church in that I open the way for a new beginning and for a new order of its leadership."[20] But Schultz, the treacherous leader of the land church, managed to get himself elected as bishop of the united Land Church of Mecklenburg on May 23, 1934, and Rendtorff accepted a call into the parish ministry.

Schultz's election as bishop was protested by half of the 430 pastors in Mecklenburg on the grounds that the election had been illegal.[21] Moreover, Schultz's administration was thoroughly political and repressive in style. Schultz frequently suspended church law and governed by decree. In pastoral placements, he located his favorites in prominent places where they could further his political goals, and he punished his opponents by deposing them and placing them in obscure parishes. Thus Beste, an opposition leader who was pastor of the *Volksmission* in Schwerin and would later be bishop of Mecklenburg, was deposed by Schultz and banished to the remote parish of Neubukow.[22]

The notorious June 1934 Schwerin Judiciary Proceedings against seven dissenting Mecklenburg pastors provided another great source of dissension under

---

18 Meier, *EKK*, 1:343.

19 Meier, *EKK*, 1:341.

20 Meier, *EKK*, 1:346.

21 Meier, *EKK*, 1:347.

22 Meier, *EKK*, 1:344.

Schultz. This trial was heard by an ad hoc judiciary rather than a regular court of law. The seven accused pastors were Gottfried Holtz, a licensed theologian; Johannes Schwartzkopff, cathedral preacher at Güstrow; Walter Pagels of Rostock; Viktor Wittrock, a retired pastor at Schwerin; Henning Fahrenheim, cathedral preacher at Schwerin; Hans Werner Ohse; and Christian Berg. The men were accused of writing malicious statements against the government in circulars addressed to the BDL, the JB, and the PNB. The attorney for their defense, Dr. Horst Holstein, pointed out that two things were being confused: the government and the GDC. The accused pastors had written against the German-Christians, not against the state. Rendtorff was summoned as a witness at the trial, where he was sharply denounced for not preventing the pastors from their actions. Despite all efforts to clear the men, most were found guilty and were subjected to fines and imprisonment.[23]

Because of such abuses, many pastors joined the Confessing Church. The movement in Mecklenburg was led by Beste, Schreiner, and, later, by Rendtorff. Other pastors who were leaders in the Brethren Council of the Land Church of Mecklenburg were Arnold Maercker, Johannes Güsmere, Heinz Pflugk, Hans Kraner, Paul Buchin, Hans Friedrich Koch, Hermann Timm, and a number of laymen.[24] Beste became a founding member of the Luther Council when it was established in March 1936.[25]

On November 20, 1936, Beste appeared before the meeting of the land church leaders (*Kirchenführerkonferenz*) at Berlin, where he read a written account: "The Churchly Situation in Mecklenburg."[26] He reported many troubling occurrences in Mecklenburg under Schultz's despotic leadership. For example, though church law required that the theological faculty at Rostock be involved in the examination of theological candidates, this was being blocked. Beste also reported that "many church members are angry that they must pay church dues to the present church power brokers, and especially those in the controverted congregations such as Teterow, Eldena, etc., where it is not allowed that the bells be rung at funerals and the churches are closed for baptisms and weddings."[27]

Beste related that despite a serious shortage of pastors, Schultz had passed over forty to fifty available vicars who were well-educated and had Mecklenburg roots, refusing to give them calls to service.[28] Instead, Schultz had brought in fifty or

---

23 Meier, *EKK*, 1:347–48.

24 Meier, *EKK*, 1:599.

25 Meiser, *Verantwortung*, 2:559–60.

26 Meiser, *Verantwortung*, 2:573–79.

27 Meiser, *Verantwortung*, 2:576.

28 Meiser, *Verantwortung*, 2:578.

sixty outsiders to supply the vacant parishes. Approximately twenty of these men had not studied theology at all, and a few others had started theological studies but had not passed their theological examinations. Many of these men had been imported because of their radical Nazi leanings or German-Christian allegiance.[29] Beste reported that of 400 clergy in Mecklenburg, about 190 were in the Confessing Church and 50 or 60 in the Lutheran Pastoral Circle. Of the remaining 150, most of these were in the National-Socialist Pastors League. There also were 50 or 60 men who belonged to the radical Thuringian Circle of the German-Christians. Beste continued: "One must speak of a deliberately planned overpowering of the pastors by infiltration, and it is working itself out in a really serious political situation in the church because these persons are the main support of the German-Christians in the land and they stand in a strong dependency upon the church government."[30] Beste closed his report with this appeal: "The Evangelical Lutheran Church in Mecklenburg presents a picture of the most fearful destruction. Antichurchly powers have an easy game. The pressure against the Confessing Church grows more and more severe. The help of the Lutheran churches of Germany is urgently needed."[31]

The German-Christians had attempted to make a distinction between the "external" affairs of the church, which should be regulated by the state, and the "internal" matters of the church, such as Word and Sacrament, over which the church was to have full control. Obviously, the form of the church service should belong to the second category. However, German-Christian spokesmen wanted to alter the liturgy and hymns to suit their own purposes. Thus Walter Lemcke, a member of the Confessing Church and pastor at Brunow, wrote a paper about the "experimental liturgies" and other changes that the German-Christians were fostering "because of the liturgical needs" of the time. Lemcke mentioned the newly invented creeds, pointing to their theology that departed from the confessions of the church,[32] and also the change in the words during the distribution of the Lord's Supper ("The bread of the earth; the wine of the earth" instead of the traditional words "This is the body of Christ; this is the blood of Christ"). Furthermore, a new version of the Lord's Prayer had been arranged by Reich Bishop Müller.[33]

---

29 Meiser, *Verantwortung*, 2:577.

30 Meiser, *Verantwortung*, 2:577.

31 Meiser, *Verantwortung*, 2:579.

32 An example of a German-Christian substitute for the Apostles' Creed: "I believe in the German mother who bore me. I believe in the German farmer who breaks bread for his *Volk*. I believe in the German laborer who carries out his work for his *Volk*. I believe in the dead who gave their life for the *Volk*. For my God is my *Volk*! I believe in Germany!" (Schmidt, *Bekenntnisse*, 3:338).

SCHLESWIG-HOLSTEIN

There were similar experiences in neighboring Schleswig-Holstein. Like Mecklenburg, this land church had also been divided into two parts. Eduard Völkel was bishop of Schleswig and Adolf Mordhorst was bishop of Holstein. Both bishops resided in Kiel. At that time, the Church of Lauenburg, later independent, was a part of the Church of Holstein, with a church superintendent residing in Ratzeburg.[34]

Schleswig and Holstein were in great turmoil. The farmers were up in arms because prices were low and they were unable to make a decent living. Industrial workers also were greatly dissatisfied with their economic situation. Many of these people joined the Communist Party in hopes of bettering their lot. A sign of the prevailing discontent came on "Bloody Sunday," July 17, 1932, when there were battles in the streets of Altona between members of the Nazi and Communist Parties. Seventeen people were killed (see chapter 3).

As was customary in Lutheran circles, pastors were forbidden to preach partisan politics from the pulpit. The rationale was that the confidence of parishioners would be damaged if their pastor favored any one political direction.[35] The church of Schleswig-Holstein had a statute dating from November 2, 1932, that prohibited pastors from joining political parties or from preaching politics from the pulpit. However, the National Socialists urged pastors to join their party and fiercely attacked this statute until it was repealed on May 4, 1933. In fact, 27 percent of the pastors in Schleswig and Holstein already were members of the NSDAP by January 30, 1933.[36]

Neither Mordhorst nor Völkel had joined the Nazi Party, but, like Rendtorff, they had welcomed the participation of the German-Christians in the land church. And like Rendtorff, they, too, were soon to be deposed and replaced by men of Hitler's choice. On September 12, 1933, the Brown Synod at Rendsburg,

---

33 Beste, *Der Kirchenkampf in Mecklenburg*, 203–4. Lemcke may have had in mind this German-Christian substitute for the Lord's Prayer, written not by Müller but by Arthur Dinter: "Unser Vater in den Himmeln, Sei geheiligt! Dein Reich komme: Dein Wille geschehe, wie im Himmel, auch auf Erden. Unser Brot für morgen gib uns heute. Und vergib unsere Schuld, sofern auch wir vergeben unsern Schuldigern. Und laß uns nicht erliegen der Versuchung, Sondern gib uns Kraft gegen das Böse. Heil!" (Schmidt, *Bekenntnisse*, 2:180). On Dinter, see Meier, *EKK*, 1:49–50.

34 *KJahr 1932*, 571.

35 This principle was sound enough. It is commonly followed in the United States today, where it is expected that pastors will keep aloof from partisan politics or at least will not publicly take sides on controversial political or social issues, an action that might alienate people who think differently.

36 See Meier, *EKK*, 1:362.

convened under Hans Aselmann of Altona, the new president, deposed the two bishops and helped bring Schleswig-Holstein under German-Christian domination. The new Land Church Commission, which had been established by the Brown Synod, appointed Adalbert Paulsen as bishop and dismissed Mordhurst and Völkel, effective January 1, 1934. On the basis of a decree of October 5, 1933, the bishop had full power to appoint pastors, transfer them, or remove them from office, thereby eliminating the choice of the local congregation.[37]

The unconstitutional actions of the Brown Synod provoked the formation of a dissenting organization, the Emergency and Working Fellowship of Schleswig-Holstein Pastors (*Not- und Arbeitsgemeinschaft der schleswig-holsteinischen Pastoren*), which was organized by seventy pastors and professors on October 19–20, 1933. Several months later, the organization had increased to 140 pastors. Led by Professors Volkmar Herntrich and Kurt Dietrich Schmidt of the University of Kiel and Johann Bielfeldt of Rendsburg, a prominent pastor who later wrote a history of the church struggle in Schleswig-Holstein,[38] this group regarded itself as a branch of Martin Niemöller's PNB.

In Schleswig-Holstein, the relation between the land churches and the Confessing Church group was not as confrontational as elsewhere. To be sure, the Confessing Church established a Lutheran Church Congregation Movement, which enrolled seven to eight thousand laypeople. This group remained aloof from the Dahlem Front and rejected its radical notion that the Confessing Church was the only legitimate church.[39] Meanwhile, the Brethren Council joined the Luther Council, the Confessional Lutheran form of the Confessing Church. Paulsen sought to moderate his course, and the PNB sought to preserve the integrity of the land churches and to avoid the free-church direction taken by the Dahlem Front.

In some ways, it could be said that Schleswig-Holstein had shed the marks of a destroyed church. Paulsen worked to restore the unity of his land church, and in so doing, he reversed some of the actions that offended those belonging to the Confessing Church. For example, Paulsen resigned from the GDC in 1934. On December 1, 1934, the commission of the land churches announced that its incorporation into the Reich Church was no longer valid.[40] Although the men from the Confessing Church had hoped that Paulsen would align himself with the VKL

---

37 Meier, *EKK*, 1:363–64. Meier discusses Schleswig-Holstein in *EKK*, 1:360–72. There is a short presentation on Schleswig-Holstein in Scholder, *Kirchen*, 1:606–7.

38 Bielfeldt, *Der Kirchenkampf in Schleswig-Holstein 1933–1945*, AGK 1 (Göttingen: Vandenhoeck & Ruprecht, 1964).

39 Meier, *EKK*, 1:369–70.

40 Meier, *EKK*, 1:370–71.

headed by Marahrens, Paulsen seemed afraid to take that additional step. However, Paulsen renewed his efforts to achieve a peaceful settlement of the differences between his administration and the Confessing Church and strove to involve all the people in his church, except the radical German Church (*Deutschkirche*) circle, whom he firmly excluded. A May 20, 1936, resolution even recognized ordination by pastors of the Confessing Church and reinstated its candidates who had been rejected in 1935.[41]

It was Paulsen's fate that despite his success in pursuing a middle course and pulling his land church back together, he gradually lost much of his power. As previously noted, a dualistic view of church polity was propounded by many German-Christians and Nazis, and because of this, the church was dissected into its internal (spiritual) and external (administrational) aspects. According to this concept, the clergy should lead only in spiritual matters and the state should govern the outward affairs of the church. Moreover, the sphere of "spiritual" matters steadily diminished. Paulsen found himself increasingly restricted in his powers as bishop. The German-Christian leader, Christian Kinder, took over the administration of the church as president of the Land Church Office (*Landeskirchenamt*).

However, Kinder, who had been regarded as too compliant with National Socialism, began to moderate his actions and to hold out the olive branch to the Confessing Church. This new attitude was exemplified by the conciliatory Christmas message he promulgated in December 1937, in which, among other things, he lauded the parsonage families for the many sons they sacrificed in World War I.[42] Kinder also began to protect pastors who had been subject to unfair political attacks. Although Kinder offended some of the pastors by supporting the 1938 demand from Berlin that pastors take an oath of allegiance to Hitler, that action was consummated, and he later could boast that none of the pastors in the Land Church of Schleswig-Holstein had ever been sent to a concentration camp.[43]

During the first years of World War II, much of the tension between church and state in Schleswig-Holstein was relieved, and the church struggle began to diminish. In 1943, the Confessing Church in Schleswig-Holstein decided to dissolve. Following Kinder's resignation in 1943, more power was returned to Paulsen. After the war, Paulsen resigned, and several years later, Reinhard Wester became bishop of Schleswig and Wilhelm Halfmann became bishop of Holstein.[44]

---

41 Meier, *EKK*, 2:265.

42 Meier, *EKK*, 2:268.

43 Meier, *EKK*, 3:389–90, 668–69 nn. 1,053 and 1,056.

44 Meier, *EKK*, 3:392–93.

LÜBECK

The picturesque city of Lübeck—beloved by artists and tourists for its narrow medieval streets, quaint brick buildings, rich art treasures, magnificent churches, and notable church music—had been a center of Confessional Lutheran faith and practice since the days of Luther. Prior to World War I, the city-state of Lübeck possessed a Lutheran territorial church under the tight control of its senate. In 1921 a new constitution was introduced that made the church independent and reduced the role of the state to that of a monitor of the church's administrative and financial operations. This was similar to the situation in the United States in which churches are independent but subject to the legal statutes of the individual states. In 1928, the church, wanting to strengthen the relationship between state and church, requested that a city senator be selected and appointed to the Land Church Council as Evangelical Church *kommissar*. During the Third Reich, this political tie would bring the church under the control of the Nazis.

In the elections to the national parliament (*Reichstag*) on March 5, 1933, the National Socialists won only 38,000 out of 88,000 votes in Lübeck, but 50,000 votes were scattered among the Social Democrats, the Communist Party, the Black-White-Red Front, the DVP, the CVDP, and the State's Party.[45] Out of this minority position, the Nazis and German-Christians in Lübeck were able to seize power and construct a National Socialist city-state.

Early on, Hans Böhmcker, a strong-headed senator and lawyer, together with Johannes Sievers, a merchant, dominated all ecclesiastical decisions, including the calling of the new bishop, Erwin Balzer, who, like the other two men, was a National Socialist. Through the intervention of the Lübeck senate, the Evangelical Lutheran Church of Lübeck was integrated into the DEK on May 30, 1934, and became a "destroyed" church. Because Lübeck was a Confessional Lutheran church, this action implied the surrender of the confessional integrity of the Lübeck church and was an illegal act according to Lübeck's church law. The German-Christian leadership of the Lübeck church promptly adopted the Aryan Paragraph of the Prussian Union and advised pastors that they should not minis-

---

45 Statistics cited by Karl Friedrich Reimers, *Lübeck im Kirchenkampf des Dritten Reiches: Nationalsozialistisches Führerprinzip und evangelisch-lutherische Landeskirche von 1933 bis 1945* (Göttingen: Vandenhoeck & Ruprecht, 1965), 50. Reimers shows antipathy toward Confessional Lutheranism (cf. *Lübeck im Kirchenkampf,* 94, 131, 158ff., 182–85, 218, 375) and a strong affinity to Barth and Barmen, Niemöller and the Dahlem Front. He shows much admiration for Wilhelm Jannasch, the provocative pastor at St. Aegidius and representative of the Dahlem Front (Reimers, *Lübeck im Kirchenkampf,* 58ff., 143, 147, 152f., et passim). Actually, the radicality of Jannasch led to a division between the Confessing Church and the majority of pastors who represented a more moderate approach (Reimers, *Lübeck im Kirchenkampf,* 171).

ter to Christians of Jewish parentage who were members of their parishes. As years passed, Balzer and some of the pastors became increasingly radical and espoused the heretical teachings and evil practices of the German Church Circle (*Deutschkirche*).

Still, the majority of pastors at the start were opposed to this direction. By the end of 1933, in opposition to German-Christian pastors, Lübeck had fourteen pastors in the Confessional Fellowship, men who aligned themselves with the JB, the PNB, or the emerging Confessing Church—all three programs were critical of National Socialism. The most determined opponent of the Nazi changes was Wilhelm Jannasch, chief pastor of St. Aegidius Church, who identified himself with the more radical Dahlem Front of the Confessing Church. The leader of the more moderate Confessing Church group was Axel Werner Kühl, pastor at St. Jacob. Others in the circle included Johannes Pautke at St. Mary Church, Erwin Schmidt at the cathedral, Johann Schulz (Schultz) and Hans Kanitz (pastors at St. Gertrude), Gerhard Fölsch at St. Matthaeus, Bruno Meyer at St. Aegidius, and Werner Greiffenhagen and Julius Jensen at St. Lorenz in the suburb of Travemünde.[46] Unfortunately, Jannasch pursued a radical course and refused to cooperate with the more moderate group headed by Kühl, which joined the Luther Council and tried to work with Marahrens and even Hanns Kerrl. Consequently, the resistance movement at Lübeck was sadly splintered.

Kerrl, Hitler's Reich Church commissioner, was a man of ability and integrity who, despite his connection with the Nazi Party, tried to counteract the extreme German-Christians in the destroyed churches. The militant Lübeck Church Commission, under the evil influence of Böhmcker, harassed the Confessional Lutheran pastors and recruited German-Christians or Nazis to fill any pastoral vacancies. Thus the church at Lübeck was increasingly under political control.[47] This radical group rejected the moderating work of Kerrl, who tried to intervene on behalf of both factions of the Confessing Church clergy in the crisis of December 1936.

Things came to a head on December 5, 1936, when Bishop Balzer discharged all pastors who were active in the Confessing Church, an action that would take effect December 31. The pastors also would lose their pensions and all financial aid.[48] Nine pastors—Fölsch, Greiffenhagen, Ernst Jansen, Jensen, Kühl, Meyer,

---

46 The moderate group of Lutheran pastors in the Confessing Church of Lübeck, shunning the radical course of the Dahlem Front, asked Marahrens of Hanover to function as their bishop (Reimers, *Lübeck im Kirchenkampf*, 141ff.). Marahrens was a source of hope for pastors in neighboring destroyed churches.

47 Meier, *EKK*, 1:355–57.

48 Schmidt, *Dokumente*, 2:1,271.

Pautke, Karl Richter, and Schulz—were dismissed without stated grounds and without concern for financial need. Balzer took action because the pastors had protested in a November 14 letter that the church council had made it impossible for them, "as men of honor, to stand in ministerial relationship with them." Balzer understood this to be a letter of resignation and fired the pastors on the grounds that the state and church in Lübeck were one entity and that a protest against the church council was an act of disloyalty to the state.[49] The moderate pastors of the Confessing Church had allied themselves with Marahrens and the RKA. The DEK and the RKA issued the following denunciation of the actions of Balzer and the Lübeck Church Council:

> They have determined that thereby the law of the church has been violated in an unheard-of manner. They request the Commission of the Reich Church to inform itself and to publish a statement in the *Gesetzblatt der Deutschen Evangelische Kirche* that the entire German Evangelical Church (DEK) stands behind the affected pastors and their congregations. They further demand that the Commission of the Reich Church (RKA) should, with great emphasis, make the plight of the affected pastors and congregations their own concern.[50]

A letter by Otto Koopmann, a member of the RKA and chairman of the DEK Chamber for Legal Questions, contested Balzer's interpretation of the November 14 protest letter. Koopmann said that it could not be called a letter of resignation and defended the nine pastors as follows: "The claim of the Lübeck Church Council in its letter of December 5 of an alleged request for dismissal is therefore legally invalid." Regarding the withholding of salaries, Koopmann wrote: "Although the dismissal was first set for December 31, the Church Council has also withheld the salaries due as of December 1, 1936, and this completely without any basis or reason. This action of the church council is legally invalid and requires immediate intervention."[51] This intervention was important because the RKA was the official leader of the DEK and was headed by Hitler's choice, Kerrl. Therefore this intervention was an act of defiance against Nazi leaders. Nevertheless, Balzer and the other radical church leaders in Lübeck simply ignored the arbitration of the DEK.

Meanwhile, the other Lutheran land churches supported the nine persecuted pastors at Lübeck. The Luther Council issued a statement with a strong denunciation of the repressive Lübeck Church Council. Even Bishop Franz Tügel of Hamburg, formerly a German-Christian and a Nazi, called for all the Lutheran churches in Hamburg to hold "supplementary prayers for the persecuted

---

49 Letter in Schmidt, *Dokumente*, 2:1,272.

50 Schmidt, *Dokumente*, 2:1,271.

51 Schmidt, *Dokumente*, 2:1,273.

Lutheran congregations and pastors in Lübeck." Marahrens issued the following statement to be read in all the parishes of the Land Church of Hanover: "The congregation of the Lutheran Church of Germany remember today a circle of nine pastors of the city of Lübeck against whom the most painful suffering has come about. These men, who until now have faithfully attended to their pastoral office, have been dismissed immediately as of now without any reason and deprived of their financial support [*Ruhegehalt*] contrary to law."[52] This bold announcement was followed by a prayer that Marahrens asked to be read in all the churches of Hanover: "Lord God, heavenly Father ... We pray for the congregations which in these weeks have been robbed of the daily ministry of their shepherds. Have mercy upon them and restore to them the unaltered preaching of Thy Word."[53]

Soon Wilhelm Zoellner, the chairman of the RKA, stated that the entire DEK stood behind the nine beleaguered pastors and their congregations:

> We know that unfairness and violence, even though they seem at the moment to prevail, can bring no blessing with them. We therefore expect from the pastors that they cling to their legally conferred office and that they continue to serve their congregations ... The pastors have no right to give up the office that has been committed to them. Likewise we admonish the congregations that they remain faithful to their rightly called pastors, carry them in their prayers, help them and take their part, accept their ministry in churchly actions now as in the past, and especially that they attend their church services whenever they are held. The congregations have no right to leave their properly called pastors in the lurch.[54]

On December 23 the president of the Lübeck Land Court (*Landesgericht*) spoke at a public meeting of the First Civil Chamber in which he expressed the verdict of the courts that the church council was obligated to keep the nine pastors in their offices and pay their salaries until a final judgment was received from the RKA. The church council ignored this legal verdict. Therefore the land court delivered an injunction against the Lübeck Church Council on December 30 on behalf of the nine pastors and ordered their salaries paid, but the church council ignored the legal verdict. All efforts to prevent the dismissal of the pastors proved fruitless.

On December 31 the Gestapo imposed a speaking prohibition, placed all nine pastors under house arrest, and ordered them not to discuss the church conflict with anyone. Kurt Dietrich Schmidt explained this development as follows: "The Gestapo gave as reason for these measures the allegation that the pastors had

---

52 Reimers, *Lübeck im Kirchenkampf,* 328.

53 Reimers, *Lübeck im Kirchenkampf,* 329.

54 Cited in Schmidt, *Dokumente,* 2:1,274.

opposed their bishop and thereby had opposed the state, since, as was well known, the [Nazi] Party, the state, and the church are all one entity in Lübeck."[55] On January 1, 1937, Kühl was ordered to leave Lübeck. In these events is the sad picture of a Lübeck Church Council that not only did not act in a Christian manner but also refused to listen to officials of the DEK and of the legal court. Rejecting the rule of law, the council ruled instead by its own decree.

Zoellner then made preparations to visit Lübeck to set matters in order, but the Nazi government wanted to prevent his intervention and refused to authorize his trip. In protest, Zoellner resigned his office on the RKA, which led to the resignation of his fellow commission members. Thus the entire RKA was dissolved, a severe setback for the DEK. Zoellner died on July 16, 1937.

Before the conflict was finally resolved by restoring the pastors who had been dismissed, an incident occurred that was all too characteristic of the bizarre events of the Third Reich. The young musician Jan Bender, who later became a renowned composer of church music, was organist at St. Gertrude in the suburbs of Lübeck. The pastors of St. Gertrude, Hans Kanitz and Johannes Schultz (Schulz), were opposed to the German-Christians, and the staff at St. Gertrude, including Bender, stated that if their pastors were repressed, they would refuse to serve under a German-Christian pastor. But the Land Church Council's dismissal of the pastors took effect December 31, 1936. As Bender related the story in August 1971, the very next day, January 1, 1937, Bender arrived at the church before the service and learned that a notorious German-Christian[56] was replacing the regular pastor. Bender told the new preacher that he could not play for a German-Christian. The preacher angrily responded, "This is treason against the state. You're going to be sorry for this." Nevertheless, Bender resolutely turned off the organ and left the church.

Shortly thereafter, Bender's predecessor entered the church. Someone rushed up to him and said, "Bender isn't here, and you will have to play for church today." They hustled the man up to the organ, but the older gentleman was confused. The motor, which was controlled by an old-fashioned circular relay switch, had to be

---

55 Cited in Schmidt, *Dokumente*, 2:1,274.

56 During a telephone conversation with Charlotte (nee Peters) Bender in early 2000, I asked her for the name of the German-Christian pastor whom Jan had defied. She said that she and Jan had not been married then nor was she in Lübeck at that time, thus she could not recall the name. Reimers mentions the name of Scheunemann as a German-Christian pastor who was forced upon St. Gertrude (*Lübeck im Kirchenkampf*, 181). He also refers to the Bender case; see *Lübeck im Kirchenkampf*, 354. For a more complete account, see Hugo Gehrke, "Composers for the Church: Jan Bender," *Church Music* 71, no. 1 (1971): 30ff. Gehrke bases his account upon his own interview of Bender in the matter.

turned on slowly. In his excitement, he started the motor too rapidly and burned out the fuse; consequently, the organ would not play.

"Bender has damaged the organ to sabotage our service!" said the angry preacher, so the service was held without the organ. While Bender was eating lunch with his widowed mother, there was a knock on the door. Several Gestapo officers entered the house and arrested Bender for damaging the organ to sabotage the service. From there, he was transported to the concentration camp at Berlin-Sachsenhausen, where he was incarcerated for nearly four months. Meanwhile, Bender's mother asked Walter Kraft, the organist at St. Mary Lutheran Church, and Rudolf Kemper, who had built the organ at Lübeck, for their help. Both men inspected the organ at St. Gertrude's, certified that Bender had not damaged the organ, and reported the burned-out fuse. Bender was set free on April 20, 1937.[57]

On March 28, 1942, the medieval city of Lübeck was almost totally destroyed in an incendiary bombing by the British Royal Air Force. St. Mary's Church, the cathedral, and St. Peter's Church were badly damaged.[58] The next day was Palm Sunday, and Pastor Karl Friedrich Stellbrink entered his pulpit and declared that the bombing was a judgment of God against the city. Stellbrink was arrested, imprisoned, brought to trial, and condemned to death for traitorous actions that

---

57 Reimers places the liberation of Bender in connection with the truce reached between the official church headed by Balzer and the moderate pastors of the Confessing Church. This occurred April 3, 1937, when the nine ministers were restored to their pastorates. Thus "the deportation of the organist of St. Gertrude, Jan Bender in the concentration camp at Sachsenhausen" was ended (*Lübeck im Kirchenkampf,* 354). However, Charlotte Bender, Jan's widow, opined in a winter 2000 telephone conversation with me that his liberation was connected with an amnesty pronounced by Hitler on the Führer's birthday. Possibly both versions are true. After this, Bender returned to Lübeck only briefly to visit his mother. Some time later he received a position in Aurich in East Friesland, where he served as Lutheran cantor at St. Lambert. At Aurich he married Charlotte Peters. Bender was drafted into military service in 1939 and sent into combat, where he was wounded, losing an eye in a battle against the Russians. He was sent back to the combat zone despite his injury, and in October 1944 he was taken prisoner by U.S. military forces. These facts were verified in a February 8, 2000, telephone conversation with Charlotte Bender. Part of this story is also chronicled in Gehrke, "Composers for the Church: Jan Bender," 30. After Bender was taken prisoner by the U.S. military, he was discovered by the Lutheran chaplain Carl Zimmermann, who pressed him into service as his organist. His work for Zimmermann during his imprisonment led Bender to begin his career as a composer of church music. I met Bender through family connections. Eventually Bender became the first organist and cantor for the Concordia Academy, which I founded.

58 Actually, two fine medieval cities, Nuremberg and Lübeck, were chosen for destruction in revenge for the German bombing of Coventry, England. (I heard some Germans say these cities were chosen on the doubtful premise that Coventry was twice as fine as these German cities.)

hindered the war effort. Despite the desperate efforts of all the pastors to find leniency for him, the lay leaders of the Lübeck Church Council, especially Böhmcker and Sievers, refused to intervene. Meanwhile, three Roman Catholic clergymen in Lübeck, Johannes Prassek, Hermann Lange, and Eduard Müller, had also been implicated for treason. On November 10, 1943, Stellbrink and the three Roman Catholics were beheaded on the guillotine.[59]

Hamburg

The Lutheran Land Church of Hamburg had freed itself from state-church ties in the nineteenth century, and in 1932 it produced a new constitution. Consisting of 140 clergy positions in 1932,[60] the church traditionally followed a collegiate system and was governed by the five "chief pastors" of the historic old congregations: St. Peter, St. Jacob, St. Katharine, St. Nikolaus, and St. Michael. Of these five men, a leader was chosen and given the title "senior." Two prominent leaders and future bishops of Hamburg were Simon Schöffel, a Franconian who had become chief pastor (*Haupt-Pastor*) of St. Michael in 1922, and Theodor Knolle, chief pastor at St. Peter since 1924. Another prominent pastor who was later to become a bishop was Karl Witte, who had held several positions in education and in inner-mission work in Hamburg since 1921. Schöffel and Knolle, both of whom, like Elert, favored a stronger leadership in the church (such as a bishop) and who held a high view of the pastoral office, opposed the parliamentary system (*Parlamentarismus*) in church government. They advocated replacing the position of "senior" with the office of bishop, a development that occurred with the May 29, 1933, election of Schöffel as the first Lutheran bishop of Hamburg.

Schöffel's first term (he would serve as bishop again from 1946 to 1954) was an unhappy experience, marked by constant conflicts with the German-Christians in Hamburg. Schöffel was a Lutheran representative on the Spiritual Ministerium (*Geistliches Ministerium*) of the Reich Church, on which Joachim Hossenfelder, leader of the German-Christians, also sat. However, Schöffel was so thoroughly turned against the German-Christians by the November 1933 Sport Palace scandal that he resigned his position in the Spiritual Ministerium in protest. This action was perhaps overly hasty because Hossenfelder also lost his power shortly thereafter. Schöffel's resignation from the Spiritual Ministerium also made him an easy target for the German-Christians, who now leveled bitter attacks against

---

59 Meier, *EKK*, 3:388; Reimers, *Lübeck im Kirchenkampf*, 371–74. Stellbrink was not a part of the Confessing Church, and Reimers, who has a strong bias toward the Dahlem Front and the Barmen Declaration, treats Stellbrink negatively throughout, except for his martyrdom.

60 Statistics in *KJahr 1932*, 584.

him. Tügel, a pastor from Hamburg who belonged to the Nazi Party and was the leader of the GDC in Hamburg, coveted Schöffel's post as bishop and worked to unseat him.[61] Schöffel was forced to resign on March 1, 1934.[62]

Following Schöffel's resignation, Tügel became the bishop of Hamburg, and he remained in office until the fall of the Third Reich. At that time, Schöffel regained the position. The years of Tügel's tenure were a period of deep turmoil in the history of the Hamburg church. The Confessing Church was fragmented into three rival groups of pastors: (1) the PNB, which was headed locally by Pastor Philipp Hermann Junge; (2) the Confessional Fellowship (*Bekenntnisgemeinschaft*), which split into two groups when Schöffel and Knolle refused to support a declaration in favor of Niemöller; and (3) a further splinter group that resulted from the actions of Pastor Heinrich Wilhelmi, who served as temporary delegate to the Conference of the Brethren Councils (*Brüder-Räte*) and who signed, contrary to the instructions given him, a statement that approved the actions of the second VKL.[63]

Meanwhile, Tügel sought to heal the rifts in his church. To show his good intentions, he tried to bring in men who supported the Confessing Church. Thus he proposed Helmut Thielicke as pastor at St. Nikolaus in Hamburg, though he was not called by the congregation. In 1942 Tügel succeeded in placing Volkmar Herntrich at St. Katharine. Tügel invited men who were known to be sympathetic to the Confessing Church to speak at pastoral conferences, including Martin Doerne of Leipzig, Gerhard von Rad of Jena, Helmuth Schreiner of Rostock, Julius Schieder of Nuremberg, and Hanns Lilje of Berlin. Tügel also had Bishop Meiser come from Munich to preach at St. Michael for the 1941 Reformation Festival.

In April 1945 Tügel renewed his earlier plans to reorganize the land church and began by inviting Herntrich to take part in the new Land Church Council. Tügel also asked the chief pastors, Schöffel and Knolle, to join the council, but they mistrusted him and refused. At the end of World War II, Tügel saved the city of Hamburg from a disastrous attack by the Allied forces by persuading the National Socialist governor, Karl Kaufmann, to defy Hitler's orders and surrender the city without a battle on May 3, 1945. On Ascension Day, May 10, Tügel, in a "Word to the Hour," called the German people to repentance; however, he refused

---

61 On Tügel, see Meier, *EKK*, 1:375.

62 Meier, *EKK*, 1:376–77.

63 Meier, *EKK*, 1:395. The second VKL was the militant successor to the first VKL, which had included moderates such as Marahrens and Breit. Wilhelmi's action seemed like an unauthorized endorsement of the radical Dahlem Front.

to endorse the so-called Stuttgart Confession because it lacked a word about the common guilt of all people.[64]

OLDENBURG

The highest ranking officer of the Evangelical Lutheran Church of Oldenburg since 1920 had been Heinrich Tilemann, who bore the title of president of the High Church Council (*Oberkirchenratspräsident*). The GDC in Oldenburg, led by Pastor Ernst Hollje, alarmed many pastors, some of whom joined the JB. A branch of the PNB also was organized in the fall of 1933 under the leadership of Pastor Heinz Kloppenburg. Although 90 percent of the pastors supported Tilemann, he was forced out of office by the German-Christians on February 1, 1934.[65]

In the presence of Müller and Jäger, the Land Church of Oldenburg was merged into the DEK on June 15, 1934, at a celebration in St. Lambert. Shortly before the service, Johannes Volkers, a pupil of Adolf von Harnack and a moderate German-Christian pastor at Ganderkesee, was called by the land synod to the office of land provost (*Landespropst*), a position that stood under Reich Bishop Müller and replaced the office of president, which had been held by Tilemann.[66] In August, Volkers's title was changed to bishop of Oldenburg. In succeeding months, the gulf widened between Volkers and the church leaders supporting Kloppenburg.

On February 27, 1935, a group of protesting pastors and laymen met at Varel to assemble the first Confessing Synod of Oldenburg. Oberamtsrichter Ricklefs, president of the former land synod, was elected president of the Confessing Synod. Rather than a Brethren Council, they chose to be led by a Presidium of the Confessing Synod, which consisted of Pastors Kloppenburg, Hans Rühe, and Hans Schmidt.[67] Kloppenburg's determined stand against persecution of the Jews and his correspondence with Althaus, who counseled Kloppenburg to support several teachers who were imprisoned for helping Christian women of Jewish background, was referred to previously (see chapter 6).

In the Resolutions of the First Oldenburg Confessing Synod, it was noted that the DEK had been launched on July 11, 1933, but that

---

64 Meier, *EKK*, 1:396–97. Tügel was not the only German church leader who considered the Stuttgart Confession deficient or even hypocritical. The objection was raised that the "confessors" paraded their own good deeds, then said, with an air of humility, that the deeds were not sufficient.

65 Meier, *EKK*, 1:399.

66 Meier, *EKK*, 1:401.

67 Meier, *EKK*, 2:285.

according to uncontested legal opinions, its foundation has been most severely injured, yes, that beyond this, there have been assaults against every legal impulse and against the duty of truthfulness. False teachers destroy faith, arbitrariness destroys order, violence destroys legality, and force destroys the freedom of confession. Congregations have had their mouths stopped and the ordination vows of the pastors have in fact been disabled by the demand of blind obedience. Where both congregations and pastors have nevertheless raised their voices, all too often their sense of national honor has been dragged into the dust by leaders of their own church, contrary to the truth.[68]

Therefore the protesters asserted that the "serious need of the church" forced the Oldenburg Confessional Fellowship to proclaim an emergency situation and to bring members of the congregations and pastors together in this Confessing Synod. They noted the lack of true leadership in the church and the decline in the life of the parish and its youth work: "We lack the needful representation of the church's needs in the matter of the sanctification of Sunday." The resolutions noted further that "the Land Church is ruled by a small group who are not trusted by those among whom the strength of the church resides, and they have 75 percent of those who hold pastoral office against them." The resolutions added that, consequently, the joy of working in the church had been seriously hindered, and the work of rebuilding the church was made impossible.[69] The resolutions now asserted: "Where such a situation prevails, the Christian congregation has, according to the Scriptures and Confessions, not only the right but also the obligation to help itself. Such self-help does not mean the breaking of the law but rather its restoration."[70] The representatives committed themselves to working under the "Provisional Leadership of the DEK," which consisted of Marahrens, Paul Koch, Breit, Paul Humburg, and Eberhard Fiedler.

BRAUNSCHWEIG

In the nineteenth century, the Lutheran Church of Braunschweig had already won considerable independence from the state; consequently, the power of governing the land church lay in the hands of the church itself. The German territorial churches were permanently abolished in 1918, and the church of Braunschweig adopted a new constitution on January 23, 1922. In it, the powers of the church were vested in the land synod, which had the authority to select members of the church government and of the Land Church Office. To strengthen and centralize its affairs, the office of bishop was created. The first bishop was Alexan-

---

68 Schmidt, *Bekenntnisse*, 3:66.

69 Schmidt, *Bekenntnisse*, 3:66–67.

70 Schmidt, *Bekenntnisse*, 3:67.

der Bernewitz, a Baltic Lutheran. As National Socialism strengthened its position in 1932, Bernewitz cautiously supported the movement. Caught up in the enthusiasm over the Führer principle (*Führerprinzip*) during the first months after Hitler's assumption of power, the diet of the land church conferred full authority upon the bishop as a church *kommissar*. During the ensuing *Kirchenkampf*, this decree of empowerment was to prove a poor decision.

Before the election of July 23, 1933, one slate of candidates was presented by the JB and another slate was presented by the GDC. The German-Christians succeeded in repressing the rival slate, which resulted in the GDC taking over every seat in the land church diet. Six weeks later, the diet convened and elected 30-year-old Wilhelm Beye as bishop. It was decreed that the land church should adopt an administrative structure after the model of the Third Reich. Henceforth, pastors would be placed by the Land Church Office rather than called by the congregation. The eighteen conferences were replaced by seven conferences that corresponded to the political entities. Also, the Aryan Paragraph of the Prussian Union, which banned pastors of Jewish blood, was approved.

On November 30, 1933, forty-two pastors, led by Heinrich Lachmund of Blankenburg, walked out of a meeting presided over by Beye and founded the Braunschweig Pastors' Emergency League. The land church was reorganized so the number of representatives to the diet was reduced from thirty-six to twelve, all of whom were German-Christians. On June 1, 1934, the newly constituted diet transferred the powers of the land church to the DEK, thus merging with the Reich Church. The Land Church of Braunschweig thereby became a "destroyed" church.

Beye fell from office because of an alleged embezzlement of funds in his previous position. A moderate German-Christian, Helmut Johnsen, the chief pastor at the Lübeck cathedral, became *kommissar* church leader on June 19, 1934. On November 15 he was called by the land church diet to serve as bishop of Braunschweig. Somewhat surprisingly, Johnsen took a mediating course and thereby exerted a beneficial influence upon the ravaged church. He was tolerant and moderate with members of the Confessing Church and reinstated a number of pastors who had been deposed by Beye, including Lachmund. Johnsen also instituted proceedings against German-Christians who had abused their positions in office.[71] On January 6, 1937, Johnsen even led the Land Church of Braunschweig into joining the Luther Council (*Luther-Rat*).[72]

A source of great mischief came with the accession of Ludwig Hoffmeister, who, as a High Church Councilman (*Oberkirchenrat*), also served from 1938 until

---

71 Meier, *EKK*, 1:412–13.

72 Meiser, *Verantwortung*, 2:367, 667.

1943 as director of finances for the Land Church of Braunschweig. While in office, he misused the church's endowments and, as a hardened Nazi, withheld funds from people connected with the Confessing Church or the Luther Council. He also interfered in church administrative matters not related to his authority and harassed the bishop, the pastors, and the lay leaders of the church in every imaginable way. In 1939 Hoffmeister cut off the salaries of the preacher, cantor, and organist of the Braunschweig cathedral. He decreed that the cathedral would no longer belong to the church but should belong to the state in its new capacity as an Aryan temple. This act of secularization was consummated in 1941.[73]

From the time of this takeover, the government spent immense amounts of money making the cathedral into an Aryan temple. Most of the ecclesiastical furnishings were removed, and great excavations were carried out in the crypt to prepare a new sepulcher for Henry the Lion and his second wife, Mathilda of England, beneath their monument in the nave. Preparing the elaborate sepulcher entailed such massive structural changes that the foundations of the cathedral were endangered and had to be replaced by a construction of steel and concrete at great expense to the government.[74]

A similar occurrence took place at Quedlinburg, an ancient city about 50 miles southeast of Braunschweig but located within the boundaries of the Prussian Union. There, in the Collegiate Church (*Stiftskirche*), a venerable structure more than 900 years old, the millennial anniversary of the death of Henry I (d. 936) was observed by transforming the church into a Hall of Old German Kings. Celebrations were led by the *Schutzstaffel* and followed by a church service at which Johannes Eger preached the sermon.[75]

Johnsen found it impossible to work with Hoffmeister. In 1939 he left Braunschweig to join the army and served as an officer on the southern front. He was taken prisoner and placed in a camp at Zrenjanin, Yugoslavia (in modern-day Serbia), where he was shot to death on September 2, 1947.[76] Upon Johnsen's resigna-

---

73 Meier, *EKK*, 3:415.

74 On the political aspects, see Meier, *EKK*, 3:415–16. On the alteration of the building, see Adolf Quast, *Der Sankt-Blasius-Dom zu Braunschweig; Seine Geschichte und seine Kunstwerke* (Braunschweig: Borek, n.d.), 19–21, 31, et passim. Quast mentions that the Nazi alterations of the Braunschweig cathedral were done under the leadership of "the professors Krüger, two brothers, who had also worked on the Tannenberg monument" (*Der Sankt-Blasius-Dom zu Braunschweig*, 19–21). Quast does not supply the Krügers' first names. I was well acquainted with Dr. Quast, an esteemed theologian and art historian, who was cathedral preacher at Braunschweig in the 1970s.

75 Meiser, *Verantwortung*, 2:366.

76 Meiser, *Verantwortung*, 2:667.

tion, Pastor Martin Erdmann was designated land church president, and he became bishop of Braunschweig on April 22, 1947.[77]

THE ESTABLISHMENT OF THE *REICHSKIRCHENAUSSCHUß* (RKA)

When Müller refused to resign as Reich bishop after the debacle of October 1934, representatives of the Confessing Church, together with the bishops of Hanover, Bavaria, and Wurttemberg and the Brethren Council of the Confessing Synod, established the VKL, which was led by Marahrens and included Meiser and Wurm. Thus the viewpoints of both the Confessing Church and the Lutheran land churches were represented. Following this action, the inner life of the churches became much more quiet and harmonious.[78] However, attempts by the VKL to obtain recognition from the Nazi government were unsuccessful.

On July 16, 1935, Hitler appointed Hanns Kerrl (1887–1941) as state minister for the DEK. Kerrl seems to have been a man of some integrity, who, in his own way, cared about the Protestant churches and honestly tried to clear up the confusion that Müller had left behind. Unfortunately, because of poor health, Kerrl was not always able to attend to official matters. He tried to steer a middle course between the less radical German-Christians and the more moderate men from the Confessing Church. The Reich Church Commission (RKA) was to be an arm of the state that would provide leadership for the DEK and relate it properly to the National Socialist state. Kerrl assembled the RKA on October 3, 1935, placing the highly respected Zoellner as chairman. Other RKA members included Christhard Mahrenholz of Göttingen, Johannes Eger of the Prussian province of Saxony, Theodor Kuessner of East Prussia, Otto Koopmann of Aurich, Bishop Ludwig Diehl of the Palatinate, Walter Wilm of Pomerania, and Friedrich Hanemann of Kulmbach in Bavaria.[79]

Kerrl's objectives were not compatible with those of Confessional Lutheranism but were more in tune with the goals of the Prussian Union and the Barmen Declaration. He wanted to achieve an "evangelical" church for Germany that would unite all Protestants—whether Lutheran, Reformed, or Union—within one church, an organization that would remove Hitler's distrust and would bring all German Protestants together in support of the Third Reich.[80]

---

77 Meier, *EKK*, 3:419. There is further information on the Lutheran land churches of Saxony, Mecklenburg, Schleswig-Holstein, Lübeck-Eutin, Hamburg, Oldenburg, and Braunschweig in Meier, *EKK*, 1:204ff., 261ff.; see also Meier, *EKK*, 2:155ff.; 3:181ff.

78 Schmidt, *Bekenntnisse*, 2:10–11.

79 See Heinz Brunotte, "Kirchenkampf," *EKL*, 2:742.

Meanwhile, Kerrl sought to counteract the influence of the German-Christians in the destroyed churches by establishing a system of church commissions (*Kirchenausschüße*) within the individual land churches (*Landeskirchlicher Ausschuß*) after the pattern of the RKA. Where these church commissions were implemented, they tended to remove power from the puppet churches and to place it in the hands of duly elected people. The more radical elements in the Confessing Church, however, particularly those within Niemöller's Dahlem Front, fought this development vehemently. They accused the bishops of the intact land churches and other leaders of the VKL, who tried to go along with Kerrl, of complicity with the Nazis. It was the conflict between these two groups over this and other issues that led to the tragic schism at Bad Oeynhausen in February 1936 when the Confessing Church was split into several fragments.

The attempt by Marahrens to cooperate with Kerrl brought the bishop much grief. We shall see later how, after being coaxed by Kerrl into signing a revised form of the Godesberg Declaration, Marahrens's relations with his allies were soured. From the start, his establishment of a Land Church Commission after the plan of Kerrl met with energetic resistance in Hanover. The Osnabrück Circle, who strongly supported the Barmen Declaration and Niemöller's Dahlem Front, rejected the RKA and its Hanoverian branch most strenuously. Moreover, when the Osnabrück Circle followed Barth and Niemöller in rejecting the "leadership principle," they were opposing Marahrens, who had been granted emergency powers as bishop by the land church. Marahrens's strong leadership was important in keeping the Church of Hanover "intact," while the churches that followed Barth's democratic principles of church government were infiltrated in church elections and were "destroyed" by the German-Christians and the Nazis.[81] When the Confessional Fellowship backed Marahrens and expressed its willingness to give the Land Church Commission a chance to prove itself, the Osnabrück Circle protested loudly, withdrew from the fellowship, and threatened to leave the Land Church of Hanover as well.[82] It must be said that the Osnabrück Circle, consisting

---

80 On Kerrl's goals, see the excellent summary in Meier, *EKK*, 2:78. It was the old story of a national church, after the Prussian Union, versus an ecumenical church, as desired by the Confessional Lutherans.

81 Insisting that their church follow the directives of Barmen and the Confessing Synods, the Osnabrück Circle declared: "Without violating our commitment to the Confessions, we cultivate our fellowship with the brethren in the Union and in the Reformed Church . . . A 'leadership principle,' even in a milder form, is unacceptable in the Church of Jesus Christ" (Klügel, *Dokumente*, 94).

82 Klügel, *Landeskirche*, 207–12; see also the documents in Klügel, *Dokumente*, 93–100, including the November 28, 1935, declaration of the Osnabrück Circle and the perceptive reply by Heinz Brunotte, with his criticisms of the Barmen Declaration. The

of people such as Hans Bodensieck, Richard Karwehl, and Paul Leo, was a coura-geous and intelligent group, but some of its militant actions made matters diffi-cult for Marahrens.

Several letters from 1936 reveal a significant argument between Friedrich Coch, the radical Nazi bishop of the destroyed church of Saxony, and Kerrl. On October 20, Coch wrote an angry letter to Kerrl in which he complained that the Saxon Land Church Commission had joined the Luther Council and was perse-cuting his own group, the German-Christians. Coch further complained that the commission had ordered him to avoid offensive words and had limited his preaching, speaking at conferences, lectures, and so forth ("muzzling decree" [*Maulkorberlaß*] of March 31, 1936) with the stated purpose of avoiding further rancor within the badly divided Saxon church. Coch wrote: "I am no longer able to recognize the Land Church Commission as of May 27, 1936."[83] This was an act of defiance against Kerrl, which the Reich minister did not take kindly. In his terse reply, Kerrl took note of Coch's tone and proceeded to put him in his place:

> The letter of October 20, 1936 gives me no reason to change my position regarding the regulation on March 9, 1936, of your official activity. It is known to you that I have worked constantly for a diminution of the difficulties in Saxony. Also, I have taken pains, with some success, to hinder some of the greater church-political actions of the Confessional Front. Therefore, I must expect that you will not one-sidedly renounce the previous regulation, and that, when a special difficulty arises, that you will turn to me to arrange a mediation. I also observe that the tone of your letter to me is totally inappro-priate.[84]

It is clear that Kerrl was seeking a middle-of-the-road position in what he regarded as a means of saving the church and averting radical actions from both the left and the right. Therefore he rejected Coch's complaints and firmly stated that he would not tolerate his actions.

In the Land Church of Saxony there were many pastors and congregations who did not feel they belonged to either the extreme position of the Nazi bishop or the position of the Dahlem Front. Accordingly, a group of church leaders and pastors called themselves "The Churchly Alliance of the Middle" (*Der Kirchliche Bund der Mitte*). They stated that they wanted to avoid the mixing of politics and church: "We want to go the legal way for the renewal and purging of the church,

---

Osnabrück Confession was signed by Hans Bodensieck, Hans Hermann Bornschein, Richard Karwehl, Paul Leo, Julius Ruprecht von Loewenfeld, and Wilhelm Thimme (Klügel, *Dokumente*, 94). Full names are supplied in Meier, *EKK*, 2:283.

83 Fischer, *Die sächsische Landeskirche im Kirchenkampf,* 233.

84 Fischer, *Die sächsische Landeskirche im Kirchenkampf,* 234.

and therefore we cannot decide upon a course of general disobedience. We have a wholesome feeling for authority and we struggle for the true establishment of the same."[85] Five superintendents of church conferences who designated themselves as belonging to the middle were Walter Berg of Bautzen, Herbert Böhme of Meissen, Willy Gerber of Chemnitz, Georg Krönert of Flöha, and Arno Spranger of Annaberg.[86] Another letter was signed by 129 pastors of the "Middle Group."[87]

The idea of developing a middle group in Saxony soon spread to other land churches. In the spring of 1937, several groups of pastors elsewhere in Germany sought to establish new groups that would take a mediating position between the more radical church leaders on the left and on the right. One such group was the Wittenberg Federation (*Wittenberger Bund*), which was founded in the Luther Hall in Wittenberg on June 21–23, 1937. If this was a "middle position," as was claimed, however, it was actually a mediating stance only between the radical German Church (*Deutschkirchler*) on the far right and the more moderate German-Christians on the near right. In contrast to the truly middle group in Saxony, this new federation stood completely on German-Christian ground. Speakers at the founding event of the Wittenberg Federation were Hans Schomerus (cathedral preacher in Braunschweig), Theodor Ellwein (High Consistory Councillor of Berlin), and Walter Jeep (a pastor in Bremen). A paper by Ernst Forsthoff of Königsberg, who was unable to attend, was also read by Schomerus.[88] This federation was ready to make itself available to Kerrl.

The RKA collapsed after the Nazi state refused to allow Zoellner to visit Lübeck during the altercation between the pastors and the Nazi-dominated church council in January 1937. Zoellner resigned in protest, and his fellow members on the RKA followed suit. This placed Kerrl in an awkward position, and he had to fill the breach somehow. Meanwhile, Kerrl was seeking ways to bring about an understanding between the Nazi state and the DEK in the attempt to renew Hitler's flagging interest and declining support for the Protestant churches. To this end, Kerrl tried to produce a statement that would seem to embody Nazi ideology without compromising the Gospel. Although Kerrl had been brought up in the church and had a fairly good grasp of theological matters, his plans for framing such a mediating position were faulty. In the winter of 1938–1939, Kerrl's efforts led to several new documents.

---

85 Fischer, *Die sächsische Landeskirche im Kirchenkampf,* 208–9.

86 Fischer, *Die sächsische Landeskirche im Kirchenkampf,* 198–99. The first names of individuals omitted by Fischer have been partly supplied from Meier, *EKK,* 2:455 n. 993; 3:688 n. 1,421, who lists thirteen church superintendents.

87 Fischer, *Die sächsische Landeskirche im Kirchenkampf,* 197–98.

88 Meier, *EKK,* 2:373.

Godesberg Declaration[89]

In this, the first of Kerrl's efforts, the first paragraph states: "With all the powers of faith and our daily life we serve the man who has led our *Volk* out of servitude and trouble into freedom and glorious greatness. We fight with determination against all elements that use religion as a disguise for political enmity." The third paragraph calls for a distinction between politics and religion. It claims that National Socialism was, politically, the continuation of Luther's work and thereby "helped us again in a religious sense to the true understanding of the Christian faith." But what is the relationship of Judaism and Christianity? The document answers: "The Christian faith is the unbridgeable opposite to Judaism." The document then raises the question of whether Christianity could be supernational and international, which it answered with a resounding *no*—ecumenical ties would bring the corruption of Christianity. Instead, "true Christian faith unfolds itself fruitfully only within the given Orders of Creation," which likely meant *Volk*, blood, and soil as understood by National Socialism.[90] In the fifth paragraph, the declaration calls for "tolerance" in the church, which means either doctrinal indifference or the acceptance of church leaders who followed National Socialism, offering this compliment to the Prussian Union: "We welcome the newly published decrees of the Old Prussian Union as an essential contribution in that direction."

The Godesberg Declaration bears the signatures of eighteen men. Of these, Helmuth Kittel objected that he had not been present and that his name had been placed there by someone else. Nearly all the signers were from regions of the Prussian Union or other Union churches; the exceptions were Siegfried Leffler of Thuringia, leader of the radical German-Christians, and two laymen from Hamburg: Wilhelm Stapel and Kurt Woermann, a merchant. In every case, the signers were from destroyed churches.[91] At an April 6 meeting in Berlin, representatives of other destroyed churches (Saxony, Schleswig-Holstein, Thuringia, Mecklenburg, the Palatinate, Anhalt, Oldenburg, Lübeck, and Austria) added their names.[92]

Because of the strong criticisms of the Bad Godesberg Declaration, Kerrl prepared a revised document called the "Five Basic Principles" (*Fünf Grundsätze*), in which some of the objectionable features were removed or watered down.[93] At the Church Leaders Conference—attended by Marahrens, Wurm, Walter Hollweg,

---

89 The text of the Godesberg Declaration, together with the names of the signatories, is given in Meier, *EKK*, 3:75–76.

90 Meier, *EKK*, 3:76.

91 The signers are listed in Meier, *EKK*, 3:76.

92 Hermelink, 474–75.

93 Kerrl's revision is given in Meier, *EKK*, 3:80.

Friedrich Happich, Adolf Drechsler, Meiser, Julius Kühlewein, Kasimir Ewerbeck, and Wilhelm Henke—the Five Principles were not accepted as presented. They were rewritten in an altered form.[94]

Later, Kerrl tried to convince Marahrens that his signature to the Five Principles was needed to convince Hitler of the possibility of a reconciliation of the German government with Christianity. With much hesitation, Marahrens added his signature to the document. This action soon brought him much grief. Meiser and Wurm reprimanded Marahrens in a public announcement.[95] The two southern bishops were deeply offended by Marahrens's action, and his previously close relationship with them was seriously impaired. Of course, Marahrens had not signed the Godesberg Declaration itself; he had signed the Five Principles, which they also had signed in their own revised form, but the effect was not much different.[96] Perhaps this breach was partly responsible for Wurm's backing away from the formation of the VELKD and support of the EKD, which caused a further rift among Confessional Lutherans after the war. Regardless, in 1947 Marahrens expressed his deep regret for having made this mistake.[97]

What had been a desperate attempt by Kerrl to win the favor of Hitler for the Christian churches ended in failure. Hitler was no longer interested in working with the churches; instead, he turned to sinister plans for the utter destruction of the churches following an anticipated German victory in World War II. Only the end of the war and the fall of the Third Reich averted Hitler's demonic plans. Kerrl himself was spared from the last deadly phase in Hitler's church politics, for he died unexpectedly in 1941.[98]

---

94 The revised form of the Five Principles by the Church Leaders Conference is given in Meier, *EKK*, 3:81. Wilhelm Niemöller claims that the nine church leaders had signed the "Godesberger Erklärung variata" (*Evangelische Kirche,* 380), but this is incorrect. What they signed was their revision of Kerrl's Five Principles, a different document from the earlier Godesberg Declaration.

95 The rebuff of Marahrens by Meiser and Wurms is given in *KJahr 1933–1945*, 305–7.

96 It must also be said to the discredit of Wurm and Meiser that their own revision of the Five Principles had included in § 3 this regrettable concession to Kerrl: "In the area of *volkisch* life, a serious and responsible racial politics is necessary for retaining the purity of our *Volk*" (Meier, *EKK*, 3:81).

97 The text of the March 26, 1939, Godesberg Declaration has seldom been published, but it is given in Meier, *EKK*, 3:75–76. The signers are listed in Meier, *EKK*, 3:76 (also given in *KJahr 1933–1944*, 293–94). Its softened version, the "Five Basic Principles for a New Order of the German Evangelical Church Which Corresponds to the Needs of the Present Time" (*Grundsätze für eine den Erfordernissen der Gegenwart entsprechende neue Ordnung der Deutschen Evangelischen Kirche*), is given in Hermelink, 476. The mistake of Marahrens in signing the second document is discussed in Meier, *EKK*, 3:82, and in Klügel, *Landeskirche*, 369–70.

During the war years, the churches were increasingly harassed by the state. Religious publishing houses were shut down; the finances of the churches were progressively cut off; persecution of Jews increased; the practices of abortion, forced sterilization, and euthanasia were expanded; church services were subject to spying by the secret police; and many preachers were arrested for allegedly subversive remarks. During the first years of the war, 46 percent of the Protestant pastors were drafted into military service, leaving the local churches in a precarious position. Many pastors were wounded or killed, resulting in a great void of spiritual leadership. On the home front, an escalation in bombing by the Western powers destroyed dwellings, businesses, and churches. Food, fuel, clothing, and medicine came into increasingly short supply. By the end of the war, Germany was totally ruined. Her great cities had been destroyed, the railroads and means of communication had shut down, and life was at a standstill. Meanwhile, the Western occupation forces were widely regarded as a means of liberation for a country ruined by the horrors of National Socialism.

---

98 Kerrl died of a heart attack on the morning of December 14, 1941, the Third Sunday in Advent; see "Nachruf für Hanns Kerrl," in *KJahr 1933–1944*, 479.

CHAPTER FOURTEEN

THE STRUGGLE OF THE INTACT LUTHERAN LAND CHURCHES AGAINST HITLER

It has been noted that the Confessional Lutherans were disappointed when the DEK showed itself as primarily interested in the outward merger of the separate land churches into one overarching Reich Church. Confessional Lutherans also were disappointed when the DEK failed to take a clear position in favor of the Lutheran Confessions or the truly spiritual purpose of the church. The Lutheran Council issued the following statement on October 5, 1934:

> A German Lutheran Church could have come to worldwide importance in ecumenical Lutheranism and would thereby have performed an important service for the German people. But a German Union Church is incapable of establishing ties with any Lutheran churches of the world. Therefore, we lift our voices loudly and clearly to protest against the weakening and robbing of the Lutheran churches in Germany of their legal rights, and warn of the unforeseeable results. We are willing to struggle for a great Lutheran Church of the German nation.[1]

Because Lutherans in Germany were part of a worldwide church, their outlook was international in scope. Their interest and involvement in the Lutheran World Convention and in the Faith and Order Movement made Lutherans a natural corrective to the unbridled nationalism of the Nazi Party and the DEK. The

---

1 "The Lutheran Council Regarding the Incorporation of the Lutheran Land Churches," in Niemöller, *Evangelische Kirche,* 192–93.

299

Prussian Union was not an ecumenical entity like the Lutheran Church; it barely existed outside the national boundaries of Germany. Thus the Confessional Lutherans transcended the narrow nationalism of Adolf Hitler and the Prussian Union (see chapter 12).

It has been noted that not only the Union churches but also some of the Lutheran churches were susceptible to Nazi takeover. It might be pointed out that except for the Land Church of Saxony, which was in central Germany, every one of these destroyed churches was located in Northern Germany, where church life tended to be rather languid. Many parishes in Northern Germany achieved church attendance of 1–2 percent of their nominal membership. In contrast, in Southern Germany church attendance reached the relatively high level of 10 percent of the total population, and churches were full on a given Sunday morning. This was generally considered a good percentage, considering that many members were ill, infirm, or working on Sunday. During the Nazi attempts at merger (*Gleichschaltung*), the Lutheran land churches of Bavaria and Württemberg in Southern Germany fended off Nazi takeovers. They were joined by the Lutheran Land Church of Hanover in Northern Germany. Although church life in Hanover lacked the ardor of that found in the south, the church struggle stirred up unexpected levels of devotion and fidelity to the Lutheran Confessions and a willingness to support a strong leader, Bishop August Marahrens. Therefore attempts at seizure by the Nazis and the German-Christians were foiled, despite the strong presence of Nazis who had seeped into the bureaucracy of the Hanoverian church. This chapter begins with a discussion of the unsuccessful attempt to incorporate the Land Church of Hanover, after which it focuses on the churches of Württemberg and Bavaria.

THE LUTHERAN LAND CHURCH OF HANOVER
AND BISHOP AUGUST MARAHRENS

The Lutheran Land Church of Hanover consisted of about two and a half million members or 82 percent of the population of the land of Hanover.[2] This church had a distinctively Confessional Lutheran character. Its Lutheran consciousness in

---

2 A valuable study by a secular historian is given by my colleague at the State University of New York at Buffalo, William Sheridan Allen, *The Nazi Seizure of Power: The Experience of a Single German Town 1930–1935* (Chicago: Quadrangle, 1965). This book about a small city within the Land Church of Hanover is exceedingly well researched and graphically demonstrates how a community in Lower Saxony was gradually taken over by Nazism. It deals with Northeim, a picturesque medieval city of about 20,000 inhabitants, which had once been a member of the Hanseatic League and is located about 15 miles north of Göttingen.

part went back to the Reformation and Luther. However, during the nineteenth century, when the state of Prussia annexed the kingdom of Hanover, a group called the Lutheran Association (*Lutherische Vereinigung*) emerged to shield Lutheran faith and practice from the inroads of the Prussian Union.[3]

Inextricably involved with the survival of Hanover during the Third Reich was its bishop, August Marahrens, who was born October 11, 1875, in Hanover. After holding various other offices in the Church of Hanover, he served as bishop from 1925 to 1947 and as abbot of Loccum Abbey from 1928 to 1950. He was chairman of the first VKL of the DEK from 1934 to 1936 and a member of the Supreme Council of the DEK from 1939 to 1945. Marahrens served as president of the Lutheran World Convention from 1935 to 1945, an organization that later became the Lutheran World Federation. Marahrens died at Loccum Abbey on May 3, 1950.

On May 23, 1933, the church senate and the Land Church Commission conferred upon Marahrens the act of a *Bevollmächtigung*, that is, full power to suspend the constitution and take over the leadership of the church with unlimited authority in case of an emergency.[4] Max Schramm, president of the Land Church Office (*Landeskirchenamt*), gave the following reason for this act:

> I have held the decree for absolutely necessary. This is because the struggle to reorganize conditions in the Evangelical churches, under which surprisingly quick changes have occurred again and again, and particularly also for the individual land churches, requires quick decisions in order to avoid dangers. The participation of the various parts of the church government in decision making, as stipulated in the constitution, could not meet this need, and therefore a legal basis had to be created which gave to one person the authorization to make necessary decisions alone that would be legally binding.[5]

Eberhard Klügel insists that this action was not done to be in accord with the "Führer principle" of the secular state but to facilitate the needs of the church to respond to sudden emergencies. Similar full empowerment was also given to Bishops Hans Meiser and Theophil Wurm by their respective land churches.

During Hitler's first year in office, Marahrens seems to have been carried along with the general euphoria of the time. Although he had advocated Friedrich von Bodelschwingh rather than Ludwig Müller for the office of Reich bishop, he seemed unaware of the potential dangers of the GDC. One gathers this from a letter that Marahrens wrote to Gerhard Hahn on August 26, 1933:

---

3 See the account in Klügel, *Landeskirche*, 8–9.

4 Klügel, *Landeskirche*, 28–29.

5 Klügel, *Landeskirche*, 29 n. 17.

I recognize, with a full personal affirmation of the National Socialist move-ment, the desires of the "German-Christians," on the basis of the recent guide-lines, as my own. . . . I certainly hope to find a basis upon which all the minis-terial brethren can agree, among whom there is to be a wide-reaching renewal of the life and forms of our church, a group that is willing with all its powers to take hold of the task. I definitely expect that a declaration for such work under my leadership can be produced before the second session of the Land Church Diet in which the willingness is expressed for fellowship with the Faith-Movement "German-Christians."[6]

Marahrens, however, stated near the end of the letter that it would be against his personal policy to become a member of the GDC.[7] In much less than a year, Marahrens was to have reached full clarity regarding the malevolence of this movement.

By May 1934, there was a strong German-Christian majority in the church senate (*Kirchensenat*) and in the Land Church Office (*Landeskirchenamt*) of the church of Hanover. At this time, Marahrens found himself in a fierce struggle against this German-Christian presence, against minister of justice August Jäger, and against the government of the Reich Church as it was led by Müller.[8] On May 15, 1934, the German-Christians, led by Hahn, tried to merge the Land Church of Hanover with the DEK, and the church senate (*Kirchensenat*) of Hanover, which was dominated by German-Christians, approved the decree of merger (*Gleich-schaltung*).

It has often been said that Marahrens refused to sign the document that would formally merge Hanover into the Reich Church. Actually, Marahrens at first signed the document but then, realizing his mistake, crossed out his name and, backed by the majority of pastors in the Hanoverian church, successfully foiled the takeover.[9] The underlying reason that led Marahrens to oppose the merger was doctrinal: The Lutheran Church of Hanover was pledged to uphold the Lutheran Confessions, whereas the DEK was a Union church, based upon the model of the Prussian Union. One of Marahrens's abiding characteristics was his deep concern

---

6 Letter in Klügel, *Dokumente*, 26–27. Because no name is given, though the letter is addressed to "Hochverehrter Herr Amtsbruder," its addressee can only be a matter of conjecture. Klügel thinks it was written to Hahn, an ardent German-Christian who later became a strong opponent of Marahrens. Hahn led the movement in May 1934 for the merger (*Gleichschaltung*) of Hanover into Müller's Reich Church.

7 Klügel, *Dokumente*, 26–27.

8 This is summarized in Hermelink, 92–93. For a more complete account, see the two exemplary volumes by Klügel.

9 Marahrens's position on the signature is discussed in detail in Klügel, *Landeskirche*, 122–24; cf., Meier, *EKK*, 1:205.

for doing things correctly and for upholding the ecclesial law that governed his church. He realized that he could not merge the church of Hanover into the Reich Church without compromising the confessional basis of his church. Marahrens's commitment to the Lutheran Confessions was what saved him from a dreadful mistake; he withdrew his signature.

On May 23, 1934, a gathering of two thousand loyal representatives, mostly men, from 560 congregations (about half of the 1,158 churches of the land church) gathered inside the Market Church of St. George and St. Jakob in Hanover to hear Marahrens preach. The service was conducted according to the traditional Lutheran liturgy. The sermon was based on Ephesians 5:25: "Christ loved the church and gave himself for it, that he might sanctify it."[10] This "confessional service" in the Market Church was followed by a "confessional gathering" in the meetinghouse (*Rusthaus*). Pastor Hans (Johannes) Bosse of Raddesstorf, leader of the Confessional Fellowship (*Bekenntnisgemeinschaft*), read a resolution that declared the motion to merge their land church with the Reich Church must be withdrawn as illegal "because it is irreconcilable with the confession of our land church as well as with the constitution of the Reich Church." The scribe stated that this declaration was unanimously accepted by the assembly "with loud applause."[11] Pastor Friedrich Duensing, who later lost his life in the war, gave the following eyewitness report:

> The Lutheran Church struggles over its confession, over the authenticity of its Lutheran nature. Therefore, it resists the way of the German-Christians, which comes not out of the church but out of politics. The Lutheran Church is intent on building the church—if it must be, also against its own past, which bears the blame that the church was not church in a clear demarcation, but has allowed the elevation of views in its midst that destroy the church. A storm is going through the Lutheran congregations. It will sweep away what is rotten, sick, what is not out of faith.[12]

Thus these meetinghouse speakers supported the stand of Marahrens against merging the Hanoverian church with the Reich Church. Like Marahrens, the speakers wanted to bring the German churches closer together, but not at the cost of surrendering the Lutheran Confessions. Some pointed out that the DEK did not safeguard the Lutheran Confessions but was actually a new form of the Union church. Therefore the gathering rejected any merger with the Reich Church and repudiated its previous ratification by the senate. Those present made the following staunch affirmation: "Contrariwise, the majority of the church senate has

---

10 Described in Klügel, *Landeskirche*, 125f.

11 Klügel, *Dokumente*, 34–35.

12 Cited in Klügel, *Landeskirche*, 125–26.

not taken note of the confessional standpoint of our land church, but has accepted a motion for merger that endangers our confessional position."[13] Therefore the Confessional Fellowship abandoned its previous reluctance toward disobedience and demanded that the members of the church senate who had supported this harmful, anticonfessional resolution resign from office.[14] The five members of the church senate who were Nazis fought back. In a statement that appeared in the secular press, they demanded the immediate expulsion of Marahrens from his office. The doughty bishop was not easily frightened and remained in office until he retired in 1947 at the age of 72.

Marahrens appealed directly to all his pastors in a letter dated August 24, 1934. In this epistle, he explained that he was supporting the Lutheran Confessions and the rules and decrees of the church. Marahrens wrote: "We must be on guard lest secular attitudes find place in the church in which the right understanding of revelation is corrupted, the Gospel obscured, and the confession of the Reformation denied."[15] Answers to a questionnaire that had been sent out at that time revealed that of 985 pastors in the Land Church of Hanover, 810 clearly supported Marahrens and only 76 were opposed to him.[16]

Shortly thereafter, Reich Bishop Müller attempted once more to seize the "unliberated" Lutheran Land Church of Hanover. In a "Reich Church Decree" of September 3, 1934, Müller claimed to remove all authority from Marahrens. In the middle of September, Müller himself came to Hanover and tried to incite the people against Marahrens. Nevertheless, 90 percent of the pastors stood behind their bishop. On November 4, 1934, a rival bishop was set up in Hanover by the DEK. Despite the treachery and intrigue with which he was surrounded, Marahrens continued the struggle.

The Enabling Act of May 23, 1934, had given Marahrens sweeping emergency powers for leading the Hanoverian church. The conscientious bishop had been slow to invoke these powers, and he actually used them only when the constitution required it or the will of the majority of his people was at stake. However, during this crisis, he proceeded with a frontal attack upon the German-Christians who dominated the church senate as he issued the following statement on November 2, 1934:

> As the responsible spiritual leader [*Führer*] I am forced to enable all the parts of the land church to work together without disturbance. It was especially the conduct of the majority in the church senate and their refusal to participate in

13 Klügel, *Landeskirche*, 127.

14 Klügel, *Landeskirche*, 127.

15 Hermelink, 93.

16 Scholder, *Kirchen*, 2:131.

regular meetings that has obliged me to issue a church decree this day by which the senate shall be given the competency to reach decisions without regard to the number of members that are present, and the chairman is hereby given the right of a veto.[17]

On November 3, Superintendent S. Cillien and Pastor Friedrich Duensing successfully occupied facilities of the Land Church Office on behalf of Marahrens. Three days later, Marahrens dismissed Hahn, Johannes Richter, and Eugen Mattiat, as well as their German-Christian employees in the Land Church Office. On November 19, Marahrens issued a statement by which he reversed the illegal actions of the German-Christians, ousted the insurgents, restored the legal constitution, and filled vacant offices according to legal procedures.[18]

But the German-Christians were not finished. On November 5, fifteen men, under the direction of German-Christian leaders, broke into the Land Church Office. A bloody fistfight ensued, in which supporters of Marahrens managed to keep the intruders within the waiting room while they blocked the door that would have given the insurgents control of the offices. Had Marahrens's supporters not prevailed, it might have cost him his position because it is doubtful that the civil government would have intervened on his behalf.

The German-Christians tried yet again to usurp control. On November 30, the Land Church Diet, which was dominated by German-Christians, held a meeting in which they deposed Marahrens. On December 5, the deposed church senate, also dominated by German-Christians, held a secret session in which they determined to send Marahrens into retirement, but these last attempts by Nazi church leaders were fruitless.

Attempts to get the civil government to depose Marahrens also were unsuccessful. On November 13, 1934, Richter, a German-Christian, had initiated a legal action in the Hanoverian land court to overthrow the bishop. The judges heard the depositions of Richter and of Marahrens and decided in the bishop's favor. Thereupon Richter appealed to the Superior Court at Celle. On March 4, 1935, the Superior Court at Celle rejected the overtures of Richter, affirmed that Marahrens stood on legal ground, and certified his authority as bishop.[19] Marahrens had appealed on the basis of the Lutheran Confessions, the legal constitution of the church, and the laws of the state—and he had won his case. After this, the Ger-

---

17 Klügel, *Landeskirche*, 145.

18 Klügel, *Landeskirche*, 145–47.

19 Klügel, *Landeskirche*, 152–55. Klügel attaches importance to the fact that Richter, not Marahrens, brought the case into court. He refutes Wendland's comment that Marahrens "had applied worldly legal measures to extricate himself from the stormflood of the German-Christians" (Klügel, *Landeskirche*, 151 n. 167). Marahrens had simply followed church law to the letter.

man-Christians lost their power in Hanover and Marahrens remained in control until Hitler's fall.

On February 26, 1935, a large spontaneous gathering was held in the Market Church of Hanover. It was attended by 2,131 representatives from 733 congregations, and the group issued a statement endorsing Marahrens. This statement was signed by 1,409 church councilmen, 806 pastors, and 47 candidates of theology, as well as by all the important church organizations of the land church. The statement said, in part: "Since the land bishop, out of the responsibility of his office, assumed the leadership of the land church, a time of rest and peace has entered in an ever stronger measure. Trust has been restored. A new period of well-planned and edifying work has begun."[20] In the end, Marahrens was able to avert every takeover attempt by adroit diplomacy, and he kept the Land Church of Hanover intact until the fall of the Third Reich in 1945.

Still, there were many difficult challenges for Marahrens. In 1935 Hanns Kerrl, the state-appointed Reich minister for church affairs, had established the RKA to replace Müller. Kerrl's attempt to mediate among the various warring groups of the DEK met with strong opposition from the radical Dahlem Front of the Confessing Church. Coming from the Prussian Union, the radical leaders in the Confessing Church seemed never to tire of finding fault with Meiser, Wurm, and Marahrens, or with their churches, which had avoided incorporation into the DEK and were still trying to cooperate as much as possible with Kerrl and the RKA. In this situation, the more radical activists argued that one must not cooperate with the RKA because it was an arm of the state and because the churches must be self-ruling. Because of their extreme positions, the Dahlem Front could not participate in the governance of the DEK or influence the course of German politics, but the group waged a relentless battle against the bishops of the intact land churches. The Dahlem Front had its adherents in the Land Church of Hanover, particularly at Osnabrück, and they caused much grief for Marahrens. But the more moderate opponents of the GDC in Hanover, the Confessional Fellowship, expressed guarded willingness to work with the RKA.

This expression drew strong objections from the pastors of the Osnabrück Circle, who denounced both Marahrens and the Confessional Fellowship for their intention to work with the RKA. The Osnabrück Circle also criticized Marahrens for placing faithfulness to the Lutheran Confessions above cooperation with the Union churches. These pastors insisted that Hanover must follow the Barmen Declaration closely and stated that working within the Confessing Church was the only approach that Hanover should take. The Osnabrück Circle also withdrew

---

20 Klügel, *Landeskirche*, 151.

from the Confessional Fellowship in protest and threatened to leave the land church if their objections were not heeded.[21]

Klügel supplies some significant statistics regarding popular attendance at the respective rallies for both Müller and Marahrens during their rival meetings in 1934. In Walsrode, Müller spoke before 2,500 people (7,000 had been expected), and at Osnabrück he experienced a good turnout. Other German-Christians had less success. Fritz Engelke spoke at Lüneburg to 200 people; in Syke and Northeim only 150 people attended the "mass rallies." When Marahrens spoke at Aurich, 2,600 people came to hear him. When his German-Christian opponent spoke, despite the fact that German-Christians had conducted a house-to-house visitation to secure a crowd, only 600 people appeared. In view of the obvious loyalty shown by Lutherans toward Marahrens, and in consideration of the powerful resistance movement in Southern Germany after the arrest of Wurm and Meiser, further actions against the bishop of Hanover were abandoned by the Nazis and the GDC. As a matter of fact, it was this successful resistance in the three Lutheran land churches that removed Müller and Jäger from Hitler's favor and toppled them from power in November 1934. Those who followed the Lutheran Confessions had won the first round.

However, youth work was a more difficult story. In December 1933, German-Christian leaders, despite energetic opposition from people in the church, had achieved the incorporation of the youth work of the churches into the Hitler Youth. During succeeding years, the Third Reich attempted to draw the youth away from the church by substituting Nazi Youth Dedication ceremonies for the church's confirmation program. The Nazis also forced boycotts of church services by holding "required" meetings of the Hitler Youth on Sunday mornings. However, these measures met resistance in Hanover. Even in the cities, only 10 percent of the children were withheld from confirmation. But in the southern parts of Hanover, the defection was much greater. In Northeim, 25 percent of the young people were not confirmed; in Altenau, 20 percent; in Barbis, 30 percent; in Volpriehausen, 50 percent; and in Wolfsburg, 75 percent. Klügel points out that in these latter cases special circumstances were partly responsible, such as long pastoral vacancies and aggressive intervention by local members of the Nazi Party. Regardless, Marahrens, in the name of the Church Leaders Conference, lodged a strong protest against the interference with confirmation education. In many places, Nazi Party members competed with Sunday church services by holding "morning celebrations" at the same hour; however, these were generally attended

---

21 Document of Osnabrück Circle in Klügel, *Dokumente*, 94–95 (signed by Hans Bodensieck, Hans Bornschein, Richard Karwehl, Paul Leo, Julius Ruprecht von Loewenfeld, Wilhelm Thimme). Rebuttal in defense of Marahrens by Heinz Brunotte in Klügel, *Dokumente*, 95–99.

only by members of their own group. In the Northeim circuit, barriers were set up around the churches to hinder attendance. The names of churchgoers were recorded, and these individuals were later threatened or even punished.[22]

Throughout the Hitler years, Marahrens, who was regarded as the senior German Lutheran bishop, played an important role in Protestant church affairs. Some people have accused him of cooperating with the Nazis. Although Marahrens was cautious by nature and hesitant to make bold moves, he managed to defend his church, protect its Confessional Lutheran character, shield his pastors from Nazi extremes, and hold together the Land Church of Hanover until the fall of Third Reich in 1945.[23]

THE LUTHERAN LAND CHURCH OF WÜRTTEMBERG AND BISHOP THEOPHIL WURM

Theophil Wurm (1868–1953), the bishop of Württemberg, was born in Basel, Switzerland. His father was a pastor with a mild attachment to Lutheranism who served as a teacher at the Basel Mission House; his mother was the daughter of a Swiss Reformed pastor. The future bishop had strong Pietistic tendencies and was moderately Lutheran in his theology and practice. He did not show the same concern for doctrinal soundness that was shared by Meiser and Marahens. Wurm's relaxed attitude was further encouraged by the *Kirchenkampf,* in which he worked shoulder-to-shoulder with members of the Union and Reformed churches. After the war, Wurm demonstrated little interest in the formation of the VELKD and pushed instead for the more inclusive EKD. During the EKD formation discussions, Wurm, contrary to Meiser and Marahrens, advocated full pulpit and altar fellowship among people of the Lutheran, Reformed, and Prussian Union churches. Wurm called for the EKD to be a church rather than a federation. Thus Wurm broke with his colleagues Meiser and Marahrens, and Württemberg remained outside the VELKD.[24]

Although Confessional Lutherans found Wurm's unionistic tendencies regrettable, one should not forget this man's courage as manifested in his repulsion of the attempts to incorporate his land church into the DEK in 1934; his steadfastness when he was twice imprisoned; and his courageous stand after 1939 against

---

22 Discussed in Klügel, *Landeskirche,* 454–55.

23 For more on the church struggle in Hanover, see the presentation on anti-Semitism (chapter 5) and how Marahrens attempted to shield his pastors of Jewish descent, including Paul Leo.

24 Konrad Gottschick, "Württemberg," in *EKL,* 3:1,874–75.

the Nazi policies of eugenics, abortion, genocide, racism, euthanasia, the destruction of "useless life," and atrocities against the Jewish population (see chapter 9).

One account in Wurm's published papers relates that on August 13, 1944, about three weeks after the assassination attempt on Hitler, Wurm was visited by a deputation from the Reich Office of the SS. At this time, when the Third Reich was struggling for its very existence, Wurm was asked to aid Hitler by delivering an appeal to the German people from the historic Wartburg castle at Eisenach. If he should consent, Wurm was promised that Hitler would initiate a new policy of warm support of the evangelical churches. Wurm did not hesitate in his reply: "My sirs, report it back to your office that Land Bishop Wurm is not willing to dirty his hands in this last minute."[25]

One of the earliest assaults of Müller's program to merge land churches into the DEK was his move against the Lutheran Land Church of Württemberg, a church characterized by a devout Pietism and a conservative biblicism. Lay members were deeply involved, and church attendance was relatively high, about 10 percent of the total population.[26] During the first months after Hitler's rise to power, Wurm welcomed the new regime as a deliverance from the ineffective Weimar Republic and spoke favorably of Hitler and of the GDC. Many pastors in Württemberg had joined the GDC in early 1933, but as the movement became increasingly radical, the pastors left the GDC in large numbers. On October 11, about 150 pastors left the GDC and joined Martin Niemöller's PNB, which at that time numbered about 800 members in Württemberg. This mass exodus came about despite the fact that many of these pastors rejected the troubling position of Karl Barth in favor of the Lutheran understanding of a revelation of God in history as well as the divine revelation in Christ as recorded in the Bible. Some prominent professors of theology at Tübingen University—Arthur Weiser, Hanns Rückert, Karl Fezer, and Gerhard Kittel—who had been members of the GDC left after the November 14, 1933, Berlin Sport Palace scandal.[27]

---

25 Schäfer, *Wurm*, 363.

26 Americans often err at interpreting European church statistics. Württemberg was a *Volk* church, and in a typical Swabish community of perhaps 5,000 people, nearly everyone had been baptized as an infant. If 2,000 people did not go to church at all, if 2,000 were shutins and 200 had to work on Sunday, 200 might go to church every Sunday and the remaining 400 every other Sunday. This does not compare unfavorably with statistics in a U.S. community without a folk church, where 40 percent of the people do not belong at all, 40 percent are sporadic churchgoers, and only 20 percent attend regularly. In addition, the pious Swabish people did attend midweek Bible studies or prayer services with great diligence.

27 The movements against the German-Christians in Württemberg are discussed in Meier, *EKK*, 1:446–47.

Having sustained heavy losses in membership and seeking to strengthen their position in Württemberg, the German-Christians, led by Pastor Karl Steger of Friedrichshafen, and Wilhelm Rehm, a former parish pastor who was now the student leader at Stuttgart, turned against Wurm. The Standing Commission (*Ständige Ausschuß*) of the Land Church Diet (*Landeskirchentag*) normally reviewed the proposed budget for the church, but the commission still had a majority of German-Christians in its composition. Thus Steger and Rehm, who were also on this commission, saw an opportunity to reestablish the GDC in Württemberg. Steger and Rehm demanded that in exchange for their support for Wurm's budget, Wurm must arrange for a majority of German-Christians to be placed on the High Church Council *(Oberkirchenrat)* when it was reconstituted on July 1. Wurm refused to make such a promise and instead summoned a special meeting of the Land Church Diet for April 16. This action made a separate meeting of the Standing Commission unnecessary. Steger and Rehm were enraged and sought to unseat Wurm as bishop; for this purpose, they called in Müller and Jäger.

As early as April 14, 1934, the German-Christians, led by Reich Minister of Justice Jäger, had tried unsuccessfully to depose Wurm. They claimed that the bishop had shown himself unfit for service in the Third Reich and that Reich Bishop Müller was coming to effect the incorporation (*Gleichschaltung*) of the Lutheran Land Church of Württemberg into the DEK. Immediately, Wurm issued a statement that was read on April 15 in all the churches of Stuttgart. The statement denounced Jäger's action as illegal and called for people to resist the merger. In his protest, Wurm distinguished this action of the German-Christians from the legitimate government of Hitler and declared "that he [Wurm] so often had proved his positive attitude toward the Third Reich that also this charge must be refuted." That evening, Wurm preached in the great Holy Cross Church (*Stiftskirche* or Abbey Church) of Stuttgart. Afterward, thousands gathered outside the church in the Schiller Place for a demonstration in support of Wurm. Before it was dispersed by the police, the crowd sang two chorales by Luther: "A Mighty Fortress Is Our God" and "From Depths of Woe I Cry to Thee."[28]

One of the striking occurrences of the spring of 1934 was the gathering at Ulm and the promulgation of the Manifesto of Ulm. In view of the aggressive actions of the GDC against Wurm and the Church of Württemberg, representatives of the Confessing Churches from Württemberg, Bavaria, Rhineland, Westphalia, and other parts of Germany gathered at Ulm on April 22, 1934. The Church of Our

---

28 Hermelink, 83–84. English texts of these hymns are found in *The Lutheran Hymnal* (St Louis: Concordia, 1941), 262, 389; *Lutheran Worship* (St. Louis: Concordia, 1982), 297/298, 230; and *Lutheran Service Book* (St. Louis: Concordia, 2006), 656/657, 607.

Lady (the Minster of Ulm) was filled to capacity; varying accounts list the crowd as numbering from 10,000 to 17,000 church members and visitors who came to hear Wurm's sermon. Wurm preached on the Epistle for Jubilate Sunday, 1 Peter 2:11–17, and developed two parts: "We serve God when we place ourselves within the order of the state" and "We serve our *Volk* when we are different from the world." Apparently, Wurm still trusted the Hitler state and expected it to hold back the assaults of the German-Christians.[29] Meiser read an "Announcement of the Evangelical Confessing Front in Germany." This announcement, which was introduced as the *Ulmer Einung*, included the following statement:

> Concern over the German Evangelical Church weighs heavily upon us. To be sure, the Reich Church government has spoken of peace in its latest edicts and decrees. Its deeds stand in contradiction to these declarations. They reveal that this "desire for peace" did not proceed from God's Word and Spirit. One cannot announce peace and immediately afterwards carry out an assault on a confessionally committed land church as was done in Württemberg. But this was done by the Church Decree of the Reich Bishop which, in violation of the Constitution of the German Evangelical Church, has blocked the meeting of the Diet of the Land Church of Württemberg.

This document was then promulgated as the Manifesto of Ulm, which denounced the actions of the German-Christians.[30]

As a result, Wurm was able to thwart the attempted merger of Württemberg with the DEK and to remain in office, but his trials were not over. On September 14, 1934, Wurm was again deposed, and in the following weeks he was intermittently placed under house arrest. This punishment ended on October 26 when Hitler, who had faced enough resistance from the Lutheran churches of Bavaria and Württemberg, called off the German-Christians and in effect declared a truce. Before this can be discussed in detail, however, the dramatic events that took place in Bavaria must first be addressed.

THE ASSAULT ON THE LUTHERAN LAND CHURCH OF BAVARIA AND BISHOP HANS MEISER

The story of the Bavarian church begins with its first bishop, Hans Oswald Meiser (1881–1956), who showed the same kind of courage as his older colleagues, Wurm and Marahrens. Meiser was born at Nuremberg and studied in Munich, Erlangen, Halle, and Berlin. After various positions as parish pastor and church leader, he was elected bishop of Bavaria in May 1933. The first twelve years of his tenure

---

29 Hermelink, 87.

30 The circumstances of the meeting and the Manifesto of Ulm are given in Schmidt, *Bekenntnisse*, 2:62–63; also in Hermelink, 87–89, and in *KZ* 58 (June 1934): 379–80.

occurred during the Third Reich. Meiser showed great courage and wisdom throughout this period and was able to keep the Lutheran Land Church of Bavaria from being incorporated into the DEK. Meiser kept a journal with careful notes of the meetings he attended. His notes from 1933 until the spring of 1937 have been published and offer a wealth of firsthand testimony regarding the events of those years.[31] After the war, Meiser was involved in ecumenical endeavors that resulted in the formation of the EKD (the reorganized Reich Church), in the VELKD, and in the creation of the LWF.

Soon after Meiser was elected bishop, he found himself involved in skirmishes with the German-Christians and Nazis. These escalated in 1934 when his opponents attempted to drive him out of office and seize control of the Bavarian church. This attack was signaled by Wolf Meyer-Erlach (1891–1982), a man who had come out of the Bavarian church and had been educated, in part, at the University of Erlangen. He had been entrusted with the position of radio preacher for the Bavarian Land Church from 1931 to 1932. Meyer-Erlach became a member of the Nazi Party and leader of the GDC in Lower and Middle Franconia (Bavaria). His political activities continued when he accepted the call in 1933 to be the professor of practical theology at the University of Jena, where he allied himself with the radical Thuringian German-Christians and took a leading role in the move to oust Meiser and seize control of the Bavarian church for the Nazis.

On May 23, 1934, Meyer-Erlach publicly incited several Nazis and German-Christians at Nuremberg to accuse Meiser of "mutiny" against the DEK and National Socialism. Among this group were Burgermeister Heinrich Münch, who charged that the Confessional Lutheran stance of the Bavarian church "was only a hindrance toward a unified land church that would be loyal to the state."[32] On July 6, Meyer-Erlach published an inflammatory article in the Nazi newspaper *Fränkische Tageszeitung,* from which the following statements can be gleaned:

> Franconia, Bavaria, do not let yourselves be led into error by the screeching lies that the Bible and the Confessions are in danger in the new German-Evangelical Reich Church. . . . Germany, think about it that the spirit of churchly divisiveness, which goes out from Bavaria over the entire Reich, gives our enemies the hope that this will shatter the work of the Führer, the holy will of the entire *Volk* toward a steely resoluteness.[33]

---

31 It is fervently hoped that Meiser's records from the subsequent years also will be published. See p. 18 for bibliographic details on Meiser's journals.

32 Meier, *EKK,* 1:461–62.

33 The text of Meyer-Erlach's attack given in Wilhelm Niemöller, *Kampf und Zeugnis der*

Fig. 8: Land Bishop
August Marahrens
(photo courtesy
of Landeskirchliches Archiv of Hanover)

Fig. 9: Land Bishop
Theophil Wurm
(photo courtesy
of Landeskirchliches Archiv-Stuttgart)

Fig. 10: Market Church, Hanover, before World War II
(photo courtesy of Landeskirchliches Archiv of Hanover)

Fig. 11: Land Bishop Hans Meiser
(photo courtesy of Karlmann Beyschlag)

Fig. 12: Collegiate Church
(*Stiftskirche*), Stuttgart
(photo courtesy
of Landeskirchliches Archiv-Stuttgart)

Fig. 13: St. Lorenz Lutheran Church, Nuremberg
(photo in possession of author)

The "Decree for the Incorporation of Bavaria into the Reich Church" followed on September 3, 1934. The plan for incorporation into the DEK, as envisaged by Meyer-Erlach, dismissed Meiser and replaced him with two *kommissar* bishops: Hans Sommerer in Franconia and Hans Gollwitzer in Old Bavaria. Meiser declared at once that the decree possessed no legality.

The picturesque medieval city of Nuremberg has been an evangelical stronghold since the city council introduced Lutheran services in 1524. During the Third Reich, the city acquired an unfortunate reputation as a Nazi resort. Its fair name was further blemished when the Nuremberg Racial Decree against the Jews was promulgated and when the Nuremberg Trials were held in 1946. Despite these blemishes, Nuremberg, the center of Franconia, was also an important hub of church resistance to National Socialism as early as 1934. Julius Schieder, the stalwart director of the Preacher Seminary in Nuremberg and later pastor at St. Lorenz Lutheran Church and district dean, related how on Wednesday, September 12, 1934, huge placards had been planted in the streets of Nuremberg with this message: "Away with Meiser. The man is un-Christian. He has no character. He has behaved like Judas Iscariot." As soon as the Nazis had distributed their placards denouncing Meiser, there were protest demonstrations from the people. On Friday evening, September 14, the Nazi Party marched in a parade past St. Lorenz Church and made its way to the Market Place, where it had been announced that a large rally would occur. At the same time, a capacity crowd of 5,000 people crowded into St. Lorenz. The overflow moved to the other Lutheran churches in the inner city, first to Holy Ghost Church, which seated nearly 2,000 people. Then the crowds moved St. Aegidius until it also was filled. Meiser had come up from Munich, and he went to each church to preach. Following the last service in St. Aegidius, an angry crowd assembled in the square in front of the church, where the bishop once more greeted the people. Afterward, they stayed and sang Lutheran chorales for nearly an hour.

On Saturday, September 15, Karl Holz, the Nazi district leader (*Gauleiter*) in Franconia (Northern Bavaria), published an article in the daily Nazi newspaper *Fränkische Landeszeitung* in which he accused Meiser of being a faithless betrayer of the people, a man who broke his word. He also accused Meiser of betraying the Führer as Judas Iscariot had betrayed Jesus. However, Holz had not anticipated the piety and loyalty of the congregation members. On Sunday, September 16, Confessional Lutheran services were held in the fifteen churches of Nuremberg, all of

Bekennenden Kirche (Bielefeld: Ludwig Bechauf, 1948), 172. Niemöller carelessly omitted the documentation, which is supplied in Meier, *EKK*, 1:463–64, 616 nn. 1,572–73.

which overflowed their capacites. Mass rallies were also held in the churches of surrounding Franconia, down to the smallest village church.[34]

On October 11, 1934, a commission appointed by the German-Christians seized the offices of the Bavarian church at Munich. Eduard Putz (dean at Erlangen from 1954 to 1972) related how earlier in the day he had intercepted the bishop, who had been preaching resistance against the German-Christians in various cities near the Württemberg border. Putz got word to Meiser, who was returning home aboard a train, that he should not return directly to Munich but should get off at an earlier stop in Augsburg. Putz met Meiser at the depot and whisked the bishop into a limousine, where the two clergymen sat in the back seat with a young couple dressed as a bridal pair, which provided camouflage. In this way they were able to evade the police and bring Meiser to St. Matthew Church in Munich, which was filled to capacity and was surrounded by thousands of supporters chanting, "Heil, Meiser! Heil, Meiser!" Meiser preached to the crowded church on Hebrews 10:38–39: "If anyone shall yield, my soul shall have no pleasure in him. But we are not of those who yield and are damned, but of those who believe to the saving of the soul." After the service, thousands of people accompanied the bishop through the streets of Munich to his residence on Arcis Street. Here, the stalwart bishop was arrested the next day, October 12, 1934, and confined to his home.[35] (In 1938 the Nazis retaliated by tearing down St. Matthew Church, the largest Lutheran church in Munich.)[36]

Putz related that on Friday, October 12, he began a journey to strengthen the congregations of the Bavarian church that had been disturbed by the recent events. He recalled his visit in Ansbach:

> I experienced in the great and overcrowded St. John Church a moving Confessional service led by Circuit Dean Georg Kern. . . . Kern extinguished the candles on the altar as a sign of the church's sorrow. I myself then entered the pulpit, delivered the greeting of the land bishop, called the congregation to engage in resistance, told them that the so-called "New Constitution of the Land Church" with two new German-Christian bishops was null and void, and that the Land Church Council had kept unchanged its leadership of the church. I exhorted, "Every person who stands faithful to his Lutheran Confessional Church is asked to enter his name with the red card in the Confessional Fellowship." This took place on that Sunday through the entire Land Church.[37]

---

34 The graphic description of the resistance movement at Nuremberg is given by Schieder in *ZwKK*, 75–76. See also Scholder, *Kirchen*, 2:314–16.

35 Eduard Putz and Max Tratz in *ZwKK*, 12–18.

36 The destruction of St. Matthew Church in Munich by the Nazis is described in Hermelink, 451–52. Photographs of the church before and during the demolition can be found in *ZwKK*, 102.

On October 16, Meiser, who was still under house arrest, issued a pastoral letter addressed to the pastors of the land church. In this letter, he strongly repudiated the action of the DEK. Meiser wrote: "Our protests against the unspiritual conduct of the administration of the Reich Church, and all the serious objections that we of the Lutheran confession must have against the total absorption of our land church within an all-encompassing church that is not governed by the Lutheran Confession, remains unchanged." Meiser continued to make it clear that the actions of Müller and Jäger that attempted to merge the Bavarian Land Church into the DEK were completely illegal and un-Christian.[38] Meiser insisted that "in questions of faith there can be no negotiating." As one who had been robbed of his freedom, he charged his brother pastors: "Stand fast in the faith, be manly and be strong!"[39] This letter shows that though Meiser might not have had a clear understanding of Hitler's motives, it was his fidelity to the Lutheran Confessions that led him to denounce the German-Christians.

The theological faculty at the University of Erlangen remained loyal to Meiser during his period of incarceration. The faculty took a determined stand against the seizure of the land church and denounced the German-Christians. The faculty held a special meeting on Saturday, October 13, and passed a resolution that was signed by all the regular (*Ordinarius*) professors. This was a firm protest against attempts by leaders in the Reich Church to split Bavaria into two bishoprics with Nazis leading each fragment. The professors stated:

> Objections must be raised against the splitting of the Evangelical Lutheran Church in Bavaria for the following reasons:
>
> 1. The measures leveled against our Land Church by the Reich Church government on October 11 cannot be regarded as legally valid since they were done in contradiction to the Constitution of the German Evangelical Church [DEK]. The fragmenting of our land church into two church bodies also contradicts the spirit of the constitution, for the constitution attempts to bring together ecclesial territories of the same confession, whereas by that fragmentation a unified ecclesial territory is actually torn apart. Neither can the tearing apart of our church be justified on grounds of the ethnic differences between the Bavarians and the Franconians because our church people have grown together to a total unity. . . .

---

37 Putz, *ZwKK*, 18. The red card identified one as a member of the Confessing Church. It is said that even the cautious Elert had taken out the red card.

38 Müller's plan for splitting the church of Bavaria is given in a document of October 25, 1934; see *KJahr 1933–1944*, 75–76. Signed by Müller and Jäger, this document provided for one bishop in Nuremberg and another in Munich.

39 Meiser's pastoral letter of October 16, 1934, is given in Hermelink, 171–73.

3. These measures offend against love for the brethren, loyalty, truthfulness, and the divine commandments, which the Church of Christ must obey. Furthermore, these measures offend against the right that was established in the confessions of the Evangelical Lutheran Church regarding the calling and dismissing of spiritual leadership that is legally valid.[40]

During this turmoil, the Lutheran laity were thoroughly stirred to action. Their outrage at the illicit seizure of power, their piety and loyalty to their church, and their fidelity to Meiser led them to stage powerful demonstrations of protest throughout Bavaria. A great swell of protest services were held in Nuremberg and throughout Franconia as the Nazis cracked down on the church. On October 16, more than 10,000 people attended Confessional services in Nuremberg. On October 21, as many as 900 citizens of Nuremberg traveled to Munich to protest the separation of the Franconian churches from Bavaria under Bishop Hans Sommerer and to demonstrate their continued loyalty to Meiser. On October 22, 850 out of the 1,350 Bavarian Lutheran pastors gathered at a service in Nuremberg's St. Lorenz Church to protest the Nazi plan of splitting the Bavarian Land Church into two bishoprics. The pastors sent a telegram to Meiser expressing their continued loyalty.

The Nazi government responded to this resistance by ordering that meetings could be held only inside churches, that every gathering had to be reported in advance to the police, and that spies be placed in the churches to listen to every sermon. Soon pastors and lay leaders were summoned to report to the Gestapo. Some were imprisoned. The question was raised whether the church should mount a resistance movement. The Bavarian Lutherans rejected such a possibility on the grounds that even a corrupt government must be obeyed, according to Romans 13.[41]

Despite the danger of Nazi retaliation, thousands of laypeople came by train to form massive protest demonstrations in Nuremberg, Munich, and other cities. In one case, fifteen members of the Nazi Party appeared before the Bavarian min-

---

40 The "Protest of the Erlangen Theological Faculty" (in Hermelink, 176) was signed by Hans Preuß, Otto Procksch, Hermann Strathmann, Elert, Ulmer, Althaus, and Sasse. As the faculty of a state university, these men ended their votum with the customary words "Heil Hitler!" Although Procksch, Strathmann, Ulmer, and Sasse were strongly critical of National Socialism, it was customary that these words be used in official correspondence. In a December 12, 1934, letter to Marahrens, Elert further criticized the seizure of power by the Reich bishop: "The [alleged] right of direct spiritual care of individual members of the Land Churches over the head of the land bishop and other instruments of the land church, [is] a right which, by analogy, even the pope did not have prior to 1870" (in ATF, file "Elert.").

41 Schieder in *ZwKK*, 78–79.

ister-president, spoke of a demonstration by 60,000 Franconian farmers, and reported that 95 percent of the peasants stood behind Meiser.[42] Putz describes an unusual meeting on October 22 when a group of thirty people, primarily farmers and pastors, confronted Nazi Governor Hans Ritter von Epp in the Bavarian chancellory in Munich. After a period of tumultuous protests, the hereditary landholder Georg Mack rose to address Epp. He recounted how his family had retained their land since the Middle Ages, throughout the Peasants' War, the Thirty Years' War, and so forth, to the present. All generations had retained their ownership of their hereditary land "because they had faith." He turned to the governor of Bavaria and said: "You know, Mr. Governor, what a piece of dirt a man is who has no faith [*Sie wissen ja selber, Herr Reichsstatthalter, was der Mensch für a Dreck is, der kan Glauben hat*]."

Putz recalls that Epp, perplexed at this unusual diplomacy, grasped the top of the table until his knuckles were white. Then he responded that he had not been informed of the measures that had been planned against the land church and its bishop and that he would immediately appeal to Wilhelm Frick, the Reich minister of the interior, to undo the changes and restore law and order to the Lutheran Land Church of Bavaria.[43] Max Tratz relates how the demonstrations and resistance by the faithful members of the Bavarian churches had finally brought down the German-Christians and secured the release of Meiser and the restoration of the rightful government to the land church.[44]

Several historians have downplayed the intentions of the laypeople who demonstrated on behalf of Meiser. Perhaps some of these farmers thought they were fighting only the German-Christians and did not realize that leaders such as Müller and Jäger enjoyed Hitler's blessing. Scholder cites Ludwig Sieber, a Nazi official and minister-president of Bavaria, to state that these supporters of Meiser remained loyal to Hitler and only opposed the actions of those who oppressed their bishop. Some of the protestors were likely members of the Nazi Party and were unaware of where the party was going. For example, Putz, an assistant to Meiser, had become a member of the Nazi Party early on and later used his party membership to the advantage of the church. Few people at that time understood what the Führer really stood for. Although Müller had been Hitler's handpicked choice as Reich bishop, and Hitler had attacked the JB for supporting a different candidate, after the unsuccessful attempt to overthrow Meiser, Hitler coldly abandoned Müller.[45]

---

42 Scholder, *Kirchen*, 2:332.

43 Putz in *ZwKK*, 21.

44 Putz and Tratz in *ZwKK*, 19–21.

45 Scholder, *Kirchen*, 2:332; Helmreich writes: "It is clear the feeling was still widespread

The stalwart Lutheran laypeople in Bavaria, as well as their pastors, continued to support their leaders and to protest the excesses of National Socialism. In February 1937, Johann Michael Reu reported that thousands of Franconian people had gathered in Ansbach "in the last month" (likely in December 1936) to listen to Meiser and to offer their protest against the cheap tactics followed by Julius Streicher, the district leader (*Gauleiter*) in Franconia. Reu also reported that new assemblies, called "evangelical weeks" (*Evangelische Wochen*), were well attended. Reu noted that "this and similar things merely show that God has his people still today in Germany."[46] The "evangelical weeks" are also described by Ernst Helmreich: "Large public meetings were to be held to discuss religious questions. . . . The first such mass gathering was held in Hanover, August 26–30, 1935, and attendance exceeded all expectations." After a number of remarkable rallies, these gatherings were banned by the Nazis, but they became the precedent for the German evangelical diets (*Evangelische Kirchentage*) and evangelical academies after the war.[47]

Another act of resistance against National Socialism took place in Nuremberg in the fall of 1937. Walter Künneth, who directed the Seminary for Apologetics in Berlin, had been the chief opponent of Hitler's court philosopher, Alfred Rosenberg. Künneth had steadfastly and firmly refuted the attacks of Rosenberg upon Christianity and upon Judaism; he was renowned for his book against Rosenberg, *Antwort auf dem Mythos* (*A Reply Regarding Myth*), the first edition of which had appeared in 1935. Künneth relates in his memoirs that in October 1937 he spoke at a Reformation service in St. Lorenz Lutheran Church in Nuremberg, which was crowded with 5,000 people.[48] Theodore Baudler, a U.S. student at Erlangen, attended that rally and told me how the church was not only filled to capacity but thousands of people were gathered in the streets in front of and to the side of the church, listening to loudspeakers and joining in the singing. The crowd was so dense that the streetcars were unable to run. Many expected that Künneth would be arrested after the service, but the Gestapo was powerless to do anything because of the thousands of people who were present.[49] In fact, Künneth was able to dis-

---

that if Hitler only knew the true situation, he would set things right" (172). Nevertheless, some historians persist in writing as though the men and women of that time possessed knowledge that was not available until after World War II.

46 *KZ* 61 (1937): 122.

47 Helmreich, 187–88.

48 Künneth, *Lebensführungen*, 149–51.

49 During the 1950s, when Künneth was lecturing at Erlangen, I heard students say that Rosenberg had protected Künneth because he regarded himself as a great scholar and was unwilling to have it said that he had used political means to destroy Künneth to avoid losing the argument.

tribute a pamphlet written against Rosenberg. Certainly, the Gestapo had confiscated the booklet, but because more copies were ready from another printer,
112,000 copies were handed out before the Gestapo could prevent it.[50]

The Schwabach Conventicle (*Schwabacher Konvent*) was a valiant but unsung
association of Bavarian pastors. It received its name because Christian Stoll, pastor at Schwabach, a town near Nuremberg, was its leader. Other members of the
Schwabach group included Sasse, Friedrich Wilhelm Hopf, Martin Wittenberger,
Hans Siegfried Huß, and Karl Krodel, the father of two U.S. professors: Gerhard
and Gottfried Krodel.

After the war, Künneth described the persecution of pastors in the Bavarian
Land Church. Out of a total of about 1,200 Lutheran pastors, 448 were summoned to a hearing before the police or a judge; 303 received warnings; 144 were
subjected to house arrest; 165 experienced confiscations; 38 were forbidden to
speak in public; 9 were forbidden to leave a severely limited locale; 58 were imprisoned; 245 were subjected to state prosecution and trial (for 179 of these the
charges were dismissed); 7 homes were searched; 27 were committed to punishment; 66 paid cash fines; 14 were punished by imprisonment; and 98 had their
right to teach religion in the schools removed. A total of 43 pastors were forbidden
to have parish meetings, Bible studies, and social gatherings; 21 were attacked
through the official press; and 33 were threatened or abused.[51]

The Intact Lutheran Land Churches: A Summary

There can be no doubt that it was their faithfulness to the Lutheran Confessions
and their sturdy church life that enabled the great land churches of Hanover,
Württemberg, and Bavaria to weather the storms of National Socialism and to
emerge from the Third Reich in 1945 as intact churches. Nevertheless, the three
bishops and their churches were subjected to constant criticism and even denunciations from church leaders in the destroyed churches. They were characterized
as doctrinally stiff, unloving, and unwilling to cooperate with the Union and
Reformed churches. An endless flow of invective was aimed against the Lutheran
bishops by such leaders in the Confessing Church as Barth, Niemöller, and
Asmussen, who could not understand how these Lutherans could take the
Lutheran Confessions so seriously that they were unwilling to sacrifice doctrinal
integrity for unionism. These men themselves seemed blind to the fact that their

---

50 Künneth, *Lebensführungen*, 151.

51 Incidents in Bavaria are summarized by Künneth in *Abfall*, 216–17. Actions against
pastors in the Land Church of Hanover are listed by name in Klügel, *Landeskirche*,
503–13.

own doctrinal indecision had been part of the reason why their Union churches had lacked the stability and strength to fend off the German-Christians.

Despite the fulminations leveled against the intact churches, the Lutheran churches also remained a bulwark and an emblem of hope for people in the destroyed churches. Marahrens, Wurm, and Meiser sometimes made mistakes, but they managed to foil the sinister program of Müller and Jäger. They prevented the DEK from swallowing up all the Lutheran churches and provided a haven for the resistance. Hitler had found the point where he had to stop. From the theological faculty of the University of Erlangen came a steady stream of theological material to strengthen the German churches in their struggle against National Socialism.

CHAPTER FIFTEEN

THE ERLANGEN THEOLOGICAL FACULTY DURING THE THIRD REICH

RETROSPECTIVE AND CONCLUSION

Founded in 1743, the Friedrich and Alexander University of Erlangen and its theological faculty rose to world prominence during the nineteenth century. Under the Third Reich, it was the only theological school in Germany to avoid a Nazi takeover and remain intact. Throughout this book, the faculty of Erlangen has assumed a dominant position. This final chapter is devoted to the special contributions made by Erlangen's professors to the movement against Adolf Hitler.[1]

A SHORT HISTORY
OF THE THEOLOGICAL FACULTY BEFORE 1933

During most of its history, the University of Erlangen has been dominated by its theological faculty, which during two distinct periods was regarded as the leading voice of world Lutheranism. The first period of greatness, which ended about

---

1 I attended the University of Erlangen from 1952 to 1955 when memories of Nazi rule and the early postwar years were still fresh in people's minds. I met many of those involved in the church struggle and this chapter presents some of their stories. Although I have tried to be as accurate and objective as possible, the reader should expect that this chapter will reflect some subjective opinions of the participants and bear some of the qualities of oral history.

1900, was characterized by such famous theologians as Adolf Harless, Johann Christian Konrad von Hofmann, Gottfried Thomasius, Theodosius Harnack, Franz Delitzsch, Gerhard von Zezschwitz, Heinrich Schmid, Theodor von Zahn, and Franz Hermann Reinhold von Frank. These men overcame rationalism in theology and reasserted the authority of the Bible and the Lutheran Confessions. At a time when much German theology was caught in a dry and secular liberalism, the University of Erlangen produced a theology that was closely related to the life of the church and produced new pastors who restored vitality to the congregations.

Two characteristics marked the theology of Erlangen: (1) Whereas other theological schools rejected traditional doctrine, Erlangen supported the Lutheran Church and its teachings; and (2) Erlangen also emphasized the religious experience of the theologian himself. Both its churchliness and its piety evoked the scorn of its opponents, the leader of whom was Albrecht Ritschl at Göttingen. Ritschl once said sarcastically that if one went to Erlangen to learn about its theology, one didn't need to get off the train; it could all be found in the train depot. (Erlangen has a severely plain depot.) Despite Ritschl, the theological faculty of Erlangen was the most popular in Germany, with enrollment often rising above 500 theological students at one time.

When considering this first period of prominence for the theological faculty of the University of Erlangen, one typically thinks of systematic theology, which culminated in Frank and suffered a temporary setback after his death in 1894. Later, the systematic department experienced renewal under the leadership of Ludwig Ihmels and Werner Elert. Straddling the earlier and later periods of great systematicians was a group of important church historians: Gustav Plitt, Theodor Kolde, Albert Hauck, Reinhold Seeberg (at Erlangen 1889–1898), and Theodor von Zahn (1838–1933). Thomasius was also important as a pioneer in the history of dogma. Zahn was famed for his phenomenal knowledge of patristics and the history of the New Testament canon. In 1903, at the normal age of retirement, Zahn began his important *Kommentar zum Neuen Testament* (*Commentary on the New Testament*), which he completed near the end of his long life.[2] Meanwhile, Ihmels, a pupil of Frank, corrected an overemphasis that was placed upon the religious experience of the individual believer, which was found in the early theology of Erlangen. He did this by basing his theology exclusively upon the Bible, which relegated the experience of the theologian to a secondary position. Ihmels moved

---

2 Zahn, *Kommentar zum Neuen Testament*, 18 vols. (Leipzig: A. Deichert, 1903–1924). Contributors besides Zahn (Matthew, Luke, John, Acts, Revelation) included Gustav Wohlenberg, Philipp Bachman, Paul Ewald, Friedrich Hauck, and Eduard Riggenbach.

to Leipzig in 1902 and became bishop of Saxony in 1922. Ihmels and Zahn both died in 1933.

After World War I, Erlangen's theological faculty entered its second great period with the enlistment of Werner Elert (1923), Paul Althaus (1925), and Otto Procksch (1925). Under these men, the "Big Three," Erlangen entered its second period of celebrity. Each of these men was noted for scholarly brilliance coupled with a strong fidelity to Martin Luther and the Lutheran Confessions. No other German university offered a faculty with such a united confessional front. The enrollment rose from 181 students in 1923 to 661 by 1933. Wolfgang Trillhaas has characterized this triumvirate as follows: Procksch, the unteachable Lutheran; Althaus, the man of humane and pastoral nobility; and Elert, the scholar of uncontrollable love for research.[3]

Other leading Erlangen theologians between the two World Wars were Hans Preuß, Hermann Sasse, and Friedrich Ulmer. Preuß wrote superb studies in the history of Christian art. His popular church history *Von den Katakomben bis zu den Zeichen der Zeit* (*From the Catacombs to the Signs of the Times*)[4] has been read by thousands of theologians and laypeople alike. He also produced outstanding studies on Luther.[5] Ulmer, professor of practical theology and founder of the Martin Luther Bund, was a decisive Confessional Lutheran whose work has been cited in this book.

There were other important scholars who were not full professors (*ordentliche Professoren*). Friedrich Hauck, son of the great church historian Albert Hauck, taught classical languages in the Erlangen gymnasium, New Testament at the university, and wrote several widely used books. Georg Kempff, a fabled organ improvisor and a musician of multifaceted talents, directed the academic choir, taught

---

3 Beyschlag, 146.

4 Preuß, *Von den Katakomben bis zu den Zeichen der Zeit: Der Weg der Kirche durch zwei Jahrtausende* (Erlangen: Martin Luther Verlag, 1936; repr., 1960). An example of his work in art history is *Das Bild Christi im Wandel der Zeiten: Einhundertunddreizehn Bilder auf 96 Tafeln gesammelt und mit einer Einführung sowie mit Erläuterungen versehen* (Leipzig: R. Voigtländers, 1915).

5 Preuß wrote a set of four books on Luther: *Martin Luther, der Künstler* (*Martin Luther, the Artist*) (Gütersloh: Bertelsmann, 1931), *Martin Luther, der Prophet* (*Martin Luther, the Prophet*) (Gütersloh: Bertelsmann, 1933), *Martin Luther, der Deutsche* (*Martin Luther, the German*) (Gütersloh: Bertelsmann, 1934), and *Martin Luther, der Christenmensch* (*Martin Luther, the Christian*) (Gütersloh: Bertelsmann, 1942). In *Martin Luther, der Deutsche*, written during the giddy enthusiasm of Hitler's first year, Preuß unfortunately tried to establish affinities between Luther and National Socialism. After World War II he paid heavily for his folly when he was summarily dismissed and stripped of his pension and all the privileges of a retired professor in the denazification process employed by the U.S. occupation forces.

liturgics, and edited the *Cantionale* for the Land Church of Bavaria.[6] During the desolate years of World War II and the harsh times after 1945, Kempff provided comfort and relief with his musical programs in the church and in the *Orangerie* (pavilion for oranges) at the old palace. In 1944 Walter Künneth ended his virtual exile under National Socialism to become dean of the church circuit of Erlangen and a part-time professor of theology.

A number of brilliant younger scholars from the the University of Erlangen who had been held back in their careers by their opposition to the Nazis included Wolfgang Trillhaas, Helmut Thielicke, Oskar Grether, and Walther von Loewenich. After the expulsion of Ulmer by the Nazis, Trillhaas, who was pastor of Trinity Lutheran Church (*Die Altstädterkirche*), took over the courses in practical theology. Elert used this ploy to avoid the dangers in the customary advertising of an opening, which might have resulted in a Nazi being forced upon the theological faculty. Thielicke, who could not get along with Elert, moved to Heidelberg, later to Tübingen, and still later to Hamburg. Loewenich, who was married to Thielicke's sister, taught in the local gymnasium and served as a part-time instructor in the theological faculty. After World War II, he was made a full professor and was joined by Friedrich Baumgärtel, Wilhelm Maurer, Kurt Frör, Eduard Steinwand, Ethelbert Stauffer, Fritz Fichtner,[7] and Künneth, who became a full-time professor as Elert's successor. Gerhard Friedrich and Leonhard Rost, who came in 1954 and 1956, rounded out the faculty. Part-time professors of eminence included Karl Schornbaum, Gerhard Pfeiffer, Georg Vicedom, and Hans Kreßel. With this roster, Erlangen possessed some of the best theologians in Germany. When they retired, they could not be replaced by people of equal stature. At the

---

6 Kempff, ed., *Cantionale für die Evangelisch-Lutherische Kirche in Bayern,* 2 vols. (Ansbach: C. Grügel & Sohn, 1941). This work employed Kempff's masterful knowledge of music and liturgics. A book in a more popular vein is Kempff, *Neues Singen nach dem Neuen Gesangbuch* (Potsdam: Stiftungsverlag, 1934). A book about Kempff with many anecdotes is *Erlebnisse mit George Kempff,* ed. by Walter Opp (Erlangen: Palm & Enke, 2001). The volume includes a CD with recordings of Kempff at the organ; as bass soloist in Franz Schubert's *Winterreise,* excerpts from his oratorio, *Die Hochzeit zu Kana,* and a speech he gave at Erlangen before the 1973 celebration of his 80th birthday. (I studied organ and harpsichord under Kempff and personally experienced some of the related anecdotes.)

7 Fritz Fichtner had been director of the Gallery for Porcelein in the famous art galleries of the Dresden *Zwinger.* During the dreadful bombing of Dresden on February 13, 1945, his wife and children were killed. He arrived at Erlangen in 1949 after this and other terrible experiences. In Erlangen, Fichtner gave courses on the history of Christian art and conducted art excursions that made him a popular professor. I gained a whole new understanding of art in its relation to history from this gifted teacher.

beginning of the new century, there is no theological faculty in Germany that can compare with that of Erlangen prior to the mid-1960s.

Elert had made a name for himself in both historical and systematic theology. Althaus was noted for his work in systematic theology, New Testament studies, and, like Elert and Preuß, for his research on Luther. Loewenich and Maurer added to the roster of Luther experts. Sasse came to Erlangen in 1933. More than any other person, he saw the dangers in National Socialism and was the first (in 1932) to sound the warning call concerning the Nazi platform for religion. Sasse's critical attitude toward National Socialism prevented his promotion to a full professorship, and because Elert was consequently unable to get him a promotion, Sasse harbored resentment against Elert. Procksch was a commanding figure who uncovered many significant findings in Old Testament studies. Unfortunately, his important *Theologie des Alten Testaments* (*Theology of the Old Testament*) was not published until after his death.[8] By that time, some of his important findings had already appeared in the work of other scholars, including his own pupils. Baumgärtel was called as successor to Procksch in 1941, but because of his uncompleted term in the military, he could not take over until 1944. Mindful of the Lutheran distinction between Law and Gospel, Baumgärtel presented a unique hermeneutics that revolved around the distinction between the Law and the promise in the Old Testament. Baumgärtel published a pamphlet entitled *Wider die Kirchenkampf-Legenden* (*Against the Church-Struggle Legends*), which debunked the writings of Wilhelm Niemöller and others who played up their own role and belittled the Confessional Lutherans for their actions during the *Kirchenkampf*.[9] Maurer became professor of church history at Erlangen in 1951. As a member of the Confessing Church, his academic career had been stalled by the Nazis. Maurer published important works on Luther and Philip Melanchthon,

---

8 Procksch, *Theologie des Alten Testaments* (Gütersloh: Bertelsmann, 1950).

9 See the important book on Old Testament interpretation by Baumgärtel, *Verheissung zur Frage des evangelischen Verständnisses des Alten Testaments* (Gütersloh: Carl Bertelsmann, 1952). Baumgärtel wrote a critical review of Wilhelm Niemöller's *Evangelische Kirche*. When Baumgärtel's review met objections, he expanded his position into a small book that reviewed literature on the church struggle: *Wider die Kirchenkampf-Legenden* (Neuendettelsau: Freimund, 1959; repr., 1976). In this study he set straight a number of fabrications regarding the churches during the Third Reich, thereby incurring the wrath of the Niemöllers. Baumgärtel served double terms as *Rector Magnificus* of Erlangen (elective head of the entire university), which was unusual. It is said that when the Americans chose him as university president, Baumgärtel said he could serve as the university's head only as rector and according to traditional academic rules. His proposal was accepted; thereby he achieved the restoration of this singularly democratic manner of governing a university. On this matter, see Loewenich, *Erlebte Theologie*, 202. During Baumgärtel's rectorate, the Roman Catholic

two volumes on the Augsburg Confession, and four volumes of collected essays, all of great significance.[10] Karlmann Beyschlag, in his summary of the history of Erlangen, calls Hofmann and Elert the two greatest of all the noted professors who adorned the Erlangen theological faculty in its more than two hundred years of distinguished history.[11] The era of Erlangen Theology ended in 1970 when the faculty voted to withdraw its subscription of the Lutheran Confessions.

THE ERLANGEN FACULTY DURING THE YEARS 1933–1934

The claim has been made that Althaus was a member of the GDC, which had connections to the Nazi Party.[12] Upon what circumstances does this misunderstanding rest? It was noted previously that Althaus had belonged briefly to the CDB, which disbanded after the 1933 elections, but Althaus never joined the GDC. Hans Preuß, the celebrated historian of Christian art and Luther scholar, expressed strong support for Nazism during Hitler's first year in power. When the Nazis tried to seize control of the Land Church of Bavaria in October 1934, however, Preuß recognized his mistake. As dean of the theological faculty that year, he drew up a strong statement in support of Bishop Hans Meiser that repudiated the aggressive actions by the German-Christians and the Nazi potentates. This statement, as we have seen, was signed by all the regular theological professors. Preuß himself never joined the Nazi Party or the GDC.

---

parliament in Munich attempted to close Erlangen. One might recall a comment by Elert that "a committee of individuals does not have a conscience." As rector, Baumgärtel carried out an energetic campaign that forced the parliament not only to withdraw its plans but also to increase greatly its financial subsidies, leading to a tremendous rebuilding and expansion program at Erlangen.

10 Maurer, *Von der Freiheit eines Christenmenschen: Zwei Untersuchungen zu Luthers Reformationsschriften 1520–21* (Göttingen: Vandenhoeck & Ruprecht, 1949); *Melanchthon-Studien*, Schriften des Vereins für Reformationsgeschichte 181 (Gütersloh: Gerd Mohn, 1964); *Der junge Melanchthon*, 2 vols. (Göttingen: Vandenhoeck & Ruprecht, 1967–1969); *Kirche und Geschichte: Gesammelte Aufsätze*, 2 vols. (Göttingen: Vandenhoeck & Ruprecht, 1970); *Die Kirche und ihr Recht: Gesammelte Aufsätze zum evangelischen Kirchenrecht*, Jus ecclesiasticum 23 (Tübingen: J. C. B. Mohr, 1976); and *Historischer Kommentar zur Confessio Augustana*, 2 vols. (Gütersloh: Gerd Mohn, 1976–1978; English translation by H. George Anderson, *Historical Commentary on the Augsburg Confession* [Philadelphia: Fortress, 1986]). Maurer was also co-author with Heinrich Hermelink of the useful handbook *Reformation und Gegenreformation*, vol. 3 of *Handbuch der Kirchengeschichte* (Tübingen: J. C. B. Mohr, 1931).

11 Beyschlag, 146, et passim.

12 James Zabel, *Nazism and the Pastors: A Study of the Ideas of Three Deutsche Christen Groups*, Dissertation Series of the American Academy or Religion 14 (Missoula, MT: Scholars Press, 1976), 25.

Several professors at the University of Erlangen who opposed Hitler's program almost from the start included Sasse, Ulmer, and Procksch. Procksch, an Old Testament professor, was beloved by the students for his witticisms at the expense of the Nazis. Everyone was expected to deliver the "Nazi salute" in public. Procksch, who was badly crippled, would hobble to the classroom lectern, lean over it, and raising his right arm in mock salute, would ironically call out "Heil, Hitler" to the delight of his students. In May 1933, Pastor Fritz Kessel (later the German-Christian bishop of East Prussia) spoke at a gathering in the ballroom (*Redoutensaal*) of the university about his goals as a German-Christian. He called for the dismissal of all Jews from the pastoral ministry and said that instead of spending their time on the Old Testament, it would be better if the students studied eugenics. In the discussion that followed, Procksch limped to the podium and said: "Hereafter I will no longer examine my students regarding the *Jewish* kings. Perhaps the Apostle Paul could at least become a Vicar at the New Town Church [*Neustädterkirche*] here in Erlangen. And so far as Aunt Eugenia is concerned . . . [Loud laughter and stormy applause]."[13]

When Alfred Rosenberg, Hitler's intellectual guru, spoke in Erlangen, Procksch had to skip one of his lectures on the minor prophets. On the day before Rosenberg's appearance, Procksch announced: "Tomorrow I must skip my lecture because Colleague Rosenberg wants to speak to you. As a matter of fact, I didn't invite him."[14] On the following Thursday, Procksch appeared at his rostrum and remarked: "Ladies and Gentlemen, on Tuesday a substitute whom I did not choose took my place. But when the 'major prophets' speak, the 'minor prophets' must keep still [*Wenn die Großen Propheten reden, die Kleinen Propheten müssen schweigen*]." Laughter and applause filled the room, and Procksch could barely speak for thirty minutes.[15] The indomitable Procksch insisted on walking to class until his lameness forced him to drive. As a last resort to silence him, the Nazis took away his gasoline ration, which made it impossible for him to teach.[16] During the Third Reich, people such as Procksch manifested great courage, even when others were afraid to speak out.

The year 1934 was a difficult time for the Erlangen professors. During May, the Confessing Synod at Barmen had promulgated the Barmen Declaration,

---

13 "Ich werde in Zukunft nicht mehr über die jüdische Könige prüfen. Den Apostel Paulus könnte man vielleicht wenigstens als Vikar von Erlangen-Neustadt anstellen. Und was die Tante Eugenie anlangt . . . " (Loewenich, *Erlebte Theologie*, 124–25).

14 Loewenich, *Erlebte Theologie*, 123.

15 Theodore Baudler, nterview by the author, July 28, 1994. Baudler was a student at Erlangen and was present during the event reported.

16 Werner Elert, "Bericht über das Dekanat der Theologischen Fakultät 1935–43," document given in Beyschlag, 285.

which was a worrisome echo of the theology of Barth. In June, Elert and Althaus had been prodded into joining the Ansbach Circle, which produced the Ansbach Memorandum. This brought about a storm of opposition (see chapter 11). In October the Nazis staged their aggressive moves against the Lutheran Land Church of Bavaria, seizing the church offices and placing Bishop Meiser under house arrest. At this time the Erlangen professors were blamed for their participation in the Ansbach Memorandum, which was alleged to have been responsible for the Nazi seizure of power in Munich. Meiser, who had been arrested on October 11, was released on October 26. Meanwhile, Elert and Althaus publicly withdrew from the Ansbach Circle in protest.

Elert wrote a brusque letter to Wolf Meyer-Erlach (see chapter 14), who had involved himself in the German-Christian demonstrations of 1934 against Meiser. This November 26, 1934, letter was a reply to a November 16 letter from Meyer-Erlach. In the reply Elert took issue with a Thuringian "liturgy," likely stemming from the Jena professor, before he discussed the Bavarian situation:

> I cannot understand your surprise over my position regarding Dr. Meiser, especially after I made this plain to you on your recent visit. Beyond this, Meiser, in a personal discussion with me, apologized for having fallen for false information about me. But even if that had not happened, he would ever remain for me the legitimate bishop of my land church. Did you really believe that the journalistic rabble-rousing, which began against Meiser right after your visit here, could move even a single decently thinking person in Bavaria *against* him? If there was anything at all that ended my previous ambivalence in the church-political struggle, it was this rabble-rousing and the ensuing measures of violence, which struck against every feeling of lawfulness, honor, and shame in the heart of any German person. When the lineups were so sketched out, then I knew where I belonged and I still know this, in spite of all theological differences.[17]

Elert exhibited less confidence regarding his standing with Meiser in a letter written on February 12, 1935, to Christian Stoll, his former pupil, who was in Munich as the bishop's theological advisor at the time.[18] Elert wrote:

> It cannot be unknown to you that in the decisions by the church during the last year the [theological] faculty has been consistently excluded by the church authorities. There was, of course, no legal requirement to consult it. . . . For a long time now, the faculty has been informed on the church's situation, and especially on the views and intentions of the church authorities, only by the

---

17 Letter to Wolf Meyer-Erlach, November 26, 1934, ATF (*Elert's emphasis*).

18 Regarding Stoll, see Hans Siegfried Huß, " 'Nunmehr geht es um die Frage, ob das Luthertum als Kirche bleiben wird!' Zum Gedenken an Christian Stoll. 6. Dezember 1946," *JMLB* 43 (1996): 67–78.

general press releases. What we know beyond that does not in any case come about through the confidence of the church authorities. The press center of the Bavarian Land Church sends us only the sheet that is sent to local church council members but not the special reports that every pastor in the land church receives. I will remain silent regarding what motives should be imagined and that this is objectively insulting. At this point, I am only concerned about the result. It lies in this, that the faculty is not informed by any place in the land church concerning the current crisis in the church, matters which are talked about even in the pastoral conferences.[19]

Elert went on to protest that, except for Strathmann, all the Erlangen theological professors had intervened on behalf of the Lutheran Confessions and had struggled for the Lutheran Church. He also related how the theological faculty had fought the attempt to move the examination of theological students from the church to the Nazi state. "That we have not participated in the *Kirchenkampf* is a plain lie," Elert asserted. He even thought that the bishop was trying to drive a wedge between the professors and their students. Elert attributed this to the land church's tendency to identify with the theology of Barmen. Elert commented that the leadership of the Bavarian land church had declared its solidarity with the Barmen Declaration and that Barth "was described as *the* teacher of *the* Confessing church." Elert declared it important that in the future the land church and its theological faculty come into communication and work more closely together.[20]

Elert's relationship with Meiser had doubtless been disturbed by two matters: (1) Elert's rejection of the Barmen Declaration, which Meiser, at first, had supported; and (2) Elert's involvement with the June 1934 Ansbach Memorandum. Stoll likely intervened on behalf of his teacher and set Meiser straight. Regardless, the relationship between the bishop and his famous professor from Erlangen did grow stronger. In fact, the aged Meiser came to Erlangen for Elert's funeral on a wintry day in November 1954. At that time, I heard him speak movingly of how important the departed theologian had been for his work as bishop.

THE ERLANGEN THEOLOGICAL FACULTY UNDER ELERT'S DEANSHIP (1935–1943)

Elert was dean of the theological faculty for nine of the twelve years that was dominated by National Socialism; therefore his name dominates its history during this time period. The reason for Elert's unusually long deanship demands an explanation because the dean of the theological faculty at Erlangen traditionally

---

19 Letter to Christian Stoll, December 2, 1935, ATF.

20 Letter to Christian Stoll, December 2, 1935, ATF (*Elert's emphasis*).

served for only one year and was chosen from all the "ordinary" (*ordentliche*), or full, professors in rotation, based on date of entrance.[21] However, during the Third Reich, to provide continuity and stability, Elert was made the permanent dean (*Decanus perpetuus*) from 1935 until he was ousted from that position by the Nazis in 1943.

Elert was sometimes regarded as a sensitive and difficult person. He could be cuttingly critical toward one person while easily taking offense from another. However, Elert, as theological dean, proved to have full mastery of himself in his dealings with the National Socialists. He displayed remarkable diplomatic skills as he steered a difficult course between placating the Nazis, on the one hand, and protecting professors and students, on the other hand. He was able to safeguard the concerns of his church while convincing the Nazis of his "reliability." Elert carried on a masquerade in which, pretending to cherish Nazi goals, he resolutely pursued the opposing values in his work with his theological faculty. It was not until 1943 that the Nazis realized that Elert was slyly preventing the placement of Nazis in the inner faculty. Mindful that Elert had repeatedly resisted suggestions that he join the Nazi Party or at least the GDC, they removed him from the deanship in 1943. Elert was replaced by Althaus, who also had avoided joining both groups.

A number of papers relating to Elert's role in the church struggles (*Kirchenkampf*) may be found in the Archives of the Theological Faculty at the University of Erlangen under the heading "Elert Papers" ("Nachlass Elert"), especially in the folders on "Church Struggle" ("*Kirchenkampf*") and "Reich Church" ("*Reichskirche*"). This archival material has not been consulted by many previous writers and provides new insights into the years under Hitler; however, the careful historian must test the reliability of each of these documents. Some of the material was written by friends of the Erlangen professors for the purpose of exculpating them at a time when they were being accused of complicity with the erstwhile Nazi government. Among these papers are characterizations of Elert and Althaus that were written by colleagues and former students after the war and during the U.S. program of denazification. These papers describe Elert's conduct as dean and professor, as well as the actions of Althaus and other professors, as seen by people who experienced those events. Included are depositions written in 1947 by two vicars of Jewish descent. These depositions relate Elert's efforts to help the two vicars during the Nazi persecutions.[22] If taken at face value, these

---

21 *Satzungen der Theologischen Fakultät der Universität Erlangen* (*Statutes of the Theological Faculty of the Erlangen University*) (Erlangen: E.Th. Jacob, Univ.-Buchdruckerei, 1926), § 8, p. 8.

documents exonerate Elert and his colleagues from the charges of undue capitulation before Nazi demands.

The archives include several firsthand reports written by Elert that describe his experiences as dean of the theological faculty. The earliest of these bears the title "Werner Elert: Report on the Deanship of the Theological Faculty of Erlangen 1935–1943" ("Werner Elert, Bericht über das Dekanat der Theologischen Fakultät Erlangen 1935–43"). This report was accompanied by a letter to Althaus, who at that time was dean of the theological faculty. In this letter, Elert remarks that there were two reasons for the preparation of this report: first, because previous deans had left such records of their tenure, and, second, to answer a certain "secret report . . . which said that I had lacked character, also in connection with my leadership as dean."[23] Elert's reference to a "secret report" undoubtedly alludes to the "Confidential Memorandum" that Sasse prepared for the U.S. military during its investigation of the University of Erlangen. This impression is confirmed by the fact that Sasse did indeed complain in that report that Elert had lacked character. Therefore Elert's motive in writing this report was not to clear his name with the U.S. occupation forces, which had already accepted Sasse's recommendation that Elert and the other professors be allowed to remain in their positions. Besides, the average U.S. soldier didn't care whether Elert had shown a strong character under duress. The proud Elert wrote these lines to clear his name in history, an observation that is supported by the first of his reasons for writing: that this report would take its place with such reports written by his predecessors in the annals of the department. As a matter of fact, this report remained unknown until Karlmann Beyschlag published it in 1993 (it shall be cited here as "Elert's Report").[24]

The second of these statements is entitled: "Prof. Dr. Elert Regarding His Position on National Socialism" ("Prof. D. Dr. Elert über seine Stellung zum Nation-

---

22 There are notarized depositions by two men of Jewish descent: Rolf Neumann, vicar at Schwürbitz (dated November 23, 1947), and Fritz Fraenkel, theology student at Göttingen (dated April 26, 1947). Neumann stated that Elert had tried repeatedly in 1941 and 1942 to achieve his matriculation without success, and though he could only audit courses without credit because of his Jewish blood, the dean twice secured scholarship funds for him against the rules, a procedure potentially dangerous to Elert. Fraenkel declared: "Elert never suggested that because of my descent I should abandon my studies in theology, and he was always friendly and met me in the most tactful and helpful manner in the course of the many consultations we had in the years 1942–1944." Obviously, Elert was anticipating a time when Jewish pastors could again function without the interference of a Nazi state.

23 Elert's August 20, 1945, letter to Althaus is printed in Beyschlag, 266–67.

24 I have a copy of Elert's August 20, 1945, letter to Althaus, which is in ATF. "Elert's Report," with the cover letter to Althaus, is given in full in Beyschlag, 266–86.

alsozialismus") and should be dated before August 1946 (this statement will be subsequently referred to as "Elert's Position").[25]

The third of Elert's statements is dated January 17, 1948, and is entitled "Prof. W. Elert Regarding His Conduct under the National Socialist Rule" ("Professor W. Elert über sein Verhalten unter der nationalsozialistischen Herrschaft") (this statement will be referred to as "Elert's Conduct"). These latter two statements were part of the papers that Elert assembled to present to the U.S. military officers on several occasions when university professors were being examined during the denazification proceedings. Hence, in assessing these documents as historical sources, care and criticism must be exercised because it is known that they were written to the U.S. investigators to justify Elert's activities during the Hitler years.

When Hitler first took over the German government, Elert, like many other Germans at that time, welcomed the change and hoped for the best. It has been stated that Elert signed the Ansbach Memorandum in June 1934, which included a pledge of allegiance to Hitler, but gradually Elert's eyes were opened. On July 1 of the same year, his confidence in Hitler was rudely shocked by the Roehm Purge within the Nazi Party. On that day, Ernst Roehm and a number of his followers were assassinated by Hitler's men. According to Wilhelm Gerhold, Elert's former student and later son-in-law, this violent event opened Elert's eyes to the evils of National Socialism.[26] However, Elert's new assessment of the situation was known only to a close circle of family and friends. The Nazi reign of terror had begun, and Elert discreetly hid his opinions and prudently[27] pretended to go along with the new government. Elert's camouflage was so convincing that he was able to hold on as dean of the theological faculty for eight years, even in a university belonging to the state of Bavaria, which had been "coordinated" into the German Reich and was therefore under Nazi control. Despite this circumstance, Elert managed to keep the theological faculty intact and free from Nazi infiltration.

---

25 Although the archivist Prof. Niels-Peter Moritzen conjectured the date of 1947 for "Elert's Position," there is a new piece of evidence for an earlier date. In "Elert's Position," Elert stated that he did not have access to his house, which had been requisitioned for use by U.S. troops. But Elert wrote in a May 20, 1947, letter to his nephew Waldemar Elert of Lübeck that he had regained possession of his house the previous August. Therefore "Elert's Position" was written prior to August 1946.

26 Wilhelm Gerhold, interview with author, Erlangen, August 24, 1997.

27 By the same token, some might argue that if Elert was so skillful in hiding his true intentions from the Nazis, why couldn't these documents in the archives have also been intentionally deceptive? Yet as someone who knew Elert rather well, I strongly doubt such a conclusion. Elert was a born historian, and it seems unlikely that he would have planted false documents to mislead subsequent scholars.

Fig. 14: Hans Preuß
(photo courtesy of Karlmann Beyschlag)

Fig. 15: Otto Procksch
(photo courtesy of Karlmann Beyschlag)

Fig. 16: Paul Althaus
(photo in possession of author)

Fig. 17: Hermann Sasse
(photo courtesy of Karlmann Beyschlag)

Fig. 18: Werner Elert
(photo courtesy of Karlmann Beyschlag)

Fig. 19: Georg Kempff
(photo courtesy of Karlmann Beyschlag)

Fig. 20: Wilhelm Maurer
(photo in possession of author)

How did people react to Elert's double play? There seem to have been three reactions. First, there was the response of the Nazis, who were duped into regarding Elert as trustworthy until they finally saw through him and deposed him as dean in 1943. Second, there was the disappointment of people who were opposed to National Socialism and who were offended by Elert's "loyalty" to Hitler's government. Third, there were the colleagues and friends of Elert who realized that he was not a Nazi at all but feigned such pretensions to fend off the Nazis in the university and in the community.[28]

Elert writes: "In the summer semester of 1937, the long expected attack against the theological faculty took place." Elert was referring to the proceedings of the Nazi Party against Ulmer.[29] He relates how Ulmer, professor for practical theology and head of the Martin Luther Bund, was forced out of office by the Nazis. It all began when Ulmer criticized Robert Ley, Reich leader of the Nazi Party and of the German Labor Front. In June 1937, Ulmer was deposed from his position as professor; later he also had to resign as *Ephorus* of the Martin Luther Home for Theological Students to avert a Nazi takeover. Ulmer's former assistant, Gottfried Werner, relates how Elert sought out Werner, told him of the Nazi plot against Ulmer and the Martin Luther Home, and advised him: "Ulmer must resign his position as *Ephorus* as quickly as possible. Otherwise the home will be closed, or, what would be worse, be taken over [by the Nazis]. You must bring this news to him in a considerate manner."[30] A circle consisting of Elert, Preuß, Sasse, and Werner functioned in place of Ulmer and was able to keep the Nazis from taking over the home; Elert himself served as *Ephorus*.[31]

Elert later opined that the real reason for deposing Ulmer was to give Rector Fritz Specht a vacancy that he might fill by appointing a Nazi Party activist. Elert noted that professorships in the department of practical theology were often used by the Nazis to gain control of a theological faculty, which had previously occurred in Jena, Göttingen, Kiel, Berlin, Königsberg, and Rostock. Therefore

---

28 I was made aware of these three opinions from discussions with two former students of Elert who were deeply offended by his expressions of political loyalty: Theodore Baudler, an American, and Ernst Kinder, a German. After the war, both men learned to appreciate Elert's dogmatics system, and Kinder became the editor of *Der christliche Glaube*. Baudler complained to me that Elert had reproved him for not saying "Heil, Hitler!" on one occasion. However, even Sasse concluded his official correspondence with the words "Heil, Hitler!" when he thought it was expected.

29 See "Elert's Conduct," 5 (ATF).

30 The painful story of Ulmer's resignation is told by Gottfried Werner, Ulmer's assistant, in "Friedrich Ulmer—Vater des Martin-Luther-Bundes und seiner Werke," *JMLB* 32 (1985): 201.

31 Werner, "Friedrich Ulmer," 201.

Elert used every possible subterfuge to avoid each candidate that Specht tried to bring in, with the result that the vacancy remained until after the war. Meanwhile, Wolfgang Trillhaas served as an adjunct professor for practical theology. Elert writes:

> Soon after Ulmer's dismissal, Specht and Molitoris informed me that also Prof. Sasse, who had been openly attacked by Rosenberg, would no longer be tolerable because he endangered the whole university. Also Strathmann stood for a while on the blacklist. I did everything I could to beat off these attacks, but I believe that the case of Sasse was mainly delayed because they first wanted to be sure they got someone who would listen to the [Nazi] Party as successor to Ulmer. At the beginning of the war, when the Old Testament scholar, Procksch, went into retirement, I also succeeded in winning Dr. [Friedrich] Baumgärtel, a non-[Nazi] Party man, as his successor. There was a rule that vacant assistantships should be posted on the bulletin boards of all other universities. As dean, I always evaded this requirement, in spite of numerous warnings from Molitoris, because it could be expected with certainty that, in this way, outside [Nazi] Party members would be placed in these positions. By managing to have the previous assistant renewed in his position for a longer time, the faculty could also at this point be protected against [Nazi] Party spies. *The Erlangen Theological Faculty is the only one in all Germany which remained without [Nazi] Party members.*[32]

From "Elert's Position" (1945–1946), the second of Elert's statements, the following information can be gleaned about Elert's attitude toward Hitler. Elert writes: "At the same time that I came to Erlangen in 1923, the Hitler putsch was taking place in Munich. Ever since, I have hated the man and could also not bring myself to attend the two meetings in which he himself appeared in Erlangen."[33] Regarding his attitude toward Jews, Elert remarks that *Kristallnacht*, November 9, 1938, had "permanently healed" him of all hopes that the Nazis would do better.[34] He mentions that the "wild anti-Semitism" of Julius Streicher in and of itself would have kept him from joining the Nazi Party, but he adds that he had studied at the Institutum Judaicum Delitzschianum at Leipzig, an institute for bringing together Jews and Christians in Hebrew and Jewish studies. While at the institute, he had been on friendly terms with noted Rabbi Jechiel Lichtenstein. Elert had even sketched a portrait of the man.[35] Elert also mentions his friendship with the

---

32 "Elert's Conduct," 6 (ATF) (*Elert's emphasis*). That Elert avoided advertising vacancies to keep out Nazis also was confirmed by Thomas Würtenberger, professor at Mainz University, in an affidavit of December 12, 1947, in ATF, "Elert."

33 "Elert's Report," 1 (ATF).

34 "Elert's Report," 4 (ATF).

35 "Elert's Position," 1 (ATF). Concerning Elert's statement that he had sketched a portrait

Nuremberg Jewish banker Albert Kohn and with another Jew by the name of Aufsesser, who was a member of the chamber of commerce in Nuremberg.

Elert relates that he had helped forty or fifty students, men who had problems either because they were partly Jewish or because they had gotten into trouble at other universities through anti-Nazi political activism. With the assistance of Herr Zinner, the business manager (*Syndicus*) of the university, Elert enrolled these students at Erlangen. Elert recalls that in 1943, while dean, a Gestapo agent visited him and demanded material related to a former student named Schläfer. This young man had been active in the Student Congregation (*Studentenge-meinde*), a group mistrusted by the Nazis. Later, Schläfer completed his examinations at Erlangen. Although Elert had the papers "at arm's length" that could have sent Schläfer to prison, he writes: "This case dealt with the life of a man who was unquestionably innocent. I succeeded in deceiving the man from the Gestapo so that he left my office without any results."[36]

In 1938 Elert attended a meeting held at the University of Halle for the theological faculty deans from throughout Germany. One item of business was a proposal to abolish Hebrew studies. In view of the fact that this step had been demanded by Nazi Party and German-Christian propaganda, deans who were present "stormily advocated" the removal of Hebrew from the curriculum. Although Hebrew was not Elert's specialty, he gave a thirty-minute speech in which he defended the need for Hebrew studies. As a result, "the mouths of the opponents were stopped up," "the Old Testament professors also took courage and defended Hebrew studies," and the attempt to remove Hebrew from the curriculum was averted.[37]

At a similar meeting in Berlin the previous year, Elert had foiled the attempt of Reich Minister Eugen Mattiat, "a brutal SA man," to remove the examination of theological candidates for the ministry from the churches and place such examinations under the state universities. "I recognized the hidden purpose," Elert related. He was fully aware that Erlangen had virtually the only theological faculty in Germany that was free of German-Christians and Nazi Party members and

---

of the rabbi, it could be added that he possessed considerable skills as an artist. As a 17-year-old, Elert had painted a watercolor entitled "John Hus at the Council of Constance." The painting was in the possession of Elsbeth Elert Peter of Fargo, North Dakota, until her death. At that time, it passed to her daughter, the late Margaret Fraase, and is now in the hands of Margaret Fraase's son-in-law, Dr. William R. Babcock of Buffalo, North Dakota. The painting is skillfully done and has the qualities of a professional piece.

36 "Elert's Position," 3 (ATF). This event is also mentioned in "Elert's Report," reprinted in Beyschlag, 280.

37 "Elert's Position," 3 (ATF).

that, though the proposal might not have harmed churches that drew their pastors from Erlangen, it would be different for other universities. Elert believed the results of Mattiat's proposal would have been disastrous for the churches. Elert's remarks moved the assembly to reject the proposal by Mattiat, who was so angry that he threatened Elert, accusing him of "acts of enmity against the state" (*Staatsfeindlichkeit*). A victory was won that day for the German churches, however.[38]

THE LAST DAYS OF WORLD WAR II IN ERLANGEN

The U.S. armed forces marched into Erlangen on April 16, 1945. Walther von Loewenich gave an eyewitness report:

> On April 16 [Monday], 1945, the first American soldiers appeared upon the castle hill [Burgberg] of Erlangen . . . For us at least the Third Reich had come to an end . . . As many others, I experienced the Americans at first as liberators. The mental pressure caused by the politics of insanity of the Führer had become unbearable at the end . . . . To be sure, he who believed that the American soldiers were all angels had of course basically deceived himself.[39]

Erlangen was one of the few cities that had come through the war with its buildings relatively unscathed. Hitler's men had ordered that the city should not be surrendered. The Americans delivered an ultimatum: If the city was not surrendered by 3 PM, it would be bombed. Loewenich relates: "Three o'clock came and nothing happened. Evening came and nothing took place. I did not learn until later that the commander at Erlangen, First Lieutenant Lorleberg, surrendered the city from a courageous sense of responsibility. On this account he was shot behind his back by a fanatical SS officer. Erlangen was saved."[40]

Althaus preached a sermon on the following Sunday (April 22, 1945) with a graphic description of the impact the occupation had made. His text was 1 Peter 5:6: "Humble yourselves, therefore, under the mighty hand of God," and his theme was "The Mighty Hand of God." He began his sermon:

> Our hearts are moved, aroused, overfilled, torn here and there by all that the last eight days have brought us . . . . As we come into the presence of God, we come to hear his word for our situation and to express to him the things that move us. The first word—and here there can be no doubt—must be a word of thanks . . . . Last Sunday afternoon, the following night, Monday noon—what

---

38 "Elert's Position," 3 (ATF). See also Kurt Meier, who refers briefly to Matthiat's unsuccessful plot in *EKK*, 3:659 n. 878. Meier does not mention the role of Elert in foiling Matthiat, however.

39 Loewenich, *Erlebte Theologie*, 185.

40 Loewenich, *Erlebte Theologie*, 186.

anxious hours .... Our fate, or at least of the greater part of Erlangen, hung by a single thread. [Would the commander dare to defy Hitler and surrender the city to the Americans, or would he let the city be bombed and destroyed?] But then we sensed the mighty hand of God. Whoever watched the long line of people leaving Erlangen, the line of families, with their old people and their children, fleeing up the mountain, into the forest, with anxious faces; whoever waited with them from quarter hour to quarter hour with pounding hearts for the explosion of a destructive war over Erlangen—how could he ever forget these hours again! We are deeply thankful for the men who helped to turn our threatening fate and to save Erlangen. But the hand of God himself worked through them. How joyful was the afternoon, as all could return to Erlangen with liberated hearts![41]

Althaus continued by saying that the mighty hand of God meant not only deliverance but also judgment: "For a long time we have felt that the blessing of God no longer rested upon our way .... The mighty hand of God was against us." Why? According to Althaus, it was because "our public life no longer knew the fear of God, which is the beginning of wisdom."[42] Althaus asked his congregation: "Do we not experience today the dreadful earnestness of God's Law: 'whatsoever a man sows, that shall he also reap'? We must unflinchingly ask God to show us our guilt."[43]

EVENTS AT ERLANGEN FOLLOWING THE WAR

A gnawing problem at Erlangen after the military takeover was the U.S. denazification program for the German universities as well as for the rest of society. This program was supposed to rid the institutions of former Nazis. It was generally agreed that the former Nazis needed to be eliminated if Germany were to return to a normal course, but even Helmut Thielicke, one of the sturdiest opponents of National Socialism during the Third Reich, criticized denazification as it came to be practiced, naming it a destructive program that made people hide their past by proving their innocence instead of repenting of their wrongdoing during the Hitler years.[44] Elert wrote in a letter to his nephew Waldemar Elert at Lübeck: "We have experienced many painful things at our university; the denazification methods here are very different from those in the English Zone. I have remained in

---

41 Althaus, *Der Trost Gottes: Predigten in schwerer Zeit* (Gütersloh: Bertelsmann, 1946), 222–23.

42 Althaus, *Der Trost Gottes*, 224.

43 Althaus, *Der Trost Gottes*, 225.

44 Thielicke, *Notes from a Wayfarer: The Autobiography of Helmut Thielicke*, trans. David R. Law (New York: Paragon House, 1995), 232–36.

office until now."[45] As a matter of record, Elert was never indicted during these investigations.

At the University of Erlangen there were three phases in the denazification procedures under the U.S. military. The first of these came in the early summer of 1945. At that time, thanks to Sasse's "Confidential Memorandum," the theological professors were all reviewed and exonerated of any Nazi affinities. The theological faculty was allowed to reopen in the autumn of 1945. During the second phase (1945–1946), the U.S. occupation installed Althaus as university president and head of a commission answerable to the military. This setup bypassed the historic democratic self-governance under a rector, which had been in place at Erlangen. Althaus was placed over a denazification program in which he was lenient in pardoning his colleagues. Althaus's mildness turned against him during the third denazification proceeding (1946–1947). This was a harsh operation, led by Wallach, a German-American officer. During these proceedings, seventy-six professors, assistants, and staff members were discharged.

Sasse's "Confidential Memorandum

An important source of information on the professors at the University of Erlangen during the Third Reich is given in Sasse's "Confidential Memorandum," prepared for the U.S. occupation force in April 1945. Because he had spent much time in the United States and England and spoke fluent English, the U.S. intelligence system regarded Sasse as a trustworthy man who had been opposed to National Socialism. Almost immediately after the military occupation of Erlangen, he was approached by the army and asked to prepare a statement regarding the reliability of the theological professors. Sasse prepared the "Confidential Memorandum," which convinced the U.S. military that there had been no Nazis or German-Christians in their midst and that the theological faculty should be allowed to resume its work. The U.S. military accepted Sasse's recommendation, and Erlangen became the first university in Germany to reopen after the fall of National Socialism.

Sasse's memorandum began with a laudatory description of the theological faculty, characterizing it as churchly in nature, devoted to the Lutheran Confessions, and dedicated to educating men to be parish pastors. Sasse pictured the serious problems the theological faculty had experienced and successfully solved during the Third Reich without sacrificing integrity to the Nazis.[46] Sasse empha-

---

45 A copy of Elert's May 20, 1947, letter to Waldemar Elert is in my possession, thanks to the kindness of their common cousin Lois Elert Veseley of Seattle, Washington. Mrs. Veseley has also provided me with family portraits, valuable genealogical records dating to the Middle Ages, and maps and photographs of their ancestral home in Rarfin, Pomerania, now part of Poland.

sized that the department had remained free of members of the Nazi Party except for Wilhelm Vollrath, who as a nonregular professor did not participate in department meetings and who, after he lost all his students because of his party affiliation, had moved to the University of Giessen. The other exception was Paul Sprenger, who had the chair for Reformed theology and who, therefore, because he was not Lutheran, did not belong to the inner faculty. Sasse concluded: "The theological faculty of the University of Erlangen had absolutely no connections with the National Socialist Party. There can hardly have been any other evangelical theological faculty in all Germany that remained intact in this manner as ours did. In this respect the department is like the land church with which it is tied very closely."[47]

If Sasse had stopped at that point, he would have won the gratitude of his fellow professors. According to an October 23, 1945, letter to Friedrich Wilhelm Hopf, at the meeting of the commission in which Sasse presented the "Confidential Memorandum," he was asked by the Americans to speak more critically of his colleagues. Possibly this was the reason he added the additional descriptions of his colleagues' relation to National Socialism. Besides presenting material from their published statements, Sasse made a number of unflattering comments about his colleagues. For example, Sasse said that at the time the Nazis had taken over, Preuß had repeatedly made public statements in which he hailed the new movement.[48] Sasse called Strathmann, the political opposite of Preuß, a man whose interest in politics had led him to sacrifice a brilliant career as a New Testament scholar. Strathmann had been such a determined opponent of National Socialism that he nearly lost his professorship. In later years, however, Strathmann had published journal articles in which he had lauded Hitler's foreign policy and his military victories in Poland, Denmark, and Norway. It was not until the invasion of Russia that Strathmann finally recognized Hitler's errors. Sasse castigated the nationalist views of Strathmann as unreal and wrong.[49]

Regarding Elert and Althaus, Sasse opined that Elert should have heeded the warnings of his Swedish Lutheran colleagues, such as Gustaf Aulén. Sasse criticized Althaus for seeking a reconciliation of Christianity with the concept of the German *Volk*; it was this type of reconciliation that helped Althaus become the theologian of the German national citizenry of the 1920s. Althaus was a

---

46 Sasse, "Vertrauliches Memorandum von Prof. D. Hermann Sasse über die Theologische Fakultät der Universität Erlangen für die Amerikanische Militärregierung vom 28. 4. 1945," 1 (ATF).

47 Sasse, "Vertrauliches Memorandum," 2 (ATF).

48 Sasse, "Vertrauliches Memorandum," 3 (ATF).

49 Sasse, "Vertrauliches Memorandum," 3 (ATF).

Melanchthonian, a mediator, the master of a theology that says both *yes* and *no* to everything. The tragedy of Althaus's life's work is that, without knowing it or desiring it, he became the forerunner of the German-Christians, who in a clumsy way did what Althaus had done in a careful manner when he filled Christian teaching with a secular ideology. He was never a National Socialist because every kind of radicalism lay far from his nature. Increasingly his eyes were opened to the demonism of modern nationalism.[50] Sasse also wrote unflattering words about Elert:

> As a strongly profiled representative of Confessional Lutheranism, called to Erlangen in 1923, he could have become the theological leader of the Lutheran Church of Germany, had he not weakly failed at every decisive hour, especially during the National Socialist Revolution of 1933 and in the following Church Struggle. In the role of professor and dean he presented himself in public as a Nazi, but he was neither inwardly nor outwardly a Nazi, and more sharply than others he recognized the demonic trends of the party and he condemned them in private. . . . From the human and ethical point of view his colleagues found him a heavier burden than Sprenger [a Nazi]. But politically there was nothing in him or in the previously mentioned men that renders them unsuitable for [teaching at] the university.[51]

Sasse concluded: "The undersigned accepted the difficult and thankless task of writing such a report so that it would not be committed to less knowledgeable hands. He has labored to be as objective as possible, but also to speak with full openness, so that this openness will be rightly understood at the place to which this report is directed."[52]

DENAZIFICATION UNDER ALTHAUS

The second period of denazification took place under Althaus. In a document presented by Lt. Ben D. Kimpel of the United States Army on May 31, 1945, it was decreed that the office of rector was abolished and that the leadership of the university would henceforth be vested in a commission, of which Althaus was appointed president. The professors were not to resume their lectures until the

---

50 Sasse, "Vertrauliches Memorandum," 3–4 (ATF).

51 Sasse, "Vertrauliches Memorandum," 4 (ATF).

52 Sasse, "Vertrauliches Memorandum," 5 (ATF). Unfortunately, Sasse's memorandum did not remain confidential but reached the hands of his colleagues, where it provoked a storm that he was unable to live down until he moved to Australia. There was an indignant reply, written anonymously but obviously by Elert, which is described in Lowell C. Green, "Sasse's Relations with His Erlangen Colleagues," in *Hermann Sasse: A Man for Our Times?* (St. Louis: Concordia Academic Press, 1998), 47–49. Other responses are also discussed there.

Fig. 21: Exterior of New Town and University Church
(*Neustädter- und Universitäts-Kirche*)
(photo in possession of author)

Fig. 22: Interior of New Town and University Church
(*Neustädter- und Universitäts-Kirche*)
(photo in possession of author)

process of purification had been completed. A list of all professors and staff members of the university was prepared, and all of these individuals were to fill out questionnaires and return them by June 10, 1945. "Aside from the elimination of Nazi personnel and of Nazi ideology, the military government will not involve itself more than necessary in the leadership and management of the university," the document stated.[53]

The Americans had assigned much discretion to Althaus, who, however, proved to be a lenient judge. Thus he reinstated the distinguished gynecologist Hermann Wintz, who, though he had been a nominal member of the Nazi Party and a Roman Catholic, had been friendly to the theological faculty during the Third Reich and had once saved Althaus from the clutches of the Gestapo.[54] In later correspondence, despite his bitter experience in 1947, Althaus did not hesitate to write letters to support others in the clutches of denazification, including the medical professor Hans-Albrecht Molitoris (December 4, 1948) and the theologian Hans Preuß (February 19, 1949).

Although the Erlangen theological faculty was the only one to remain intact throughout the Third Reich, it became the object of jealous denunciations after the war. On January 22, 1946, Martin Niemöller spoke in Erlangen. Originally, he was to have held an address in the university *Aula*, a small, formal auditorium, but so many people wanted to attend that the lecture was moved to the New Town Church (*Neustädterkirche*) because it had a seating capacity of more than 1,300. In his address, Niemöller called the German people to repentance and labeled the students who were former draftees in the army as war criminals (*Kriegsverbrecher*). This was tactless, insofar as many of the students, lacking other clothing in this time of poverty, were clad in former army uniforms. Some of the students walked out of the church in protest. In a personal letter to me, Gerhard Krodel portrayed the discussion period that followed Niemöller's lecture:

> Yes, I was there when Niemöller tried to sell us the *Stuttgarter Schuldbekenntnis* (Stuttgart Confession). And I denounced him in no uncertain terms when he arrogantly rejected the distinction between "Scham" [*shame*] and "Schuld" [*guilt*]. If my father had been a murderer, I would be ashamed of him and

---

53 The document is titled: "Abschrift. / DET H3B3 / CO B, 3d Ecar / 31.Mai 45." This is a German translation of the original, which was signed by Ben L. Kimpel, 2d Lt. AUS. Supply Officer, H3B3," and countersigned: "Erlangen, den 5.5.1945. Althaus." From "Althaus Papers" in the possession of Gerhard Althaus, of which I have a photocopy.

54 How Wintz saved Althaus from the Gestapo is related in a July 22, 1947, deposition by *Oberkirchenrat* Hans Schmidt, at that time pastor to the university students. This paper is in "Althaus Papers" in the possession of Gerhard Althaus.

would have to bear that burden. But surely I would not be guilty of murder. Niemöller rejected this.[55]

Niemöller was furious at the cold reception he received from the Erlangen students. He told the press that Erlangen was a holdout for the Nazis. The newspapers exaggerated this event. For example, in the Communist East Zone the media reported that there had been violent demonstrations and fighting in the streets of Erlangen; this, of course, was a pure invention. However, Niemöller's claim that Erlangen was supporting Nazis suggested that a new purification was needed.

A few months later, Sasse wrote a letter that produced a devastating effect on the university. In correspondence with Dr. Fendt, the Bavarian minister of education in Munich, Sasse called for a crackdown on former Nazis at Erlangen and announced that because of their continued presence, he was resigning in protest as pro-rector of the university. Sasse stated: "I am simply not in the position that my name should be used any longer to conceal the course in which the university has been steered for a prolonged period of time." Sasse then implied that the *Concilium Decanale* (which consisted of the deans of theology, law, medicine, philosophy or liberal arts, and natural science) was sympathetic toward National Socialism, that its composition was not legal, and that its decisions were invalid. He added these fateful words: "I hold that a humane but just and relentless denazification of the university is an urgent task, and, yes, also for the question of the further existence of German universities, if these once more shall win back their intellectual leadership among the German people." Sasse continued: "I cannot with a good conscience apply the rules laid down by the American military government for the screening of prospective students . . . while professors, who in word and writing supported National Socialism and accepted the plaudits from political leaders of the Third Reich in the Nazi university of that time, should today still stand in leading positions."[56]

It is doubtful that Sasse realized the devastating impact his words and resignation would have on the university. Sasse discusses his intentions in a February 15, 1947, letter to Frederick Emanuel Mayer, a professor at Concordia Seminary, St. Louis. This letter reflects the backlash against him that resulted from the new misfortunes at Erlangen instigated by his missive to Fendt. Sasse wrote:

> The military government pronounced a number of dismissals at the University of Erlangen. Among these was also Althaus, who, as president of the first

---

55 June 19, 1995, letter from Gerhard Krodel, Gettysburg, Pennsylvania, to me. Also present at this lecture was Loewenich, who states that some students left the church early, which caused a commotion, but he denies there was a riot (*Erlebte Theologie*, 189).

56 Sasse, letter to Minister for Education and Culture Dr. Fendt, with copy sent to Hans Liermann, from Erlangen University Archives E-UA 76b.

"Commission for the Implementation of De-Nazification," was held responsible. The occasion of this action had been the case of Suess from the law faculty, the first rector under the praesidium of Althaus, who proved himself to be a sort of white-collar swindler [*Hochstapler*], and who, for falsifying a questionnaire, was summoned to the court of the military government. At that time, I, as pro-rector, tried to do everything I could in order to end the injustice that had taken place, but it was all in vain, and then I resigned my pro-rectorate since nothing else could be accomplished. Suess, with the help of Althaus, was even called into the *Ministerium*! Now judgment has fallen over the university.[57]

Sasse explained to Mayer that his central concern had been the men in the school of medicine who had cooperated with Hitler's program of racial cleansing but who now were being treated as if they had done nothing wrong:

The occasion for the action of the military government came, among other things, from the fact that the leadership of the university did not dismiss those physicians who, during the war years, upon the command of the notorious man, Himmler, and without a legal basis, in countless cases committed crimes against humanity in that they performed abortions upon women workers from the east. Such things cannot be concealed permanently, so that the office of control in Berlin has intervened. Now I am held responsible for everything. I am supposed to have given the Americans the writings of Althaus in order to overthrow him. That was not the case. I am going to step in at once against this slander, which is now going through the whole land church. I hope this comes to order before a big propaganda [campaign] once more carries it into foreign countries.[58]

It appears that Sasse's letter to Fendt, combined with Niemöller's defamations, had a devastating effect upon the university.[59] Niemöller and Sasse's allega-

---

57 Mimeographed February 15, 1947, letter from Sasse to Mayer, Concordia Historical Institute, 200-SAS Box File 16 (66–70). Copied with the author's possession, courtesy of Ronald R. Feuerhahn, Concordia Seminary, St. Louis.

58 February 15, 1947, letter from Sasse to Mayer, Concordia Historical Institute, 200-SAS Box File 16 (66–70).

59 Although both men differed greatly in their understanding of theology and the church, Althaus had supported Niemöller when he was sent to the Dachau concentration camp. Althaus announced Niemöller's incarceration from the pulpit and included him in the prayers of the church, actions that were forbidden by the Nazis. Althaus also helped gather funds to support Niemöller's wife and children. Niemöller's attacks against Erlangen in 1946 and during the denazification process, which led to Althaus's troubles, did nothing to repay the Erlangen professor for his kindness to the Niemöllers at a time when such acts of support might have brought Althaus interrogation and imprisonment by the Gestapo.

tions evidently led to the third denazification proceeding, which was launched in early 1947. Wallach, a German-American officer in the U.S. military administration, started a particularly bitter inquisition, during which seventy-six professors and staff members from the university and its clinics were dismissed without pay.[60] Those who were dismissed included four theologians: Althaus, Strathmann, Preuß, and Friedrich Hauck.[61] The reasons reported in the February 3, 1947, edition of *Die neue Zeitung* often lacked substance. Althaus was criticized for statements in two pamphlets that appeared in 1933 and 1936 respectively.[62] Regarding Hauck, it was reported that he was "an author of school prayers in honor of the Führer."[63] The newspaper reported that Preuß "glorified National Socialism in his book, 'Hitler and Luther.'" The newspaper also reported that Preuß "is said to have taken part in the burning of books and to have welcomed the Nazi seizure of power" in 1933.[64] A further charge against Althaus stated that "as chairman of a denazification commission at the University of Erlangen he had supported the restoration of anti-democratic professors."[65]

---

60 The author could locate little information on Wallach—not even his first name! However, Loewenich, at Erlangen at that time, later reported in his memoirs that Wallach was a German-American of Jewish descent who wanted to cleanse all the German universities of suspected Nazi sympathizers and had previously denazified Heidelberg. Wallach's army career ended when he was convicted of bigamy and dishonorably discharged (Loewenich, *Erlebte Theologie*, 189).

61 Account in *Die neue Zeitung* (February 3, 1947). Thielicke sent an unsolicited letter in which he strongly supported Strathmann, whom he called the boldest of the Erlangen professors in opposition to National Socialism. Strathmann was not restored to his professorship until September 25, 1948 (Otto Hass, *Hermann Strathmann: Christliche Denken und Handeln in bewegter Zeit* [Bamberg: Wissenschaftliche, 1993], 416–29; Thielicke's letter, 422–23).

62 It was alleged that Althaus, in *Die deutsche Stunde der Kirche*, "had welcomed the events of the year 1933." It was further held against him that in *Obrigkeit und Führertum* (Gütersloh: Bertelsmann, 1936) he had criticized the Weimar Republic and "had made democracy laughable" (*Die neue Zeitung* [February 3, 1947]). The newspaper's allegations are given without page references to the cited works.

63 I knew Hauck to be a gentle and kind man who seemed out of touch with events around him and who had no interest in politics. He was only following a general directive of the government that required all public schoolteachers to have the pupils recite a classroom prayer that included the words "God bless the Führer."

64 The charges as reported in the February 3, 1947, edition of *Die neue Zeitung* were carelessly thrown together. Preuss did not write a book by that title; they likely meant his book *Martin Luther, der Deutsche*. Furthermore, one should not discharge a professor and rob him of his pension on the basis of hearsay. None of this encouraged a positive impression of the American sense of justice.

65 *Die neue Zeitung* (February 3, 1947).

Künneth, the dean of the Erlangen circuit of the Land Church of Bavaria, speaking at his circuit conference, issued a strong statement of protest that was adopted by the conference.[66] Künneth mentioned that during the horrors of the Third Reich, the church had not remained silent but had resisted the government's evil designs: "The Confessing Church stood like a dam against the dark flood. But when we look back, we must admit that it was too little."[67] Künneth acknowledged:

> The great world powers have destroyed the rule by force of National Socialism, and have become the instruments of God to carry out God's judgment on our people. We understand therefore the concern of the victors lest the spirit of National Socialism revive, and we understand their effort to do everything they can to render impossible any resumption of National Socialism.[68]

Künneth added that no power of the world could take away from the church its duty to proclaim the truth of God to the world: "The church wants to help, wants to improve, edify, bring things to order. Its actions come from love, from the will to truth. Therefore today she must plead with those of our time who bear responsibility that they listen to her . . ."[69] This was difficult because a word of criticism could easily be misconstrued as sabotage directed against the efforts to remove National Socialism. Nevertheless, Künneth felt obligated to warn that the well-intended measures of denazification might have the opposite effect. He spoke especially concerning the dismissal of professors of theology, "who for many years have served our church with much blessing. We cannot act as though their discharge had nothing to do with us. We are also affected by this misfortune."[70] Künneth pointed out that many of the charges against the professors and staff that were published in the newspaper were based on mere rumor and that the accused had no chance to defend themselves. Why was there no hearing? This was not true justice. As one example, Künneth mentioned Althaus:

> I do not need to explain to those who are present who Professor Althaus is and what he has represented. We must be clear about this: A highly valued person

---

66 Künneth's speech and the subsequent resolution by the circuit conference are found in a two-sided imprint titled "Vom Öffentlichkeitsauftrag der Kirche: Vortrag von Dekan Professor D. Dr. Künneth, gehalten auf der Bezirkssynode in der Christuskirche in Erlangen am 9. Februar 1947" ("Regarding the Responsibility of the Church on Publicity: A lecture by the Dean and Professor Künneth, Dr. theol., D. theol., given before the Circuit Synod meeting in Christ Church at Erlangen on February 9, 1947"). Cited as "Publicity," recto or verso.

67 "Publicity," recto, column B.

68 "Publicity," recto, column B.

69 "Publicity," recto to verso.

70 "Publicity," verso, column A.

who is known in the whole world, a very prominent teacher in our church, whom hundreds—yes thousands of pastors and students—thank as the best and the greatest, the celebrated and blessed university preacher who for twenty years has been active in our congregation and church and who, through his sermons, has given power, comfort, and hope to innumerable people in the worst of times, has suddenly and without any possibility of self-defense been robbed of his academic rights. *This occurrence we experience as an injustice.*[71]

Künneth next referred to the chaos that had arisen in the university hospitals and clinics by the discharge of many physicians and health-care professionals.

We are no less concerned about the suffering, afflicted sick people in the clinics and their families, who are afraid of what will happen to their loved ones. What else can it mean, when the faculty of medicine appears to be so good as destroyed? How many human lives are endangered, whose recovery is delayed or completely destroyed? We are unable to see how such sweeping changes can be brought into harmony with the basic human rights of a democracy, which should rather serve the advancement of humanity.[72]

Künneth added that all people present had heard Althaus and Strathmann when they preached and could vouch that they had had nothing to do with National Socialism. "Rather, we heard from them a clear and firm repudiation of the spirit, being, and method of National Socialism."[73] With these powerful words, Künneth called upon his assembly to endorse this statement and to take a position regarding the dismissals at Erlangen. They were to call for hearings, to engage the administration of the land church, and to work toward preventing further aggressive actions and disturbances so the university might find the necessary peace to carry out its work for the students.[74]

Another defense of Althaus was given in an October 13, 1947, "Opinion of Experts" (*Sachverständigengutachtung*), which was signed by Künneth, Loewenich, and Hans Liermann. This defense concentrated upon the charges that Althaus had held a *völkisch* (racist) position. Referring to statements made in the 1916 Lodz address, they point out that the word *völkisch* had developed later and that the term as Althaus used it at that time had a different connotation from the radical meaning of *völkisch* under National Socialism. The men added that when Althaus wrote about *Volk,* he placed it under the context of the theology of orders, that is, the concept that the people, or *Volk*, were God's creation and answerable to him. They clarified that this had nothing to do with the mindless glorification of *Volk*

---

71 "Publicity," verso, column B (*Künneth's emphasis*).

72 "Publicity," verso, column B.

73 "Publicity," verso, column B.

74 "Publicity," verso, column B.

under National Socialism. Regarding the charge of racism, they pointed to Althaus's efforts to support Jewish people and to defend the three teachers at Bremen who had been arrested for helping Jews. They also referred to Althaus's writings against Nazi programs of eugenics and euthanasia. In a reference to the Erlangen Opinion on the Aryan Paragraph, which was drafted for the theological faculty by Althaus and Elert, the men cited these words from section 7: "The church cannot simply take over the assertions of the secular lawgivers, but must act according to its own rules as they correspond to its nature as a church."[75]

Partly through intervention by men such as Künneth and partly by a legal investigation that established his innocence, Althaus was restored to his position late in 1947. However, Hermann Wintz suffered a worse fate. Although he had been a nominal Nazi Party member, he had never been an active Nazi. He was not restored to his professorship, however, and was forced to earn a living by menial labor (for which he was ill-prepared). Deprived of his grocery ration card (*Lebensmittelkarte*) and given only an emergency ration (*Notration*), the celebrated physician and medical scholar was unable to sustain himself and consequently died of hunger.

The theological faculty at the University of Erlangen was at a high point from the accession of Elert in 1923 until the death of Althaus in 1966. Several of the old masters still remained after Althaus's death, but Maurer and Baumgärtel had previously retired and Loewenich took this step in 1968. For 150 years, Erlangen had been the chief citadel of Confessional Lutheran theology, but by the time that Karlmann Beyschlag, a pupil of Elert and Althaus, retired in 1988, the theological faculty had changed completely. Most of the successors to the older scholars were men of lesser achievements. There was a tendency to espouse generic Protestantism rather than Lutheranism. In 1970, the theological faculty voted to annul its historical commitment to the Lutheran Confessions. Despite the fact that hundreds of foreign students had visited Erlangen to hear Elert, Althaus, Procksch, Sasse, Künneth, Maurer, and others during its prime, Erlangen voluntarily ended its tradition as the world citadel of Lutheran theology.

---

75 From Künneth, Liermann, and Loewenich, "Sachverständigungengutachten," October 13, 1947, from Althaus Papers, file "Entlaßung," in the possession of Gerhard Althaus.

The Continuation of the Church
Struggle after 1945

During the years of World War II, various opponents of Adolf Hitler from within Germany tried to establish contact with the Western allies for support in their attempt to overthrow Hitler and bring about a conditional German surrender. The Western leaders refused such offers, taking the position that there must be no partial capitulation: Germany must surrender unconditionally. When the war came to an end, Germany was battered and nearly destroyed. Highways and bridges had been bombed, railroads were at a standstill, and newspapers were unable to publish. Germany had ground to a halt. As the widow of Count Helmuth von Moltke commented, the only institution that had survived the war was the church. Soon the church bells were ringing, and local residents were joined by starving and emaciated refugees who streamed into crowded churches.

Acknowledgments of German Guilt
and the So-called Stuttgart Confession
of the Confessing Church

At the end of hostilities in 1945, German theologians struggled with the question of individual and collective guilt. From a Lutheran standpoint, this was a problem within the discipline of ethics, but Karl Barth had belittled the study of ethics. How would his disciples deal with the problem of guilt for National Socialism and German responsibility for the war? Barth's followers dealt with this problem in the public media rather than on the university podium. A group from the

Confessing Church gathered at Stuttgart on October 18–19, 1945, for a meeting attended by a number of ecumenical leaders from outside Germany.[1] At this time, one German attendee gave this rather eloquent response, which became known as the Stuttgart Confession:

> We are all the more thankful for your visit, as we with our *Volk* know ourselves to be not only in a community of suffering, but also in a solidarity of guilt. With great anguish we state: Through us inestimable suffering was inflicted on many people and lands. What we have often witnessed before our congregations we now declare in the name of the whole church: Indeed we have fought for long years in the name of Jesus Christ against the spirit that found horrible expression in the National Socialist regime of force, but we charge ourselves for not having borne testimony with greater courage, prayed more conscientiously, believed more joyously, and loved more ardently.[2]

The Stuttgart Confession has been widely regarded as an important step in rehabilitating the German churches after the Hitler years. However, after the passage of more than fifty years, some nagging questions present themselves.

A confession of sins normally relates to infractions against the Law of God and particularly to one's guilt before the Ten Commandments. Did the Stuttgart document really deal with infractions of divine Law? It states: "We testified but we should have testified more boldly, we prayed but we should have prayed more fervently, we loved but we should have loved more ardently." Is this a confession of one's sins, or is it a statement of one's virtues? It continues, "We testified, we prayed, we believed, we loved." Weren't these really noble and meritorious deeds? Was there also the suggestion from the German church leaders that their friends from Switzerland, Britain, the United States, and other countries who had not experienced the brutality of a totalitarian state had not testified, prayed, believed, and loved nearly so much because they were in more comfortable circumstances? One heard such expressions of self-chastisement afterward among many Americans. At least the Stuttgart Confession evoked a series of "confessions" from church leaders from other countries, even if they had by far fewer virtues in which they could boast. Also, the Stuttgart Confession did not mention the Ten Commandments, which the Germans had so grievously broken under Nazi rule.

Among the observers at Stuttgart representing the ecumenical movement, this confession was regarded as a statement of heroism. Many German Lutherans were highly critical of the Stuttgart Confession, however, because it opens the question of whether there is collective guilt as well as individual guilt. Walter Künneth suggested that not only were all Germans responsible for the evil of the

---

1 There is a helpful description of the meeting at Stuttgart in Helmreich, 420.

2 Text in Helmreich, 421.

Third Reich but also all human beings on earth.[3] Werner Elert accepted the concept of group guilt on the premise that all people, descended from Adam, are sinful and that all members of humanity share in the disgrace of deeds of inhumanity. Were all Germans, however, guilty for the persecution of the Jewish population, for the confiscation of property, the forced labor camps, the concentration camps, the euthanasia of handicapped persons, the abortion and genocide, the medical experiments, and so forth—matters on which they were never informed by the totalitarian press?[4]

To whom does one confess one's sins? To God or to one's pastor or to a press conference? To confess one's sins before the news media might become a process of mutual exhibitionism and voyeurism. A much more impressive confession of guilt is contained in this October 23, 1945, letter from Hermann Sasse to a pastor. This wasn't a "we/they" statement like the Stuttgart Confession but a full confession. Sasse, the prophet and pastor, wrote as follows:

> Why should we theologians not confess our share of the guilt that we bear for the fall of the German university and for the ruin of Germany? Certainly, we are not outwardly so implicated like those in the faculty of medicine. We had it easier to avoid the terror of the [Nazi] Party. But in the emergence of National Socialism we were just as guilty as the rest. Weren't we theologians just as susceptible to the national intoxication that brought the [Nazi] Party into power as the representatives of the other faculties? What did we really do to strike up a wall against the National Socialists in the German universities? We must ask such questions today if at least we men of the church still want to know what repentance is. Also, as I know, you, honored brother pastor, were horrified at the number of [Nazi] Party members among the Bavarian pastors. These were our pupils. We have to answer for that, just as we are also responsible for this war, which Hitler had declared with cynical openness already in *Mein Kampf,* and, for the propagandistic justification of which, Lutheran theologians were helpful [namely, Hermann Strathmann]. How would we fare in churchly institutions if, out of concern for collegiality, one could no longer confess one's own guilt?[5]

---

3 Künneth, *Abfall,* 243–44.

4 Elert taught both universal guilt (*Gesamtschuld*) of all people on the basis of original sin and the consequent collective guilt (*Kolletivschuld*) of all people in the world. Emigration to another country did not remove the guilt. Elert believed that the whole human race was degraded by the atrocities of the twentieth century, but this is not the same as the individual guilt a person bears for personal sins (see Elert, *Christian Ethos,* 169–73, 357–61).

5 Sasse, October 23, 1945, letter to a Bavarian pastor, page 2 (ATF).

CONFESSIONAL LUTHERANS AIM TO RETAIN DOCTRINAL INTEGRITY AND REMAIN AN INDEPENDENT CHURCH

In 1944 Lutheran leaders sensed that the Third Reich was about to end and they began to consider what the relationship of Confessional Lutherans should be toward the DEK after the war. On December 7, 1944, a number of Bavarian pastors issued "Church Order and Confession," a declaration in which they gave their reasons why their land church should maintain its independence.[6] They explained that they could not sacrifice the traditional Lutheran freedom concerning outward order so they could adopt a statement that speciously claimed the Bible as its source. Despite the insistence of their opponents that they adopt the church order of the DEK and thereby give up their distinctively Lutheran position, these pastors countered: "From this it follows that the Lutheran Church cannot have a joint church order with other churches that have a different interpretation of the Scriptures and thereby hold to other confessions. . . . If various confessional churches are to live together, each confession, independent of the rest, must develop a church order, all the steps of which correspond to its confession." The Bavarian Lutherans then noted that because the other parties had a different confession, any closer arrangement would have to hold the character of a federation rather than a church: "Such an alliance, if it is not to bring more harm than usefulness, must have the character of a free brotherly federation [*Kirchenbund*]. Therefore, the right of forming laws and the exercise of the functions of church government cannot be delegated to its structure."[7]

The writers noted that Lutherans had been hindered in the past from developing their own distinctive church order by two outside factors: the former territorial church system and the nineteenth-century Prussian Union (see chapter 12). The abiding meaning of the *Kirchenkampf* should be that the Lutheran Confessing Church and the Reformed churches, with which it had worked shoulder to shoulder, would continue to work toward a confessionally bound church government, even if this proved to be impossible. However, when this approach had been tried in the past it had led to a complaint from the Prussian Union, which asked: "Can and should the Lutherans and the Reformed live together within a common church order as representing different churchly-theological tendencies, or must every confession set up its own confessionally bound church government and its own church order, so that thereby the Union sooner or later finds its own end?"[8]

---

6 Document in Reese, 590–93.

7 Reese, 591.

8 Reese, 592.

The Bavarian Lutheran church leaders then said that the first task in rebuilding the DEK should be to gradually bring together churches with the same confession: the Lutheran, the Reformed, and possibly also the various Union churches. The pastors expressed a critical opinion regarding the problems raised by the Prussian Union and the question whether it could any longer continue:

> In the total connection the question of the Union needs a fundamental solution. The existing Union churches arose out of historical situations (rationalism and state church organizations), which meanwhile have changed completely. To be sure, the modern relocation of the population might seem to point today toward a union. Nevertheless, the deepening of churchly and theological understandings has shown that preaching, the divine service, and church leadership require a nonambivalent and confessionally sound foundation. The Barmen Theological Declaration cannot be regarded as a new Union Confession for the future church.[9]

The Bavarian pastors closed their "Church Order and Confession" by expressing their desire for unity and their concern for the ecumenicity of the church, which, they said, were best served by fidelity to God's Word and firm practices in doctrine and life. Of course, by *ecumenicity* they meant not the amalgamation of unlike churches within a nationalistic German framework (the union), but increasing ties with the churches outside Germany and particularly with other Lutherans.[10]

This document was signed by some of the most prominent leaders in the Bavarian Lutheran Land Church: Friedrich Langenfass, a leading church councillor in Munich, Hermann Dietzfelbinger, who later would become bishop; Kurt Frör, who later would be full professor at Erlangen; Künneth, dean at Erlangen; Wilhelm Bogner, dean at Augsburg; Georg Merz, dean at Würzburg; Heinrich Riedel, dean at Kulmbach; Gerhard Schmid, dean at Regensburg; and Christian Stoll, dean at Schwabach.

Some of these men belonged to the Schwabach Conventicle (*Schwabacher Konvent*), a league of pastors opposed to National Socialism, which was founded in 1940 by Christian Stoll. Friedrich Wilhelm Hopf, a member of this group, writes: "The Schwabach Conventicle brought together theologians who stepped in for the renewal of the Lutheran Church in regard to the pastoral office, life of the congregation, theology, and church government." The members of the Schwabach Conventicle, all stalwart supporters of the Lutheran Confessions, also included Hans Siegfried Huß, Karl Krodel, and Sasse. These men worked together at considerable personal risk during the Hitler years, and following the war, they con-

---

9 Reese, 592.

10 Reese, 593.

tinued the struggle for the Lutheran Confessions. These men were members of the Confessing Church but not of its radical wing, the Dahlem Front.[11] After 1945 they reached out to those of similar convictions in the Lutheran land churches of Hanover, Hamburg, Braunschweig, Thuringia, and Saxony in support of the VELKD and in the attempt to limit the scope of the EKD.[12] They were troubled by this question: How long would the Lutherans be allowed to remain a separate church body in Germany, the homeland of the Lutheran Reformation?

CONFESSING CHURCH MOVEMENT REGROUPS AS THE DEK BECOMES THE EKD

After the war, the Prussian Union, following 128 years of operation, faced a major crisis. Part of this was the result of its disgraceful record of compliance with the Nazi state, but the division of Germany into the east and west zones made a reorganization imperative. Because the name "Prussian" was not acceptable to the Soviet conquerors of Eastern Germany, the name was changed to Evangelical Church of the Union (EKU). Additionally, because there was no longer any state of Prussia, the former Prussian Union provinces were changed into independent "provincial churches," which were regarded as equal in rank to the traditional land churches. The newly constituted EKU saw itself as the model for the Evangelical Church in Germany (EKD), and it strove to transform the EKD from the federation of churches, which Lutherans had regarded as acceptable, into a new Evangelical Church after the model of the EKU, which was not acceptable to Confessional Lutherans. In the end, the EKU, abetted by the Reich Church Brethren, prevailed.[13]

The old Reich Church, the DEK, was reorganized as the EKD at an August 27, 1945, meeting at Treysa, near Kassel, deep within the Union church in Hesse. It was decided that the new organization would be built upon the existing land churches and their administrations, not on the Confessing Church organizations. This decision was a temporary setback for the Brethren Councils, which had hoped to perpetuate themselves in a Provisional Church Leadership (*Vorläufige Kirchenleitung*). Six days before Treysa, the Brethren Council had met at Frankfurt am Main. Barth and Niemöller were in attendance, and it was decided not to

---

11 It might be added that even Elert possessed the "red card" of one who belonged to the *Luther-Rat* of the Confessing Church. Regarding Hopf, see Jobst Schöne and Volker Stolle, ed., *Unter einem Christus sein und streiten: Festschrift zum 70. Geburtstag von Friedrich Wilhelm Hopf* (Erlangen: Verlag der Ev.-Luth. Mission), 1980.

12 Most of the information on the Schwabach Conventicle was supplied by Hopf in his article, "Schwabacher Konvent," *EKL*, 3:873–74.

13 Wilhelm Maurer, "Ausklang und Folgen des Kirchenkampfes," in *Tutzing*, 1:250.

insist upon becoming a Provisional Church Leadership for the German churches at large. Instead, the local units, the land church Brethren Councils, would remain in force with communal powers similar to those they had held during the Third Reich. Where they did not already exist, councils would be instituted in all the land churches.

On August 25, 1945, the Luther Council (*Luther-Rat*) met at Treysa to discuss Lutheran strategies. The representatives determined that Lutherans were ready to take part in a loose federation with the Reformed and Union churches but that they also would pursue their goal of total unity for the Lutheran churches in Germany. When Theophil Wurm told the assembled Lutherans that the Reich Brethren Council was coming back to life, there was much resentment. It was clear there were strong differences between the Lutheran land churches and the Reich Brethren Council. Wurm, who was primarily interested in pan-Protestant unity, was displeased with the plans for forming the VELKD and kept the Land Church of Württemberg out when it was formed.

Wilhelm Maurer has written about the Dahlem Front's attempts to seize power in the EKD and its disastrous effects upon Confessional Lutheranism in the postwar period.[14] Circles of the old Brethren Councils were established in the land churches where they competed with the duly elected church leaders. The more radical holdouts from the Confessing Church stated that it would remain "as an advisory and controlling instrument of the church leaderships and of the Council of the EKD [*als beratungs- und Kontrollorgan der Kirchenleitungen und des Rates der EKiD*]."[15] At Treysa, Niemöller stated that many did not want a church led by regular church officials (*Behördenkirche*). The existing church officials should be "purged." The people whom he represented did not want a bishop church but a congregational church. Nevertheless, when the opportunity presented itself, Niemöller was willing to become a church president (bishop) and to betray a former comrade in so doing. Maurer reports:

> The conflict between Niemöller and [Hans] Asmussen was widely known, a conflict that characterized the entire church situation after 1945. The struggle burst into flames over the position of president of the newly constituted Church of Hesse and Nassau. (If one wanted a spot in the Central Church Office, one must have the leading position in a land church.) Niemöller was the victor and shortly thereafter Asmussen was forced out of the church chancellory.[16]

---

14 Maurer, "Ausklang und Folgen des Kirchenkampfes," in *Tutzing*, 1:247–48.

15 Maurer, "Ausklang und Folgen des Kirchenkampfes," in *Tutzing*, 1:249.

16 Maurer, "Ausklang und Folgen des Kirchenkampfes," in *Tutzing*, 1:248.

Although it had been agreed upon at the second conference at Treysa in June 1947 that the EKD would be only a federation of confessionally stipulated Lutheran, Reformed, and Union churches, the Reich Brethren Council met on August 8, 1947, in Darmstadt and decreed that "there can be no return to a Confessional [Lutheran] stance. Church fellowship cannot be based upon a static agreement regarding doctrines established by the confessions; church fellowship—the *Kirchenkampf* taught us this—consists in each actual and specific common hearing [*in einem jeweils aktuellen, bestimmten gemeinsamen Hören*] of the Word of God."[17]

It was tragic that people from the Union churches, which had weakly surrendered to Nazi pressures, should now denounce church leaders who, by their firm Confessional Lutheran teachings, had foiled Nazi takeovers and kept their churches intact and that these critics should now demand that they renounce their "Confessional stance." This seemed to be a demand that the church of Luther no longer had any right to exist in Germany.[18] As Maurer pointed out, this led the way to a program of political lobbying, media exploitation, and influencing voters at synods, thus diverting control from the legitimate church leaders to serve its own agenda. These militants seemed to have learned their lessons well from the infiltration methods of the German-Christians.[19]

Although the *Kirchenkampf* against National Socialism had ended, some of the Confessing Church adherents in West Germany were not willing to give up their power, and they remained as political action groups.[20] In East Germany, where the *Kirchenkampf* continued under the Communist occupation, the leaders of the Confessing Church failed to provide any real leadership for the distressed

---

17 Cited in Maurer, "Ausklang und Folgen des Kirchenkampfes," in *Tutzing*, 1:249.

18 In his presentation titled "Die Kirche und ihre Dogmengeschichte" ("The Church and Its History of Dogma"), Elert criticized these followers of Barth for reducing the church to an existential moment (*Ereignis-Charakter*) and to the decisionism of political or theological romanticism (in Elert *Ausgang*, 318–21).

19 Hermann Diem, a disciple of Barth, admitted in 1972: "The veterans of the church struggle are dying out. To the extent that they entered Lutheran Church councils after 1945 through the Confessing Church's 'half-seizure of power,' they were unable to alter the ecclesiastical structure along the lines of Barth's order of the community." The attempt to seize control of the Lutheran land churches was only partially successful, but they did get the Confessional Lutheran churches into the EKD and achieved recognition of the Barmen Declaration and acceptance of open Communion after the Union church model. Thereby the Confessional Lutheran position was devitalized. See Diem in Georg Hunsinger, ed. and trans., *Karl Barth and Radical Politics* (Philadelphia: Westminster Press, 1976), 121.

20 Hunsinger, *Karl Barth and Radical Politics*, 121. See also Maurer, "Ausklang und Folgen des Kirchenkampfes," in *Tutzing*, 1:254.

churches.[21] In fact, leaders from the Confessing Church, such as Niemöller and Barth, publicly argued a political position favoring Communism. Indeed, Niemöller accepted the Lenin Peace Prize in 1967.

There was also a serious theological conflict among the members of the EKD. The Confessing Church had included some notable liberals such as Hans Freiherr von Soden and Rudolf Bultmann. Bultmann taught that the Bible was written in a mythological language that the theologian or pastor must "demythologize" to make its message acceptable to modern people.[22] It was this development that Künneth called "the Second *Kirchenkampf*" as he launched his rival program, *Kein anderes Evangelium!* ("No Other Gospel"). Künneth opined that this second church struggle was more difficult than the one against Hitler. Dietzfelbinger, Lutheran bishop of Bavaria and chairman of the EKD council, who had made a name for himself in the resistance to Hitler, declared in 1971: "If I am not deceived, we stand today in a Faith Struggle, in a Church Struggle, in comparison to which the *Kirchenkampf* in the Third Reich was only the preliminary skirmish [*Vorhutgefecht*]."[23]

Sasse, with clear vision, saw all of this coming and fought manfully but to no avail to keep the Lutheran Land Church of Bavaria from an entangling alliance with the EKD, an entanglement that would deny the position of the Lutheran Confessions on church fellowship. Sasse, who was out of favor with the other professors on the faculty of the University of Erlangen, received little support. However, Elert attempted to stave off unionistic fellowship that violated the teachings of the Lutheran Confessions in his own way. He wrote a scholarly book titled *Eucharist and Church Fellowship in the First Four Centuries*,[24] which clearly showed that the Lutheran Church, in refusing sacramental fellowship where doctrinal agreement was lacking, was following the position of the Christian church from its earliest times. Sasse was supported at first by two high church councillors in Bavaria: Christian Stoll and Wilhelm Bogner, but both men met a tragic death in a collision with a U.S. army vehicle that was driving on the wrong side of the road near Würzburg. After their passing, Sasse found that he no longer had a voice in Munich. Bishop Hans Meiser seemed to be misled and was no longer listening to Sasse. It was this disillusionment that led Sasse to resign and move to Australia.

---

21 Maurer, "Ausklang und Folgen des Kirchenkampfes," in *Tutzing*, 1:253.

22 Maurer, "Ausklang und Folgen des Kirchenkampfes," in *Tutzing*, 1:254–55.

23 See Dietzfelbinger, 304.

24 Elert, *Eucharist and Church Fellowship in the First Four Centuries* (St. Louis: Concordia, 1966) was a translation by Norman E. Nagel of *Abendmahl und Kirchengemeinschaft in der alten Kirche hauptsächlich des Ostens* (Berlin: Lutherisches Verlagshaus, 1954).

Years later, Dietzfelbinger, Meiser's successor as bishop, expressed his appreciation for Sasse's warnings in a memorial essay written in 1977 after Sasse's death.[25] By then, however, the Lutheran Church of Bavaria had given up its confessionally Lutheran stance by accepting the practice of intercommunion with churches that held different teachings and had also introduced the requirement that candidates for ordination accept the Barmen Declaration. This gave the Barmen Declaration a quasi-confessional status and denounced the positions of Elert, Althaus, Sasse, Ulmer, and Stoll, among others. At the University of Erlangen, the theological faculty formally revoked its commitment to the Lutheran Confessions in 1970. This brought to an end a period of 150 years in which the University of Erlangen had been widely regarded as the principal voice of the Confessions in world Lutheranism. Only time will tell whether such changes might be reversed— whether Erlangen will return to its former glory and whether the Bavarian Lutheran Church will become again what it was when tens of thousands of loyal lay members boarded the trains to Nuremberg and Munich and swayed the evil Nazi leaders by their devotion to their God and their church.

---

25 See Dietzfelbinger's memorial essay on Sasse, "Aus Treu zum Bekenntnis: Hermann Sasses Vermächtnis," *Lutherisches Monatsheft* 6, no. 1 (1977): 6–7. Dietzfelbinger resigned from office and retired in 1974 in a situation not unlike that which had led Sasse to leave Bavaria. He discussed the factors that brought about his resignation and retirement, including his opposition to the ordination of women and to intercommunion as introduced by the Leuenberg Concord, in Dietzfelbinger, 317–26.

Glossary

Allgemeine evangelisch-lutherische Konferenz (AELK), General Evangelical Lutheran Conference. A federation of Confessional Lutheran churches in Germany.

Altona Confession. Prepared by the Lutheran churches in Holstein as a formal statement concerning the class conflict in Germany. Delivered January 11, 1933, by Georg Sieveking. Authors included Hans Asmussen.

Altpreußische Union. See Prussian Union.

Ansbach Memorandum, *Ansbacher Ratschlag*. Prepared in 1934 by Hans Sommerer. Others in the discussion group included Ludwig Beer, Paul Althaus, Werner Elert, and several pastors in Ansbach. Intended to counteract the Barmen Declaration and the positions of the GDC.

Antinomianism. An ideological position that denies the validity of the divine Law of God, as in the case of those who reject the distinction between Law and Gospel (Karl Barth) or the German-Christians, who believed that the will of the people was the Law of God.

Arbeitsgemeinschaft Völkisch-Soziale Pfarrer Württembergs (AVSPW), the Study Association of *Völkisch*-Social Parsons of Württemberg. This group of pastors was concerned about social and political matters. Its earliest work dates to 1925.

Auschuß für das niederdeutsche Luthertum, Commission for Lower-German Lutheranism. Launched by the October 7, 1935, Lüneburg Agreement, this commission sought a closer collaboration among the churches of Hanover, Schleswig-Holstein, Hamburg, Lübeck, Mecklenburg, Braunschweig, Oldenburg, and Schaumburg-Lippe (Bückeburg).

Barmen Declaration. Prepared in 1934 as a foundational document of the Confessing Church. Relied heavily on the theology of Karl Barth, who saw the declaration as a replacement for the Bethel Confession.

Berneuchen Circle. Promoted high liturgical views and supposedly influenced the JB. Leaders included Wilhelm Stählin and Karl Bernhard Ritter.

Bethel Confession. The first and best manifesto in the Lutheran struggle against the GDC. Authors included Hermann Sasse, Dietrich Bonhoeffer, and Georg Merz.

369

Brüder-Rat, Brethren Council. A leadership group within a Confessing Church.

Bund deutscher Lutheraner (BDL), Federation of German Lutherans. A group of Lutheran pastors in Mecklenburg who were opposed to the machinations of the GDC and were loosely connected with the JB. The group also opposed Heinrich Rendtorff's early attempts to appease the Nazi Party and the GDC.

Christliche-Deutsche Bewegung (CDB), Christian-German Movement. A moderately nationalistic group of Christian theologians and laypeople, not to be confused with the GDC because it avoided becoming politicized. Leaders included Walter Wilm, Ewald von Kleist-Schmenzin, Heinrich Rendtorff, Bruno Doehring, and Otto Lohss.

Christlicher Volksdienst Partei (CVDP), Christian *Volk*-Service Party. A small political party that opposed National Socialism and drew its members largely from Protestant people, for example, Hermann Strathmann.

Center Party. The moderate Roman Catholic party in the Weimar Republic. Moderates of other religious backgrounds, such as Paul Althaus, also belonged.

Christian-Germans. *See Christliche-Deutsche Bewegung.*

Christian Student Movement. *See Deutsche Christliche Studenten-Vereinigung.*

Confessing Church, *Bekennende Kirche*. An underground church devoted to a program of resistance against the DEK. Leaders included Karl Barth, Martin Niemöller, Heinz Brunotte, and Dietrich Bonhoeffer.

Confessional (Lutheran) Church, *Bekenntnis Kirche*. Church body that follows the Lutheran Confessions as contained in the 1580 or 1584 *Book of Concord*.

Confessional Fellowship, *Bekenntnisgemeinschaft*. More conservative than the PNB but did support the Confessing Church. Leaders included Friedrich Denting.

Dahlem Front. This group drew its name from the Berlin suburb where Martin Niemöller, one of its leaders, was pastor. It consisted of the more radical elements of the Confessing Church.

"Destroyed" church. One of the Protestant denominations in which the German-Christians or Nazis seized control of church leadership. As a result, the denomination lost its independence and was merged into the DEK or Reich Church.

Deutsche Christliche Studenten-Vereinigung, Christian Student Movement. German youth association led by Hanns Lilje.

Deutsche evangelische Kirche (DEK), German Evangelical Church. Organized in 1933 in response to Hitler's desire to deal with only one Protestant church, this group sought to bring all German Protestants together into a new federation. Including most German Protestants, the DEK quickly became Hitler's Reich Church.

Deutsche Glaubens-Bewegung (DGB), German-Faith Movement. Its members, called the *Deutschgläubige* (German-Faithful), were much more radical than those of the GDC. They sought to restore a Teutonic heathenism in place of some form of Christianity. Leaders included Ernst Bergmann.

Deutscher evangelische Kirchen Bund (DEKB), German Evangelical Church Federation. This federation of German evangelical churches was founded in 1923 as a pioneering effort to bring together Lutheran, Reformed, and Union churches. The DEKB remained a federation and did not include fellowship among the member churches. The federation was replaced in 1933 by the DEK.

Deutscher Lutherischer Tag, German Lutheran Diet. This conference was first held July 2–5, 1935. All Confessional Lutheran churches were eligible to send representatives to its annual meetings.

Deutschnationalen Volkspartei (DNVP), German National *Volk* Party or Nationalist Party. The DNVP tried to dissociate itself from the Nazi Party but joined in the "Battle Front Black-White-Red" coalition to give Hitler 52 percent of the votes in 1933. After this, the Nazis gradually relegated the DNVP to oblivion. The *Stahlhelm* (Steel Helmets) was a military adjunct.

Deutsche Volkspartei (DVP), German *Volk* Party. In 1933 the DVP formed a coalition with the NSDAP and the DNVP, the "Battle Front Black-White-Red," giving Hitler a 52 percent majority in the 1933 election.

Erlangen Opinion. Statement prepared by the theological faculty of the University of Erlangen at the request of the Union Church of Kur-Hesse. Specifically addressed the validity of the Aryan Paragraph of the Prussian Union.

Evangelical Church of the (Old) Prussian Union. *See* Prussian Union.

Evangelische Kirche in Deutschland (EKD or EKiD), Evangelical Church in Germany. The DEK as it was reconstituted after 1945. Originally considered a federation rather than a church possessing fellowship, the EKD gradually established pulpit and altar fellowship among the various confessions and came to be regarded as a church.

Evangelische Kirche der Union (EKU), Evangelical Church of the Union. The postwar name for the Prussian Union in the East Zone of Germany after the Communist government proscribed the word *Prussia*. In Western Germany, the surviving churches of the Prussian Union followed suit and became known as provincial churches of the EKU.

Federation of German Evangelical Churches. *See Deutscher evangelische Kirchen Bund.*

First Article. The opening words of the Apostles' Creed: "I believe in God the Father Almighty." Also referred to as the "Article of Creation" as developed by Luther in the Small Catechism. A First Article theology emphasizes the article of creation.

Gauleiter. A Nazi official who was in charge of party operations in a specified local area; a district leader.

Geistliches Ministerium, See Spiritual Ministerium.

General Evangelical Lutheran Confession. *See Allgemeine evangelisch-lutherische Kirchen.*

German-Christians. *See Glaubensbewegung Deutscher Christen.*

German Evangelical Church. *See Deutsche evangelische Kirche.*

Glaubensbewegung Deutscher Christen (GDC), the German-Christian (Faith) Movement. This religious party supported National Socialism within the German Protestant churches. Leaders included Joachim Hossenfelder.

Gleichschaltung. The incorporation or merger of various bodies into one total whole. Prussian King Frederick William III introduced this procedure when he forced 7,000 Lutheran congregations to unite with fewer than 130 Reformed congregations. In the Third Reich, Hitler merged the various political entities into his Reich, thereby suspending their local liberties. This was also Hitler's program for subjugating the German Protestant churches.

"Intact" church. A Protestant church that avoided a German-Christian or Nazi takeover and remained relatively independent throughout the Third Reich; principally the Lutheran land churches of Bavaria, Württemberg, and Hanover.

Jung-evangelische Konferenz, Young Evangelical Conference. Originally called the Hanoverian Conference of Younger Theologians. Grounded in the Lutheran Reformation but listened to Barth. Led to the Sydowa Brotherhood.

Kapler Commission. This group assembled by Hermann Kapler met at Loccum Abbey. On May 26, 1933, the commission published the Loccum Manifesto, which laid the groundwork for the DEK constitution. Members included Hermann Hesse, August Marahrens, Kapler, and the uninvited Ludwig Müller.

Kirchenbewegung Deutsche-Christen (KDC). The more radical Thuringian German-Christian Movement. Leaders included Julius Leutheuser and Siegfried Leffler.

Kirchenkampf. The church struggle against Hitler and National Socialism.

Landeskirche, land church. A church formed when the territorial or state churches were abolished in 1918.

Landeskirchliche Sammlung, Land Church Gathering. First met June 26, 1933. Leaders included Hans (Johannes) Bosse.

Landeskirchlicher Ausschuß, Land Church Commission. This committee within the local land churches linked the churches with the RKA.

Loccum Manifesto. *See* Kapler Commission.

Lutheran Confessions. The codified and official doctrinal writings adhered to by Confessional Lutheran churches as collected in the 1580 *Book of Concord.* The documents include the three ancient creeds (Apostles', Nicene, Athanasian), the Augsburg Confession, the Apology of the Augsburg Confession, the Smalcald Articles, Luther's Large and Small Catechism, and the Formula of Concord.

Lutherische Konferenz, Luther Conference. Group of Confessional Lutherans organized within the Union churches with the purpose of maintaining a Lutheran consciousness.

Luther-Pakt or *Lutherischer Pakt,* Luther Pact or Lutheran Pact. Founded February 13, 1935, this association of the bishops of Bavaria, Hanover, and Württemberg coordinated administrative, liturgical, and other practical matters to achieve greater uniformity.

Luther-Rat, Luther Council(s). A leadership group analogous to the *Bruder-Räte* (Brethren Councils) within the various jurisdictions of the Confessing Church. A primary Lutheran Council was founded August 25, 1934, to provided leadership for Confessional Lutherans.

Nazi Party, *Nationalsozialistische Deutsche Arbeiterpartei* (NSDAP), National Socialist German Workers Party, National Socialists. This political organization was established in 1920 by Hitler and his associates from a nucleus of the earlier German Workers Party.

Osnabrück Confession. Spoke convincingly of the autonomy of the church and offered a clear distinction of the two governances. Prepared by the Osnabrück Circle, which was a group of Lutheran pastors in the Land Church of Hanover who favored Barth and the Dahlem Front and were critical of Marahrens. Leaders included Hans Bodensieck.

Pastors Emergency League, *Pfarrernotbund* (PNB). Organized September 21, 1933, this arm of resistance against National Socialism was an important part of the Confessing Church. Leaders included Martin Niemöller.

Provisional Church Leadership, *Vorläufige Kirchenleitung* (VKL). The first VKL, established by the Confessing Church in November 1934, was a moderate group that was introduced to provide temporary leadership for the DEK, in the sense of the Spiritual Ministerium. At the schismatic synod of Bad Oeynhausen in February 1936, the VKL resigned and was replaced by the more radical second VKL.

Prussian Union, *Die Altprußische Union* (APU), Evangelical Church of the (Old) Prussian Union. This German Protestant denomination originated in 1817 and was supported by the decree of Prussian King Frederick William III, a Calvinist, who forced Lutherans and German Reformed churches to combine into one unified state church. This "organization" existed in various manifestations until it was taken into the DEK.

Reich Church. *See Deutsche evangelische Kirche.*

Reich Church Commission, *Reichskirchenausschuß* (RKA). Headed by Hitler's appointee Hanns Kerrl, a moderate Nazi and a church leader with some religious knowledge. Kerrl sought to restore Hitler's diminishing support for the Reich Church. He attempted to set up an LKA (Land Church Commission) in each "destroyed" church to counteract the more radical German-Christian infiltration. Although Marahrens and the first VKL endeavored to cooperate with Kerrl, the Dahlem Front bitterly opposed Kerrl and the RKA.

Schurmabteilung. The Nazi storm troopers, also known as the Brownshirts.

Schutzstaffel (SS). The Nazi elite guard.

Schwabach Conventicle, *Scwabacher Konvent.* A group of Lutheran pastors in the Land Church of Bavaria who met in Schwabach and who supported the Lutheran Confessions and were critical of the GDC and National Socialism. Leaders included Christian Stoll.

Seminar for Apologetics (Berlin). Led by Walter Künneth.

Spiritual Ministerium, *Geistliches Ministerium.* A committee of councillors provided for in the DEK constitution. The committe was comprised of three men chosen from the clergy and a jurist. Along with the Reich bishop, the ministerium was to have led the DEK; however, Ludwig Müller's dictatorial policies prevented the Spiritual Ministerium from fulfilling its intended purpose.

Stahlhelm. The Steel Helmets, a militaristic group that was an adjunct of the DNVP.

Sydowa Brotherhood, *Sydower Bruderschaft.* Grew from the Young Evangelical Conference. Called for church and liturgical renewal. Supposedly influenced the JB. Leaders included Georg Schultz.

Theocracy. A form of polity that rejects the two-governance theory of Lutheranism and places political power into the hands of religious authorities. Historical examples are the Puritans of Geneva, England, and the United States, as well as Justinian's Byzantium, where the emperor claimed to be a holy personage, ruling supremely in the stead of Christ. The "marriage of throne and altar" in Prussia was another example. The teachings of Karl Barth and the Barmen Declaration were rejected by Confessional Lutherans as theocratic enthusiasm.

Theology of creation. A theological approach that begins with the doctrine of creation, that is, an approach that emphasizes the sanctity of created things. This approach is sometimes called theology of the First Article (of the Apostles' Creed), as taught in Luther's Small Catechism

Union church. Any of several Protestant denominations in which Lutheran and Reformed congregations were amalgamated into one church body, the largest of which was the Prussian Union.

Vereinigte evangelische-lutherische Kirche in Deutschland (VELKD), United Evangelical Lutheran Church in Germany. Founded July 6–8, 1948, the VELKD tried to unite all German Lutherans despite opposition from more radical individuals in the EKD.

Volk and its derivatives. *See* the discussion on pp. 109–11.

Young Evangelical Conference. *See Jung-evangelische Konferenz.*

Young Reformation Movement, *Jungreformatorische Bewegung* (JB). This society aimed to strengthen the evangelical churches by a renewal of the principles of the Lutheran Reformation. Leaders included Walter Künneth, Hanns Lilje, Gerhard Jacobi, and Martin Niemöller. Its periodical was called *Junge Kirche.* After the abortive church elections of 1933, the JB was partially replaced by the PNB.

BIBLIOGRAPHY

Allen, William Sheridan. "Die deutsche Öffentlichkeit und die 'Reichskristallnacht'— Konflikte zwischen Werthierarchie und Propaganda im Dritten Reich." In *Die Reihen fast geschlossen: Beiträge zur Geschichte des Alltags unterm Nationalsozialismus*, edited by Detlev Peukert and Jürgen Reulecke. Wuppertal: Hammer, 1981.

———. *The Nazi Seizure of Power: The Experience of a Single German Town 1930–1935.* Chicago: Quadrangle, 1965.

Althaus, Paul. *Grundriss der Ethik.* 2d. ed. Gütersloh: Carl Bertelsmann, 1953.

———. *Leitsätze zur Ethik.* 2d ed. Erlangen: R. Merkel, 1928.

———. "Theological Responsibility." *Luthertum* 1, no. 1 (1934).

———. *Der Trost Gottes: Predigten in schwerer Zeit.* Gütersloh: Bertelsmann, 1946.

Barth, Karl. *Not und Verheißung im Deutscher Kirchenkampf.* Bern: Buchhandlung der Evangelischen Gesellschaft, 1938.

———. *Theologische Existenz Heute!* Munich: Christian Kaiser, 1933.

Baumgärtel, Friedrich. *Wider die Kirchenkampf-Legenden.* Neuendettelsau: Freimund, 1959; repr. 1976.

Becker, Karl-Heinz. "Zur Auseinandersetzung Prof. Elert—Pfr. Steinbauer." *Korrespondenzblatt für die evangelisch-lutherischen Geistlichen in Bayern* 65, no. 15 (August 15, 1950): 82.

Berghahn, Marion. *Continental Britons: German-Jewish Refugees from Nazi Germany.* Oxford: Berg, 1988.

Besier, Gerhard. *"Selbstreinigung" unter britischer Besatzungsherrschaft: Die Evangelisch-lutherische Landeskirche Hannovers und ihr Landesbischof Marahrens 1945–1947.* Göttingen: Vandenhoeck & Ruprecht, 1986.

Beste, Niklot. *Der Kirchenkampf in Mecklenburg von 1933 bis 1945: Geschichte, Dokumente, Erinnerungen.* Göttingen: Vandenhoeck & Ruprecht, 1975.

Bethge, Eberhard, ed. *Gesammelte Schriften: Dietrich Bonhoeffer.* Munich: Kaiser, 1965.

Beyreuther, Erich, ed. *Die Geschichte des Kirchenkampfes in Dokumenten 1933/45.* Wuppertal: R. Brockhaus, 1966.

Bielfeldt, Johann. *Der KirchenKampf in Schlewig-Holstein* 1933–1945. Arbeiten zur Geschichte des Kirchenkampfes 1. Göttingen: Vandenhoeck & Ruprecht, 1964.

Bonhoeffer, Dietrich. *Ethics.* Edited by Eberhard Bethge. Translated by Neville Horton Smith. New York: Macmillan, 1955.

Brunner, Emil. *Das Gebot und die Ordnungen: Entwurf einer protestantisch-theologischen Ethik.* Zürich: Zwingli, 1939.

Brunotte, Heinz. "Kirchenkampf als 'Widerstand.'" In *Reformatio und Confessio: Festschrift für D. Wilhelm Mauer zum 65. Geburtstag am 7. Mai 1965,* edited by Friedrich Wilhelm Kantzenbach and Gerhard Müller. Berlin: Lutherisches Verlagshaus, 1965.

Cochrane, Arthur C. *The Church's Confession under Hitler.* Philadelphia: Westminster, 1962.

Conquest, Robert. *The Harvest of Sorrow: Soviet Collectivization and the Terror-Famine.* New York: Oxford University Press, 1986.

Cramer, Karl. "Die deutschen Kolonisten an der Wolga." In *Lutherische Kirche in Bewegung: Festschrift für Friedrich Ulmer zum 60. Geburtstag,* edited by Gottfried Werner. Erlangen: Martin Luther-Verlag, 1937.

Cullmann, Oscar. *Christ and Time: The Primitive Christian Conception of Time and History.* Philadelphia: Westminster Press, 1950.

Dietzfelbinger, Hermann. "Aus Treu zum Bekenntnis: Hermann Sasses Vermächtnis." *Lutherisches Monatsheft* 6, no. 1 (1977): 6–7.

Elert, Werner. "Der 'Ansbacher Ratschlag von 1934' und die kirchliche Lage in Bayern." *Korrespond-enzblatt für die evangelisch-lutherischen Geistlichen in Bayern* 59 (October 29, 1934): 479.

———. *Der Christ und der völkische Wehrwille.* Theologia militans 15. Leipzig: A. Deichert, 1937.

———. *Ecclesia militans: Drei Kapitel von der Kirche und ihrer Verfassung.* Leipzig: Dörffling & Franke, 1933.

———. *Die Herrschaft Christi und die Herrschaft von Menschen.* Theologia Militans 6. Leipzig: A. Deichert, 1936.

———. "Die Lutherische Kirche im neuen Reich." *Luthertum* 48, no. 2 (1937): 38–39.

———. *Morphologie des Luthertums.* 2 vols. Munich: C. H. Beck, 1932; 2d ed., 1952.

———. "Politisches und kirchliches Führertum." *Luthertum* 1, no. 4 (1934): 102–17.

———. "Randbemerkungen," *Luthertum* 49, no. 12 (1938): 372–73.

———. *Stand und Stände nach lutherischer Auffassung.* Berlin: Verlag des Evangelischen Bundes, 1940.

———. "Unter Anklage." *Korrespond-enzblatt für die evangelisch-lutherischen Geistlichen in Bayern* 65, no. 14–15 (July 31 and August 15, 1950): 55–56, 59–60.

Field, Geoffrey G. *Evangelist of Race: The Germanic Vision of Houston Stewart Chamberlain.* New York: Columbia University Press, 1981.

Fischer, Joachim. *Die sächsische Landeskirche im Kirchenkampf 1933–1937.* Arbeiten zur Geschichte des Kirchenkampfes 8. Göttingen: Vandenhoeck & Ruprecht, 1972.

Fischer, Martin. "Wilhelm Gross, sein Werk und sein Auftrag." In *Der Fels der Mitfolge: Christus im Alten Testamen: 18 Kohleskizzen von Wilhelm Gross.* Berlin: Lettner, 1953.

Ford, Charles E. "Dietrich Bonhoeffer, the Resistance, and the Two Kingdoms." *Lutheran Forum* 27, no. 3 (August 1993): 28–34.

Frör, Kurt. "Evangelische Erziehung im Dritten Reich." *Luthertum* 1, no. 3 (1934).

Fuller, B. A. G., and Sterling M. McMurrin. *A History of Philosophy.* New York: Holt, Rinehart & Winston, 1966.

Fuss, Gottfried. "Gruß an Altbischof D. Hahn." *Allgemeine evangelisch-lutherische Kirchenzeitung* 10 (September 15, 1956): 373–75.

Gehrke, Hugo. "Composers for the Church: Jan Bender." *Church Music* 71, no. 1 (1971).

Green, Lowell C. *Adventures in Law and Gospel: Lectures in Lutheran Dogmatics.* Fort Wayne, IN: Concordia Theological Seminary Press, 1993.

———, trans. "The Confessions and the Unity of the Church," by Hermann Sasse. Pages 351–68 in *The Lonely Way: Selected Essays and Letters (1927–1939)*, edited by Matthew C. Harrison. St. Louis: Concordia, 2001.

Hahn, Wilhelm. "Zum Heimgang von Altbischof D. Hugo Hahn." *Allgemeine evangelisch-lutherische Kirchenzeitung* 11 (December 15, 1957): 430.

Harleß, Gottlieb Christoph Adolph von. *Christliche Ethik.* 7th ed. Gütersloh: Carl Bertelsmann, 1875.

Hirsch, Emanuel. "Die wirkliche Lage unserer Kirche." *Pastoraltheologie* 29 (1933).

Hunsinger, George, ed. and trans. *Karl Barth and Radical Politics.* Philadelphia: Westminster Press, 1976.

Huß, Hans Siegfried. "Friedrich Wilhelm Hopf—Evangelisch-lutherischer Pfarrer zu Mühlhausen (Oberfranken) (1936–1951)." In *Unter einem Christus sein und streiten: Festschrift zum 70. Geburtstag von Friedrich Wilhelm Hopf,* edited by Jobst Schöne and Volker Stolle. Erlangen: Verlag der Ev.-Luth. Mission, 1980.

———. " 'Nunmehr geht es um die Frage, ob das Luthertum als Kirche bleiben wird!' Zum Gedenken an Christian Stoll. 6. Dezember 1946." In *Lutherische Kirche in der Welt: Jahrbuch des Martin-Luther-Bundes.* Berlin: Martin Luther Verlag, 1996.

Karwehl, Richard. "Politisches Messiastum: Zur Auseindandersetzung von Kirche und Nationalsozialismus." *Zwischen den Zeiten* 9 (1931).

Kittel, Gerhard, ed. *Theologisches Wörterbuch zum Neuen Testament.* Stuttgart: W. Kohlhammer, 1932–79.

Klepper, Jochen. *Unter dem Schatten deiner Flügel: Aus den Tagebüchern der Jahre 1932–1942.* Edited by Hildegard Klepper. Stuttgart: Deutsche Verlags-Anstalt, 1955.

Kusukawa, Sachiko. *The Transformation of Natural Philosophy: The Case of Philip Melanchthon.* Ideas in Context. Cambridge: Cambridge University Press, 1995.

Lazareth, William. "Orders of Creation and Preservation." In *Baker's Dictionary of Christian Ethics*, edited by Carl F. H. Henry. Grand Rapids: Baker, 1973.

Liermann, Hans. *Kirchen und Staat.* Munich: Isar, 1954.

Ludolphy, Ingetraut. "Franz Lau (1907–1973): Kirchenhistoriker und Anwalt evangelischer Diaspora." In *Lutherische Kirche in der Welt: Jahrbuch des Martin-Luther-Bundes.* Berlin: Martin Luther Verlag, 2001.

Mau, Rudolf, ed. *Evangelische Bekenntnisse: Bekenntnisschriften der Reformation und neuere Theologische Erklärungen: Im Auftrag des Rates der Evangelischen Kirche der Union.* Bielefeld: Luther Verlag, 1997.

McNeill, John T. *The History and Character of Calvinism.* Oxford: Oxford University Press, 1970.

Niemöller, Gerhard, ed. *Die erste Benenntnissynode der Deutschen Evangelischen Kirche zu Barmen.* Arbeiten zur Geschichte des Kirchenkampfes 5–6. Göttingen: Vandenhoeck & Ruprecht, 1959.

———, ed. *Die Synode zu Halle 1937: Die zweite Tagung der vierten Bekenntnissynode der Evangelischen Kirche der altpreußischen Union. Text—Dokumente—Berichte.* Arbeiten zur Geschichte des Kirchenkampfes 11. Göttingen: Vandenhoeck & Ruprecht, 1963.

Niemöller, Wilhelm. *Kampf und Zeugnis der Bekennenden Kirche.* Bielefeld: Ludwig Bechauf, 1948.

Preuß, Hans. *Von den Katakomben bis zu den Zeichen der Zeit.* Erlangen: Martin Luther-Verlag, 1936.

Reimer, A. James. *Emanuel Hirsch und Paul Tillich: Theologie und Politik in einer Zeit der Krise.* Berlin: de Gruyter, 1995.

Reimers, Karl Friedrich. *Lübeck im Kirchenkampf des Dritten Reiches: Nationalsozialistisches Führerprinzip und evangelisch-lutherische Landeskirche von 1933 bis 1945.* Göttingen: Vandenhoeck & Ruprecht, 1965.

Reu, Johann Michael, and Paul H. Buehring. *Christian Ethics.* Columbus: Lutheran Book Concern, 1935.

Riemenschneider, Ernst G. *Der Fall Klepper: Eine Dokumentation.* Stuttgart: Deutsche Verlags-Anstalt, 1975.

Rose, Paul Lawrence. *Revolutionary Antisemitism in Germany from Kant to Wagner.* Princeton: Princeton University Press, 1990.

———. *Wagner: Race and Revolution.* New Haven: Yale University Press, 1992.

Rössler, Hans. "Das Ende einer Freundschaft—Rektor D. Hans Lauerer und Pfarrer Hans Sommerer im bayerischen Kirchenkampf (1934)." *Zeitschrift für bayerische Kirchengeschichte* 57 (1988): 77.

Sasse, Hermann. *Here We Stand: Nature and Character of the Lutheran Faith.* New York: Harper & Bros. , 1938; repr. Minneapolis: Augsburg, 1946.

Schjorring, Jens H., et al., ed. *From Federation to Communion: The History of the Lutheran World Federation.* Minneapolis: Fortress, 1997.

Schöffel, Simon. "German Lutheranism at the Turning Point of Time." *Luthertum* 1, no. 1 (1934).

Schöne, Jobst. "Georg Philip Eduard Huschke (1801–1886): Ein Rückblick." *Lutherische Beiträge* 6, no. 3 (2001): 205–13.

————, and Volker Stolle, ed. *Unter einem Christus sein und streiten: Festschrift zum 70. Geburtstag von Friedrich Wilhelm Hopf.* Erlangen: Verlag der Ev-luth. Mission, 1980.

Siemon-Netto, Uwe. *The Fabricated Luther: The Rise and Fall of the Shirer Myth.* St. Louis: Concordia, 1995.

Smith, Preserved. *The Reformation in Europe.* New York: Collier-Macmillan, 1962.

Stapel, Wilhelm. *Die Kirche Christi und der Staat Hitlers.* Hamburg: Hanseatische Verlags-anstalt, 1933.

————. *Über das Christentum.* Hamburg: Agentur des Rauhen Hauses, 1951.

Stauffer Ethelbert. *Die Theologie des Neuen Testaments.* Gütersloh: Bertelsmann, 1948.

Steinbauer, Karl. "Paulus und Nero: Bedenken zu dem dritten in *Zwischen Gnade und Ungnade* erschienenen Vortrag von Werner Elert." *Korrespond-enzblatt für die evan-gelisch-lutherischen Geistlichen in Bayern* 65, no. 3–4 (February 15 and February 28, 1950): 9–11, 13–16.

Stephan, Horst. *Luther in den Wandlungen seiner Kirche.* 2d ed. Berlin: A. Töpelmann: 1951.

Stoltzfus, Nathan A. *Resistance of the Heart: Intermarriage and the Rosenstrasse Protest in Nazi Germany.* New York: Norton, 1996.

Strohm, Theodor. *Theologie im Schatten politischer Romantik: Eine wissenschafts-soziolo-gische Anfrage an die Theologie Friedrich Gogartens.* Munich: Kaiser-Grünewald, 1970.

Tal, Uriel. Published address in *Luther, Lutheranism and the Jews: A Record of the Second Consultation between Representatives of The International Jewish Committee for Inter-religious Consultations and The Lutheran World Federation,* edited by Jean Halpérin and Arne Sovik. Geneva: Department of Studies, The Lutheran World Federation, 1984.

Tilgner, Wolfgang. *Volksnomostheologie und Schöpfungsglaube.* Arbeiten zur Geschichte des Kirchenkampfes 16. Göttingen: Vandenhoeck & Ruprecht, 1966.

Voigt, Gottfried. "Gottesgesetz und Volksgesetz: Ein Vergleich zwischen Gogarten und Luther." *Luthertum* 50 (1939): 114ff.

Werner, Gottfried, ed. *Lutherische Kirche in Bewegung: Festschrift für Friedrich Ulmer zum 60. Geburtstag.* Erlangen: Martin Luther-Verlag, 1937.

Wirth, Günter. *Jochen Klepper.* Berlin: Union, 1972.

Wolf, Erik, ed. *Zeugnisse der Bekennenden Kirche.* Tübingen: Furche-Verlag, 1946.

Wolf, Ernst. *Peregrinatio.* 2 vols. Munich: Christian Kaiser, 1954–65.

Zabel, James A. *Nazism and the Pastors: A Study of the Ideas of Three Deutsche Christen Groups*. Dissertation Series of the American Academy of Religion 14. Missoula, MT: Scholars Press, 1976.

INDEX OF NAMES

TOPICAL INDEX